INVASION OF THE SALARYMEN

INVASION OF THE SALARYMEN

The Japanese Business Presence In America

Jeremiah J. Sullivan

PRAEGER

Westport, Connecticut
London

Library of Congress Cataloging-in-Publication Data

Sullivan, Jeremiah J.
    Invasion of the salarymen : the Japanese business presence in
America / Jeremiah J. Sullivan.
      p.   cm.
    Includes bibliographical references and index.
    ISBN 0–275–94404–2 (alk. paper)
    1. Corporations, Japanese—United States—Management.
2. Investments, Japanese—United States.   I. Title.
HD38.S785   1992
338.8′8952073—dc20   91–43435

British Library Cataloguing in Publication Data is available.

Library of Congress Catalog Card Number: 91–43435
ISBN: 0–275–94404–2

First published in 1992

Praeger Publishers, 88 Post Road West, Westport, CT 06881
An imprint of Greenwood Publishing Group, Inc.

Printed in the United States of America

The paper used in this book complies with the
Permanent Paper Standard issued by the National
Information Standards Organization (Z39.48–1984).

10 9 8 7 6 5 4 3 2 1

Contents

Introduction:
Shall It Be War?

Nations have engaged in economic conflicts for thousands of years, and the economic war which some Americans want to wage against Japan is remarkably similar to that proposed by ancient Greeks long ago.

In 432 B.C. a representative of Corinth rose in the assembly of the Lacedaemonian States to warn them of the growing threat of Athens. Part of his speech as recreated by Thucydides in *The Peleponnesian War* is included below. Wherever "Athens" is mentioned, I have substituted "Japan"; the "you" refers to Americans.

"You have never yet considered what sort of antagonists you will encounter in the Japanese and how widely, how absolutely different they are from you. The Japanese are addicted to innovation, and their designs are characterized by swiftness alike in conception and execution; you have a genius for keeping what you have got, accompanied by a total want of invention, and when forced to act you never go far enough. The Japanese are adventurous beyond their power and daring beyond their judgment. In danger they are sanguine. Your wont is to attempt less than is justified by your power, to mistrust even what is sanctioned by your judgment, and to fancy that from danger there is no release.

"Further, there is promptitude on the Japanese side and procrastination on yours. They are never at home. You are never from it. The Japanese hope by their absence to extend their acquisitions. You fear that by your advance you endanger what you have left behind. They are swift to follow up a success, and slow to recoil from a reverse. Their bodies they spend ungrudgingly in their country's cause; their intellect they jealously husband to be employed in her service. A scheme unexecuted is with them a positive loss, a successful enterprise a comparative failure. The deficiency created by the miscarriage of an undertaking is soon filled up by fresh hopes; for the Japanese alone are enabled to call a thing hoped for a thing got, by the speed with which they act upon their resolutions.

"Thus the Japanese toil on in trouble and danger all the days of their life, with little opportunity for enjoying, being ever engaged in getting. Their only idea of a holiday is to do what the occasion demands, and to them laborious occupation is less of a misfortune than the peace of a quiet life. To describe their character in a word, one might truly say that the Japanese were born into the world to take no rest themselves and to give none to others."

This speech, almost 2500 years old, could have been made yesterday by Clyde Prestowitz or James Fallows, two well-known "Japan bashers," in testimony before a Senate subcommittee investigating the supposed economic threat of Japan. The points that were made are:

- Americans must realize that the Japanese do not look at things the same way we do.
- The Japanese are aggressive. They take risks. We don't.
- When the Japanese move, they move rapidly, especially in the international arena. They build on their successes and learn from their failures.
- Each American does his own thing. Each Japanese works tirelessly in his country's service.
- The Japanese never take a day off. They are most comfortable when they are working. Americans love their vacations.

The Corinthians wanted the Lacedaemonian States to declare war on the Athenians. Their reasons: the Athenians were different, innovative, unified, and hard working. One would be pressed to find in history less compelling reasons for making war. Yet they fought for over twenty years. In the end, both sides fell back, exhausted, and were easy prey for even more aggressive raiders from the north; namely Alexander, and later on from the west, the Romans. The Japanese are often described by their critics in the same way the Corinthians described the Athenians, and often the goal is similar: to declare war. The war in this instance, of course, will be economic, with the defense of U.S. borders appearing in the guise of tariffs, quotas, onerous reporting requirements for investors in the United States, restrictions on investing, and swift retaliation for not moving quickly enough to remove barriers to U.S. investment in Japan.

What had the Japanese done to cause the U.S. Congress and the press to call for defense of our shores against this invader? Simply put, the Japanese had the audacity to invest in America. And how did all of their investment come about? Briefly, the surge of Japanese investment in the United States and the movement of perhaps 50,000 Japanese managers and their families to America was the end result of a process triggered by a massive U.S. government deficit which had developed by 1982. Taking federal, state, and local governments together, the United States had a small budget surplus in 1979, while Japan and West Germany had deficits. The U.S. deficits incurred over the next three years set off a wave of demand in this country in which Americans wanted to buy and the Japanese and Germans wanted to sell. All of the importing which followed should have driven the dollar down quickly. Soaring U.S. interest rates, however, attracted Japanese stock and bond capital instead, which kept the dollar high and imports cheap for several years. Americans bought and bought until by 1985 their savings available for consumption were exhausted. At the same time, available Japanese savings (gross savings minus gross investment) had grown from 3.8 percent of GNP (Gross National Product) to 4.5 percent. This hoard of cash poured into America to purchase more stocks and bonds and was later available to fund direct investing. The dollar finally started to fall in 1986 after interest rates declined and the United States felt the weight of the growing trade deficit. Knowing that a weak dollar could not last forever, especially given the U.S. propensity to fight inflation with dollar-raising high interest rates, Japanese corporations hurried to invest in America. Their rush was further spurred by American threats to raise trade barriers and to make future investing difficult.

There are other elements to the story, discussed later in Chapter 2, but none of the events of the last ten years suggests that the Japanese are deviously trying to provoke economic warfare. Nonetheless, the inevitable precursor to war, the lining up of opponents on either side, has been occurring as critics, scholars, politicians, and journalists scurry to take a stand either for or against Japan. Ezra Vogel in *Japan as Number One* and William Ouchi in *Theory Z* argued that Japan's political, educational, and managerial philosophies were miles ahead of America. Both books sold well but were criticized as pandering to Japanese interests. Then came Clyde Prestowitz's *Trading Places* and Karel van Wolferen's *The Enigma of Japanese Power*. These were criticized as overly hostile attacks on Japan. Van Wolferen received special censure from some Japanese quarters, since his focus on power rather than trust or loyalty as the key concept in Japanese business and political life struck an exposed nerve. Unfortunately, these authors did not create a tone of balance or objectivity in their writing. As observers of Japan know all too well, it is very easy to either love or hate Japan. It is very difficult to find a middle ground.

In this study I will focus on the experiences, successes, and failures of Japanese managers in America. Along the way I will discuss the ideologies, philosophizing, and values which influence their behavior and American reactions to them. Many of my insights will be useful to managers of both countries, especially those who must work with each other on a day to day basis. But this is not a "how to manage" book. Nor is it a quick journalistic summary based on quotes from several interviews strung together and fleshed out with biographies of key players. This is not to say that I do not quote Japanese managers or employ narrative and dramatizations to illustrate a point. I do, and the results of my interviews in Tokyo, Osaka, Kyoto, New York, Nashville, Seattle, and Portland are sprinkled throughout the text, as are findings from my surveys of several thousand Japanese and American managers over the last fifteen years. In this book, however, I interpret, criticize, explain, and reach conclusions about what managers have said to me and what the data implies.

I would like to stop here and offer a word on balance and bias. Without in any way excusing Japanese faults, I am firmly in favor of Japanese direct investment in America. In writing about Japan in general and managers in particular, I have tried to be fair. Occasionally I say harsh things, but these are based on my experiences, data gathering, and wide reading. Over a long period of time I have come to admire the Japanese people, but at the same time I have developed a highly critical stance on Japanese political and economic institutions. The Japanese are a first-rate people saddled with second-rate institutions. Because of this they have not yet fully enjoyed the fruits of their remarkable labors over the last half century, and much of their thinking and actions during the next fifty years will be focused on making government and big corporations responsive to the people rather than to narrow constituencies. My biases will color my remarks, but they will not determine them. Thus, at times I will attack some of the foibles of the Japanese people while praising their organizations. At other times I will reverse my stand. All that my Japanese friends and interviewees have asked of me is to speak with honesty and conviction. This I have done.

The story that emerges on Japan's investment in the United States is not the story one reads about in the press, which often focuses on the menace of Japan, Inc. in its relentless pursuit of power over America's "economic independence." Instead, Japan's move to America is an act of submission, a final recognition that Japan must internationalize and be internationalized in turn. The fact that some Japanese industries are wonderfully competitive and eventually might even dominate should not obscure the overall reality of American hegemony. In the long run as in the short run, America will dominate Japan. Sheer size alone makes this inevitable, but superior American productivity and managerial skills, augmented by well-functioning political and social institutions, ensure the outcome. Japan certainly will narrow the gap over the next few decades, and some Americans will see this as a sign of American decline. Nothing could be further from the truth. Americans will benefit from Japanese job-creating investments and high-quality imports. The Japanese will prosper as American firms enter Japan in greater numbers. Talk about dominance will become irrelevant as people simply engage in enterprise without worrying about whether a firm builds its headquarters in America or Japan. Chapter 1 sets the stage for discussion by giving vivid examples of good and bad Japanese managers in America. Subsequent chapters describe reactions of the Japanese to their American assignments within a context of the economic and strategic forces driving Japan's investment in the United States. The middle chapters discuss the impact in America of Japanese approaches to job security, trust, communicating, and decision making. In the latter part of the book I examine Japanese management in various manufacturing and non-manufacturing industries. I conclude with extensive notes and a bibliography of relevant works.

I began by asking, "Shall It Be War?" *Invasion of the Salarymen* shows that the answer is neither "yes" nor "no" but, "How could such a silly question be asked in the first place?" As you will read in Chapter 1, the question of economic war on Japan has indeed been raised. I hope to convince you, however, that people who say such things should be ignored. You should instead listen to those of us who can shed light on the first significant movement into the economic life of the United States of non-Westerners who are not immigrants, the Japanese.

INVASION OF THE SALARYMEN

ONE

The Invasion

In 1841, fourteen-year-old Manjiro stood on the beach of the small island where he and his four fishing companions had washed ashore after being driven from the Japanese coast by a storm. They lived on the island for six months until the New Bedford whaler *John Howard* sailed into view, Captain William H. Whitfield commanding. The young Japanese were frightened by the bearded, tough sailors who landed on the island to hunt for turtles, especially by the two blacks among them— a reaction shared by some Japanese managers 150 years later. When the Americans treated them well, however, fear soon gave way to happiness. On the trip back to the United States, Manjiro's four friends were put ashore in Hawaii under the care of missionaries. Captain Whitfield asked Manjiro, clearly the brightest of the young men, if he would like to see America and study there. Like a good Japanese, the boy conferred with his group. Then he decided to go.[1]

Soon christened "John," Manjiro loved America and America loved him. Within the next five years he rose from illiteracy (he could not even read and write Japanese) to second in command of the whaler *Franklin*. As the first Japanese to visit and work in the United States, Manjiro could be considered the first Japanese manager in America. His career advancement was, to say the least, a bit more rapid than he could have expected back home in Japan, where, as today, status and seniority sometimes counted more than raw talent. But even an up and coming "manager" like John Manjiro could not prosper in a declining industry. As the days of New England whaling came to an end, he decided in 1849 to return to Japan. He shipped out on a lumber schooner bound for San Francisco. Once there, he headed straight for the gold fields. Within two months he had over $600, enough to book passage for Honolulu. There he picked up two of his former companions who wanted to go home, built a small sloop which he named *Adventurer*, and stowed it on the deck of a Shanghai-bound merchant vessel. On February 3, 1851 he landed the sloop on the southern tip of Okinawa, ten years and one month after leaving Japan for a day's fishing.

Japanese officials wary of foreign things arrested him at once and held him in jail for over a year, a treatment, metaphorically speaking, not too unlike that meted out to returning Americanized Japanese today in some companies. Manjiro was questioned endlessly about his visit to America, and the transcripts have survived. They go something like this:

Question: How are men judged in America?

Answer: Americans judge a man by his competence and ability.

Question: That cannot be so.

Answer: It is true!

Question: Tell us about their machines.

Answer: Their steam engine car is called a *reiro* (railroad), and twenty or thirty people ride this so as to travel without exerting themselves.

Question: What are their leaders like?

Answer: The ones who occupy high positions are men of lofty ideas, wiser and more intelligent than the ones we have in Japan. On this point the difference between Japan and America is like the difference between heaven and earth.

What does one do with a bright fellow who has developed an American sense of personal worth and sings America's praises every chance he gets? You watch him very closely, but being Japanese, you also learn everything you can from him. By 1855 Manjiro had become personal secretary to Egawa Toraemon, an influential official. In 1860 he was a member of the first Japanese mission to America, but he was so distrusted as an America lover that he was not allowed to contribute much to the undertaking. Finally in 1870 he returned to New York and journeyed to Fairhaven, Massachusetts to see his old mentor, Captain Whitfield. When Manjiro had gone, the Captain commented, "John Manjiro has paid me a visit. It is wonderful to see the workings of Providence or of God, to bring about His ends."

The first Japanese mission to America in 1860 consisted of three envoys, seventeen officials, fifty-one clerks and six cooks (perhaps Manjiro, like other returned expatriates, had warned them about the food). One of the officials, Yukichi Fukuzawa, was overwhelmed. "One day, on a sudden thought, I asked a gentleman [probably with Manjiro translating] where the descendents of George Washington might be," he recalled years later. "His answer was so casual and indifferent that it shocked me. Of course, I knew that America was a republic with a new president every four years . . . but I could not help feeling that the family of Washington would be sacred above all other families." This belief that rulers and their families should forever be treated as royal has not entirely disappeared from Japan. *Business Tokyo*, an excellent monthly magazine on economic issues, until recently ran articles on the business careers of Japanese royals and their royal-like school chums. To be fair, most Japanese are not interested in outright worship of rank, and even Fukuzawa later wrote, "It is said that heaven did not create one man above or below another man." Rank does count in Japan, however, even if today it is based on tests passed and university attended.

The Japanese visitors' reactions in 1860, which are well known to modern Japanese, helped set the tone of future observation of the United States. The Americans, said one of the mission, "are a people without etiquette . . . we had not entirely been wrong in calling them Western barbarians." Lest this sound too offensive, the same official then noted, "I would forgive their impoliteness because of their friendliness." *Crude* but *friendly*, every Japanese manager of the 1990s probably has heard these words before he embarked on his first assignment to the United States.

The senior Japanese found American casualness about class and status distasteful. The lower-level, younger Japanese loved it. "The ordinary people need not flatter high officials," wrote one. "Thus the nation prospers and the people are secure." This observation tells us a good deal about the forces that drove the Meiji Restoration in the 1860s and that still drive Japan today. The chief goal of Japanese society is the establishment of a secure, orderly nation. The chief means to do this is not a self-appointed, self-perpetuating elite before whom the people must constantly bow. Rather it is an openness and freedom in which "ordinary people" can pursue their interests. Japan has *not* yet reached that goal, no matter how well off Japanese are today. But they are reaching it in their usual incremental Japanese way.

Walt Whitman watched the progress of the first Japanese delegation in the United States.

Sultry with perfume, with ample and flowing garments.
With sunburnt visage, with intense soul and glittering eyes,
The race of Brahma comes.
    . . .

Over sea, hither from Niphon,
Courteous the Princes of Asia . . .
This day they ride through Manhattan.
. . .
You Japanese man or woman . . . ,
Health to you! good will to you all, from me and America sent!

Courteous but *intense*, these are reactions Americans still have to Japanese. So when the crude, friendly Americans work with the courteous, intense Japanese in the 1990s and beyond, what will the result be? Will courtesy blunt crudity? Will friendliness mute intensity? If so, Japanese-owned companies in America will be pleasant, civil environments. If not, they will be stressful and rancorous. As we will see, they are sometimes one, sometimes the other.

When the Japanese ambassadors returned to Japan, the most able of these, Tademasa Oguri, urged his countrymen to develop commercial dealings with other countries. As a result, he was assassinated in 1868. More fortunate was Yukichi Fukuzawa. In his long career he founded a great university and an influential newspaper. After further visits to the United States and Europe, he became Japan's leading champion of modernization. In the minds of Japanese managers in the United States today, his spirit is probably more influential than that of his more conservative traveling companions of 1860. Manjiro and Fukuzawa got the Japanese in America off to a great start. In fact, American-Japanese relations, with the ghastly exception of 1925–1945 (and some West Coast racism), have been remarkably friendly. The Japanese like Americans, even if we are crude, and Americans admire Japanese energy and elegance, even if they are at times stuffy and arrogant.

ECONOMIC WARFARE IN THE 1990s

The history of Japanese visitors to the United States is mostly a record of cordiality. Yet the Japan-U.S. discourse of the 1990s is filled with war talk. William Piez is a career foreign service officer who in 1990 was serving as a senior policy person in the office of the U.S. Trade Representative. Heavily involved in U.S.-Japan trade negotiations since 1971, he notes the militant tone Japanese journalists use to describe discussions. "The Japanese press uses the language of warfare to describe trade talks," he says. "They typically will use words like 'demands,' which usually are associated with the most tense diplomatic exchanges that could even lead to outright hostilities. The press also employs phrases like 'invasion,' 'assault,' 'the landing of foreign products in Japan,' or 'attacks on Japanese industry X from foreign suppliers'—all of which send the wrong set of emotional signals."[2]

War talk is even more inflammatory in the United States. Writing in 1985, journalist Theodore White said, "Today, 40 years after the end of World War II, the Japanese are on the move again in one of history's most brilliant offensives."[3] "The U.S. economy is under siege, and the battlefronts are many," claim Douglas Frantz and Catherine Collins in *Selling Out*.[4] Even worse, America appears to be losing the war. "Japan is creating an economic success where Pearl Harbor failed."[5] On Wall Street, where traders and salesmen like to use military language to put a gloss on the rather banal work they do, the talk is even more fevered. "From a financial point of view, we are being colonized," says investment banker Felix Rohatyn.[6] Economist Kenneth Courtis notes, "What used to happen only on the battlefield, they are doing through the stock market."[7] Journalist Daniel Burstein, hearing all this chatter from the street, concludes, "In financial services the growing Japanese attack will lead to a bloody shakeout."[8]

If the rhetoric on Japanese investment in the United States must be warlike, then let us put it to use. Yes, an invasion is occurring. The Japanese have moved beyond the beaches and are advancing into the heartland. Many state governments are clamoring to surrender to them. The Japanese even are manufacturing their army's vehicles on American soil. Their managerial soldiers are streaming in, corrupting our simple folk with promises of high quality products and superior service. Rotary clubs have been infiltrated. School systems have been poisoned with their educational ideology. What will become of us poor, weak, helpless Americans?

What *might* happen is the following: If the Japanese succeed in establishing economic front lines in every state, our productivity will improve, as will our standard of living. We will enjoy the products Japanese sell and we will revel in their excellent service. Our workers will feel more secure in their jobs in Japanese factories and will be treated with respect. Our children will begin to learn again as schools imitate Japanese ways.

I say *might* because in fact the Japanese do not appear to be having much success in their invasion. Later I will examine economic and managerial explanations for Japanese problems in America, but for now let me say this: Japanese employees often are not as loyal to their companies as Americans are. Japanese are group-oriented, but they also have a highly developed sense of self, and group life can be just as much a torment for them as it is for their employees in America. The practice of lifetime employment in large firms is a World War II development and not rooted in age-old cultural values. Indeed, Japanese managerial values depend more on economic, institutional, and demographic conditions than they do on culture. Without deep roots, Japanese managerial practices can be remarkably flexible, and in well-run firms like Honda and Sony they are. In later chapters, however, I show that in fact many Japanese firms in America are rather clumsily managed. For example, before they knew better, Japanese executives wanted senior Americans to punch a time clock in their Japanese-owned Wall Street securities firm. In an Ohio factory the Japanese forbade Americans to chew gum. Japanese owners of a New England ball bearing plant removed chairs from the factory floor so workers could not sit down. At several Japanese factories employees are only allowed to go to the bathroom on their breaks.

Most of the talk about economic warfare arose because Japanese corporations rushed to invest massive amounts of dollars in the United States during the late 1980s. Americans saw this ill-planned deluge of capital as a menace to their economic independence. By 1992 Japanese foreign direct investment in the United States was about $150 billion. One-third was in manufacturing, with most of it in autos, machinery, chemicals, metals, food processing, and wood and paper products. Non-manufacturing capital was mainly in real estate ($25 billion), financial services ($17 billion), and sales ($14 billion).[9] Japan ranks second behind Britain among foreign investors in the United States, but it holds only about 18 percent of foreign direct investment.

Japan must adjust its economy to the United States, but it is not as dependent as some people think. Only about 5 percent of Japanese domestic and foreign industrial activity serves final users in the United States. Auto manufacturers receive 28 percent of their sales from America, and consumer electronic producers 23 percent. No other industry is above 20 percent. Electronics, computers, machinery, and steel industries represent between 10 and 20 percent.[10] This is important, but it certainly is not enough to engage in economic warfare. After all, American business receives 20 percent of sales from production in other countries, about four times more than the Japanese do. Loose talk about America conducting economic warfare abroad is heard, but it is no longer taken as seriously as it once was. If Japan keeps expanding its American investments, however, which it will, hostile comments will multiply. According to MITI (Japan's Ministry of International Trade and Industry) surveys, 30 percent of Japanese firms plan to establish overseas headquarters in the 1990s, mostly in the United States.[11] If this investment occurs, Japan will rapidly approach the United States' level of foreign investment, and journalists will be looking frantically for fresh military metaphors to describe the "onslaught." By the end of the decade up to one million Americans could be working for 100,000 Japanese managers in the United States. Currently there are about 2600 manufacturing and non-manufacturing Japanese affiliates in the United States. Aside from forty to fifty of them that are large and profitable, most are small and many are unprofitable. They threaten no one except their Tokyo- and Osaka-based parent companies that must continually subsidize their operations. If this somewhat modest Japanese investment is provoking an outcry, what will happen when Japan's investment reaches big league proportions? The future depends to a large extent on how Japanese expatriates conduct themselves in America.

THE GOOD JAPANESE MANAGER

Mr. K., a small gray-haired man in a blue company jacket, walked slowly along the assembly line. On the line about fifty employees, mostly women, were occupied in maintenance and service tasks. The real work of putting the VCRs together was being performed by robots.

"Of course, these robots are not nearly as sophisticated as the ones we have in Japan," he casually remarked. "But here the workforce is not as well trained as the workers in Japan." His matter of fact honesty carried no trace of arrogance. This was simply the way he saw the world, and he had adapted to it.

Many of the employees smiled at Mr. K. as he showed his visitor around. He appeared to be at ease with these Americans and they with him. Yet it was just as apparent that the workers were being polite rather than ebullient. He paid the going wage, kept the place clean and warm, and sometimes slowed the line to keep everyone working on three shifts. The daughters of some of these employees probably worked the night shifts, and their paychecks helped a lot. They appreciated Mr. K.'s thoughtfulness and respected him for it. But no one treated him as a father figure in an extended family. He did what he did because a clever manager paid attention to employee needs. These American women liked that, but he was still an employer and was kept at arms length.

"I can't really get through to them," Mr. K. said. "The loyalty and commitment I see in the Japanese worker just isn't there."

"Well," said the visitor, "You don't offer the kind of job security and training a Japanese 'lifetime' employee gets. You can't expect as much allegiance."

"That's correct," he responded quickly. He had thought much about this. "We have to adopt American-style relations with our workers, but I wish I could figure out a way to develop a more Japanese approach."

"I don't think you can do much more than you've done," said the visitor. "Even though your business here is owned by a Japanese firm, it is not a Japanese company in the real sense."

"This is true, and my American personnel director and I have discussed this many times. He criticized me for thinking of the plant as Japanese," said Mr. K., smiling. "I will have to go back to Japan and let a more sophisticated manager take my place." The visitor laughed, for Mr. K. was as good as most Japanese managers he had observed. Even better.

They walked on until the visitor stopped behind a woman who seemed to be doing the same tasks as the robots on either side of her. She was the only human on that part of the line.

"Why not a robot?" he asked.

Mr. K. hesitated a moment. Then he explained. "We have created jobs in the plant for local people. It is politically sensible." Then he moved on.

The next stop was at the station of a woman in her mid-forties. She was checking an oscilloscope as each VCR passed her.

"Hi, Mr. K.," she said, smiling. Mr. K. smiled in return.

"It is very strange to me," he mused when they had walked on. "That lady is very nice, a fine lady. But she is suing the company. I cannot understand this."

He explained. A few months earlier one of the American foreman had asked her to speed up a bit since she was slowing the line. She did. Later at home she casually mentioned the incident to her husband, who was an out-of-work union member. He had heard that a lawyer in town specialized in age discrimination suits. Within a few days the woman sued.

"It seems so routine to her," said Mr. K., "as if it happens every day. I can't get over it." Each day as the suit dragged on, the woman cheerfully came to work and went about her job. She was polite and friendly to Mr. K. He was the same because she was really a good employee. But the tendency of Americans to sue bothered him. He said it was the major difference he had encountered in America.

"My personnel director tells me to expect a lot more nuisance suits," he said, "but I will never get used to it. Such things should not be routine."

Mr. K. and his visitor walked through a set of doors and arrived at an office, one large room with desks and chairs. A woman sat near the front door. She was the receptionist, telephone operator, and private secretary to Mr. K.; there were no other secretaries. Mr. K's desk was in a small closet-like room behind the switchboard.

"Your VCRs are fine ones," the visitor said as they sat in two soft chairs separated by a low table, the only plush items in the building. "But so are the Korean and Taiwanese sets. How will you compete with them as they enter the American market?"

Mr. K. folded his hands. "Our strategy will be to move upward in the market. We have developed many 'bells and whistles' in Japan, and we will add them to attract a more affluent customer."

"But what if the competitors also enter the upscale markets?"

"Eventually they will, but we are taking some steps. Within a year or two all of our parts and raw materials will be American made. Our goal is to make a 100 percent American VCR."

"How will that help?" the visitor asked, although he expected Mr. K.'s answer.

"Who can tell? Perhaps the pressure of foreign imports will become great in America. Actions may be taken."

"Quotas on VCRs?"

"It is possible."

"But what if that doesn't happen? Then how will you compete?"

"We will compete on price."

"Tokyo will subsidize you?"

"Of course. As long as I cut some cost to show my effort to compete."

"How will you cut cost?"

"Workers can be replaced by robots, cutting cost by perhaps 10 percent. Then I can lower prices."

"I suppose you can," said the visitor, remembering the woman alone amid the robots. "But you will be criticized for not practicing Japanese management. Japanese are not supposed to lay employees off."

Mr. K. shook his head. "This is not Japan," he said. "However, we will never take such steps unless the competition becomes overwhelming. I don't think that will happen. Our marketing department is tireless in creating an image of a superior product, which ours is." He smiled. So did the visitor.[12]

Mr. K. is honest, thoughtful, friendly, and politically sensitive. He represents the majority of Japanese managers in America. His simple, no-frills approach is appreciated by Americans used to high-handed, status-conscious American managers. But like most Japanese he is confused by the legalistic system in which he finds himself, and American ideas about the nature of work, loyalty, and commitment are not his ideas. He copes because he must, and thirty years of assignments in over fifty countries have given him the adaptive skill he needs. Nevertheless, his lot is a hard one. He is very much under the thumb of Tokyo, to which he reports as a manufacturing manager. But he also reports to the marketing people at U.S. headquarters. What they want is not always what manufacturing wants, so he spends perhaps a third of his time traveling one way to Tokyo and the other way to the New Jersey regional office in an endless round of coordination. Of course, he is good at this. He is a *bucho*, a senior general manger without technical expertise whose task is to create conditions in which the technical people can do the best possible job. American managerial theorists lecture about the need for "buffers" to "protect the technological core" from external forces. Mr. K. is a buffer. Right alongside him is a technical manager of roughly equal pay but somewhat lower status. This man takes care of the machines and the production process while Mr. K. deals with everything else. The generalist-specialist team approach works very well and is at the heart of most Japanese successes in America. However, what evidence there is suggests that many firms, perhaps 45–50 percent of Japanese manufacturing plants, are not doing very well in the United States. Markets may be weak and the inherent risk of direct investment are always a trial, but to complicate matters, some remarkably bad managers also have journeyed to America.

THE BAD JAPANESE MANAGER

Matsushita has been selling in the United States since the 1960s, but its real involvement in this country began in the 1970s, when it began building one plant after another. Astonished Matsushita executives rushed to expand U.S. production even faster in the 1980s, after General Electric (GE) withdrew from consumer electronics. Matsushita had been in big trouble in the 1970s, but thanks to GE and Matsushita's own bootstrap efforts, it prospered in the 1980s. During this rollercoaster ride the firm learned what kind of manager is suitable for overseas assignments and what kind is not. Officials at Matsushita's Overseas Training Center near Osaka have put together a composite picture based on real incidents of the bad Japanese manager. It tells us something about what American employees currently are enduring in poorly-administered Japanese-owned firms.[13]

Let us call the composite bad manager Mr. Moto. He is a rather rigid person, dependent on tried and true practices and unwilling to change. He carries a long narrow stick to point out things to his staff as he walks through his plant and has been known to rap American workers sharply on their hard hats when he sees them deviating from the programmed motions they are required to perform on the production line. Rarely does he treat employees as individuals, preferring instead to rely on stereotypes he has picked up in Japan. To him Americans are a lazy people whose time in the sun has come and gone. Getting work out of them, in his view, requires constant pressure. Often this takes the form of searching out bad behavior and then yelling at the offender, preferably in front of other employees so that they get the message. In Mr. Moto's division only perfect performance will be tolerated, and since there is only one way to do a job with maximum efficiency, no deviations are allowed. Moto-san can get very emotional sometimes, and he is noted for making the women employees cry when he screams at them. "You are stupid! stupid! stupid! Why do you work here?" he will say.

Moto-san finds he must carefully explain his directives to his harried staff. "Why do Americans ask so many questions?" he wonders. The fact that he gives inconsistent, arbitrary directions does not bother him. He is the boss and their duty is to obey. The staff would not mind Mr. Moto's confused decisions if they at least got the division somewhere, but Moto-san rarely makes decisions about important things. His job is to please his superiors and do what they tell him, not to make judgments on his own. With the plant manager Moto-san is unassertive and passive. His Japanese colleagues, who dislike him just as much as the Americans do, call him a "dark" person. Yet they welcome him at their after work social hours and often cover up for his blundering. When Americans complain, his colleagues close ranks and defend him vigorously. They must spend their careers with Mr. Moto, and it would not do to have him as an enemy back in Japan.

Luckily, the Mr. K.'s are easy to find while the Moto-sans are few and far between. But there are enough of them to notice.

WHAT THREAT?

The Japanese "invasion" of the United States is not a threat to anyone. Indeed, except for a few notable successes in a few auto manufacturing and some consumer electronics firms, Japan's investment in America in the 1980s was ill-planned and unsuccessful. This is not to say that the Japanese will not eventually become more successful in the United States. They will, but the 1990s will be a period of floundering about as Japanese companies develop a customer base and try to find American employees who are both submissive order-takers, which Japanese managers are used to in Japan, and creative idea-generators, which the Japanese desperately need.

In this book Japanese managers will tell their stories and I will present data and analysis to back up those stories. It is not the tale currently being told in the American press or the Japan-bashing books. For example, it is not the story of the fierce competitive nature of Japanese business that forces companies to develop strengths transferable to America. On the contrary, a number of highly uncompetitive (economists use the term "oligopoly") industries have provided a low-risk base for firms to undertake high-risk American ventures. Oligopolization in Japan has enabled firms to pile up huge profits, which wisely have been used to develop high-quality products and flexible manufacturing processes. Big-name firms like Matsushita have exported their acquired knowledge in electronics to their American factories in the United States, and have been strong competitors there. But about 1400 Japanese factories are in the United States, and generally they are not profitable. Why not? For one, American markets are freely competitive, and Japanese are often not used to that. American suppliers are independent, and that is hard to deal with. American workers do not want to accumulate overtime like Japanese workers do. Unlike Japan, the government wavers between disinterest and hostility. The press is not as docile, the education system is disorganized and failing to provide good workers, no web of friends, relatives, and school chums exists to help a manager over the rough spots, and quality is a function of price rather than an end in itself. Life is tough for Japanese managers in America, and knowledge of great technology alone has not been enough to crack the American nut.

The usual response of the threat-mongers at this point is, "Yes, but the Japanese are very long-term oriented. They are establishing themselves now in a manner which bodes ill for America." Later I will look at the likely future of the Japanese manager in America. It is not a pretty picture—for him. His customers will be pulled away by dazzling prices offered by Korean and Taiwanese firms and by newly invigorated American competitors. His friendly Japanese bank will not be so friendly anymore, beset by rising costs and bad Third World debts. His hardball lobbying tactics in Washington will backfire on him. His American employees will be second raters unless he figures out a way to share power with them. The barriers to success are many and high.

As our story unfolds, the real nature of Japanese management will become clear, as will the character of the Japanese "invasion" of the United States.

What drives Japanese managers is not loyalty, commitment, trust, or a warm communalism in the workplace. It is rather an extreme intolerance of uncertainty and risk and a belief that more than anything else managing is the exercise of power.

Japanese labor productivity is often poor. What managers are good at is using workers to improve quality. Making a fetish of quality is good business, but it is also a way to more easily control employees and vendors.

In the 1980s Japanese direct investment was driven by United States government threats of protectionism and a need to do something with massive amounts of trade surplus dollars. It was rushed and ill-planned. Over the long term, however, what makes foreign investing possible is oligopolization in Japan.

As a proportion of the American economy, the direct investment by Japan in the United States is much smaller than most people realize. It has, however, the potential to be quite large.

Japanese managers in America are both delighted and appalled by American workers. They like the hard work, but they are aghast at the low education levels. They value American creative spirit, but they dislike American individualism. They admire Americans' commitment to their families; in a nation riddled with divorce this has been a big surprise. But they resent the American's need to drop everything and leave for home at 5 o'clock.

Many Japanese managers in the United States are carbon copies of Americans in Europe in the 1950s and 1960s. They are sometimes arrogant and heavy-handed. They see their domestic approaches to managing as automatically transferable to any nation at anytime. They live in enclaves, send their children to their own schools, and party among themselves.

In the 1990s Japan's American investment will change. There will be more acquisitions than start ups and more expansions than acquisitions. Some movement to America by small and mid-sized companies will occur, but large firms will still dominate. Japanese management will become Americanized. This is what usually happens to foreign investment in the United States, but also the Japanese are changing. Their move to America was something that had to be done if Japan was to be a full member of the emerging global society. They no longer will be able to maintain their wariness of outsiders and conservative adherence to unique domestic business practices. None of this is easy for Japan, which adapts readily on the surface of things but resists change at the core. In a sense the invasion by Japan is not a set of considered choices. It is more a whole string of hasty and reluctant responses to American economic activities at home and abroad. Behind everything, then, the real forces driving Japan's surge of investment in America, the real CEOs of Japan, Inc., are people named Jones and Smith.

TWO

Why Are They Here?

Michael Porter, in *The Competitive Advantage of Nations,* explains why companies of some nations are more successful at globalization than others. They continually innovate and upgrade, spurred on by capable domestic suppliers, sophisticated customers, and specialized skill and knowledge, all in close proximity to each other.[1] Most of this is certainly true for Japan, whose globalization is taking the form of heavy investing in the United States. It is the *lack* of well-developed domestic competition, however, that is the engine of Japanese foreign direct investment. This is quite commonsensical, since firms locked into freely competitive markets rarely develop the surplus capital needed for overseas investing. The oligopoly environment which prevails in many Japanese industries has created the conditions in which "competitive advantage" could be developed. Without those low-competition conditions Japan would not have been in a position to take advantage of all the opportunities and stimuli to invest in the United States that came its way during the 1980s. Japanese companies in America can afford costly trial and error tactics in American markets because they have low risk conditions at home. This is an important point for Americans trying to figure out why the Japanese tolerate so many blunders in their U.S. operations. When you own the mine, the company store doesn't have to make much of a profit.

WHO ARE THEY AND WHERE ARE THEY?

About 6000 foreign manufacturing firms have set up operations in the United States.[2] About 1000 are West German, 900 British, and 850 Canadian.

Japanese Companies in the United States

How many?	About 1400 goods producers and 1200 in financial services, insurance, trade, sales, and entertainment. About 50,000 Japanese managers and their families live in the U.S.A.
How big?	Most are small, averaging a few hundred employees. In terms of dollar investments, the entertainment and auto industries lead.
Where are they?	Concentrated in the NYC and LA areas. Sizable outposts in Pennsylvania, Georgia, Illinois, North Carolina, Texas, and Florida.
What do they do?	Most firms operate only one plant. The largest number of Japanese investors is in: plastic products, motor vehicle parts, pharmaceutical preparations, inorganic chemicals, prerecorded tapes and records, and printing and publishing.

Most plants were started in the 1980s, a sign of just how new Japan is to the United States. Only eight firms were started before 1970.[3] The oldest affiliate is Hawaii Hochi, Ltd., a newspaper publisher in Honolulu. Started in 1912, it employs 100 people. In 1954 Alaska Pulp Co. opened a wood pulp plant in Sitka. It now employs 300. In the 1960s Taiyo Fishery Co., one of the world's largest firms, started Western Alaska Fisheries, Inc., to produce frozen fish for Japan. During that decade Sumitomo Metals acquired Western Tube and Conduit in California, and Matsushita started a plant in Puerto Rico. It now employs close to 500 people and produces stereo speakers and cabinets. Mitsubishi started a small chemicals plant in Alaska, while Sekisui Chemical Co. acquired plants in Lawrence, Massachusetts, and Coldwater, Minnesota. Interestingly, recent investments follow the same pattern as early investments. The Japanese of the 1950s and 1960s focused on wood, fish, consumer electronics, and chemicals, as they still do. The only change in the 1990s has been the addition of auto manufacturing and entertainment as major investment industries.

The list of 1980s investors is revealing. Until recently, most companies from Japan began in America by building their own plant. Rarely did they acquire and rarely did they own multiple facilities. The exceptions to this pattern are the following:

Multiple Facility U.S. Acquisitions of Japanese Companies

Acquiring Firm	Acquired Firm	What the Japanese Got
Sakata Inx	Acme Printing Ink	24 small plants in the South, East, and Midwest
Mitsubishi Heavy Industries	Beloit Corp	20 percent ownership of ten plants in the paper machine business
NEC	Bull HN Information Systems	15 percent of a 9000–employee computer manufacturer
Kirin Brewery	A Coca-Cola subsidiary	13 bottling plants in New England
Nippon Mining	Gould, Inc.	12 plants producing electronics equipment
Nippon Sanso	Matheson Gas Products	50 percent of nine plants producing gas handling equipment
Dainippon Ink	Reichhold Chemicals	27 facilities employing 2000 people
Settsu	Uarco	17 plants and 5500 employees producing business forms

The reasons for these purchases of extensive physical assets are two-fold. First, some Japanese firms want to buy market share. These companies are in it for the long term and want a major presence right away. Second, others simply identified a profitable investment and grabbed it with cheap dollars. If more U.S. firms with good market shares and profit potential come up for sale in the 1990s and the dollar remains low, Japanese firms will buy them. The list of Japanese buyers, however, far exceeds the list of American sellers, so new Japanese investment is likely to continue to be mainly the one-plant-start up, or acquisition, or expansion of an existing facility. Start up of multiple-unit investments is unlikely.

The South has been an attractive destination for Japanese manufacturers for a decade.[4] Wages are only 80 percent of the national average, unions are few, and states have offered lower taxes and higher incentives than elsewhere. Although the Japanese avoid the South's poorer, blacker counties, Japanese-created Southern employment grew at a 35 percent greater annual rate than the national rate of Japanese job creation. This is an indication of the attractiveness of the South, but also suggests that Japanese firms with low-labor productivity—a big problem in Japan—are congregating there. Real estate investors, on the other hand, are focusing on California, New York, Hawaii, Illinois and Washington State. With the exception of Illinois they avoid the Heartland and Dixie.[5]

THE OLIGOPOLY EDGE

A freely competitive market exists when the actions of no individual firm or set of firms can control entry to the industry, prices, wages, or other costs. In this environment consumers enjoy the lowest prices for goods, and the welfare of society is maximized. An oligopoly exists when a few firms dominate sales in an industry over a long time. If, for example, three or four firms collect over 50 percent of the sales in a market, they probably can control prices by colluding or simply imitating each other. Prices will be above what they should have been in a freely competitive market, and the excess profits, which are more than those required by owners as an adequate return on their capital, can be reinvested. When these profits (which often do not show up as bottom line numbers) are enormous, as they have been in Japan for the last eight years or so, good domestic opportunities to reinvest cannot absorb all the cash. Companies then start looking overseas. One of the most oligopolized industries in Japan, autos, has been the most aggressive investor in America, and similar patterns can be observed in other industries. Oligopolization does not cause foreign investing, but in Japan's case it was a condition which allowed other investment stimuli—such as the trade surplus of dollars and threats of U.S. trade barriers—to trigger a massive response. Indeed, it is something of a mystery as to why that response has not been even more massive.

In a study of twenty-five Japanese industries, all but six had concentration ratios above 50 percent.[6] That means the top three firms held more than 50 percent of market share in Japan. In autos, Toyota, Nissan, and Honda hold 80 percent of the market. In detergents Kao, Lion, and Procter & Gamble's subsidiary hold 94 percent. Ricoh, Canon, and Fuji Xerox share 84 percent of the plain paper copier market, and NEC, Fujitsu, and Toshiba divide up 77 percent of the personal computer market. Large portions of Japanese manufacturing clearly are oligopolized. Although consumers pay higher prices than they would in more competitive markets, the Japanese government has made little effort to break up oligopolies, preferring instead to guide them. It is much easier to control an industry with only three important firms than one with no important firms. The bane of oligopolies is new entrants to the industry offering lower prices, and the least manageable entrants are foreign investors. Until only a few years ago Japan had strong legal barriers against them. These barriers are down now, but through a variety of techniques foreigners in large numbers are kept out. As a share of the total economy, foreign investment in Japan is only about one-tenth of what it is in America and one-twentieth of European levels. Importers, who also could undercut oligopolies with low-priced products, have not done so. As the dollar fell during the late 1980s, prices of U.S. goods in Japan should have fallen at the same rate. They did not, suggesting either aggressive profit-taking by importers of price inelastic U.S. products or collusion. Probably both are occurring.

We looked at the behavior in the United States of the top three oligopolized Japanese firms in comparison with the top three non-oligopolized firms. On average the oligopolized firms controlled 38 percent of Japanese-owned firms in their corresponding U.S. industries. Non-oligopolized firms controlled only 29 percent in their industries. Moreover, the greater the domination of Japanese investment in an American industry by oligopolized firms, the bigger their U.S. subsidiaries and affiliates tended to be in terms of employees.[7] The top Japanese three in VCR production, Matsushita, JVC, and Hitachi, control 50 percent of Japanese firms producing in the United States and 32 percent of employees. The top three in autos control about 80 percent of Japanese-owned U.S. auto firms (including sales and marketing firms) and 68 percent of employees. What we see, then, is that Japanese investment in the United States is dominated by oligopolized firms. They tend to own the largest number of Japanese-owned firms within a given industry and control the largest number of employees. The non-top three firms in oligopolized home industries do invest in the United States, of course (Sony, not being a big player in Japan, being the most noteworthy example), but they are in the minority.

According to Kagayaki Miyazaki, chairman of Asahi Chemicals, "Few Japanese corporations develop overseas operations because, in actuality, few even today have the strength to do so."[8] To test this claim, we examined thirty-five manufacturing industries, ranging in size from a few firms to over eighty firms in the industry. Regardless of industry size, only a few firms in each industry had invested in U.S. operations.[9] In the pharmaceutical preparations industry, for example, only six out of eighty-two firms had U.S. operations. In industrial inorganic chemicals, only nine out of sixty-five had gone to the United States. Mr. Miyazaki is correct. On average, about five Japanese firms per industry have established an American presence. These five were undoubtedly the top firms.

Thus, only a small number of top firms, predominantly from oligopolized low-competition industries in Japan, have been able to accumulate enough capital (still, a very large sum of money) to finance direct investment in the United States. These firms do not fit the description of globalizers offered by Michael Porter, who emphasized strong competition in Japan as the domestic base required for launching world-class competitors. If we assume that these firms in America are world-class competitors, which may or may not be the case, their strengths really are based on the *lack* of freely functioning competitive markets in Japan. The Japanese oligopolists do compete fiercely with a few rivals within each industry, but they need not worry about new entrants endangering their position or about second-tier firms making a bid for supremacy. It is all quite orderly and managed in comparison with the fluid markets of economic theory. Economists call the excess profits that oligopolists accumulate "economic rent," and it is rent that has financed the invasion of the salarymen. As noted earlier, the competitive markets in the United States are quite a shock to some Japanese managers, and it will take them time to learn how to become successful. They probably will make it, given their technology, quality emphasis, and flexibility, but these strengths more often than not are rooted in the highly circumscribed competition of oligopolized markets at home. When American managers see their Japanese bosses perplexed and even terrified by the fluid entry and exit strategies of American companies in U.S. markets, they should remember that little of this coming and going occurs in Japan. It is all very strange to the Japanese.

WHERE IS THE MONEY COMING FROM?

In 1987 Japan invested $7 billion in American manufacturing and non-manufacturing companies. In 1988 about $14 billion was invested. Estimated investing in 1990 ran about $2.3 billion a month, including purchases of and loans to U.S. subsidiaries.[10] Over $100 billion in total was invested in the United States by 1990, most of it within the previous six years. By 1991 the figure was $132 billion. Where is all of this money coming from? Economists would say that it is trade-surplus dollars simply being recycled. They are correct, but only in a very general sort of way. The specific processes followed to gather capital together have been different for different types of investors.

During the mid-1980s, when the surge of direct investing in the United States began, Japanese manufacturers depended mainly on retained earnings as a source of foreign investment capital. Retained earnings came from profits, and profits in part came from trade-surplus dollars. Currently retained earnings still are a major source of funds, but the trade surplus has declined. By 1990 the profits were coming from the Japanese domestic market. In addition, firms raised about $186 billion in 1989, up from $33 billion in 1985. Most of this money came from selling warrant and convertible bonds, and part of it was used to build or acquire companies in America. As for non-manufacturing investors, mostly banks, securities companies, and trading firms, their 1985–1986 capital came in large part from borrowing. By the end of the decade equity issuing was the preferred source, especially for the banks. That has now come to a crashing halt because of the 1990 stock market collapse.

Stimulated by an expanding Japanese money supply, the Tokyo stock market grew dramatically from 1987 to the end of 1989, and some firms turned away from their major lines of business to speculation. About 50 percent of bank profits in the period came from investing in financial markets, but the killing made by the banks was nothing in comparison with that of a few big industrial firms. For fiscal year 1989, Toyota earned *$792 million* and Matsushita *$766 million* (at 150 yen/dollar) in loan interest, dividends, and interest payments on bonds held.[11] Toyota could have funded, and probably did, almost all of its billion dollar investment in Kentucky right out of investment profits. Other firms with substantial yields from the financial markets were Hitachi ($413 million), Kirin ($189 million), Sharp ($177 million), Fuji Photo ($172 million), Sumitomo Corporation ($167 million), Sony ($158 million), Mitsubishi Heavy Industries ($157 million), and Nissan ($151 million). Big American investments by Matsushita and Sony in the last few years probably are directly related to these speculative gains. The other firms undoubtedly will be looking for high-powered U.S. acquisitions in the 1990s.

As the trade surplus fell, then, firms generated funds for U.S. investment from issues of bonds and stocks, from growing profits in domestic markets, and from speculation in financial markets. Bank borrowing does not appear to have been a major fund source, although it certainly was used, especially for company expansion, real estate purchases, and some industry acquisitions. The big headline-grabbing issue has focused, however, on the use of bloated land values as the ultimate underlying basis for raising investment capital. A firm owning land that has risen several hundred percent from the purchase price could borrow against the land, speculate in the equity markets, pay back the loan with profits, and still have plenty left over to invest overseas. In the late 1980s the CEO of a large energy company decided to sell an old barracks-like building in Tokyo which the firm had used for years to house its trainees during their indoctrination. Since the Imperial Army approach to training had had its day in Japan, replaced by more modern techniques, the firm no longer could get recruits to spend months cooped up in a barracks. The executive was astonished to find that the structure, which cost a few thousand dollars, sold for about $300 million. "I made my profit that year simply by selling the building," he said. "Of course it was really the land that had value."

Sixty-six percent of Japan's wealth is in land, and only 23 percent is in buildings, plant, and equipment. In America 24 percent of its wealth is in land and 42 percent in buildings, plant, and equipment.[12] By 1988 Japanese corporations were holding land valued at $2.9 trillion above book value. Borrowing or raising equity against 25 percent of these unrealized capital gains would have provided $700 billion. Little of this potential corporate borrowing occurred, although the banks showed great eagerness to make this kind of loan. They turned to lending to real estate speculators instead.

One reason for inflated land values is the mismatch between supply and demand. It is considered bad form in Japan to sell land, especially land used for farming. "Japanese farm land is like a family treasure, not just a tool to grow crops," said a Japan Agricultural Council official. "The Japanese farmer is ashamed to sell his land. We know that land is land, but the Japanese feel it is to be treasured." Keeping land out of circulation is not only rooted in culture. Real estate speculators and their friends in government like the practice, too. To make sure that landowning farmers or corporations do not waver in their mystical bond with their land, capital gains taxes on the sale of real estate can be as high as 94 percent. This keeps land off the market. So that owners are not penalized for not using it efficiently, property taxes are kept low, at rates only 2.5 percent of what they are in New York City. In addition, large tracts in cities are designated as "agricultural" land to keep them from being built on. All of these tactics keep land supply down and, as the Japanese economy grew rapidly between 1983–1990 and demand soared, values high. The banks liked this, since their corporate lending was weak and they wanted to increase land-based loans to real estate speculators. The speculators used much of the money to buy buildings in Los Angeles, New York, and Hawaii with cheap dollars. When the dollar eventually rises to an appropriate level, probably 180 yen to the dollar (give or take 20 yen), they will try to sell their holdings. If the American economy goes into a deep recession in the meantime (deeper than 1991) and building revenues do not provide enough funds to service their loans, the speculators will fail. The banks will end up with massive losses and a lot of land they cannot sell for cultural and economic reasons. If their Third World debts go sour at the same time, a number of second-tier Japanese banks will be forced to merge with other banks to save themselves.

The future will not look like the past. Interest rates in Japan are rising and stock values falling, thus reducing both bond and equity sources of capital for U.S. investments. Bank lending will have to become much more cautious, thus putting a stop to massive purchases of American real estate. American exports to Japan are gradually increasing, so that the trade surplus will become less of a source of investment funds. The only remaining capital generator is the booming Japanese economy, but even this engine of profits has begun sputtering under the pressure of inflation-busting brakes on money supply growth. Even if profit opportunities continue, Japanese workers may lay claim to them. Manufacturing productivity increases have been several percentage points above wage increases for a number of years, but the gap is narrowing.

If Japanese employees begin to reap the rewards of increased productivity, profits will decline rapidly. In effect, the subsidization of the American economy by Japanese workers will come to an end. Profits generated by their productivity increases will return to them instead of being used to create jobs for people in Ohio, Tennessee, and Kentucky.

ECONOMIC IMPERFECTIONS

As the trade deficit grew after 1985, Japanese firms had to send back all of the dollars they had piled up in the form of portfolio investment in U.S. stocks, bonds, and loans or direct investment in U.S. manufacturing or service industries. They did both, but the share of the total given to direct investment has been rising. One reason is that as Japanese executives looked to America they saw what seemed to be incredibly cheap assets. Bridgestone acquired twenty-seven Firestone plants for the cost of building one large Japanese facility. If the world were working as economic theory says it ought to, this kind of disparity would not occur. If capital flowed freely everywhere, the cost of assets would be roughly the same in all places since capital would flow into a country until prices were equal. Actually, in the early 1990s this seemed to happen, but when the 1980s began this was not the case. Economic "imperfections" in capital markets existed, meaning that capital did not flow freely to where it could buy the cheapest assets. Many explanations for this are given—government barriers, lack of adequate information, weak telecommunications—but the most interesting reason is simply that the Japanese are uncomfortable overseas and the firms could not get managers to go. Only under the pressure of the immense trade surplus did they take action to surmount barriers and compete with the foreigners in their own land. Armed with low-cost capital and strengthened by a high yen, Japanese corporations flooded into the United States.[13]

The Japanese cost of capital was indeed lower than that of the United States, another sign of imperfections in capital markets, since freely flowing capital should have the same cost everywhere. During the 1980s the gap widened considerably, mostly due to the low cost of raising equity on the booming Japanese stock market and the low returns demanded by company owners.[14] Moreover, Japanese tax policies discouraged risky investments less than U.S. tax structures did. It is not surprising that Japanese companies until 1988 undertook the riskiest of all investment, start ups, as their preferred type. Foreign investors in the United States almost always choose acquisitions instead of the so called "greenfield" method because of the chance to get a functioning, profitable company right away. The problem is that not much can be done to change it, corporate culture and employee intransigence being what they are. The Japanese could afford to take the risk of starting from scratch and moulding organizations into their own image. Eventually the greenfield mania diminished, however, probably because firms decided to become a bit more conservative. Since 1988, investment has been shifting toward acquisitions, with 130 friendly takeovers in that year and 170 in 1989 at a cost of $13.7 billion.[15] This American activity parallels a similar growth of mergers and acquisition (M & A) activity in Japan, but cross-border M & A is more difficult to accomplish. "The biggest problem I encounter in friendly Japanese acquisitions of American firms is the *ringi* system of slow decision making," says a Japanese M & A consultant. "Nobody wants to take responsibility, and the American side demands quicker action. Often the Americans can't wait and they look for another buyer." Since more and more investment will be by acquisition and Japanese owners will have to work with the Americans on hand rather than hire from scratch, we probably will see even more severe employee problems cropping up in Japanese firms than occurred in the 1980s.

Besides market imperfection disparities in the value of assets and the cost of capital, U.S. government barriers to Japanese imports and threats of further actions have stimulated Japanese direct investment to replace exporting. When AT&T talks, the government listens. In 1989 the company won its battle against Japanese and other telephone makers when a 158 percent tariff was imposed against their imports in retaliation for dumping. The act forced the Japanese to invest in the United States. Iwatsu America now produces at its New Jersey plant the same number of telephones it used to import. NEC America expanded its Dallas facilities and also began importing telephones from its Thailand plant, which was not affected by the tariff. The Japanese firms expect prices to rise because of the tariff, and they have positioned themselves to benefit. American protectionist sentiments wax and wane, but the fear of barriers weighs heavily on those firms which depend on exports to survive. Over 75 percent of Minolta's and Canon's sales come from exports, mainly to the United States. For Casio and Honda, 1988 exports were over 60 percent, and Honda's continuing movement of operations to America certainly has been spurred on by trade barrier talk in Washington, D.C.[16] In addition, the institution of "voluntary" restraints on Japanese machine tool, structured iron and steel, and auto exports all set off investment moves to the United States. It is this rush to avoid U.S. import barriers that has led some Japanese investment to be ill-planned and poorly implemented. Since Congress raises trade barrier issues every three years or so, many frightened Japanese will continue to herd unthinkingly into the United States.

ACCESS TO RESOURCES

Distortions in the transnational values of corporate assets, in the cost of capital, and in the free flow of trade all stimulated a rush of Japanese companies to America in the 1980s. These things come and go, as does the investment that follows them. One thing that is always around, however, is Japan's need for agricultural resources. Over 15 percent of Japan's imports are foodstuffs. No other developed nation must devote such a large share of its purchases to agricultural commodities—the EEC total is around 10 percent and in the United States it is 6.3 percent. Over 35 percent of food imports are fish and fish products, with 29 percent devoted to meat and cereals. Thus 64 percent of food purchases are concentrated in three products, and Japanese investment in American agriculture is similarly concentrated.[17]

Most fishing industry investment occurred in 1973–1978, just before and right after the passage of the Fishery Conservation and Management Act (FCMA), which extended U.S. ownership of ocean fish resources to 200 miles. Japanese trawlers could no longer harvest twenty-five tons of bottomfish an hour in the Gulf of Alaska without first getting permission from the U.S. government. It was clear early on that that permission would be gradually rescinded as control of resources was shifted to American harvesters—the "conservation" element to the FCMA really meant re-allocation of resources away from foreigners to U.S. citizens. To maintain access to those resources, Japanese fishing and trading firms began acquiring American processors. A low dollar at the time made American assets inexpensive. The biggest purchase was Kyokuyo's acquisition of Whitney Fidalgo for $11 million in 1973. Most fish processing in Alaska is now dominated or influenced by Japanese-owned companies. So Americanized have these firms become that they often argue for a government-mandated share of the harvest in competition with floating processing vessels on the basis of maintaining the local cultures of the communities in which they reside. By the late 1970s, when it looked like the Japanese would buy up the whole West Coast processing industry, they suddenly pulled back. Their reasons then will be heard again in the 1990s. First, the Japanese economy was booming, and capital was needed at home. Second, the price of American assets had risen in response to Japanese demand and bargains no longer existed. Third, the U.S. government was threatening to erect foreign investment barriers.[18]

In the last decade a few grain businesses were purchased by Japanese investors, but the lion's share of resource-seeking capital went elsewhere. With the opening of Japanese markets to American beef, fruit and wine, Japanese firms have been searching for U.S. acquisitions. The intensity of their search also has been driven by the growth prospects in the U.S. food processing industry. The industry needs massive capital infusions and better integrated operations. With Japanese capital it will get some of it. Kagome, Japan's largest ketchup producer, has built a plant in California, a state which also has attracted Japanese brewing companies to the wine business and textile firms to the cotton industry.[19]

Throughout the 1980s U.S. farm exports to Japan—mostly grain, meat, soybeans, fruit, and cotton—hovered around $6 billion. They are now at $8 billion and likely to grow. In the beef industry Japanese investors want to develop the highly marbled, fatty beef preferred by Japanese consumers and then export it to Japan. Since Americans prefer leaner meat, the Japanese will guarantee supplies by buying beef producers and processors. In 1988 Otaka International bought a 31,000 acre ranch in Colorado, and Zenchiku Corporation purchased Montana's 28,000 acre Selkirk Ranch. About forty Japanese food companies have established operations in the United States. By the mid-1990s quotas in Japan on beef, oranges, orange juice, tomato sauce, apple juice, and ice cream will all but disappear. As demand increases, Japanese distributors will be eager to get their hands on low-cost supplies. Unless they own their own U.S. facilities, they won't find them. Nevertheless, what ought to be a deluge of Japanese capital into American agriculture has not materialized. While Japanese ownership of farms rose 40 percent in the 1980s, the total is small, only about 0.02 percent of U.S. farm land. What should have been a rush into the apple juice business, for example, has been a trickle. To the author's knowledge, only one small company had been acquired by 1990, a Wenatchee, Washington, plant employing perhaps 50 people. It appears that Japanese trading companies and food processors, while attentive to the opportunities in beef, have not yet focused on other food industries. One suspects that their strategies may involve waiting until trends in Japanese demand become clearer.

IN THE AGE OF STRATEGY

Economic explanations for Japanese investment focus on generalizations but rarely look at individual firms. At the firm level strategic thinking focuses on such things as investing in the United States to build a platform for exporting to Europe and to force American competitors to think about their domestic markets rather than moving more into Japan.

Japan has only about $45 billion invested in Europe, less than half of its American involvement and, astonishingly, about the same as its Latin

American investment. European nations have made it clear that the Japanese are not very welcome until they open up Japan more, and so capital that ordinarily would have gone to the EEC had ended up in America to finance American exports to Europe. In Mitchell, South Dakota, Toshiba America Information Systems runs a 145-person plant manufacturing toner and developers for office copiers. It sells domestically but also exports to Europe. Canon exports copiers to Europe from its 1000 employee plant in Virginia. Other manufacturers are exporting audio and video tapes and audio recorders (Sony), microwave ovens (Sharp), television equipment (Toshiba America), and autos (Honda). Starting in 1991 Honda attempted to export Accord station wagons to Europe. France and Italy are pushing for restrictions against these and other exports, claiming that if the U.S. added value is less than 80 percent, a product should be considered Japanese. They will have trouble keeping Honda out, since it probably has or will soon have over 80 percent local content. Some Chrysler cars would have to be considered Japanese, however, since so many of their components are produced by Japanese companies.

Besides creating export bases in America, some Japanese firms have invested to counter strategic moves of competitors. The saga of Komatsu is a classic example. In 1961 Caterpillar set up a joint venture with Mitsubishi to market earth moving equipment in Japan. Komatsu executives determined that they could best fight off Caterpillar by developing an American presence. This was an exceedingly difficult goal, and the employees rallied around the battlecry, "Encircle Caterpillar!" By the late 1960s the company had established a Belgian subsidiary to produce lightweight farm machinery. Some of its output was exported to America. Caterpillar barely noticed. Little by little, however, Komatsu added to its American product line. To force its managers to become competitive, Komatsu instituted its "Yen 180 Program" in 1977. Although the yen was at 240/dollar, all budgets had to assume a 180/dollar rate. The effect on cost cutting was dramatic, and Komatsu was able to underprice Caterpillar. By 1984 Komatsu held 5 percent of the American EME market and went up to 12 percent in 1986. Then the roof caved in as the dollar fell to the 120s. Komatsu's prices rose 20 percent and market share declined. To keep Caterpillar from exploiting its advantage, Komatsu stepped up its efforts. It formed a $1 billion joint venture with Dresser Industries in Libertyville, Illinois. The goal was to use Dresser's excess capacity and dealer network in combination with Komatsu's sophisticated R & D (research and development) and management expertise to go head-to-head with Caterpillar. All of this activity is supposed to keep Caterpillar from thinking about Japan. Caterpillar has expanded its relationship with Mitsubishi and wants to develop a new integrated sales network in Japan, but it may rethink that move if the Komatsu challenge develops strength again.

Very little of these strategic struggles are picked up in the aggregate economic data. In fact, regardless of the value of the dollar, and despite the impacts in the 1980s of U.S. government deficit spending as a stimulus to imports and a Japanese trade surplus which must be reinvested, Japanese direct investment in the United States has been going up every year since the mid-1970s at an almost exponential rate. The dollar, deficit, and cost of capital issues influence the rate of growth, but the growth is always there. It is as if the Japanese suddenly decided to integrate their nation more fully into the U.S.-dominated economic sphere. One hears that a global triad is emerging focused on the EEC, the United States, and Japan. This may be so, but Japan's trade is still mostly in dollars, its defense is in the hands of the United States, it responds in a polite manner to even the most outrageous U.S. intrusions into its domestic economic life, and it creates jobs in its American subsidiaries which destroy export-related jobs at home. The Japan Automobile Workers Union, for example, estimates that 270,000 jobs will have been lost by the mid-1990s due to production at U.S. transplants. Seen in this light Japan's economic invasion of America has been more a journey of submission than attack.

Of course, some Japanese industries will come to dominant positions at the expense of American firms and Japanese strategic moves may hurt American competitors, but in the long term America will retain its overall hegemony. The reason is simple. At some point the United States will compel Japan to allow and even encourage expanded American direct investment in Japan as a *quid pro quo* for Japanese investment in America. Contrary to popular belief, American firms are generally more productive and better managed than Japanese firms, and their growing successes in Japan will change that nation forever. Japan is only Americanized now on the surface. In the future it will be Americanized to its core. Sophisticated Japanese know this. Indeed, even the woman and man on the street know that the deluge of investment into America inevitably will provoke a similar U.S. deluge in Japan. The result could be a dramatic improvement in their material well being, something the Japanese people have been waiting for for a long time, as American producers in Japan stimulate increased competition and lower prices. In a very real sense, Japan's decision to invest in the United States shows that it finally has begun to cast off the mercantilist and totalitarian theories of political economy that have guided national thinking for a hundred years. It has signalled its acceptance of European and American ideas about the way economies should work. What this means for Americans who work for Japanese firms or who do business with them is that they gradually will start to see Japanese managers, however reluctantly, acting more and more like American managers. By 2020, for example, the only differentiating factors will be the accent and the love of sake. The road to 2020, however, will be a bumpy one.

THREE

How Are They Doing?

In 1984 the 1,422 Japanese-controlled firms in the United States averaged $46 million in sales per firm. This number rose to over $79 million by 1987. However, net income fell from $1.2 million per firm to $101,155.[1] In effect, Japanese firms were not making any money. The Internal Revenue Service (IRS) began investigations in 1990, suspecting that parent firms in Japan were deliberately charging their subsidiaries above-market prices for components to raise their affiliate's expenses artificially so as to reduce net income and avoid paying U.S. taxes. The IRS ploy, which has been tried before without success, probably will go nowhere. The reality is that some Japanese parents are likely to be *undercharging* their subsidiaries as a form of subsidy to prop them up. It may be that the spectacular successes of a Honda or a Sony are obscuring the generally weak performance of Japan's U.S. investments.

Weak performance, nonetheless, may be in the eyes of the American beholder, since what counts for success to Japanese may be quite different. Consider these differences between American and Japanese corporations:[2]

- Japanese carry inventory to cover 1.55 months' sales, while U.S. firms carry 1.67 months. This difference leads to lower Japanese inventory costs. (The idea that Japanese firms follow a no inventory, just-in-time approach, however, while true for a few firms, clearly does not apply overall.)
- Japanese depreciation expenses are usually about 9 percent of fixed assets. American depreciation is around 7 percent. Thus the Japanese replace equipment faster.

Return on assets in Japan is a little over 2 percent. In America it is 5 percent. Return on sales is 2 percent in Japan and 4 percent in the United States. Dividend rates in Japan are about one-half of American rates.

These data suggest that Japanese firms—and presumably their subsidiaries in the United States—focus on cost control and technological improvements rather than profitability. In other words they keep their eyes on competitors and consumers rather than owners. They hold prices down by controlling material and overhead costs and work on quality and product improvements by investing heavily. Developing market strength and staying power are what count, although some small profit must be earned if they are to stay in business.

PRODUCTIVITY AND PERFORMANCE

Productivity, which is input divided by output, is the key ingredient for success, and Japanese firms which are more productive than American firms will thrive in America. Such firms are a minority, however. According to Japan Productivity Center data, U.S. manufacturing labor productivity is about 42 percent greater than that of Japan.[3] Only in chemicals, iron and steel, and electrical machinery is Japan's greater. Except for the outstanding performance of chemicals, electronics, and perhaps a few auto plants, labor productivity is not a strength of the Japanese and not likely to have been much of a success factor in their U.S. investments. Japanese productivity has been growing steadily during the last ten years, occasionally at rates quite a bit higher than in America. Even if this growth could be sustained, which is unlikely, Japan would still take over thirty years to catch up to the United States. In food processing, an industry targeted by Japanese firms for American investment, productivity rose 45 percent between 1970 and 1988, but U.S. productivity in food processing went up 110 percent. Japanese agricultural productivity is only 29.6 percent of the United States, construction productivity is 89 percent, and retailing productivity is 59 percent.[4]

Productivity data for Japanese firms in America are hard to come by. The figures one usually sees are for auto transplants, and they show Japanese firms in a very good light. Other data tell a different story, however. In television set manufacturing Japanese assembly plants in the United States produce on average about 1250 sets per employee per year, about twice the labor productivity of non-Japanese manufacturers. Japanese plants engaged in total production rather than just assembly, however, are only about one-third as productive as fully integrated non-Japanese plants.[5]

We also have data to compare Japanese investors in the United States with American investors in Japan.[6] American manufacturers in Japan are concentrated in petroleum and machinery and hence are different types of companies from Japanese firms in America, but the data tell the same story as above. American sales per employee are roughly twice Japanese sales per U.S. employee, and American firms show about $9000 profit per employee while the Japanese show none. Non-manufacturing firms, which can be compared more easily, are different, with Japanese investors in the United States doing much better. They have $469,000 in sales and $1,700 in profit per employee, while American firms in Japan are at $21,900 in sales and $432 in profit. What probably is going on here is the success of Japan's trading companies in the United States which have been here for a long time and are well entrenched. In contrast, American marketing and sales as well as banking and financial services firms are new to Japan and often are not well managed, due often to lack of parent company support rather than the lack of skills of American expatriates. Japanese barriers to investors also must be taking their toll.

Although labor productivity, both in Japan and in manufacturing in the United States, seems to be a problem for Japanese managers, this may not be the way to look at it. For Japanese the labor force is to work on constantly improving quality, flexibility, and service. Labor costs must be controlled, but capital investment is really what keeps costs down, as does clever inventory and overhead management as well as the use of low wage labor at subcontractors for some labor-intensive work. The Japanese say, *"jigyo wa hito nari,"* which means "business success depends on people." What they mean is that the benefits of a workforce turning out high-powered products and getting them in the hands of consumers fast are worth the low labor productivity costs. Naturally when a Honda or Matsushita can get both quality and labor productivity, they become virtually unbeatable. Luckily for American firms, this seems to be the exception rather than the rule.

In terms of 1988 sales, Honda's various U.S. operations are Japan's largest effort in America at $4.2 billion.[7] The profit generated by these revenues appears to be a company secret. The other big investments, which also do not reveal net income, are Mazda ($2.5 billion sales), Nissan ($2.1 billion), Toyota ($1.8 billion), Toyota's joint venture at NUMMI ($1.7 billion), and Sony ($1.4 billion). Those few firms that do provide data on performance are not doing well. Dainippon Ink's Polychrome earned 2.6 percent return on sales in 1988 and 2.7 percent return on assets. These are only about one-half of American average rates. Fujitsu Microelectronics reported a $75 million loss in 1988. NKK-owned National Steel lost $100 million in 1991, and Bridgestone-Firestone lost $350 million. Other losers in 1991 were NEC's home audio-visual equipment maker, Juki's sewing machine operation, and most auto transplants and their Japanese-owned suppliers. Japanese-owned firms in 1987 had 0.2 percent return on sales, 1.4 percent return on investment, and 0.2 percent return on assets. In 1990 Japanese return on sales for acquired U.S. firms was 2.1 percent and return on assets was 1.3 percent. Contrast this with American firms in Japan that had a 21.8 percent return on investment in 1987. One reason Americans do better in Japan, even with all its barriers, than Japanese in America is that they do not overcapitalize. Manufacturing investment by American firms in Japan is about $32,000 per employee. In America Japan has about $66,000 per employee. It takes a lot of profit per employee to create a respectable return on investment in these conditions, and the Japanese manufacturers are not doing it. In the 1987–1991 period, then, Japanese firms overall were not profitable or made only weak profits in the United States. For the time being Japanese managers appear to be operating their American firms more like cost centers, with adherence to budgets a measure of success, rather than profit centers.

JAPANESE OWNERS WILL NOT BE PLEASED

In 1950 individuals owned 75 percent of Japanese equity. Toward the end of the 1980s they held only 22 percent.[8] Mostly corporations bought each other's shares to strengthen ties among *keiretsu* members. Less important but also practiced was pyramid holding in which companies of higher rank own shares in the companies under them. On average the top twenty shareholders in a Japanese corporation own about 46 percent of the equity, roughly double the concentration of ownership—and double the risks of ownership—in the United States. They almost never sell the stock, an indication that the stock market in Japan functions differently from its American counterpart. Traditionally, stock markets serve to fragment ownership, thus reducing risks of investment by spreading them out. In Japan, however, the market is used by corporations to stimulate the coordination of suppliers with producers, contractors with sub-contractors, and loan providers with borrowers. In effect, the Japanese are willing to increase their risks in the market for ownership in return for reducing risks in other markets. A manufacturer which owns an important share of a vendor's equity takes a big chance that the firm will not go under, but in return it can control the price and quality of components it purchases from the vendor. Similar kinds of influence can be exerted on other firms that owe money to the manufacturer or that do sub-contracting for it.

Even competitors can become indirectly linked through all of the various crossholdings. The result is a state of highly managed markets in Japan—although not as highly managed as some Japan bashers have claimed—which make a buy and never sell strategy of stock ownership less worrisome. The reduction of domestic risks is also a stimulus to engaging in high-risk foreign investing. Foreign markets can not be so well managed, however, and the greater a firm's foreign involvement, the more the risks of stock ownership. So the crossholding-managed market system has stimulated foreign investment risks, but as foreign investment grows, it threatens the system which created it. While Japanese firms have tried to set up their supplier and sub-contractor networks in the United States, public reaction has made it inevitable that such collusion, legal or not, will not be tolerated. As a firm increases investment in the United States, its control over business transactions decreases, and so do the net benefits of ownership concentration. Holding large blocks of company stock and never selling it becomes riskier if—contrary to domestic investment—one is unable to predict what large-scale American ventures hold in store. The crossholding system could start to crumble as Japanese foreign investment soars.

An example of this could occur in the auto industry. Two of Japan's biggest steel manufacturers hold shares in five leading automakers. Will the steel and similar companies continue to hold and never sell as they see massive investing in the United States? They may begin to treat their auto stock in a traditional manner, perhaps looking at yield on a semiannual basis and selling when better yields can be obtained elsewhere. If this happens, Japanese car makers will see their stock prices fall, and they will begin to hear rumblings from owners. Like corporate executives worldwide, the auto firms' managers will increase pressure on all units, especially foreign plants, to improve Return on Investment. The weak profitability of Japanese firms in America will have to improve to compensate owners for the unmanageable risk of American markets.

As investments in America grew dramatically in 1988–1990, rational cross-shareholders in Japan should have acted to reduce their crossholding, which now is becoming more risky. This seems to have begun to happen. The share of Japanese stocks held by corporations decreased in 1989 for the first time in fourteen years by 0.2 percent to 77.4 percent. Thus the very thing that encouraged Japanese companies to make enormously risky investments in America, the willingness of corporate cross-shareholders to hold and not to sell, is now being undermined by that same foreign investing. Even worse, the collapse of the stock market in 1990 revealed the bubble-like nature of its rise in the 1980s. Firms will not be eager to hold steadily declining stocks, even those of companies with which they have a relationship, unless those companies can increase profits and dividends. This will be hard to do, since dividend payout ratios hit an all time low in 1990. All in all, the pressure will be on Japan's U.S. subsidiaries to make much larger profits than they seem to be making.

TRADE AND JOBS

If Japanese stockholders are worried, the American public ought to be delighted with Japanese investment, since it will foster a reduction in the trade deficit and will create jobs. Until recently Japanese-owned firms have been major importers, providing components from their Japanese suppliers. As noted above, public pressure is putting a stop to some of this activity. In addition, the Japanese government, to stimulate imports from the United States, now offers tax incentives covering 2300 capital goods and consumer goods products. Manufacturers who increase imports, probably from their American subsidiaries, affiliates, and joint ventures, will get either a tax credit of 5 percent of the increase or an accelerated depreciation on foreign machinery they purchase. U.S. exports to Japan could jump by $3 billion a year at a cost to the Japanese government of about $1.3 billion in lost revenue.

This activity plus a set of related events could lead to a decline of the U.S. annual trade deficit with Japan from its current $40–45 billion level to about $13 billion by 1995.[9] As companies transfer production to America, their exports from Japan to the United States will decline. This impact, combined with increased Japanese transplant exports to Japan, will be a major one. It will be offset somewhat by Japanese-owned companies purchasing components and capital goods from Japan, but the effect should be relatively minor. Exports of consumer electronics products and autos from Japan already have started to fall, and Japanese-owned U.S. firms' imports also may be falling.

A decline in the trade deficit will be associated with job creation in America. Until 1989 most Japanese investment was in the form of start ups rather than acquisitions. These accounted for about 200,000–250,000 jobs. The net figure may be much less, however, if one subtracts the jobs lost at U.S. competitor firms and at U.S. suppliers replaced by imports from Japanese vendors. Most of this impact is in the auto industry, where 40,000 autoworkers lost their jobs. Only a few were hired by Japanese transplants, which, contrary to the general Japanese trend of lower labor productivity, are able to produce a car in only twenty-five man hours compared to General Motors' thirty.[10] The recent shift to acquisitions may not create new jobs at all, but the move towards exporting to Japan and Europe will help. In America about thirty jobs are created for every million dollars of exports.[11] The $3 billion increase fostered by the Japanese governments' tax policies alone could create 90,000 new jobs, many of them at Japanese-owned firms. Moreover, if the EEC puts up barriers to Japan's exports and investment, Japan's U.S. companies will increase exports. In the 1990s, then, net job creation is likely, mostly due to exporting and a decline in importing supplies from Japan.

IS THE PUBLIC HAPPY?

Japanese investment will reduce the trade deficit and create jobs. The public ought to be delighted. It isn't. In a 1985 *New York Times* poll 87 percent of respondents expressed friendly feelings toward Japan. By June 1989, 74 percent felt that way, and in January 1990, only 67 percent did. Some Americans are beginning to waver in their support for Japan. Who is strong for Japan and who is not?

In a 1988 Japan Society study of the response to Japanese investment conducted in California, Michigan, and Tennessee, employees of Japanese-owned companies overwhelmingly saw Japanese investment as good for the economy.[12] As might be expected, they saw it as increasing competitiveness, creating jobs that would not otherwise exist, and adding new technology to the United States. Unexpectedly, given the furor over Japan's investing, both the public and community leaders in the study held similar attitudes to the employees but with less certainty. The man in the street and his political leaders could not make up their minds on which nation gained the most from technology transfer. They were certain, however, that Japanese investment was a threat to America's "economic independence."

Accordingly, the survey respondents, even the employees in Japanese-owned firms, called for laws requiring local content. These would counter the Japanese subsidiary's tendency to purchase components from Japan by mandating that a certain portion of a products' value-added components come from domestic sources. Respondents also called for Japanese firms to start new businesses rather than to buy them.

Although respondents did not want Japanese firms meddling in American political campaigns, they saw them as having little current political influence. Things they did not like involved the secrecy surrounding the nature and extent of Japanese investments and the use of state incentives to attract investment. They wanted Japanese investment to slow down.

What the Japan Society's survey indicated was not hostility to Japanese investment, but to its *pace*. It was all going too fast for Americans. Indeed, the real benefits of Japan's efforts were recognized: high quality products and pressure on American-owned firms to improve their management practices. The Japanese, according to respondents, showed greater attentiveness to employee feelings and concerns, as well as created greater work discipline. But they were seen as anti-union and somewhat questionable in their commitment to equal employment opportunities. While 70 percent of their own American employees liked working for them, other respondents would be hesitant to accept employment with a Japanese-owned firm and would rather see Canadian or British investment in their communities. Mostly this reluctance stemmed from ignorance about Japanese culture and values rather than any perceived danger.

The pace of investment increased after the survey was taken, and as we might expect, American concerns also grew. A Japanese poll conducted in early 1990 found almost twice as many Americans with bad feelings about Japanese investment (44 percent) as with good (27 percent), yet only a year earlier 65 percent of respondents had found Japanese investment helpful.[13] A late 1989 survey of U.S. CEOs by a Japanese newspaper found that 60 percent saw Japanese investment as "welcome" and 40 percent as "unwelcome." Most thought Japanese capital would strengthen the U.S. economy, but 42 percent worried about Japan gaining too much economic power in the United States. A *New York Times* poll showed that while the public did not fear Europeans, 64 percent of those surveyed saw Japanese investment as a threat to American economic independence. One-half felt that Japan would be the world's leading economic power in the next century. Fortunately, all respondents generally were friendly towards Japan, suggesting an economic rather than a racial basis for fears.[14] What triggered much of this uneasiness was a series of sensationalist media stories on Sony's purchase of Columbia Pictures and Mitsubishi's investment in Rockefeller Center, along with a growing recognition of the barriers Japan had thrown up to investment. If *they* are so worried about foreign investors, the thinking went, then we should be too. A final blow may have been the results of a *Business Week* poll which showed 43 percent of Japanese respondents believing that Japan eventually will take America's place as the world's leading economic and political power.[15] In the same survey only about 35 percent of Japanese were willing to express admiration for America and Americans.

Spurred on by the speed of Japanese direct investing in 1988–1990, Americans are beginning to believe that the Japanese do not like them, are out to dominate them economically, and are not fighting fairly. The Japanese, in response to American carping, are also getting angry. To make matters worse, the Japanese reluctance to be of much help during the Iraq conflict outraged many Americans. Before the emotional indicator reaches the hate level, we need to step back and remind ourselves of a few things. To begin with, Japan is in no position to threaten U.S. "economic independence." Its economy is only one-half the size of America's and is approaching some kind of growth limit due to a labor shortage. Its productivity problems must be solved before it can take on anyone, and the growing dissatisfaction of Japanese workers with their lot must be dealt with.[16] Moreover, Japanese investing in the United States is small compared with the market value of American investments in Europe, and the Europeans are no longer wringing their hands over the American "challenge." Finally, while the Japanese have had successes in America, their overall performance suggests a struggle to hang on and cope rather than a growing dominance. The failure of Japan to fully open up to foreign investing—legal barriers are down but nonlegal ones remain—is a sign of weakness, not strength, and the Japanese people suffer for it. The great glory of Japan is its well-educated populace, but it is also a great danger to the ruling elites. The Japanese people know that they would pay lower prices if import and investment constraints were lifted. Until recently, they have acquiesced in the argument that Japan's homogeneity and culture would be threatened by a liberalization of trade and direct investment. But the Japanese are coming to realize that like all industrialized peoples they must internationalize if they want growth in material well-being to continue. A great debate over these issues is taking place, and the result will be dramatic changes in both political and economic life. During all this, American claims that the Japanese are engaged in some sort of conspiracy to control America's economic destiny must seem rather bizarre. The Japanese are just starting to get their own house in order and are in no position to buy someone else's house.

THE STRANGE CASE OF HAWAII

Public worries and confusion are illustrated in the response to Japan's direct investment in Hawaii, which took off in 1986. The majority of investment was in hotels and real estate, with small amounts in golf courses. The reaction of the Hawaiian public was interesting. At first the public was generally positive about the Japanese investment.[17] Favorable news stories and political commentaries outnumbered negative stories in the press in 1987. In 1988, however, a dramatic negative shift occurred as the tone of editorialists and political statements became quite hostile. By 1989, although the politicians were still hostile, the editorial writers had become generally favorable again. Presumably the politicians soon followed their lead. What was going on here? One year the Japanese were good fellows, the next they were an evil presence, and the third year they were U.S. friends again. What did they forget to do in 1988 that they remembered to do in 1987 and 1989?

Some critics say the Japanese are excessively centered in the hotel industry. Concentration of economic power, however, has been a fact of life in Hawaii for most of its existence. Why are the Japanese suddenly singled out, as they were in a 1989 statement by the Office of State Planning, which wants to control Japanese investment in the islands? According to David Lohmann of Hawaii Pacific College, the Japanese threaten the political power structure in the state. Japanese investors tend to acquire existing facilities rather than building new projects. In doing so they need not come up against the zoning commissions which dole out favors to politically wired developers who support the politicians. Thus, Japanese capital is a kind of loose cannon on the deck of a tightly run ship. To whip up public sentiment for controlling Japanese investors, politicians claimed that their purchases of real estate were driving values and property taxes up. This is not the case, however. Speculative land buying in Hawaii was greater in 1975 than in 1989, and careful analysis showed that Japanese land purchases made up only a small portion of total transactions. More important worries about the Japanese have to do with their obvious eagerness to speed up acquisitions and the possible introduction of Japanese organized crime. It is their potential for destabilization that worries the public, not anything that they have done already. The up-down-up levels of public sentiment noted previously reflect occasional worries, not ongoing harm. Nevertheless, Lohman notes that politicians are waiting for the next round of Japan bashing to propose laws against "speculation," to restrict golf course construction and limit growth of retirement communities, and to channel investment. He suggests that Japanese investors stop concentrating on hotels and diversify into ocean technology investment, make long-term commitments to building the kind of infrastructure that fosters economic development, and be less secretive about their activities. One proposal is for Japanese firms to offer housing benefits to their American employees. A step of this kind would help alleviate Hawaii's affordable housing problem.

An American banker who keeps his eye on Japanese investing in America sums it up: "The Japanese guys here are only concerned about how to survive until tomorrow."[18] In the rush to take advantage of cheap U.S. assets many Japanese companies came to the United States without a clear idea of what they wanted to accomplish. They had low cost capital available to them and so could afford to take a leap into the unknown with the hope that their successes would outweigh their failures. This may well turn out to be the case, but for now performance has been modest. Anecdotal evidence suggests that some Japanese subsidiaries which produce and market goods and services have not yet achieved the status of profit centers, and managers are evaluated in terms of their adherence to a budget rather than their sales and margins. These and other firms have not established the customer bases for attaining economics of scale in production, nor are they producing the wide variety of products which could give them economies of scope. Mazda, which has large sales in the United States and factory personnel problems, could be caught up short if demand declines for the small number of car models it sells. Several Japanese banks and securities firms with miniscule shares of their markets could be driven out of the United States in the next big recession. Even worse, if the growing concerns of the American public are not muted somehow, the Congress could come up with legislation highly damaging to Japanese interests. Japanese managers, when they meet, often ask each other, "How's business?" The obligatory answer is usually something like, *"Anmari yoku nai desu ne"* (not very good). Things have not reached the stage yet in America where that response is anything more than ritual, but the next few years will be make or break time for many Japanese-owned firms.

FOUR

Japan Bashers versus the Chrysanthemum Club

What region has been the source of most of the world's instability for the last thousand years? Answer: Europe. What country was a danger for about twenty of those thousand years? It's Japan. Which is considered the better candidate to replace the Soviets as a threat to America? We all know the answer. Let's look at the issue another way. Which region is busily erecting trade and investment barriers to keep American goods and capital at bay? Europe. Which country, reluctantly, unwillingly, but inexorably, is slowly reducing those barriers? Although it takes constant pressure to keep them at it, the Japanese are responding. Imports from the United States are increasing, as is (at a low rate, to be sure) American portfolio and direct investment. Japan bashers, represented by Clyde Prestowitz, James Fallows, Karel van Wolferen, and Chalmers Johnson, are either economic nationalists (Prestowitz and Fallows) or disgruntled Japan scholars (Johnson and van Wolferen). The first group worries about America losing control of its economic destiny, whatever that is, while the second is really made of people who love Japan and want it to improve. Many Japanese are in this group, as well. A few years ago an editorial writer in Tokyo offered his plan for improving the lot of the Japanese people. It is all quite simple, he said, just give in to every American demand and all will be well. Prices will come down as imports flood in. Houses will become affordable as artificially propped up land values decline. Productivity in the whole nation—which except for a few industries is lower than America's—will rise as Japanese firms are forced to compete with foreign investors. Wages will go up. It is all so very, very easy.

The Chrysanthemum Club is made up of people whose mission is to sing the praises of Japan. The American public is often told by club members that Japanese eduation—which while good is chronically underfunded and rooted in rote learning—is the best in the world. Japanese management—which is characterized by extreme employee conformity and submissiveness—is supposedly awash with communal feelings, harmony, and trust. And Japanese investment in America—which like all investment is a mix of good and bad—is the salvation of American competitive failings. Lesser lights of the club are often sent by public relations firms hired by Japanese companies to appear at seminars and public forums on American-Japanese issues. Occasionally their remarks are quite eloquent and based on sound economic and political theories, but often their strident defense of Japan ends up as an attack on America.

As long as one discounts the foolish ravings of the hired guns among club members and focuses on the more temperate remarks of genuine scholars, the Japan bashers/Chrysanthemum Club debate on Japanese investment will be won by the club. I will review the basher's claims about the Japanese in America and show why they do not stand up.[1]

BASHERS' CLAIMS ABOUT THE JAPANESE IN AMERICA

We don't know how much Japanese direct investment there really is in the United States. This assertion comes out of the confused information collecting approach of the U.S. government and the reluctance (required by law) of the Bureau of Economic Analysis, that really does know all, to reveal data on individual firms. Every January, however, the Japan Economic Institute releases a list of all Japanese manufacturing investments in the United States. Every firm is listed with information on employees, what it does, and so forth. If we want to know about Japanese investment, it is all available in this or other resources.

The Japanese have a master plan for "economic supremacy" (according to Douglas Frantz and Catherine Collins) in the world. According to Bennett Bidwell of Chrysler, "We are having our pants removed an inch at a time by a centrally orchestrated, totally committed aggressor."[2] Frantz and Collins are less graphic: "The Japanese have demonstrated a grim determination to undergo any sacrifice to obtain economic supremacy at home, and abroad."[3] One would think that at home they already had and were entitled to economic supremacy, but let us focus on "abroad." In his massive study of power arrangements in Japanese society, Karel van Wolferen described the "hole and doughnut" structure of institutions in which government ministries, manufacturers' associations, and elements of the Liberal Democratic Party all circle around each other in an unceasing pursuit of their interests. No central office or person, certainly not the hapless Prime Minister, exists to coordinate, mediate, and occasionally dominate as occurs in America with its President and various state governors. This emptiness at the center ensures that no master plan ever can be decided on and implemented. Of course, Japan has followed until recently a mercantilist policy of running a trade surplus as a stimulus to growth and of protecting powerful corporations in domestic markets, but that's about it. The surge of investment interest in America happened because of economic processes working themselves out, not because of some master plan.

The Japanese will end up controlling America's economic life. "It is essential to recognize that foreign investment in the United States, particularly the strategic purchases by the Japanese, threatens to rob the nation of the ability to control its economic and political destiny." So say Douglas Frantz and Catherine Collins in *Selling Out.* Their argument, echoed by other economic nationalists such as Clyde Prestowitz, Lester Thurow, Peter Peterson, and Felix Rohatyn, usually involves the claim that by 2000 over 1 million Americans will work for Japanese firms. That may very well be, but so what. Since the American work force is 100 million, that is only 1 percent, hardly cause for alarm. Japanese own about 2 percent of total U.S. assets, a figure which could rise to 4 percent by 2000 when total investment may reach $200 billion.[4] These are not large figures for a country as immense as America, and they certainly do not suggest the kind of clout which would lead to control over U.S. economic destiny.

We will surrender our competitive edge to Japan. The idea here is that Japanese firms will find it easy to steal U.S. technology by investing in the United States. Let us grant that, but it will do them no good since we will be able to steal theirs. It is a staple of international business that technological advantages rarely last long. When the Japanese put their mind to it, Xerox's advantages disappeared quickly. When Ford decided to tap into Japanese assembly-line knowledge it did so quite easily, and Ford productivity is now near Japanese levels. Whatever anyone does to keep technological processes secret, they inevitably fail. Remember the atom bomb secrets; they were transferred to the Russians within months of their development. Another angle on the loss of competitive edge argument is the supposed shutting down of American R & D. As Japanese buy up American firms, they are accused of reducing R & D so that American innovation cannot threaten the homeland. In fact, corporate R & D spending per worker in the United States is about $470,000. Japanese-owned firms spend $1.5 million per worker.[5] A final claim is that Japanese investors save the high-paying jobs for Japan and only provide assembly line work for Americans. Economic analysis of early 1980s data by E. M. Graham and Paul R. Krugman suggests that this is not the case, and 1990s data probably will show an increase in highly-paid value-added work by Americans in Japanese-owned firms.[6] Clearly Japanese firms are quite similar to American firms and perhaps even more willing to foster competitive edge R & D work and to create good value-added jobs.

They may decide some day to pull out and leave us high and dry. In the Third World large firms often enter a country and set up assembly operations which can be quickly dismantled when an economic downturn occurs. This has happened in the west of Ireland, where Japanese firms sometimes will operate under subsidy from the Irish government and then quickly leave when subsidies are reduced or European markets go flat. In the mid-1980s some Japanese firms in America gave every sign of behaving in the same way. Consumer electronics, auto plants, and auto components suppliers operated mostly assembly operations and imported more from Japan than they exported. Indeed, in 1986 imports per worker in Japanese-owned manufacturing firms were about three times the imports of other foreign firms and ten times the imports of U.S. manufacturers. Clearly these firms were not deeply entrenched in the U.S. economy of that time and were depending on the home country for supplies. So the claim that the Japanese were positioned to pick up their marbles and go elsewhere had merit—in 1986. In the 1990s they can not pull out. In the first place they have become more entrenched. Honda's U.S. cars are now the product of an American auto company, and Matsushita's products are rapidly becoming localized. The first tentative steps into American markets in the 1980s have bècome giant leaps in the 1990s as Japanese-owned firms turn themselves into American firms which happen to be owned by Japanese. Second, the American market is immense. Only a madman would work hard to get into it and then leave when the going got rough. Besides, the Japanese, as the bashers tirelessly point out, are long-term players of the game. The British invested heavily in the United States in the nineteenth century and are still here a hundred years later. Like it or not, the Japanese will be here for at least that long and probably forever.

The Japanese are different. According to Frantz and Collins, "Japanese investment here is different from that of other nations." Different, as so often happens in America, means threatening. Are they really different? As we have seen, Japanese investment in start ups rather than acquisitions during the 1980s was not the usual route followed by investors. Nor has it been common for as many foreign managers to come to the United States as the Japanese have sent. These are differences. Also, Japanese-owned firms seem to export and import more than American firms or other foreign investors, and their R & D spending is higher. They pay employees about the same as other firms, but seem to be less profitable. Overall productivity is about the same or better than American firms. These are not the kind of differences, however, which worry Frantz and Collins, who note that Japanese "strategy is different from that of other foreign investors."[7] Supposedly they are "not interested in simple return on their capital," but focus instead on "seizures of power." It is hard to argue against such vague statements. The best thing to say at this point is to admit that, yes, Japanese firms tolerate or endure weak profitability and generally do seek market power; but given the chance, all firms seek market power if it can lead to long-term profits. The differences Japanese investors exhibit are not worrisome.

They will corrupt our government. Critics who follow this line usually argue from an implied model of American governmental processes which is highly idealized. One is supposed to be shocked, really shocked to learn that 150 Japanese organizations spend $300 million a year on lobbying and public relations, as if such things do not go on in Washington.[8] While Americans have a right to be angry at firms like Toshiba, which probably deserves censure for its frantic and quite successful lobbying attempt to avoid heavy sanctions over its sale of defense-related products to the Soviets, this does not mean all Japanese firms should be penalized. In any case, the American consumer has suffered much more from U.S. firms' successful attempts to get "voluntary" quotas slapped on Japanese imports than from anything the Japanese have done. And the cost to America of thrift industry lobbying probably renders the savings and loan industry as the champion corrupter of government of all time. The Japanese are pikers.

Japanese firms may threaten U.S. national security. Imagine a country involved in a war. It wants a neutral nation to help it, so it orders its companies' subsidiaries in that nation to withhold key technology from that nation's armed forces until the nation decides to get on the team and play ball. The war-making nation was the United States, and the target country was France in the late 1960s. The French reacted by creating technology sources for its military independent of U.S. subsidiaries.[9] If the United States can behave this way, say some Japan bashers, so can Japan. Perhaps it might get into a confrontation with, say, South Korea and order its U.S. high tech subsidiaries to stop exporting military-related products to South Korea. Or it might become involved in a dispute with the United States itself and seek leverage through the actions of Japanese-owned firms. These are real possibilities but unlikely to be of much consequence. The United States is simply too big and too powerful relative to Japan for it to be much of a threat. The U.S. government can seize a foreign firm's subsidiary during a national emergency under the International Emergency Economic Powers Act of 1976. Also, the president can block parent-subsidiary trade if he wants to. If Japan tells its Nissan truck plant to stop selling trucks to the Defense Department, the government would seize the plant and keep it operating, and neither Nissan nor the Japanese government could do much about it.

We should treat Japanese investors the way Japan treats American investors. Until the 1980s Japan actively sought to keep foreign investors out of the country. Even today, direct foreign investment in Japan is no easy proposition. Although government policy overall is modestly neutral or reluctantly accepting of investment, individual Japanese ministries often pursue their own agenda, and bureaucrats are known to make up the rules as they go along to fit their biases or to respond to domestic pressures. The rule of law in Japan is weaker than in America. The result of all this is that foreign investment as a share of assets in Japan is about 1 percent, in comparison with 10 percent in the United States and about 20 percent in the EEC. Although the Japanese will gradually open their doors wider, the societal fear of foreigners has been so great that foreign investing is unlikely to grow to U.S. levels anytime soon. Critics say the United States should retaliate against Japan in its barriers by instituting onerous reporting requirements, by applying the "national security" argument more liberally to keep Japanese out of certain industries, and by developing "performance" requirements. These last are rules, typically employed by developing nations, which would force a Japanese subsidiary to purchase a certain minimum percentage of its supplies from U.S. vendors. Another possible rule would require a minimum share of total value added of a product to be produced locally. The EEC seems to be moving more and more towards inefficiency-causing performance requirements, and the United States will be tempted to follow suit. Arguments like these are of the form: "You are being nasty, so we will shoot ourselves in the foot." Nonetheless, Japanese subsidiaries are taking them very seriously. Knowing full well that barriers in Japan will not come down as far as Americans would like, they are moving towards local content and value-added production in America. Matushita is a leader in this drive. The next step will be to increase exports, explicitly to Japan. These initiatives may be enough to forestall serious attacks on the Japanese.

The Japan bashers who raise mostly spurious issues about Japanese "threats" are not helpful. Contrary to their claims:

· We know a lot about Japanese investing in the United States.

· Japan has no master plan to invade America.

· Japanese investment is too small to control U.S. "economic destiny."

· America's competitive edge is probably enhanced by Japanese capital.

· Japanese will never pull out of the immense U.S. market.

· The Japanese firms are similar to other firms in terms of behavior.

· The corrupting influence of the Japanese in Washington is small relative to such titans as the thrifts.

· Japan is not powerful enough to affect U.S. national security through manipulation of its subsidiaries.

Japanese investment in America is well worth our attention, but not because Japan is "Number 1." The Japanese are the first non-European foreign investors to come to America with a large influx of capital. Moreover, they apparently want to manage many of the firms they build or acquire. This is in contrast to European investors, who hire Americans. Eventually the Japanese may turn to American management, but then again they may not. More and more Japanese people are finding to their surprise that they like the United States, with its flattened society and its valuing of the individual. Freedom is more real in America than Japan, and it intoxicates the Japanese.

BASHERS—OR GOOD OL' BOYS?

The spectre of increased foreign investment caused an extraordinary public debate in the country. The front pages of the nation's leading dailies were full of discussions of a possible "foreign capital invasion" and the pluses and minuses of "capital liberalization." One newspaper ran an "insider" story on prominent foreign industrialists who had been seen visiting the nation secretly to look for investment prospects. The government was pressured to restrict direct foreign investment by representatives of oligopolized firms fearful of new entrants to their industry from abroad. Is this America in 1992? No, it is Japan in 1964, when IBM, Texas Instruments, and other big American multinationals urged that the U.S. government increase demands on Japan to allow more foreign investment. Japan waited three years and then made minor changes. Foreigners could raise the limits of their equity ownership of a Japanese firm from 5 to 7 percent. Over the following decades some U.S. firms received special treatment. Texas Instruments (TI) was allowed to set up a wholly-owned subsidiary in Japan in 1968, but only because Japanese firms wanted access to TI's integrated circuit technology. TI was forced to set up an equal-partnership joint venture with Sony, which presumably then learned what it needed to learn from TI. TI also agreed to "consult" with MITI on its production levels and market share. The benefits to TI and a few other American firms in similar situations were that they came to enjoy the fruits of Japanese oligopoly policies. Once in the group, TI and IBM benefitted handsomely.[10]

Those bashers who want to give Japan a dose of its own medicine by setting up selectively applied barriers to Japanese investment may be motivated by a desire for revenge or perhaps a genuine fear of loss of autonomy. A few of them, however, know that there is a great deal of money to be made in the barriers game. If Toshiba has technology X that, say, Chrysler wants, then Chrysler might argue in Washington, D.C., that a Japanese firm ought to be permitted to invest in the United States only if it benefits the United States. Assume that Chrysler successfully gets Congress to raise barriers. Its next step will be to argue that Toshiba ought to be allowed to build a plant, but only if it is willing to share technology X with Chrysler, with which it has been negotiating. Congress agrees, and a rider on a bill slips through. Now Chrysler gets technology X and makes use of it to outcompete Ford and GM. Instead of complaining, however, they keep quiet and begin looking around for other technologies which they can capture from other Japanese firms. The object of the schemes is to reduce competition. This is what has gone on in Japan, at no small cost to the people of Japan. Is this the direction America should go? Do we want our oligopolists and budding oligopolists to get all the help they need in holding on to their market shares? It took Japan until 1980 to finally get rid of most of its barriers to foreign investment, yet even today no one would claim that it welcomes investors. In the 1990s, some scholars argue, American investment in Japan is really in the hands of Japanese oligopolists, who only will recommend admission to the government for those U.S. firms possessing assets and skills useful to the Japanese giants. Clearly America does not want to go this route, putting decisions about admitting Japanese investors in the hands of GM, General Electric, or Kodak. It is good to recognize that not all the Japan Bashers in America are solely patriots. Some of them, like the oligopolists of Japan, want investment barriers out of pure self-interest.

The claims of the Japan bashers are not compelling. America's economic independence is not in danger, since the Japanese invasion, while big, is not big enough to win any war. Nor is Japan itself capable of plotting, let alone carrying out, a Japan, Inc.-like takeover. Many of the Japan bashers are patriots, although some are clearly corporate greedheads looking for a chance to erect competition-reducing barriers in their markets. Some have pet theories. Chalmers Johnson wants to set up a U.S. Department of International Trade and Investment dedicated to fostering "good domestic industrial health," meaning managed trade and investment with Japan.[11] The good ol' boys would have a field day with this organization. What we would see is a group of D.I.T.I. advisory committees set up under harmless-sounding titles like, "Midwest Commission on Investment and the Environment" or "Southern Council on Conserving America's Resources." Under the guise of protecting

the environment and conserving resources, these groups would con-
spire to restrain capital and trade flows to pump up prices and profits
for their firms. We know that this would happen because it already is
happening in the fishing industry. Regional "conservation" councils
meet regularly to advise the government on fish harvest limits. Often
these limits are set more with an eye on prices rather than endangered
biomass.

The Japan bashers like to point out that it is fruitless to try to force
Japan to play on a level playing field since the Japanese are not in the
same ball park and do not play by the same rules. More concretely,
they say we should engage in the highly managed, highly politicized
control of trade and investments that the Japanese do. This argument
is based on a set of assumptions about Japan which do not stand up to
scrutiny. Karel van Wolferen has shown that while the Japanese tendency towards the management of economic life is very real, checks
exist in the form of inter-ministry squabbling and the ineptitude of Japanese politicians. In my own experience the disgust of corporate leaders with both bureaucrats and politicians has been quite evident, suggesting that the business sphere is not all that well coordinated with
the government and political spheres. Japan's ability to develop and
implement an integrated global economic initiative is weak. Although
some Japanese elites would like to do just that, the likelihood of its
occurrence is small. The second assumption is that Japan's regulated,
barrier-ridden, mercantilist approach of 1960s and 1970s is the approach of the 1990s. As noted, there are powerful forces which would
like it to be, but Japan is slowly moving away from its old ways and is
poised to enter an era of dramatic change. Japanese consumers are
starting to make their voices heard, and workers are beginning to get
a fair share of the rewards. Due to the pressures of change and an
inability to mount a coordinated policy, then, Japan is not the threat
the Japan bashers make it out to be. Indeed, America is a real threat to
Japan's rulers. As some Japanese managers and visitors in the United
States experience a society characterized by freedom, autonomy, openness, informality, and material well-being, they may want Japan to
change, and change it will.

FIVE

Japanese and American Ideologies

Stereotyping about "the Japanese" is always risky, but various Japan-watchers have offered their description of the values and qualities infusing the Japanese people. One commentator, perhaps carried away a bit, lists them: "Discipline; courage; loyalty; sacrifice; an adaptive genius; a meticulousness of the heart; an aesthetic tradition both simple and dazzling; . . . a spirit, a most troublesome spirit, of purity, whose other face is madness."[1] A Japanese author recalled a daily school ritual of his childhood:

Teacher: What would you do if the emperor commanded you to die?

Student: I would die, sir. I would cut open my belly and die.[2]

Few Japanese today would hold such extreme views, but many would say of such an exchange, "How pure the child's spirit is!" The idea of uncontaminated, selfless dedication is still much admired in Japan. Contrast this with the American student's "I pledge allegiance to the flag . . .," a ritual utterance, designed to affirm shared sentiments that pose no threat at all to self.

Who is the more ideological? Americans, of course. Americans actually believe in principles worth fighting and dying for, principles of great moment associated with the United States of America. No amount of vapid rhetoric from grandstanding politicians or contentless ritual pronouncements about the flag in classrooms ever is allowed to interfere with the deep commitment of the American psyche to democracy, freedom, the self, individualism, and equality. An American businessman abroad is not just an economic creature maximizing his own and his firm's utility. He (or she) is a missionary, usually of the closet kind, and his economic life will always be tinged (or singed) by his ideals. Nothing of the sort is true of the Japanese manager abroad. He may do the bidding of the Ministry of Finance or MITI, but that is because he has no choice. There is little of patriotism in his actions. It is mostly pure self-interest and self-preservation. When Americans see Japanese in the United States as agents of some overarching purpose, they really are seeing a bit of themselves.

The ideology of democracy has been summarized many times:

Our constitution does not copy the laws of other states; we are rather a pattern to others than imitators ourselves. Its administration favors the many instead of the few; this is why our land is called a democracy. If we look to the laws, they afford equal justice to all. If to social standing, advancement in public life falls to reputation for capacity, class considerations not being allowed to interfere with merit. Nor again does poverty bar the way; if a man is able to serve society, he is not hindered by the obscurity of his condition.

Another, more fevered spokesman for democracy is barely contained by his syntax:

This august dignity I treat of, is not the dignity of kings and robes, but that abounding dignity which has no robed investiture. Thou shalt see it shining in the arm that wields a pick or drives a spike; that democratic dignity which, on all hands, radiates without end from God: Himself! The great God absolute! The centre and circumference of all democracy! His omnipresence, our divine equality.

The first passage is from Pericles' speech to the Athenians in 431 b.c. The second is Melville in *Moby Dick*, about 2,300 years later.

American ideology, then, has most ancient roots and flowers stronger today than ever before. Contrast its intellectual edifice, tightly bound together with powerful emotion, with this thousand-year-old passage from Japan:

Harmony is to be valued, and the avoidance of wanton opposition to be honored. All men are influenced by partisanship, and there are few that are intelligent. Hence there are some who disobey their lords and fathers, or who maintain feuds with the neighboring villages. But when those above are harmonious and those below are friendly, and there is concord in the discussions of business, right views of things spontaneously gain acceptance. Then what is there that cannot be accomplished?[3]

Prince Shotoku, with the help of Confucius in this passage, says that if the Japanese, whom he sees as a rather disorderly lot, will but be in harmony with the order of the universe, they will prosper. This ideology is not the kind of thing to stimulate adventuring abroad to carry out lofty missions. Indeed, when the Japanese went international for the first time in the 1930s and 1940s, they blundered badly.

In the Union of East Asia, the Japanese Empire is at once the stabilizing power and the leading influence. . . . Since the Japanese Empire is the center and pioneer of Oriental moral and cultural reconstruction, the officials and peoples of this country must return to the spirit of the Orient and acquire a thorough understanding of the national moral character.[4]

This document hints at how resistant the Japanese people were—and are—to missionary activities in foreign lands. Japanese managers in America bear no heavy ideological burden, no sense of deep purpose in service to a national cause, and no deep emotional commitment which binds them together in unspoken union.

What we do see in the Japanese manager in this country is often a selfless dedication to his job which some Americans find rather strange. Other distinctive traits will occur, but very little of what Japanese managers think and do is likely to be very different from what American managers think and do. After all, many Americans are also workaholics. So why do we often have an image in the back of our mind of some menacing, driven Asian forcing himself on us? Part of the answer has to do with American racism. The Japanese press and politicians like Shintaro Ishihara love to highlight American "yellow peril" talk, and they are right to do so in moderation. But American racism clearly is a minor issue. What frightens many Americans is Japanese exceptionalism: the Japanese sense, more as a belief than as a guiding ideology, that they are a chosen people possessing supramoral rights. Over the last decade various Japanese commentators have pointed out that the Japanese believe their brains are different from those of other humans; Japanese are likely to be the first people to be able to talk to animals; Japanese snow is different; Japanese competitive success versus American is rooted in Japanese racial purity; and Japanese intestines are longer than anyone else's. The list goes on and on. These claims worry Americans, although they should not. It is highly unlikely that there are more than just a few Japanese businessmen in America who believe such things to the point of being guided by them in their economic dealings.

If Americans wonder about the pose of exceptionalism getting the Japanese into trouble in the United States, they should welcome Japanese direct investment with open arms. Generally that is what the United States has done, mostly for economic reasons, but also because of a faith in the American melting pot process. Ethnic identities and feelings of superiority become muted in America as different peoples mix, do business together, and intermarry. Although Japanese businessmen stay only five years in America, it is enough time to make them realize that Japanese are not necessarily better than other people, only different in a few respects. These managers develop a genuine admiration for America along with a realistic sense of American problems and failings. Akio Morita in *The Japan That Can Say No* is harsh but fair in his remarks on America. His business experiences here in the United States have matured his vision. Shintaro Ishihara, his co-author, is a politician with no U.S. business experience, and his remarks are isolationist, racist, and xenophobic. An American firm ought to hire him to be its spokesman—that would soften him after a while—just as Japanese firms might hire a Carla Hills or an Ezra Vogel.

Japanese firms use slogans to articulate corporate philosophy. Look at Matsushita's for the years when Toshihiko Yamashita led the company into renewed prosperity and a dramatic increase in its American presence.[5] See if an ideological theme emerges:

1978   Within the spirit in which our company was founded, we should be positive and aggressive.

1979   Reach for the pinnacle.

1980   React quickly. Respond wisely.

1981   In the 50th year of our corporate mission, let us prove our ability to the fullest extent.

1982   Link the world together with all our hearts and technology.

1983   Build strength into our products.

1984   Build today—challenge tomorrow.

1985   Create the future.

1986   Move forward in harmony with the world.

From 1978 to 1981 the tone is one of pleading and reaction rather than proaction. But then in 1982 the United States began its great spending binge. Buoyed by a low yen, Matsushita's sales in America boomed. A new note of globalism emerged in the slogans, as did a more confident tone and a more vigorous and strategic emphasis on the future. That spirit energizes the company's American investments today. There is no sense of grand national ideology behind Matsushita's slogans, however. Indeed, Matsushita as an organization almost seems like an end in itself rather than an instrument of national purpose or of owners' wealth-generating desires. Japanese management theories do emphasize the socially useful nature of Japanese firms, but that is as close as they get to an ideology.

THE SELF-CENTERED JAPANESE

When accusations by critics that Japanese managers are ideologically motivated servants of Nippon do not pan out, critics completely change their tack and accuse the Japanese of selfishness. "They think only of themselves and don't really care about anybody else," is a common refrain. Other comments one hears are "they are so self-centered," "they lack humanity," "they are manipulative and sly," and "they take what they can get and plow nothing back."[6] Even people familiar with Japan argue that the Japanese cannot become "global citizens." Has any country yet managed to produce global citizens? Behind these attacks is a reality that is not what it seems to be. Japanese expatriates are no more sly or selfish than other people, but they are sometimes remarkably insular and provincial. The Japanese manager in America who from afar looks like a clever manipulator often turns out to be somewhat unsophisticated. Many Americans react to people who are quiet, defensive, and withdrawn as if they are somehow dangerous. Rather, they are often desperately anxious.

When quiet Japanese do speak up, especially after a few drinks, they often blurt out things that smack of arrogance. "You Americans are too racially mixed to succeed," one will say. "Why don't you work harder," chimes in another. These statements emerge out of deeply felt feelings of inferiority, not superiority or selfishness. Japan has been under the U.S. thumb for a long time, and Japanese are entitled to blow off steam occasionally. It means very little, just as American squawking means little.

Americans depend on their newspapers to educate them, so business people are receptive to journalists who come calling. They view an interview as their chance to tell their story to the world. The Japanese on the other hand are horrified at the thought of their words appearing in the media. A reticent people, at least with foreigners, they see their dealings as nobody's business but their own. One American journalist recounted his all too familiar tale with a Japanese firm. "If I called someone in New York, he would almost invariably refer me to someone in Tokyo, pretend that he did not understand my request, or simply not respond. When they referred me to their so-called public reactions department or outside public relations firm, I fared no better."[7] With few exceptions Japanese firms have used public relations not as an informational vehicle but rather as a barrier defending the inner truth of the organization (called *honne*) with a smokescreen of obfuscation or distortion *(tatemae)*. This is normal practice in Japan, where people recognize that truth is always tailored to its context. That way society remains ordered and stable. The more ideological Americans believe that truth is "the way things really are." Recently another journalist on the West Coast did a story on Japanese banks. He quoted a Sumitomo executive, who spoke sensibly and honestly about some of the problems facing his firm in the United States. The quotes were not hostile to Sumitomo. The day after publication, the newspaper's editor received a call from the head of the bank, furious that true but revealing statements had been made about Sumitomo in public. The journalist's editor, used to dealing with attacks on his reporters' veracity, was nonplussed. The Japanese banker, used to arranging these things ahead of publication with Japanese reporters, could not understand why the paper was so impolite. After all, the public should be given "suitable" information, jointly agreed on in negotiations with Sumitomo.

To be fair, Japanese journalism, usually accommodating, is riddled with pockets of left-wing rabble rousers who often play fast and loose with facts. A businessman can never tell who the reporter is who knocks on his door, so he often takes the risk-averse path and tries to rewrite the article in such a way as to counter a possible left-wing bias. The businessman is not by nature devious; rather he is self-protective. Indeed, Japanese reticence or manipulativeness with journalists evaporates when a professor comes calling, surrounded by an aura of objectivity and modest status. Japanese managers enjoy unburdening themselves with "warts and all" truth telling as long as they know their story will be treated fairly (and they remain anonymous). Many American managers, in contrast, even when promised anonymity, resort to the long-winded newspeak of corporate gobbledygook. Presumably Japanese senior executives will also soon learn to keep the prying world at bay with verbal smokescreens. For the moment, however, they are remarkably forthcoming under the right conditions.

BURDENED RATIONALISTS

If the Japanese managers and executives are more self protective and reticent, especially with the press, than selfish, and are not particularly ideological, what are they, then? Although burdened by racial and stereotypical notions that can get them into trouble, they are mostly rational. In 1989, the Japanese External Trade Organization (JETRO) conducted a nationwide survey of Japanese managers in the United States. The findings (up to this point available only in Japanese) tell us a great deal about what is on the minds of Japanese expatriates as they go about their business in America.[8] They are quite sensible, and there is nothing ideological about them.

When a Japanese firm decides to develop a plant in the United States, it looks at markets, geographical conditions and development policies in the locations being considered, environmental policies, transportation facilities, quality of the available workforce, and state incentives.

Of particular importance is the level of unionization in the area and the likelihood of minority hiring problems. Japanese executives surveyed advise firms to consider carefully whether they want to place their plant near their sales division. They also urge consideration of the pros and cons of being yet another Japanese firm in New York or Los Angeles versus becoming the first Japanese company to move into a new area. When a firm finally decides to build on a site, it often finds that American construction schedules are much looser than in Japan, as are deliveries of machinery. Environmental and pollution control regulations shock the Japanese. Equally disturbing is the infuriatingly slow approval process by local authorities after the big welcome they received from state officials.

Once a manufacturing concern is situated, it begins the hiring process. A big surprise is the genuine seriousness with which Americans treat equal opportunity issues. Another surprise is the credentials factor. Japanese firms have found that American supervisors tend not to hire subordinates with an educational background superior to their own. In Japan, a boss is a boss. He doesn't worry about threats to his power. In America power is on much shakier ground. Once the employees are on board, a few key people will be sent to Japan for up to three months training. According to JETRO, occasionally the home company treats the American trainees like honored guests, and the training is ineffective. Other firms focus on indoctrinating Americans into corporate cultures. A few actually impart skills. Back in America, the Japanese find that absenteeism is an issue, due in large part to women's childcare problems. Since Japanese wives rarely work when children are young, working American mothers are a novel situation for Japanese managers.

Many Japanese firms like to promote people out of blue collar jobs into management, but they find that sharp divisions between "blues" and "whites" exist in America. Another division that bothers them is between day and night shifts. Americans tend to put new employees on the night shift and productivity suffers. To cope with this some Japanese-owned U.S. firms have reduced night work and initiated a system of four long work days per week. Moreover, instead of providing overtime to regular workers, a few Japanese firms now prefer to hire part-time workers. Most, however, stick with overtime.

Dealing with employees is a ticklish business. Japanese tend to conduct performance appraisals in a gentle, oblique manner. They have found that their attempts to be pleasant and non-threatening often result in American workers who were actually rated as poor demanding higher pay based on their "good" performance review, and good workers becoming resentful over lack of recognition. Another no-win situation involves a break in communication when a Japanese manager who has established rapport with his employees by practicing an open-door policy, drinking with his people after work, and fully explaining why important decisions have been made is rotated back to Japan. The Japanese are frustrated by such headquarters' policies, because inadequate and infrequent communication is the single biggest complaint they hear from American employees.

When it comes to production issues, the Japanese are struck by the high rates of defective parts they encounter. This problem and a certain American carelessness about deliveries make them plan for more lost time in their American plants. The Japanese cannot understand why American suppliers do not practice a philosophy of continuous improvement. As they see it, American vendors use high defect rates and slow deliveries as bargaining chips in price negotiating. The more the Japanese seek high-quality parts delivered on time, the more they must pay. When Japanese insist on low defect rates, some American firms refuse to do business with them. A number of Japanese manufacturers have been working with their vendors on these issues, even offering cash incentives to motivate suppliers. Since the American government insists on more local content in Japanese products made in America, Japanese firms are working to raise the proportion of domestic supplies. Auto makers claim that they will have 75–80% local content by the early 1990s, up from 50–60% in the 1980s. Most of these U.S. suppliers, however, will be Japanese-owned companies.

Japanese firms recognize that they cannot become too automated in America. Indeed, they are expected to create jobs, a process that requires elaborate technical training. This is much harder for them in the United States than in Japan, since America is a conglomeration of languages, cultures, and beliefs. The Japanese in America have been forced to depend on manuals, operational standards, and rules to a greater extent than in Japan, where workers can be trained into figuring out what to do without formal rules. Nevertheless, the firms that can send key American workers to Japan for training generally are quite pleased with the results. In the Japanese view, however, the big barrier to enhanced productivity is unions. Again and again Japanese manufacturers complain of bizarre union work rules, a rigid division of skills, and an us-them kind of attitude. Where unions are helpful, total quality control activities have been instituted. Some companies find it best not to force Japanese-style quality controls on employees but rather to introduce them gradually, perhaps with union advice, and to offer financial incentives to employees for participation in quality circles.

When it comes to sales and marketing, Japanese firms, used to oligopolized markets, are struck by the extreme competitiveness they encounter, the fluidity of manufacturing industries, and the wide variety of their customers. Many American firms have a habit of "leaning on the trade"—not paying their bills until well after the due dates. Other companies are much shakier than the Japanese are used to. When firms merge or are acquired, the Japanese are annoyed at the speed with which relationships must be renegotiated, literally overnight. American salesmen for Japanese firms are viewed as often going too far to please their customers, and sometimes the Japanese company gets hurt. Another problem with salesmen is their eagerness to get out of sales and into service. Japanese are not used to such rapid turnover in a salesforce.

Americans expect corporations to be good citizens. One problem for Japanese firms in the JETRO survey is the U.S. government's insistence that companies doing business with it give orders to minority companies. Another problem is the "Buy American" requirement. A company is urged to use at least 50 percent parts in a product. Then there is "Ship American," in which the company must ship at least 50 percent on U.S. vessels, even though Japanese manufacturers feel they are expensive and provide inferior service. On a local level Japanese companies find that they must become more involved with their communities to a greater extent than in Japan. Firms donate a set amount or a percent of sales or profits, as well as volunteer activities in education, parks, or the United Way. Some Japanese managers even become volunteer fire fighters. The Japanese realize that they must be more than givers; community involvement is also a must. Thus some firms see to it that their managers and their wives avoid enclave living and take part in local activities. The firms are beginning to realize that formal training in English and in appropriate roles to be adopted in the United States will be required prior to assignment to America.

A final problem facing the Japanese in the survey is the litigiousness of American business culture. All business is based on contracts, and the procedures for bringing suit are, to Japanese, resorted to for resolving even trivial disputes. Americans sue the Japanese for breakdowns of machinery manufactured by another Japanese firm, for injury caused by the machinery, for sex and racial discrimination, and so forth. One American sued an electronics company because they discharged him during dinner and drinks instead of on the job. Japanese firms have become exceedingly gun shy. They take great care now over legal procedures and documentation and have learned not to invite further suits by hastily settling out of court.

All in all, Japanese manufacturers see themselves as doing moderately well in America. The unions bother them, as does the "sue the bastards" mentality of Americans, but these problems can be turned into opportunities. Unions can be partners rather than adversaries. At the least they can be articulate spokesmen for worker needs and concerns. As for the hothouse legal system, it may be feverish, but it does work to protect a firm's interests as well as employees' interests. This is not always the case in Japan, where entrenched bureaucracies are not always as concerned with justice as they ought to be. In the JETRO survey, little in the responses hints at ideology or selfishness. It is simply what one would expect from businessmen trying to do their job. Americans are the great ideologues of the modern world, and in the post-cold war era of a new Pax Americana, the United States has shown itself ready to defend truth, justice, and the rights of man in various regions of the world, especially when business interests are involved. The American struggle with Iraq, with its mix of self-interest and ideology, is not the kind of conflict the Japanese would ever allow themselves to become involved in. Indeed, Japanese national ideology (*nihonjinron*) is so ineffectual that it could not possibly have much influence over Japanese managers. The Japanese sometimes may look selfish, but closer observation reveals either a self-protective reticence or an unsophisticated provincialism rather than greed or rapacity.

SIX

"Those Who Depart Are Forgotten, Day by Day"

An assignment to the United States used to be considered a death sentence by Japanese managers in large companies. As the old Japanese proverb above suggests, the longer one is away from the center of Japanese power and advancement, the less likely one is to prosper in a career. This out of sight, out of mind perspective still prevails, but it has diminished in companies where American sales now are the major source of income. Today a tension exists that forces Japanese expatriates to be keenly attentive to both the American business environment and the needs or foibles of the home office. Japanese often march boldly into the United States with their heads turned back towards Tokyo lest they be forgotten by headquarters. It is not surprising that they sometimes stumble.

LOS ANGELES, JAPAN

"I worked in what we call Los Angeles, Japan," says a Japanese trading company textile manager now based in Tokyo. "My secretary was Japanese, my boss Japanese, all my colleagues were Japanese or Japanese-Americans. We read Japanese newspapers, watched Japanese television, and ate Japanese food. I only spoke English when I called on customers." This is not quite the melting pot experience one had hoped the Japanese would encounter. A Fuji Bank executive felt the same way. "American culture is easy to adapt to," he said. "It's American food that's a problem. At my age, it is difficult to eat hot dogs. That's why I liked working in L.A. and Seattle, where I could buy Japanese food. Our managers in the Middle East or other Asian countries have a much more difficult time." When the Japanese manager comes to New York City, which is an expensive place to most Americans, he finds prices on the average 28 percent lower than in Japan. Food is 31 percent lower, autos 19 percent less, and housing 46 percent less. Only health care and education are slightly more.[1] If he is a senior executive, the expatriate can join the Nippon Club on Manhattan's West 57th Street and play bridge with other executives on Saturday night. He and mid-level people most likely will live in Scarsdale, a small suburb with twice as many trees as Tokyo. So many Japanese now live in Scarsdale that the Monday morning train to New York is called the Orient Express.

Let's look at a typical young Japanese manager in Japan, Suzuki-san. He is employed in central Tokyo. Recently he and his wife purchased their first "home," a seventy-five square-meter flat forty kilometers outside of Tokyo, for only $200,000. His monthly mortgage payment is $1000. He spends four hours a day on the train, eight hours at work, and three hours of obligatory after-work socializing, a total of fifteen hours a day. On Saturday he comes in for half a day. Some days he misses his train home and stays in a capsule hotel: a bed over a sink in a room. Suppose that Suzuki gets transferred to his firm's American marketing center on the Meadowlands Parkway in Secaucus, New Jersey. Now, he lives twenty miles away in a beautiful suburban town in a small house. It also cost $200,000, but it is twice the size of Suzuki's Tokyo flat. He drives to work in thirty minutes and finds that the American subsidiary doesn't require much after-work socializing or Saturday work. His children attend a Japanese language school. The Suzukis have learned to avoid American hot dogs and other *gaijin* horrors, but generally they like American food. Suzuki is amazed that his wife and children are learning English so quickly. Life is sweet. The only anxiety Suzuki has is that he may soon be asked to return to Japan. Although he misses his country, he wonders how he can get his stay extended.

Because living is good in America, Suzuki-san wants to stay there. He also worries about his reception in Japan. When he returns to headquarters, he may not fit in very well. Decisions he made unilaterally in New Jersey now must go before committees. Suddenly his advancement will once more depend on seniority and membership in favored groups rather than expertise. His rabbit hutch and long commute will now be seen by him as poor. His wife's and his English will start to fade, and his children may be taunted at school, forcing him to send them to an expensive school which specializes in reindoctrinating offspring of returned expatriates. "Americans can go to Japan and spend years there, but they don't have much problem readjusting to life in the states when they get back," said a Japanese trader. "Not so for the

Japanese who come to America for any length of time. It is very difficult for them." When a Japanese says "very difficult," he means virtually impossible.

THE WIVES

At least in the large American cities, then, life can be quite livable
for Japanese managers, with the price to be paid once they are back in
Japan. Wives too can benefit. In Japan, 65 percent of the wives are still
using manually operated washing machines.[2] A manager's wife can enjoy
conveniences in the United States to which she is not accustomed in
Japan. What's more, in America she won't have to live with her mother-
in-law and fight constant battles over who rules the household. The
home is the only place where a Japanese woman has a chance to exercise power. If she loses control to her husband's mother, she loses that.

Not all Japanese women, however, want the liberation which America offers. Many in fact are used to living within a small circle of relatives and friends. They are painfully shy, and American informality
can be a torment for them. Bigger companies try to help. Matsushita's
marketing center in New Jersey puts on fashion shows, golf and tennis
tournaments, and seminars for the wives so they can mingle with other
Japanese women in a structured, semi-formal way which is more attractive to them than the informality of American-style picnics and bar-
becues. Still, the lot of the salaryman's wife is not easy. "Japanese men
are married to their company and neglect their spouses," comments
former Matsushita president Yamashita. "A total commitment to the
job leaves little time or energy for family life."[3] Husbands and wives
can become strangers to each other. Mr. Yamashita tells the story of
one couple who tried to learn to communicate. "They put a little doll
on the dining room table and directed critical remarks to it. In a typical
scenario the husband says, 'Mother seems to be in a bad mood to-
night.' The wife replies, 'Tell him I've been busy all day and I'm tired.'
The doll is an intermediary. Each can speak freely; neither resents criticism addressed to a third party." This chilling anecdote suggests, first
of all, how badly Japanese married life has fared in the corporate age.
But second, Mr. Yamashita attempts to paint this dismal scene in a
positive light. The idea that husbands should simply spend more time
with their wives and children apparently never crosses his mind. Instead he suggests little dolls be used to communicate. Perhaps he will
add high tech consumer electronics to the next addition to the line.
What will happen to this couple when the husband comes home and
says to the doll, "Tell mother we have been transferred to Tennessee"?

The tough lot of the wife in America, even with conveniences and
freedom, is recounted by a trading company executive. "Each day I

arrived home at 10 or 11 P.M. Then on Saturday and Sunday I played golf. I don't like to play golf in Los Angeles, but we received many visitors from Japan. It was my job to entertain them while they waited for the jet lag to disappear." During all of this time his wife was on her own, and with a slender Japanese salary there was not much to do. "For the first two years she watched television all day and couldn't understand a word. She couldn't drive a car because she had never learned to drive in Japan." Eventually her English improved, she enrolled at the local community college, and she received her driver's license. "After two years my wife started to like America. I was lucky." Not all managers are so lucky. Beset by her constant nagging to return home, a Japanese manager murdered his wife a few years ago in Oregon. Many Japanese families prefer not to face the trials of America, and the husband arrives alone for his five-year tour of duty. He will return every six months or so for a few days' visit, but rarely will he take his full vacation time. In many firms a week or so is all the lonely expatriate can expect. Absence, even legitimate absence to see one's family during vacation, is frowned on as a sign of disrespect in Japanese companies. No wonder Americans see an excessive alcohol consumption by some Japanese managers.

THE SHOCK OF INDIVIDUALISM

A returned manager now working in Tokyo put it well, "Japan is like a group of people on a train. Everyone goes in the same direction. The train cannot stop for one person. In the United States you travel by automobile, and when you want to stop, you stop—very individualistic." Every Japanese notices it as soon as he steps off the plane. He sees it in the way the baggage handlers hand his luggage to him. He hears it in the taxi driver's voice on the way into the city. In the office individualism is palpable. "The American businessman is very aggressive compared to the Japanese businessman. But on a company basis, Japanese companies are more aggressive," noted a Bank of Tokyo branch manager commenting on American individualism. "That's because the Japanese manager is always thinking about the company and how to achieve its goals. The American thinks about his own personal needs and the personal results of business. The Japanese is 50 percent for himself and 50 percent for his company. The American is 80 or 90 percent for himself." Another manager had similar observations. "Japanese staff feel a strong identification with their company. Let's say I'm a staff person and another staff member makes a mistake. Even though I didn't make the mistake, I will feel sorry about it. I will try to explain it to the boss and even apologize." The idea that a mistake is in part everybody's fault and that everybody is responsible for the organization sounds like something out of Tom Peters. Listen to this manager as he talks about traveling in America. "I travel a lot by plane. Often there are overbookings or mistakes. Generally, American airlines don't care. Their attitude is, 'Oh, someone got bumped. Too bad.' In Japan the counter people will say, 'I'm sorry. I'm sorry.' "

Individualism, simply put, is an ideology in which the person is valued more highly than the community.[4] The consequences of this system of values are profound. The individual ought to be free to act as he or she thinks is most conducive to self-interest. The most moral society is one in which initiative comes mainly from private individuals, property is owned mostly by individuals, and wealth is generated through competition, the rivalry among individuals. Individualism, however, requires respect for human dignity, autonomy, and privacy. Japanese, who are at least 50 percent individualistic and thus think about these things, nonetheless wonder how one is to show respect for a business competitor whom one is trying to destroy.

Individualism is rooted in a view of humans as atoms in the social universe, fully functioning either in harmony with each other (Adam Smith) or colliding violently (Hobbes). Defenders of individualism from the British and American business classes have argued that Adam Smith's harmony would emerge if and only if Hobbes' collisions went unhindered. Edmund Burke, their early spokesman, put it best when he warned in 1795 against "breaking the laws of commerce, which are the laws of nature." No one should interfere with the economic processes of individuals pursuing self-interest, even though it dooms some to "innumerable servile, degrading, unmanly and often most unwholesome and pestiferous occupations." This kind of talk may be heard on a given work day at about 5:45 P.M. in any of several taverns in the financial district of New York City. One wonders how the Daiwa Securities manager, sipping his scotch, reacts to it. His view of individualism is quite different. For him a person is not so much an acquisitive creature as he is a developing creature, reaching out, often with mighty effort, to be all that he can be. This idea of effort in service to personal development is fixed on by many Japanese, who value motivation more than ability as a precursor to success. To the Daiwa man, a good employee is diligent. If he is diligent, he will develop as a person. If he develops as a person, he will help the company be successful. The employee who is admired is not an acquisitive atom, a "spinning globule of desire." He works hard to cooperate with others. What he learns he shares with his group. Their success is a joy to him. Imagine the Daiwa man sipping his scotch and sighing, for tomorrow he must return to work where his American stock salesmen and bond traders will spin and collide once more. How can he cope with them? How can they cope with him?

ROLES AND TASKS

"When a bell announces the finish time," said a manager at Sharp's Memphis plant, "the Americans quickly drop their work. Japanese workers always finish what they are doing. But productivity is about the same." American workers are a pleasant surprise for the Japanese. They work hard and are just as productive, even more productive, than Japanese workers. But what strikes the Japanese as odd are the American habits of stopping exactly at 5 P.M. and only doing what their job description calls for. Both of these things are related. They signify an American's willingness to play a role, and only that role, for the required work time and not a minute more.

As a young man, a Japan Agricultural Council official stayed with an American farm family. "I was trying to wash my clothes by myself one Sunday," he recalled. "So I asked the lady if I could use her washing machine. She didn't like that at all and said, 'Why are you doing your wash by yourself, away from everyone else?' She thought I was trying to separate myself from the family. I should have put my dirty clothes in the same pile with everyone else's. Then she would wash them, dry them and fold them and put them on my bed. When I discovered that she would do all that for me, I was very pleased." This Japanese learned to his surprise that Americans can be quite group-oriented and that role responsibility often is more important than task responsibility. In Japan getting a job done is a first priority. In America this is not always the case, and sometimes one must let another do certain work because his or her role encompasses the task. Americans, lacking a class system and hostile to status, will eagerly differentiate themselves at work by a "that's my job" role focus. Japanese do not do this; any job is everyone's job.

The agricultural official quoted above was trying to "be a good boy," as he put it, by doing his own wash and not giving the family cause to think he was lazy. The idea that he had infringed on the housewife's role never crossed his mind. This is not to say that Japanese are not role-oriented. They are. It just isn't the main issue for them at work. In an office setting a Japanese manager expects any staff person available to volunteer when something needs doing. In that way the employee shows he knows his relationship to the boss as a subordinate and signals his commitment to company objectives. Not so with an American. A task is somebody's duty, not everyone's, and while Americans appreciate help from colleagues, they are protective of the role behaviors which identify them. This drives Japanese managers in America to distraction. They will have to learn to understand American ways about roles, however. Americans in turn would do well to recognize that when a task needs to be done, Japanese expect the first employee available to do it.

A good example of task-role confusion occurred in 1988–1989 at Mazda's Flat Rock, Michigan, plant. Japanese managers had failed to hire or train enough skilled specialists. Union officials considered this a power-grabbing tactic, since often the most vocal workers are the most skilled. Given the Japanese need for control in the workplace, there is likely to be some truth in this assertion. But it is not the whole story. Japanese do not like employees who say, "I do my job and only my job," and that is a typical role-oriented pose of an American craftsman. They prefer to hire less-skilled but more task-oriented workers. At Flat Rock they counted on being able to assign workers to tasks as the tasks came up, regardless of roles. This did not work, and Mazda has been floundering in its attempt to manufacture in America.[5] Over 100,000 cars, almost a whole year's production, had to be recalled for ignition problems in 1990. Mazda has no trouble shifting employees in Japan, because Japanese are task-focused in the workplace. The company trains these workers in the skills they will need, but it does not worry that the Japanese blue collar worker will suddenly start wearing a "Machinist and Proud of It" tee shirt and refuse to do non-machinist jobs. This worry may have been behind Mazda's failure to train non-skilled workers adequately in Flat Rock. Without enough craftsmen or adequately trained unskilled workers, quality fell, defects rose, and the accident rate accelerated.

THE BUSINESS ENVIRONMENT

With one eye on the job and one eye on Tokyo, the Japanese manager may be caught unaware by Americans' individualism and their circumscribed conception of what they are supposed to do at work. But the American business environment in some respects is quite different from Japan's and requires full attention of expatriate managers. One big difference is the level of competition. Japan has been called "the kingdom of regulation" by economists. Over 24 percent of the industries in the Japanese economy are strongly regulated, a figure unmatched in any modern industrial nation.[6] Most of the regulating involves entry barriers or price controls. While only 17 percent of manufacturing is controlled, mining, construction, finance, utilities, transportation, communications, and agriculture are almost completely regulated. The explanation for control is always the same: to secure "fair" competition. What this really means is the protection of established firms through the creation of oligopoly conditions. These regulated firms have no strong impetus to control costs. Consequently their labor productivity is often poor. Japanese productivity in wholesale and retail trade is only 81 percent of that in America. In transportation and communications it is 58 percent. Generally, service industries in Japan are only 91 percent as productive as in America. One wonders how these coddled firms cope with their investments in the United States, where new competitors are always lurking and control of labor costs often is the name of the game. The blundering for which some Japanese firms are noted in their dealings with American employees may be due to desperate attempts to learn more efficient ways of managing people in the United States. Such efficiency was not needed in the old country.

Luckily, Japanese managers have developed strengths in their domestic markets which may compensate for their labor productivity shortcomings. A 1990 Japanese Fair Trade Commission study of American and other foreign managers' attitudes to Japan's business environment found that complex distribution channels and government barriers to foreign investment were not major stumbling blocks. Instead, the real problems for the Americans were the Japanese firms' skills in developing quality products and rapidly delivering them.[7] Defect rates for electronics products in Japan are 0.5–1.0 percent. In the United States they are 8–10 percent. Average Japanese delivery times in Japan for machine tools are one to two months. In the United States, five to six months.[8] Quality and service superiority, communicated to the public through brand image, are the major competitive strengths of the Japanese in America. Mazda, for example, is trying to overcome negative publicity over its production problems by increasing its marketing and advertising effort with the emphasis on Mazda as a company dedicated to quality and service.

Another competitive strength, at least in the eyes of some Japanese, is the absence of MBAs in Japanese-owned firms. The Japanese head of a sales office for a bicycle company noted, "I can tell you the major mistake that American companies are making. They are hiring people out of business schools who have learned certain tools for modeling, projecting, forecasting, etc., but they have no idea about what's happening in the back rooms. They put their money into figuring out a strategy rather than investing in advanced technology and better facilities for their employees." A Tokyo management consultant with 28 years experience working with American hosiery manufacturers was also critical. "American firms cut quality and marketing expenses to raise profits for stockholders this quarter. This has led to a deterioration of American products. I see this all the time." Both of these managers are self-proclaimed America-lovers. One wonders what the America bashers are saying.

IN THE OFFICE

"American girls, especially young girls, do not usually like to work for Japanese companies," admitted one manager. "It is due to the social structure in Japan." He commented that a recent Japanese visitor to his more liberal office had been shocked to see both Japanese men and American female secretaries sharing dishwashing duties in the office kitchen. "Usually Japanese men just leave a big pile of dishes in the sink and assume a woman in the office will take care of them. You can imagine what kind of problems they will run into when they are assigned as manager in America!" The American woman is not the only fear Japanese have about office life. "In Japan we learn to say 'How are you?' in the morning," said a cement company executive. "But here you must say 'How are you, Patrick?' or 'How are you, Ann?' This is very important in America. My name is Sumio—very difficult for most Americans. So I chose 'Sunny' as my American name. Now everyone says 'Good morning, Sunny' or 'How are you doin', Sunny?'"

Following prescribed rituals and formalities is very important to the Japanese. The cement firm executive also was bothered by his company's flex time policy. "All the Japanese start at 8 A.M., take an hour for lunch, and leave at 5 P.M. But the Americans may come at 8:30 and leave at 5:30. Or they may come at 7 A.M. This is one of the major conflicts I have." This typically Japanese manager wants an office filled with routine, rituals, symbols, formalities and all the paraphernalia which make social life orderly and predictable. One of the rituals, noted frequently by American observers, is described by a Fuji Bank manager. "Japanese businessmen work very hard. But at the end of the day, if the boss is busy doing something, they sit in their chairs even when they finish their work. They stare at the boss until he leaves." Long hours in a Japanese office may add up to paper shuffling and staring out the window. Obviously influenced by his American experience and tired of playing the waiting game with his staff, the bank manager says, "It's a waste of time, it's not efficient, and I don't like it. When I go back to Japan, I'll keep the American style [of going home]. I don't like my employees staring at me."[9]

The layout of an American office distresses many Japanese, since they have a different concept of personal space. A trading company manager recounted the story of an uncle, who had been a POW in a Soviet prison camp with German prisoners during World War II. "The first thing the German soldiers would do was to stake out their territory by placing their belongings in a certain area. They created a mental wall. In the case of the Japanese, wherever they happened to be was their space." This manager was dumbfounded when he visited a large American company office with its endless number of partitions. "It's an amazing sight for a Japanese to stand up and look out over the partitions. I don't know why they're necessary. In Japan, even in a small, crowded office, it's possible to have your own space without partitions. It is second nature for us to respect somebody's space." Personal space to Japanese is where they are now, however. To Americans it is where their desk and file cabinets are. This difference leads to some nasty encounters, since Americans see Japanese as more nosy and intrusive in the office than they have a right to be. In a Japanese office, very little is private and there is no place to hide.

THE STAFF

American employees are a source of pleasure and frustration for a Japanese manager, who, with his one eye always on Tokyo, probably takes less care with employee relations than he should. The Fuji Bank man, who does take care, tells this anecdote. "In Japan I often visit clients simply to give them the bank's calendars. When my subordinate travels with me, he will say, 'Don't take them, boss. I will carry them.' In America, I carry the calendars myself through strong wind and rain." He recognized that his power is reduced in America. "The boss is an emperor in Japan who says 'Do this' or 'Do that' or 'You should obey my order.' Such obedience does not occur in the United States. My American employees have opinions and like to discuss every order. I need to keep things very frank and have a mind open to free discussion." A Los Angeles sales manager had similar observations. "Doing business with customers is important, of course, but managing Americans is our biggest problem. Most Japanese do not even know what can go wrong." Age discrimination, sexual harassment, affirmative action hiring? "Japanese are ignorant of these things because they are not issues in Japan. We become very confused and have to consult lawyers. Things that take a day to resolve in an American company can take much longer for us because we don't know what to do."

This sales manager, who has since returned to Tokyo after eight years in the United States, had trouble finding the right balance in his exercise of power. "If I flattered them too much, I lost control. But if I treated them severely, that would not work." In Japan this kind of balance is not a problem. "Without saying much to them, my Japanese employees sense what I want and do it." He once hired an American secretary whose day began at 9 A.M. However, she tended to show up around 10 A.M. each day. "I called her and wrote letters to her. Finally I fired her. Then I received a call from her lawyer, threatening a suit. We were well prepared, so nothing happened."

The Japanese manager can be naive when it comes to power perhaps because it comes to him so easily in Japan. A senior American bond trader at a Japanese securities firm on Wall Street says, "My first boss was a stock salesman. When he went back to Tokyo, a new guy, a bond trader, came in. The first thing he did was hold a meeting at which he said, 'The old president did not understand what we do. I know what to do.' For the next six months anytime I asked the new bond trader to do a trade a little differently, he agreed. I thought I was a brilliant negotiator until I realized that he had to say yes. I had him by the balls." The new president had committed himself to being different from his predecessor and would lose face if he showed the same old conservative streak. Many Americans have noticed this Japanese tendency to categorize themselves or others and then be unable to modify or change labels. "I know this," says the crafty American trader, "and it gives me infinitely more power around here."

In Japan, where the emperor-manager enjoys power beyond the wildest dreams of Americans, office routine can take on a highly regimented tone. In one company the work day begins at 8:30, but by 8:10 A.M. most of the staff are in their work uniforms sipping coffee or tea in the cafeteria. Ten minutes before work the loudspeaker suddenly comes alive with a stirring rendition of the company song. This is followed by music to accompany physical exercise. The employees jump up and wave their arms about. Very little physical exertion occurs, but that really is not the purpose of the exercise, which is more an effort to start the day on a note of conformity and submission. However, the exercise also builds team spirit and a feeling of harmony. At 8:30 the workers line up in their respective groups while the foreman makes a short speech and asks for ideas about the day's tasks. One employee failed to show up for work and the foreman brings the absence to the attention of the workers. It is a serious breach, and the employee's name is announced to all present.

Even with all their power, the Japanese hate to fire people. A Tokyo bank spent a fortune on recruiting a class of entry-level graduates from the best universities in Japan. The group started out together and trained together for several months. During this time, the bank realized it had overhired and would have to let about one-half of the 100 or so young people go before the end of their probationary period. Bank officials announced that the class would attend a training seminar at the firm's mountain retreat for a week. Everyone was told to clear out his desk and board one of two assigned buses. The buses pulled out and headed for the highway. When they reached the onramp, one bus proceeded to the mountain retreat, but the second bus drove to the nearest train station. When it stopped, a recorded message announced that the company had decided it could no longer employ the people on the bus and they were being laid off. The driver handed out small severance checks to each person as they stepped off the bus. The ex-employees meekly took the envelopes and returned home on the train.

"When I was in L.A., I had a very bad experience with an employee review," recalled one bank manager, still smarting from the threat to his power. "An American employee argued with me for two or three hours about why I did not raise his pay. This would never happen with a Japanese employee. With Americans it's like a baseball player negotiation. It's a completely different system for the Japanese staff when they come to the U.S." A trading company branch manager also was upset by American employee aggressiveness. "Basically, Japanese don't like to be pushed," he complained. Japanese managers are used to doing the pushing and have trouble handling resistance and especially being pushed themselves.

While power is the major issue in the Japanese work setting, Japanese managers are not tyrants. In fact, when they have control of things, their behavior can be exemplary. George Ruccio was a manager at the Firestone plant near Nashville when Bridgestone took over in the mid-1980s. "The Japanese arrived and told mid-level supervisors to begin treating employees like human beings," he recalls. This involved showing each worker how to do multiple jobs and seeking employee ideas on how to become more efficient. Some American managers, used to treating workers like interchangeable parts, hoped to outwait the Japanese, whom they believed would soon return to Japan and leave the plant in the care of its former management. The Japanese stayed put, however, and hundreds of supervisors eventually went looking for other jobs.

The Japanese in America are acutely sensitive to their source of power: Tokyo, Osaka (etc.). If they have a mandate from headquarters and maintain communications channels, then Americans' individualism and role playing can be dealt with, and the mysteries of the highly competitive business environment can be solved over time. Americans who criticize the Japanese boss for spending hours on the fax machine and days on the plane to Narita must realize that the power he builds up in these activities will help him endure and gradually cope with the problems he faces in the United States.

SEVEN

Competitors, Reluctants, and Knowledge Seekers

The story of Japanese managers in America looks as follows. Growth in investment rose in the early 1970s as firms sought to gain access to natural resources. Japanese capital flowed into the fishing industry so rapidly and in such great amounts (great to 1970s observers) that talk began to be heard about total Japanese ownership of West Coast processing. That did not quite happen, although Japanese firms today are the major players in the industry. The "yellow peril" worries which surfaced among fishing people had become muted by the 1990s as Japanese became Americanized and other issues took the spotlight. This mini-invasion replayed itself on a much larger scale in the 1980s as Japanese capital flooded in, stimulated by macroeconomic phenomena in the United States and Japan and by the growing global interests of leading firms in oligopolized industries. Japanese managers have been both confused and delighted by America. While the United States and Japan have similar economies and both are free-enterprise nations, competition in America is less orderly. Many American economists have given up on the idea that equilibrium conditions ever can exist except in text books. Japanese government and corporate leaders, on the other hand, try very hard to see that equilibrium occurs in key industries. Japanese used to managed markets—the management often is worked out by senior executives visiting each other or meeting at trade associations—are discomfited by the unexpected uncertainties they find in America. They also are bewildered since in many cases their companies have no clear strategic goal. They simply got into American markets as fast as they could and told their people to cope until plans could be worked out.

Japanese, being well educated, know the Declaration of Independence, and many managers find great joy in seeing it in action when they come to America. While some young Turks are arrogant and criticize America for its crime and weak education, most Japanese expatriates are intoxicated by the freedom and material well being available to them in the United States. This came up again and again in my interviews and is starting to become a theme in newspaper stories wherever Japanese plants and offices have congregated. Nevertheless, all is not rosy. While cultural differences are far fewer than most people realize, they do exist and are causing problems. Americans are more ideological and individualistic than Japanese, and Japanese managers are more concerned about status and power than Americans are. Employees are happy to see the Japanese boss park in their lot, eat in their cafeteria, and wear the same uniform they do. But they are caught up short when they encounter the underlying verticality of Japanese organizational life, where bosses are mini-emperors and employees are expected to be submissive and respectful.

The story of Japanese investment is not the gloomy tragedy of the Japan bashers. Nor is it the "Japan will show us how" narrative of the Chrysanthemum club. Although the overall impact of Japan in the United States can be simply stated as either harmless or beneficial, the specific effects of a firm or set of firms can be quite complex. In order to analyze these effects it is important to break down the 2600 Japanese-owned American firms into manageable categories. Researchers have been doing this for the last few years, and some recognizable types of Japanese investors are beginning to emerge. One way to categorize is by strategic mission, and I have called the three varieties of firms here *competitors, reluctant followers,* and *knowledge seekers.* This is the most useful way to analyze Japanese firms, but I also will examine briefly attempts to categorize Japanese companies by size and structure.

COMPETITORS

Competitor firms like Honda and Matsushita are the largest category among Japanese investors. They are in the United States (1) to exploit a competitive advantage, usually associated with product or process technology, (2) to maintain their leadership roles in their home industries, and (3) to keep U.S. competitors preoccupied to avoid their expansion in Japan. Competitor managers emphasize productivity and profitability, try to be good citizens in America, and constantly talk about "Americanizing" their U.S. subsidiaries.

The competitive focus emerged in a 1989 Wharton School study of over 900 Japanese firms.[1] Researchers found that Japanese investors seeking to exploit a technological advantage outnumber those who are seeking to acquire technology through American investments. These firms are driven by high returns which can be anticipated from American ventures. Why do they not simply stay at home and export their wares, thus avoiding huge start up or acquisition costs? One reason has to do with maintaining or gaining a leadership role in Japan. Take the case of Honda. In the late 1970s it expected quotas to be instituted on Japanese autos coming into the United States. By establishing plants in America Honda removed constraints on the amount of revenue it could earn in this country *and* ensured that high profit margins—the result of high demand for its technologically advanced cars and low, quota-caused supply of Japanese cars—eventually would result. Growth of this kind can lead to the maintenance, or in Honda's case the attainment, of a recognized leadership role in the domestic industry. This recognition assures Honda that the Japanese government will treat it better than its lower status competitors when "guidance" is offered and subsidies doled out.

Second, by expanding into American production, the Japanese signal to their American competitors that the battleground will be on U.S. territory. These Americans then may be less likely to move forcefully into Japanese markets as Japan's barriers gradually come down. This strategy of "the best defense is a good offense" may be looked on favorably by important government bureaucrats who, while lowering trade and investment barriers to U.S. firms under pressure from the U.S. government, would like to see conditions created which hinder Americans from taking advantage of newly open Japanese markets. When American chemical processing firms started to show some movement into Japan a decade or so ago, companies like Dainippon Inc. reacted quickly by buying a number of American firms.[2] In this way they became immediately competitive with U.S. companies in America and compelled the Americans to focus on domestic concerns.

RELUCTANT FOLLOWERS

Competitor firms are in America to make profits and are active in pursuit of that goal. A number of other firms are much less certain of their course of action. I have called these firms the reluctant followers. They generally have been committed to the domestic market in Japan with perhaps an added focus on exporting. Japanese auto parts suppliers fit into this category. Few of them came to America as the end result of a thoroughly considered competitive strategy. More likely they simply had to follow their major customer abroad. Other reluctant followers have had to follow a competitor. When one Japanese forklift firm came to America, five others soon followed. They had little choice. If the first firm enjoyed major growth in the United States, its status in

Japan would grow. To forestall possible dominance in the domestic industry, the other firms had to follow and compete with it in America.

Sometimes Japanese firms have reluctantly rushed to America because they feared a growth in U.S. tariffs, quotas, or other barriers to trade. These fears have spurred investors in both fishing and the beef industry, who worry not so much about their exports to America as they do about their imports of raw materials. The same could be said of Japanese wood products investment in pulp and logs. Interestingly, the reluctant Japanese fish processors have done more than sit on their assets. Over the last fifteen years they have opened up U.S. markets for surimi-based products, and Americans have come to enjoy crab- or shrimp-like fish slices in their salads at reasonable prices. Similarly, Nippondenso, which followed Toyota to make oil and air filters, now has formed Purodenso, a joint venture in Jackson, Tennessee, to manufacture similar parts for American-owned firms. These firms are becoming competitors.

Not all reluctant followers will make something of themselves in the time-honored fashion of immigrants to America. Some will continue to keep their focus steadily on the Japanese markets. Consider the maker of electronic instruments who is having cost control problems in Japan. It finds that both American imports and a leading domestic producer both are underpricing the products. A visit to the United States shows the CEO why: low-cost labor in rural American communities. If the firm wants to stay close to the Japanese leader, it must move to America. It does, but it only goes to make use of middle-aged American farm wives getting $4.50 an hour for assembling components made in Japan. The finished product is shipped to Japan without any consideration of American markets. This kind of firm is usually spotlighted by Japan bashers who want managed investment and trade relations between the two countries. But the media stories usually miss a fascinating story buried within the main story. Our firm probably is deeply committed to its Japanese employees and has implicitly promised lifetime employment to perhaps 90 percent of them. Consider the dual image of the firm. In America it is an exploiter with no interest in American issues and no commitment to its community. In Japan it is the finest type of business, one dedicated to the needs of society and the stability of the country.

It seems that the more our electronics firm shows itself as a worthy Japanese firm, the worse it will look to American eyes. Clearly this process has been occurring over the last few years, but just as clearly it will not continue for much longer. Why not? Currently the electronics firm cannot afford to lose domestic market share in Japan to the industry leader and to imports. If it did, it would have little work for its lifetime employees. What it does now is keep them busy building added-value components for the American assembly plant. But like many other Japanese firms, it is quietly dismantling the lifetime employment system. New employees will be treated as American firms treat theirs, with no guarantees about employment. This will suit young Japanese just fine. The new generation is not as desirous of security as its parents. What it wants are interesting jobs and good pay. The electronics firm sooner or later will change the focus of its American plant from assembly to a full-scale manufacturing facility with attendant distribution and sales operations. It will do this to provide exciting, growth-oriented work for a cadre of new young Japanese managers and engineers. The best will be offered tours of duty in the United States as a sign of their fast-track status. As they succeed in expanding American operations and as repatriated profits return to Japan, the domestic operation will be able to fund growth and to develop enhanced competitiveness. The young stay-at-homes also will find work exciting. While all this is going on, the American employees will have opportunities in the growing American operations and the local community will come to love its Japanese investor (one hopes).

In sum, then, even some reluctant followers who would rather have stayed at home are likely to find their American experience more of an opportunity than they had initially recognized. While those who followed a competitor or a customer may never amount to much, those who sought access to raw materials may find new markets. And those who were driven to America by cost-control needs and a desire to keep lifetime employees working may soon see that a serious American presence will serve the needs of the aggressive young workforce which is emerging in Japan. Yes, some reluctant firms will have Japanese managers who provide only minimum wage jobs to desperate rural Americans and who will pull up stakes at a moment's notice. But others will be manned by young managers who like life in America and who are always on the lookout for new products and markets in the United States. Their older, conservative bosses in Japan will have to pay attention to them or lose them to competitor firms, to other emerging reluctants, or to the third type of Japanese investors, the knowledge seekers.

KNOWLEDGE SEEKERS

When Kao purchased Jergens and Kubota invested in Silicon Valley software firms, they were not reluctant participants in American manufacturing; nor were they fiercely pursuing a competitive strategy. Instead, they sought to build the asset base of their firm through contact with American technology. These knowledge-seeking firms have had a tremendous advantage in the United States based on the low-cost financing available to them in the 1980s. When small high-tech U.S. firms came on the market, Japanese seeker firms had the ability to outbid American rivals. Once acquired, these high-tech firms are a mine of several different kinds of knowledge. Certainly new product ideas will become available, but other valued learning will occur. For example, as the Japanese pharmaceutical market becomes less regulated and more like the American market, Japanese firms owning innovative U.S. drug companies will learn from them how to cope in a new environment. This kind of knowledge adds up to what economists call "intangible assets," and they are the hottest thing around right now in the competitive jungle.

Intangible assets, such things as managerial expertise or innovative design approaches, are thought to be a major driver of global expansion. A Japanese firm with such assets can expect to overcome the cost differential between exporting and the establishment of a greenfield manufacturing operation overseas. Often a firm exports because the cost of foreign direct investment is so high, what with the need to build buildings and send managers overseas. The negative side of exporting, however, is that agents and distributors eat up the margin. If a firm can offset investment costs with high margins based on the exploitation of its intangible assets, then investment becomes a better deal than exporting. This is what Japanese seeker firms are doing when they have their American regional headquarters' managers spend their days buying U.S. firms. The U.S. firms will supply the intangible assets needed to make investing worthwhile. Japan bashers will say that the process is similar to the condemned criminal supplying the rope with which he will then be hung. Chrysanthemum clubbers and their economist friends will call it an example of efficient allocation of resources.

Whatever one's viewpoint, the Japanese manager in a seeker firm will not be looking to quickly exploit a technological advantage like competitors; nor will he be searching for cheap American labor and control over raw materials. He will be constantly on the move, visiting new "comer" firms in his industry. Here is one scenario of the way he will operate in one year.

January: Teruhiko Kondo visits Tech-Wow in Palo Alto. He dines with the founder/chairman/CEO/chief designer—all the same person. He tells the CEO about his firm.

February: Kondo-san, working with a U.S. Big Six firm, sets up a two-day seminar on financing for high tech firms. He runs into Tech-Wow's CEO again.

March: The CEO receives a survey questionnaire from a business school professor who is gathering information on high-tech markets and distribution channels. The professor follows up with an interview. During the interview he mentions that the research is funded by a grant from Mr. Kondo's firm.

April: Kondo-san returns to Tech-Wow with an offer. His firm will help Tech-Wow purchase an important piece of equipment. All Tech-Wow has to do is issue a five-year bond to be purchased by the Japanese firm at a 6 percent coupon rate. The CEO jumps at the chance.

May: The CEO and his wife travel to Japan with Mr. Kondo to meet the chairman of the parent firm. A full-scale Japanese-style welcome occurs.

June: Monthly sales in the industry are low, but Mr. Kondo offers a low-cost working capital loan. A note is signed by the CEO for six months.

July: A journalist shows up to do a story on innovative firms like Tech-Wow. It turns out that he has been funded by a foundation which is a recipient of money from Mr. Kondo's firm. His article, which is very comprehensive, appears in an important industry journal read by HQ people in Kondo-san's firm. They now are familiar with Tech-Wow's potential.

August: The CEO is approached by a securities firm which wants Tech-Wow to make a new stock offering.

September: The offering occurs. Kondo-san's firm takes up most of the shares.

October: Mr. Kondo visits the firm again. This time he reminds the CEO that the note is due in December. Since cash flow is not so good, the CEO is worried that he may have to use proceeds from the stock sale to pay it. Kondo asks him to wait while he talks to Tokyo.

November: A deal is proposed. Tech-Wow will swap equity for both the bond and the note. This will give the Japanese control, the CEO points out. Not to worry, says Kondo.

December: The swap occurs. The CEO and his top managers and technicians retain a substantial minority interest in Tech-Wow, and they are given five-year management contracts by Mr. Kondo, who becomes the new chairman. Massive new capital infusions occur. Young Japanese show up to learn from their American counterparts.

It would be easy to see something sinister in Mr. Kondo's machinations. Easy but wrong. Nothing he did is illegal or even very deceptive. Tech-Wow's CEO probably knew from the start what Kondo was up to and welcomed the attention. Very few large American firms are involved in the venture capital business, and those that are are pulling back. Even fewer Japanese firms are in the business, but they are not pulling back. More seekers will wend their way to America. In 1989 Pioneer Electronics paid $200 million for the California-based Disco Vision to acquire state-of-the-art knowledge in the optical disk market. A similar knowledge seeker was Otsuka Pharmaceutical Corporation, which wants to learn magnetic resonance systems from its new affiliate, Chemagnetics. To develop knowledge of genetic probe technology, Chugai Pharmaceuticals purchased Gen-Probe in San Diego. In 1990 the Ishida Group decided to develop state of the art tilt-wing aircraft. To get a factory it purchased Crestview Aerospace from Fairchild Aircraft. The Japanese firm will locate in Fort Worth, which just happens to be near Textron's Bell Helicopter division. The idea may be to lure top engineers away from Bell, thus acquiring the knowledge needed to make a go of it.[3] Another way to gain knowledge is through joint ventures. The pharmaceuticals also have been active here. Fujisawa works with Smith Kline; Beckmann, Takeda with Abbott; and Yamanouchi with Eli Lilly.

Overall, Japan is a net importer of technological knowledge and has been since data began being collected in 1950. In 1987, about 8200 cases of technology imports occurred, while only 7600 exports were recorded. In 1989, Japan imported $1.5 billion in technology from the United States—about twice the technology imported from the rest of the world combined.[4] The industries that clearly are knowledge seekers, the net importers of technology, are fabricated metal products, nonelectric machinery, electronics, aerospace, and precision machinery. Big U.S. investors from those industries are Daido Steel (bearings and specialty steel), Daiichi Jitsugyo Co. (industrial machinery), Shindaiwa (machinery), Shizuki (electronics), Mitsubishi Heavy Industries (aircraft and parts), and Horiba (measuring and controlling devices). They undoubtedly are on the lookout for knowledge, as are the builders of American R & D centers. Over the last decade thirty-seven of these have been acquired or built to research such things as optical disks, copiers, electronic materials, automobiles, haircare, pharmaceuticals, and software. R & D in Japan, by the way, has not been the sacred cow described by Japanese public relations firms. When profits decline in Japan, so does R & D funding. Presumably the spread of R & D to America is not only to capture American knowledge but to keep research efforts strong by funding them with American affiliates' earnings when domestic business in Japan experiences a profit decline.

BIG, SMALL, VITALIZED, BUREAUCRATIC

People in southernmost Japan neither look like nor talk like inhabitants of the northern islands. Indeed, some northerners are indistinguishable from white Westerners in looks. The point here is that while Japan is a more homogeneous country than the United States, a great deal of differentiation still exists. This is also true of Japanese corporations. About 12.5 percent of Japanese firms with more than 200 employees have invested overseas. Only 8 percent of small firms with less than 200 have foreign investments, and most of those are in South Korea and Taiwan.[5] When they do go to the United States, they do it to expand or maintain markets and they favor full ownership over joint ventures. To reduce their risks, sometimes a group of small firms will band together. This happened when Mitsubishi linked up with Chrysler to produce autos in the United States. Faced with production cuts in Japan, sixteen parts suppliers formed Eagle Wings Industries, Inc., an American sheet metal processing company with 250 workers, to develop a market with Diamond Star, the Chrysler-Mitsubishi company. In the 1990s small firms are likely to move more towards joint ventures with American companies as they shift from reluctant follower to competitor and knowledge seeker status. This is particularly true for the auto parts suppliers, who are small in Japan and even smaller in America. Out of 120 Japanese-owned suppliers examined in one study, about one-half had less than 100 employees.[6]

Another differentiating factor is corporate culture. In a 1987 study of eighty-eight large Japanese corporations, 39 percent were categorized as "vitalized" and 36 percent as "bureaucratic."[7] The vitalized firms focused on innovation, keeping in touch with markets, learning from failure, and showing a reliance on team approaches. These "Japanese management" firms, such as Canon, Hitachi, and Sony, were contrasted with bureaucratic companies, mostly manufacturers of basic materials, that rely on rules, procedures, technical expertise, getting things done right the first time, and hierarchical management. Over the 1977–1986 period the vitalized firms' average annual sales growth rate was 46 percent greater than that of the bureaucratic firms, and return on assets was 28 percent greater. The fact that their sales grew faster than profitability suggests that these firms often seek market share, even when it does not lead to increased profitability. The vitalized firms fit the image of a typical Japanese investor in the United States, but Americans will be surprised to see that lots of Japanese subsidiaries will be just as bureaucratic as their parents. Indeed, Japanese-owned U.S. firms are quite varied. If we multiply the three strategies (competitor, reluctant, seeker) by size (large, small) and then by corporate culture (vitalized, bureaucratic), we get twelve categories of Japanese direct investment. Many generalizations can be made about the Japanese in America and I have made them, but it is good to keep in mind just how differentiated they can be. They do not all look alike. Moreover, a fourth way of categorizing can be added: Is a firm a Japanese-owned U.S. company or a Japanese company in America?

AMERICAN OR JAPANESE COMPANY?

This is the most controversial category of all. In some companies the American subsidiary is treated as an American company owned by the parent in Japan. There are both bad and good aspects to this. Take the example of dual meetings. Typically both Japanese and American man-

agers will work together on local tactical issues, but when strategy re-
lating to global integration and parent objectives is discussed, the Japanese go off by themselves. An American who thinks he is working
for Nomura or Sharp may find that he is not, regardless of company
pronouncements. Like Taiwanese or Indonesians, he is a subsidiary
employee, a local who is not part of the parent's staff. As such he is
not eligible for extensive headquarters training or the wide variety of
assignments which can lead to promotion. He probably cannot even
seek transfer within the United States. Japanese managers often complain that American managers are not as loyal or as motivated as they
would like, and it is easy to see why.

The good side of all this is that the Japanese, probably without thinking much about it, have committed themselves to Americanization. The
company is "American." Contrast this approach with that of the Japanese manager in the "Japanese" company who says, "Why can't these
American employees adapt themselves to a Japanese-style system? After
all, this is a Japanese company." This kind of firm keeps Japanese managers in all key posts. When an American of necessity is put in a high
position, a Japanese "advisor" often is appointed to keep him in check.
Instructions flow in a constant fax stream from Tokyo or Osaka, and
information useful for strategic decision making flows back the other
way. Several banks and securities firms are run in this fashion.

When these firms are criticized for not Americanizing their managerial staff, they often take the position that Japanese cultural values,
norms, and practices are deeply embedded in a company and its foreign subsidiaries, and only Japanese expatriates can function successfully in the subsidiaries' senior positions. This explanation is self-de-
feating, since it implies that all staff and technical experts ought to be
Japanese. Such a prospect would not be tolerated politically, and economically the loss of American knowledge would be disastrous—indeed it has been a disaster for a number of financial services firms.
Moreover, the "we Japanese are simply too unique" argument offends
American sensibilities (they are not all that unique, in any case) and
contributes to media Japan bashing. It is much better to admit that a
desire to maintain tight hold of power in Tokyo is behind most claims
that Japanese subsidiaries cannot be Americanized. A subsequent willingness to give up some power makes both political and economic sense.
Localization programs, in which Americans begin to move into top spots
and have a shot at company-wide posts, attract high-quality managers
with valuable skills who are eager to represent the company in its war
with Japan bashers and their allies in Washington, D.C.

Those firms which have declared themselves American clearly have
the jump.[8] The most notable of these is Honda. While it is still very
much a Japanese-managed manufacturer in Ohio, the company has de-

clared its intention to Americanize. The Accord Coupe is made only in the United States, and it is supported by American design approaches and systems. Nissan's Tennessee plant complex is American, as is Sony's San Diego television plant. Matsushita, where older managers have exhibited the "Japanese company" approach, nevertheless is changing with its recent policy of localizing supply, production, and marketing in the United States. The future will favor those firms that become American. Many of them have come to the United States proclaiming that their subsidiaries are American, but they have emphasized the negative dimensions of this by treating their U.S. firms as stepchildren not eligible for certain favors from the parent. Most Japanese investors started out like this, and most of them eventually will see that while they are in the correct half of the Japanese/American category, they need to exploit its advantages better. Members of the other half of the category, the "we are a Japanese company" managers, are doomed unless they change. Firms like Nomura on Wall Street are trying to do this now.

The typical Japanese company in the United States probably is a 150-employee firm wholly owned by a giant in Japan. It has come to America to compete, and with its vitalized, "Japanese-management" approach it is beginning to make its mark. A lack of a customer base is its biggest problem, and acceptable profits have not yet occurred. Its parent has generously provided the latest technology, but return on investment is low and not expected to increase for a long time. The firm has Japanese managers in all senior positions, but it is planning to Americanize the operation during the 1990s. By 2000 only one or two Japanese managers will be on hand, and Americans will be transferring in and out of the parent's other holdings in the United States as employees of the multinational rather than of just the one subsidiary. "Typical" in this case, it should be noted, means the largest single category, perhaps 20–30 percent of the firms. That is as close as we can get to an image of the Japanese company in the United States, given the varied strategies, sizes, and managerial approaches described previously. Fortunately, the theories of management that guide Japanese managers are not so varied, and these are described in the next chapter.

EIGHT

Japanese Management Philosophies: The Brainless and the Brilliant

Japanese managers do not pay much attention to national ideologies, but they are exposed in college and the popular press to a body of writings, the *nihonjinron*, which purports to create a legitimizing basis for the economic and business life of the nation. To an American elements of the *nihonjinron* are offensive and brainless, but since they occasionally crop up in the pronouncements of Japanese executives, they must be taken seriously. More important is the brilliant collection of ideas and values on the nature of work, the function of a company, the duties of managers, the role of failure, and the place of groups in the organization. These add up to what we know about "Japanese management." Much of this knowledge, however, does not appear in the American business press, which often has obtained its material from Japanese propaganda mills of one sort or another. While Japanese business propaganda generally is truthful, it presents a much too simplified vision of the actual behavior of Japanese managers.

NIHONJINRON

Japanese managers, we can all be thankful, do not come to the United States with any grand ideological model guiding them. Most of their college life has been spent perfecting their tennis and drinking skills, and they have not paid much attention to their professors. In magazines and television, however, they inevitably will have come across the discourse of *nihonjinron* ideologies. Shintaro Ishihara of *The Japan That Can Say 'No'* is the most visible of this group, but beneath the surface is an intellectual biomass of considerable size. American Japanologists have harvested some of the more interesting species of ideas and translated them. They give us a glimpse of the sheer nuttiness to which managers occasionally are exposed and which sometimes influences them to see Japan and Japanese managing as unique in the world ("unique" implying best). *Nihonjinron* is a basis for some of the arrogance Americans have noted in a few Japanese expatriates.[1]

In their younger days, Japanese managers may have heard that Japanese "animal sociology" is making great strides. One line of research, praised widely in Japan, explores the difference between "Japanese" and "Western" honey bees. The Western bees are insensitive to the dirt of other bees, intolerant, divisive, and bellicose. Japanese bees build clean nests, are tolerant and peaceful, and live in harmony with each other. Moving right along to humans, the managers may have been exposed to a 1978 best seller on the "Japanese Brain" by Tadanobu Tsunoda. It appears that Japanese brains are different from Western brains, a difference which forces Japanese language to be a "vowel language" rather than the "consonantal" Western variety. It can be downright unhealthy for Japanese, according to Tsunoda, to tax their unique minds by studying other languages such as English. Another scientist, Tadao Umesao, "discovered" in 1960 that Japanese are better than Westerners at probing animal mentality because Westerners are more alienated from nature than Japanese. "For Europeans, of course, there is an unbridgeable gap between man and the animal kingdom," he noted.[2]

One *nihonjinron* writer, Yuji Aida, attributes the tendency of Japanese managers to be fiercely competitive to racial characteristics.[3] It may appear that the sociability of Japanese bees has not transferred to Japanese businessmen, but other writers make the case that harmony is a within-group characteristic of Japanese, who are then competitive outside their groups.[4] None of these writers has ever shown any interest in empirically testing or supporting their claims, but then a lack of empirical focus is a characteristic of *nihonjinron* work. There are two things wrong with Aida's assertion. First, the use of race to explain social behavior is offensive, but second, Japanese business is not fiercely competitive. Many industries are oligopolized, and *keiretsu* try to see to it that their markets are "orderly." As noted earlier, the highly competitive American environment is something of a shock to Japanese managers, who are used to competing mainly with two or three other firms, often under strong guidance from the government. Within this context Japanese go at it tooth and nail, but it is not the kind of competition envisioned by Adam Smith.

Another *nihonjinron* theme picked up by a few Japanese corporations is the idea that individualism is a threat to society and that Japan is unique in being a nation where identity is a function of group and corporate membership. When observers point out that Western ideas about the individual are having a profound influence on young Japanese, *nihonjinron* writers trot out the concept of *kokutai*, the national essence which always remains unchanged and which eventually brings Japanese back to their true path. This is a comforting thought for CEOs worried that their submissive, conformist employees may start asserting themselves. *Kokutai* allows Japanese corporations to absorb foreign ways without really being changed by them. Thus, foreign investment can be undertaken with every confidence that the corporation will not need to develop in response to the new techniques of managing which its executives pick up in Europe and America. As a self-fulfilling prophecy, the *kokutai* idea probably explains some of the slowness Japanese multinationals have shown in globalizing. Internationalization can bring material rewards, but Japanese spirit will not be affected. An "indigenous purity"[5] is always sustained, no matter how much is borrowed from Western ideas, and this purity defines and defends the status quo.

Japanese are seen as a "tribe" in *nihonjinron* ideology. A corporation is a household *(ie)* within the tribe. A salaryman has allegiance to household vertical relations, expressed as submission from below and benevolence from above, and to tribal values as articulated by *nihonjinron* writers. Households in the tribe do not compete like *gaijin* do. Rather they negotiate and allocate (presumably they negotiate fiercely, as Aida would have it). Power in the tribe or the household emerges from the *kokutai*, the nature of Japanese things, rather than from command of resources, charisma, or some other Western notion such as mutual exchange. When a Japanese manager barks harshly at a subordinate ("They sometimes treat each other like dirt," noted a horrified American manager in New York), he does so because he can assert power without fearing a challenge. Behind him (supposedly) is the immutable order of Japanese existence to legitimize his behavior. Moreover, private loyalty to his group and firm is admired and takes precedence over loyalty to abstractions like the "public" or "society." That is why bribery or illegal price fixing is not punished severely. The salaryman merely is exhibiting Japanese spirit. When Americans talk of the "people," it must seem quite odd to a Japanese manager inculcated with *nihonjinron* ideology.

Talk about *kokutai* reminds one of the *volk* concept. It should, since *nihonjinron* theories were heavily influenced by European romantic thinking of the nineteenth century and fascist thought of the twentieth. But it is important to point out that Japanese managers are not fascists. They have no commitment to *nihonjinron* ideology except when it is a convenient support for whatever they happen to be doing—such as yelling at a subordinate. The elites who run the government and the big corporations will use *nihonjinron* a bit more deliberately and more cynically, but they also seem to treat it all as a set of excuses and legitimizations which no one should take too seriously. An American arguing with a Japanese will know when *nihonjinron* is about to be used to defend a point. The Japanese will preface his remarks by saying, "We Japanese . . . ." What will come next is an argument implying the following: "The *kokutai* justifies and excuses our actions. Therefore, you should accept what we have done or are going to do as a culture-bound act emerging out of the essence of Japaneseness. To argue against it would be like arguing with the wind or the rain." The Japanese will be delighted if the American falls for this line of reasoning, but he probably does not expect him to. It is simply a ploy worth trying with gullible Yankees. Americans should not let Japanese get away with it. A polite response is, "Yes, but we are all humans, and no one of us is more special than another. Also, we Americans believe in the rule of law and in fair dealing. You do too, don't you?"

WHAT IS WORK?

One night an American securities firm manager stationed in his firm's Tokyo office worked late. On his way out he encountered a Japanese employee still at his desk. "Why are you still here?" the American asked. "Do you have something to do?" The Japanese shook his head. "No, but if I go home early, the people in my block will think that I'm not a good worker." The American who told me this story is a self-admitted workaholic, but his idea of work and his Japanese employee's idea are not the same. Americans use work as a tool to pry loose rewards which can purchase enhanced leisure. To Japanese work is an end in itself— what one does if one is human. In a series of studies on why employees are willing to work hard, American workers at both Japanese-owned companies (Sony and Kikkomen) and American-owned firms agreed with the statement, "It is my responsibility to do whatever work is assigned to me." The Americans viewed work as driven by the economic transaction. In return for promised compensation, they willingly performed work. Japanese workers in Japan were different. They tended to agree with the statement, "I want to live up to the expectations of my family, friends, and society."[6] For them work is simply living as one is supposed to live in accord with the order of society. It is a process of carrying out obligations owed to society and to oneself as a social being.

According to some *nihonjinron* writers, the national commitment to hard work is the key to Japan's success. In *The Japan That Can Say 'No'* Akio Morita is eloquent in stating what he perceives to be the difference between American and Japanese approaches to business. "Business, in my mind," he says, "is nothing but 'value-added.' We must add value and wisdom to things, and that is what America seems to have forgotten. This is the most deplorable aspect of America today."[7] Morita's co-author, Shintaro Ishihara, is so committed to this proposition that he proclaims, "The more technology advances, the more the United States and the Soviet Union will become dependent on the initiative of the Japanese people." What will be the basis for this Japanese initiative to add value and wisdom to high tech products desperately needed by the United States and the Soviet republics? Hard work. Ishihara says, "Looking at history, in cases where the whole society was using their brains instead of their hands, no one has lasted to prosper today." According to Ishihara, as long as Japanese continue to dedicate themselves to working hard to manufacture complex, high value products, the nation will continue on its way towards the enhanced power in the world which Japan deserves.

The work as process of living idea may have deep religious overtones. According to Shosan Suzuki, a seventeenth-century Zen Buddhist, "When you toil, your heart is at peace. In this way you are always engaged in Buddhist practice."[8] Work is a religious exercise which cleanses an impure heart. Suzuki says, "If you cast aside all attachments and work hard, the gods will favor you, and your profits will be considerable. You will become a person of virtue and wealth, but you will care nothing for that wealth." The idea is to work hard, not necessarily to work productively, but if you are productive and profitable, you will not care. All you will care about is working hard as an end in itself. This vision is a neat twist on the Protestant ethic, in which the fruits of hard work were seen as signs of God's favor to the chosen few. If you truncate the inference chain, you get work itself as a sign of salvation. The Japanese Buddhists, however, refuse to treat work as a sign of some state one will be awarded in an afterlife. It is simply what one does if one is a good person. Some Japanese managers accordingly see work as a moral rather than an instrumental act. It is associated with good, not utility, and workers who slack off are not just unproductive. They are downright bad. When Japanese managers expect their American employees to spend thirty minutes before their work starts doing unpaid labor or to stay on after 5 P.M. to finish a task without overtime, they are offering a chance to act in a moral manner. Rather than thanking or praising the Americans, they expect the workers to thank them for providing an opportunity to be moral. Since a moral person is happy, the Japanese in their view are creating conditions for happiness.

Cynics and sceptics will accuse these Japanese of hypocrisy in their religious beliefs. They will be right to do so. Zen Buddhism's contribution to the workplace is like a high quality tool found lying on the shop floor. "Let's pick it up and use it," says the manager. "When we don't need it anymore, we can discard it." It is only fair to point out, however, that Japanese and Americans do not differ much in their use of hypocrisy, only in the content. Some kind of ideology is crucial if work is to have any meaning which makes it seem a sensible thing to do. Americans rarely bring God into the workplace, but they do infuse the work environment with pious oratory about progress and "you too can be CEO"—often to $7 per hour laborers who will be making $7.50 an hour (inflation adjusted) thirty years from now in the same job.

Another source of the theory of work as process for Japanese is the code of *bushido*. According to this model, the employee, especially the skilled people and the white collar managers, are like samurai of old who worked on behalf of their lords without question or complaint. The *Hagakure*, a samurai's guide to life, quotes what is in the heart, "I am but a servant of my liege lord. Let him be cruel to me, or kind, as he pleases . . . . At the thought of my dear lord, my eyes swim in tears and I am filled with thankful ecstasy."[9] Work is but the act of allegiance in this view; it is the expression of loyalty. To reduce the work effort or to stop then becomes the decline of loyalty, which brings forth a corresponding decline in the lord's benevolence and the "bliss" of the master-servant relationship. This kind of talk often is analyzed with great seriousness by American theorists looking for the secret of Japanese management. Japanese themselves usually are less taken by *bushido* in business. As they say, "Never be late, never take a day off, never work." Indeed, as one Japanese manager noted in my interviews, "If you visit a Japanese company after 3:00 P.M., you won't see many managers working. They are all reading the papers and being complacent. It happens all the time." As for the samurai-like loyalty which Japanese employees supposedly exhibit, it is not so. In a study of several thousand workers in the United States and Japan, researchers found that Americans exhibited more loyalty to their employers than Japanese did.[10] What looks like loyalty in Japan often is really submission to inevitable and not easily assailed managerial power.

Karoshi is a Japanese word referring to death from overwork. In Japan presence is productivity, and time logged at one's desk or work station is often a symbolic statement of submission rather than a useful generator of work. A popular pastime in Japan is wondering just how much a Japanese employee can take. How much overtime does it take before a salaryman flips out? How much drinking after work is required to rot his brains? How much unnecessary pressure is needed to destroy him? A tradition of using overtime from permanent employees rather than seeking new hires often gets out of hand in Japan, as does the use of speed up in various white and blue collar forms to raise productivity. Well-managed firms like Sony do not encourage total submissiveness and tell workers to take their vacations. Others, more concerned with order and authority, tacitly let employees know that vacations are not encouraged and overtime, even for no functional purpose and without pay, is a ritual of obedience. On average, Japanese put in 225 more hours a year in the workplace and are substantially less productive than Americans.

Work, then, is a human activity expected by Japanese society. It is what one does if one is a respected member of the community, regardless of whether or not anything productive comes of it. Japan does not have daylight savings. One reason is that many Japanese see it as an idea which the Americans tried to force on them during the occupation. Another reason, and probably the more important one, is that Japanese workers would feel uncomfortable going home in daylight. Somehow it would not seem right. This way of defining oneself as a responsible citizen through long hours of work attendance is taken up by nationalist thinkers who see work as the path to Japan's enhanced economic power in the world. Others define work as a moral act associated with the attainment of the good. To some, it is an ancient way of expressing allegiance to one's betters, while for many power-oriented managers their employees' long hours are a ritual act of submission.

All of these definitions except the first are a misuse of a sophisticated philosophy of work developed by Japanese culture in which toil is simply the act of being human. It is one of the things one does to affirm existence as meaningful. American economic theory is crystal clear: work is a "disutility," something to be done only to acquire leisure. Every American business school graduate hears this from his or her finance and economics professors, and most unions represent workers in a way which suggests their adherence to the theory. When the American and the Japanese work together, fundamental and unresolvable problems can arise because of their different beliefs about the nature of work. To Japanese work is human; Americans are trained to see work as inhuman. Fortunately, Americans *actually* tend to enjoy their work, and their faith in economic theory is rather weak. Thus, problems which crop up are endurable among men and women of good will. More dangerous, however, are those Japanese who see work as a ritual of submission to managerial power. Their rigid transference of such a perspective to America has created alarm and discord in some Japanese-owned companies.

WHAT IS A COMPANY?

Every time Akio Morita enters into a joint venture in America, he runs up against a set of problems he has encountered before. "When we spend capital on facilities investment," he says, "we are entitled to tax benefits. I like to utilize the extra profits generated by these tax benefits to get rid of debt service. Whenever I suggest that my American partners ask, 'Why do we have to sacrifice our profits now for people in the future?' "[11] Morita's partners want to increase disposable profits in the short run. While the usual rhetoric of maximizing shareholder returns is offered, the real reason is that the American executives want to increase their personal incomes as quickly as possible. In America, managers like them are called "agents;" they represent owners while also pursuing their own interests. To Japanese like Morita, they are destroyers of their companies' long-term survivability.

Morita and his American partners define a company differently. To them the company is simply a convenient tool to serve the interests of owners, managers, and employees. To Morita it is "a community bound together by a common destiny, like the relationship between a married couple. All must work together to solve common problems." A company is a "fate-sharing" institution, and it is the duty of an executive like Morita to create conditions in which an employee can spend twenty to thirty years and conclude at the end that he has had a good life. Morita feels that his California Sony plant illustrates his point. Opened in 1972, the firm soon was hit with a recession. Instead of layoffs, Sony subsidized the American plant, using the slack time to develop training programs. The result was a better trained and dedicated workforce. Morita argues that in a fate-sharing organization a bond exists rather than an exchange relationship, and the bond creates mutual obligations. In poorly run Japanese companies the obligations involve employees' groveling submission to managers who respond with paternal care. In well-run companies employees offer loyalty and receive appreciation in the form of pay, recognition, and career development.

Besides being a fate-sharing community, a company is also society's servant. To an executive like Yotaro Kobayashi, president of Fuji Xerox, the question "Who owns a company?" is not controversial. "In broadest terms," he says, "the company is, of course, an institution belonging to and serving society."[12] In light of this definition, seeming oddities of Japanese financial dealings begin to make sense. For example, many Japanese firms own stock in other firms, often their customers and suppliers. Since all firms jointly are "owned" by society, all have a link which stimulates mutual assistance when one firm is in trouble. This even pertains to competitors. In Japanese baseball, players on a team which is walloping another team sometimes are told to ease up so that morale on the losing team is not threatened. According to Mr. Kobayashi, those who invest in firms "derive a sense of satisfaction whenever the company upgrades its operations or begins marketing improved products." Can "satisfaction" be considered a form of shareholder wealth, so that the T. Boone Pickens' of the world will be happy when the firms in which they have invested improve, even though profits do not? Obviously not, and here we come squarely up against the fundamental difference in Japanese and American concepts of what a company is. Although lots of overlap exists, Japanese see a company as a set of obligations to society, with the abstraction "society" usually represented by the employees, first, and then by customers and suppliers. Americans see a company as a set of claims by owners on the wealth-generating potential represented by the organization.

The problem these varying definitions create when a Japanese firm moves to America are illustrated in the following dialogue between an American planner and his company's Japanese CEO.

David: The strategic plan is ready, Shintaro. We've focused on squeezing as much margin as possible out of each product. Our profit picture will be outstanding this year.

Shintaro: That's good. I'm really delighted. But there is one small thing. How will we stand in terms of the budget imposed on us by Tokyo?

David: We will achieve remarkable efficiencies through work force reductions and better coordination. I expect us to be 30 percent under budget.

Shintaro: Oh, well, that is good. But what will Tokyo say?

David: I don't understand. They will love us.

Shintaro: Perhaps. But we may be sending the wrong signals. Tokyo may think we are cutting quality just to grab market share which we will lose later to a Korean competitor which puts more into production.

David: I thought our goal was to increase market share?

Shintaro: It is one goal, and an important one in a growth market. However, Mr. Fuji, our chairman, is a very traditional person. To him a budget is not just a limiting constraint. It embodies social thinking too. We spend funds in response to our values about what our company should be doing in society to fulfill its destiny.

David: I don't understand. What is our destiny?

Shintaro: We must continue to be seen as a strong company creating quality products in the world. Sometimes our spending reflects our vision.

David: This is mumbo-jumbo. We are in business to make money.

Shintaro: Up to a point, of course. But really we are in business to serve society.

Should this firm spend to reduce costs and increase profits? Or should it spend to reflect a vision of the company as a major servant of societal values (often quite vague)?

These questions do not come up for American executives, who by law act primarily to attain the profit goals of owners. Life is more complicated for Japanese, who must accommodate an array of often conflicting obligations. Companies try to soften the tensions created by these conflicts by stressing civility and harmony in organizational life. Indeed, studies of terms employed in Japanese corporate philosophy statements reveal that "sincerity" and "harmony" are the most frequently mentioned.[13] Honda Motor Company tells employees to "strive constantly for a harmonious flow of work." Matsushita's "Seven Spirits" emphasizes courtesy, humility, harmony, and cooperation. Sharp stresses sincerity, harmony, politeness, creativity, and a positive attitude.

Japanese value sincerity in business, yet the concept does not mean the same thing to them as it does to Americans. In America a sincere person acts so that another person becomes aware of his or her beliefs. The idea is that sincerity breeds truth. Japanese have no such focus. To them a sincere person acts so as not to offend another. To be sincere is to foster for others an orderly, harmonious world. When Japanese corporations proclaim their commitment to sincerity, they are stating their desire to help create a stable, ordered society, not a society rooted in reality. In America sincerity is often an excuse for having committed a civil disorder. "Oh, he truly believed that his stock manipulation would increase shareholder value," we say in letting a Wall Street scoundrel down easy. That kind of response would baffle Japanese. The genuinely sincere Japanese stock manipulator would apologize and promise to behave. Whether he was lying or not is irrelevant. The important thing is that he is publicly admitting a disorderly act and affirming that such acts are wrong. He thus helps strengthen society's commitment to ordered harmony and can be called sincere.

Ideas about work and the nature of a company in Japan reflect enlightened views of economic life as an ongoing process rather than merely a set of transactions which have no relevance except in their outcomes, labeled "utilities" by American economists. The utility for Japanese is the doing, not the results of having done. Put more concretely, a Japanese company produces products while an American firm produces profits. Japanese sometimes are better at manufacturing than they are at marketing, and one reason is that maintaining the ongoing organizational life of the factory often is a more important goal than reaping profits from selling the product. Creating orderly, meaningful work, in theory at least, is what a Japanese company does. When we turn to the art of managing, we see a set of ideas supporting this vision. Managing is the benevolent use of power to foster order and harmony. The power may be misused by Japanese executives at times, but its underlying function is to create socially sanctioned control and social welfare.

MANAGING IS CONTROLLING

Americans have formed the belief that Japanese management involves the development of warm, communal environments in which loyal employees communicate freely with each other in an atmosphere of mutual trust and a shared focus on achieving company goals. This is the theory of management articulated by Honda in the early 1980s when it first came to the United States and echoed by Nissan, Mazda, and Toyota in turn. The auto companies, especially Mazda, have been especially vocal in putting forward a model of how their American factories would be run along "Japanese" lines. As recent books such as David Gelsanliter's *Jump Start* and the Fucinis' *Working for the Japanese* make clear, however, the model never was applied with much vigor, and serious labor problems have surfaced at Mazda and other auto transplants. In fact, Japanese are having employee problems in many of the industries in which they have invested. We will examine these problems, but the underlying causes are what concern us here. In good *tatemae* fashion, Japanese have told Americans what they wanted to hear. It is true that warm, caring management is one ideal in Japan in service to the company's social function and the humanitarian vision of work, but the reality is something quite different. Managing turns out to be the exercise of power to control the workplace so that society's needs can be served. American managers maximize profits, Japanese maximize order. In an authoritarian society like Japan this approach works well. It can even work in the United States in those Southern locales where workers find benevolent dictatorships congenial. But the United States is not Japan, and it cannot work in all places.

The exercise of power by those above has been a characteristic of Japanese society throughout the nation's history. One recent source of the managerial focus on power, however, is World War II, referred to by Japanese as The Pacific War. Kihachiro Onitsuka, now the retired chairman of ASICS, a major sporting goods manufacturer, was a Japan-based officer in an army regiment during the conflict. He watched his friends and colleagues march off again and again to China, Manchuria, Southeast Asia, and the South Pacific. Few ever returned. As a good soldier, his job was to help keep his regiment intact, ready to defend the home islands when the time came. In a sense that is what he did, only he did it by transforming the regiment from a military to a business organization.[14] Men like Onitsuka formed the *Kezai Doyukai* (the Committee for Economic Development) in 1946 to represent the views of a newly emerging managerial and entrepreneurial elite. Their theory of "revised capitalism" involved coordination of ownership rights of shareholders with the needs of management and labor, promotion of a guaranteed minimum wage, and the creation of company unions to promote employees' welfare by tying it to their productivity. This may sound like liberal capitalism, but it is not. Little emphasis was placed on the idea of personal or corporate gain through risk taking. Indeed, the focus on profits, while important, took a back seat to the task of maintaining coherence and balance among potentially competing interests within the business institutions of Japanese society. It was as if the end result, profit, would take care of itself as long as the process of orderly managing was attended to.

Contrast this idea of managing as a benevolent force in society with the American emphasis on success as a social good. To a Rockefeller the results of business achievement, money, could be used to improve society. To Onitsuka and his friends, skilled managing was all that was needed to create a social orderliness which itself was a noble end but which also set the stage for economic development and material well-being. Like the regimental officer of the war, the manager felt that society depended on him. He developed—or should develop—a deep sense of obligation and duty. Until only a few years ago, Kihachiro Onitsuka trained his new employees, the "recruits," by living with them and sharing his views on the purpose of business in a barracks-like dormitory built to foster group cohesiveness, shared objectives, and mutual trust. Other militaristic trappings included work songs, written exams, careful technical training for specialists, the idea of moral as well as functional leadership, and the stress on mission and dedication. The three-month indoctrination of the 1950s has now been replaced by a ten-day course for new employees, and the military approach is fading, but it is not likely to die out. ASICS still sends mid-managers to the Japanese Naval Academy for training in self-discipline, leadership, endurance, and cooperation.

Another senior executive influenced by The Pacific War was Matsushita's former president, Toshihiko Yamashita. After his wartime civilian service he had a chance to visit IBM's New York headquarters. What did he admire? "By that time [the mid-1950s] even some Matsushita employees wore colored shirts at work, so I was very surprised that every IBM male worker had a white shirt and short haircut. There was an impressive sense of order."[15] To men like Onitsuka and Yamashita, a military-style regimentation creates an environment in which managerial power will have its greatest effect. Today, this approach is often reflected in the promulgation of petty rules designed to constantly remind employees of their subservient status. In their wildest fantasies IBM executives would never dream of doing what many Japanese managers do as a matter of course. At Daihyaku Mutual Life Insurance Company employees must jump up at 3:00 P.M. every day to perform exercises at their desks. In the Tokyo branch of Yasuda Fire and Marine Insurance no double-breasted suits are allowed. Employees with dirty desks at Ube Industries will have their pictures posted on a bulletin board under a "Failed Office Inspection" sign. Women must not allow their hair to cover their eyebrows at Yamaichi Securities. In some Japanese-owned firms in the United States, employees have been forbidden to chew gum, executives have been asked to punch time clocks, chairs have been removed from work areas, women have not been allowed to go to the restroom except on breaks. While these actions may serve some immediate purpose, their real function is to put employees in their place.

The goal of this power grabbing is not the self-aggrandizement of the managers, as is usually the case among American administrators. Japanese managers are simply maintaining their work regiments so that an orderly progression towards the creation of societal value can occur. Many Japanese employees recognize this and approve. This is not the case in America, where the road to progress supposedly is based on initiative, creativity, individualism, and equality. This last is a horror to Japanese, who see the world almost solely in vertical terms. A manager exists in a hierarchy of those above *(sempai)* and those below *(kohai)*, as does each person in the office. This verticality enables him to develop a set of emotional connectors finely tuned to each level. To higher-level people he will show deference and respect. He will not question the petty rules imposed on him, recognizing their symbolic value legitimizing power. To subordinates he will be sometimes paternal, sometimes tyrannical. The system at its best establishes consistent, predictable relations among people so they can attend to their tasks without endlessly trying to figure out what tone to adopt in their next meeting or telephone call or what actions they are empowered to undertake.

Japanese management, then, is the continual exercise of power and the maintenance of control to establish an order in which work can be done efficiently without endless negotiations between superiors and subordinates. Society benefits from this control focus and responds by providing Japanese managers with a freedom of action unavailable in other countries. Employees are protected by rules of employment, but unions are weak. Consumers clamor for lower prices, but the government makes sure favored managers get a high price for their products. Accountants and auditors monitor expenditures, but as a Japanese colleague of mine puts it, accounting is mostly "window dressing." No corporate raiders exist to strike fear in the hearts of executives. Regulatory officials are an annoyance, but generally they try to be helpful, and bankers, always accommodating, rarely think of foreclosing.

None of this freedom is available in the United States, nor do employees subscribe to the power-order-societal value model. Unless a Japanese manager is carefully prepared for his American assignment, which is not usually the case, he may be quite bewildered by the managerial environments he encounters. The anxiety and confusion which occur can be a stimulus to quick learning and adaptation, or they can lead to petty power mongering on an even grander scale than in Japan. Americans have been amazed by the selection procedures of some Japanese firms, for example. Potential employees are battered by an array of written tests, interviews, field tests, more interviews with spouses, and so forth. The need to find good workers is important, of course, but part of the reason for onerous selection processes is the establishment of power, so that workers are primed to see themselves in a submissive role within a highly controlled workplace. There is nothing wrong with this as long as American employees recognize what they are getting into. Often they don't, because the operation is sugarcoated with a rhetoric in which words like *trust, community,* and *team spirit* are used.

THE FAD-VALUE OF THEORY Z

The first management book to become a best seller in the 1980s was William Ouchi's *Theory Z.* It presented American business readers with a new, elegant theory of managing which had widespread influence. Ouchi offered his theory as something which already was in use in Japan because of more favorable cultural conditions for its development and implementation. Theory Z became a description of "Japanese management" for many Americans. At first bewildered, Japanese business leaders soon hopped on the bandwagon and began articulating Z-like statements to receptive American audiences. State governors offering subsidies to Japanese investors were told how democratic and communal the new workplace would be. Wary unions were offered consensus decision making. Prospective employees were promised autonomy in their jobs. The Japanese were not lying about promising these things. They were simply picking up a management theory congenial to Americans and using it as a basis for their negotiations. Bits and pieces of Theory Z do occur in Japan, and most Japanese, like many Americans, would like to see management guided by it. The problem is that Japanese management is not driven by Theory Z, nor is it likely to be. Its fad-value in the early 1980s paid off handsomely five years later, however, when Japanese executives had to answer the question posed by politicians, unions, and workers: "How are you going to manage your new plants in America?" Theory Z gave the Japanese something to say which, for all they knew, just might work out.

The idea of Theory Z is rooted in the Japanese view of the corporation as an agent fostering moral and material well-being in society.[16] The Japanese firm is an "industrial clan" which can and does claim the allegiance of its employees because of its important social roles. In the Japanese corporate clan loyal employees are given lifetime employment, which fosters a sense of cooperation and motivation. Slow but automatic promotions put a damper on intra-firm competitiveness. Nonspecialized career paths for managers keep everyone dependent on everyone else; no expert can wall himself off from his fellows. Collective decision making of the bottom up variety builds consensus and involvement. All of these together create a meaningful, communal environment fostering interpersonal trust. In an organization where people have strong trust relationships, no sets of rules are needed to tell employees what to do. They just do what needs to be done. No rigid hierarchies of managers, controllers, and lawyers are required to monitor workers. Instead, the workplace is egalitarian, behavior is open, everyone is treated equitably and employees develop mutual understanding and a willingness to be obligated to each other without contracts or negotiations. They are motivated to want as individuals what the organization wants as an enterprise, because their values become strongly linked to corporate values. Management along Theory Z lines liberates the worker and empowers him, since everyone knows that he will work hard for the firm without supervision.

Would that Theory Z were so! Unfortunately, in Japan it is not. The firm is indeed looked on as a moral agent, but that does not seem to be enough to bring out employee loyalty. Japanese are loyal to their families, but their loyalty to their companies is more a form of submission to a highly controlled environment. Lifetime employment, as we will see later, is a tool to give managers power over workers rather than a motivating device. Decisions are usually top to bottom, although lengthy discussions are held to make sure everyone understands what is happening and gets on board. Slow but automatic promotions create resentment in able employees and lassitude in poor workers. The development of general rather than specialized management skills does force people to talk to each other, but the loss of expertise is a costly trade-off. Trust is important in Japanese organizations, but power-oriented managers often will not tolerate trust-fostering conditions to develop. Employees in Japanese organizations are not autonomous free spirits eagerly taking part in creative rap sessions with managers and then rushing back to their work stations to implement some new idea.

The reality is that the Japanese workplace is characterized by order, stability, predictability, and cohesion emerging from the subtle and not so subtle controls devised by powerful managers. In well-run companies all of this methodical regimentation can be quite effective. Managers provide employees with the training and resources to do what is expected of them and are eager to hear any employee ideas about how to do the job better. But make no mistake about it. What comes first is getting the job done, not the employee's psychological well-being. Changes will be implemented gradually so as not to disrupt existing power relationships, and proposed radical innovations, no matter how worthwhile, will be studied until they quietly die. As long as workers do what is required of them and avoid complaint, they will be well taken care of. If they must complain, a quiet heart-to-heart talk with relevant supervisors will be in order. This approach, which does not make waves, shows sincerity, defined earlier as an implicit acceptance of the existing order, and almost always results in positive action. Americans who follow this scenario in Japanese companies rave about what nice places they are in which to work. Some Japanese firms take great pains to select employees who have demonstrated their skill at communicating of this kind, and all parties have benefitted from it. None of this, however, is Theory Z, and many American employees in Japanese companies are unhappy about it.

WHAT ABOUT THEORY F?

A number of observers in both Japan and America have recognized that Japanese managers can be very tough people, not the warm pals of Theory Z, and have castigated the Japanese approach to managing as nasty and brutish. This also is not so. In fact, powerful managers, secure in their positions, can be quite tolerant and will allow employees to make lots of small mistakes as long as something useful is learned from the errors.

One stream of literature which compares Japanese and American corporate culture is "Theory F" (for fear). In this theory large Japanese organizations are characterized by a growth bias, a preoccupation with the actions of competitors, and the ruthless exploitation of competitive advantage.[17] Coupled with this fierce growth bias are high-fixed costs rooted in a reliance on debt and the use of permanent employment for workers. In this kind of environment failure is not only a shameful act, it is a threat to the firm's survival. The Japanese *kaisha* not only desires to succeed, it *must* succeed if it is to cover fixed costs. Pressure on senior executives to perform well thus is intense, and failure can not be tolerated long.

According to an American manager working in Japan, "Theory Z-like theories do not talk about how the system actually works. . . . There is no tolerance for failure. The penalty for failure is out, finished."[18] Failure may result in transfer to a remote subsidiary, early retirement, or plateauing, which Japanese call "sitting by the window." Plateaued managers (*madogiwa-zoku*) are given functionless jobs without the possibility of career advancement. These people can be seen in many Japanese organizations reading newspapers at empty desks near windows. They have failed to perform and are suffering the consequences in a system where employment is guaranteed but, after the age of thirty-five or so, advancement is not.

At one time in Mitsui 700 of its 11,000 employees were *madogiwa-zoku*, so Theory F clearly does describe a few Japanese organizations.[19] American employees have noted how wary some Japanese managers are of making mistakes, even to the point of avoiding decisions which might lead to an error. But in many more cases failure is tolerated and even protected. Here is part of an interview with a Japanese trading company manager stationed in one of his firm's American offices.

Interviewer: You said that a Japanese worker will feel sorry if someone makes a mistake?

Trading Company Manager: Yes, he feels sorry for the customer who was hurt and for the co-worker who made the error.

I: Does the one who made the error get punished?

M: He is responsible, yes, but the other workers feel sorry for him.

I: Do the co-workers in a Japanese company feel responsible for the error of another?

M: There is a kind of feeling . . . it's hard to explain . . . but direct responsibility should be on the one who committed the error.

This manager expresses an interesting tension which Japanese must deal with even in their group-oriented culture. No one likes to get burned by the foul-up of someone else, but sometimes a bullet must be bitten.

I: How do Japanese companies discipline someone who makes a mistake?

M: If a young staff person makes a mistake, the manager usually will take responsibility. If it was a big mistake, the general manager may also take responsibility. As a result, bonuses might fall 10 percent. In the U.S. if a big mistake is made, getting fired seems to be common [for American employees].

In the U.S. office, Japanese will be punished for errors, but Americans may be fired. "Japanese employees belong to the parent company," noted an American manager in a Japanese securities firm, "but Americans are under the control of the subsidiary." The Americans have a contract, and if they perform poorly, they can be let go. The Japanese manager may be transferred back to Tokyo. If he is not, he may be scorned by his fellow expatriates. "What those Japanese guys do to each other is incredible," said a chief trader for a Japanese firm. "They'll scream at a guy who's on the outs to humiliate him." Americans who are to be fired receive much gentler treatment. "When the Japanese fire an American," said an equities trader, in the same firm, "they give little hints for months so there's no surprise. This gives the manager time to develop a face-saving way out."

Failure, then, is a complex phenomenon for Japanese. Sometimes an erring manager is severely punished or humiliated. At other times his fellow employees will close ranks to protect him. American managers may be fired, but only after a long let-him-down-gently period. In a study of tolerance of executive failure in American and Japanese firms, Coral Snodgrass and I found that both American and Japanese firms tolerated failure for the same amount of time. An executive will be allowed about four years in which he fails to achieve 25 percent of his goals. After that he is plateaued. He can fail to achieve 50 percent of his goals for three years. With 75 percent failure he will last only two years.[20] The Japanese did differ from Americans in their strong efforts to learn from small failures. Indeed, small failure often is encouraged. At Sumitomo Bank a former chairman's motto was "Don't be afraid of the *muko kizu*." This refers to a minor sword wound and is a metaphor for little failures. President Yamashita of Matsushita says, "I think it is extremely important that managers in senior positions have experienced frustration and setbacks." Contrast this approach with American corporations, where tough assignments are a weeding-out device rather than a learning process. Some Japanese firms institutionalize constructive failure by transferring managers to units where they are bound to err. The head of production may be told that he is now chief of sales, while the salesman finds himself on the factory floor. They usually will not like the assignments and will blunder around quite a bit, protected from doing serious damage by their staffs. In the process of making mistakes they learn to appreciate each other's jobs. In the future the marketing man will not look down on the fellow with dirt under his fingernails, and the production manager will be sensitive to how hard it is to move the product. American employees who see a novice Japanese boss thrashing around and doing dumb things need to realize that (1) this is the way the system works, (2) they are supposed to help him learn, and (3) they should protect him from making giant blunders. "There may be severe punishment for big failures," says Richard C. Koo of Nomura Research Institute. "Consequently, making small mistakes in succession is preferable to one big mistake, even if the cumulative losses from small mistakes become larger."[21]

In American firms, tolerance of a manager's failures depends on the labor market. If the supply of managers is low and demand for their services is high, failures of people currently on board will be tolerated longer than in low-demand/high-supply conditions. This is not the way things are done in Japan or in Japanese-owned U.S. companies, where small failures are accepted as long as they stimulate learning and development. Often nothing will be done about a manager's failure until its consequences become clear. "Japanese will take failure and put it in a corner and let it sit there for a while. Eventually they will deal with it," said an American female manager at a Japanese firm.

Incremental learning from error is one of the key characteristics of Japanese management, and Theory F, in which failing managers are treated very badly, comes into play only in a few firms and only for giant errors which damage the firm. If a manager rises to a really high position in a Japanese firm, however, he becomes unassailable. Except in extreme cases when a public outcry forces his resignation, senior Japanese executives can make one big error after another without fear of repercussions. This is what has been occurring in companies in the securities industries for a number of years now, and new executives who take over the firms' American operations in the 1990s will have to dig themselves out of some very large holes.

THE FUNCTION OF WORK GROUPS

In a series of experiments, my Japanese colleagues and I found that American and Japanese managers differ in their theory of the function of work teams. Japanese managers saw a work team as an environment where information is shared in pursuit of improved performance. Americans were not against this idea, but they mainly used groups to share responsibilities and reduce risks.[22] Japanese mobilize teams to tackle hard, complex tasks. Americans employ them for dangerous jobs, the kind in which failure can threaten the careers of individuals. The Japanese, who use failure as a learning device for individuals, can afford to concentrate on having groups tackle positive things rather than avoiding the negative.

American employees are impressed by the Japanese insistence that teams communicate to collect and discuss data and develop methods for solving problems and improving performance. American firms certainly use work teams, too, but they don't do it as well as the Japanese. For cultural reasons, Japanese are a group-oriented people, but culture is not what is driving the clever use of teams in the workplace. It is simply cleverness. Japanese managers take the theories they find and put them to use. A theory of work as meaningful living primes employees for socialization in groups, as does the belief that the company has a legitimate social mission. Add in a regime of powerful managers who demand that employees participate and do not worry about little mistakes, and you get a team spirit which may look Japanese but in fact is not. The same team approach occurs in Japan's American companies which cultivate the same ideas about work, the company, power, and failure.

These ideas are not strange to most Americans. They have just been strange to American managerial elites and to the doctrinaire economists who provide them with theories. These people see work as a disutility, the company as a wealth-generating machine for owners, managing as the implementation of behaviorist stimulus-response processes, a worker as a kind of purposeful pigeon, failure as a spur to competitiveness, and groups as barriers to functional economic exchange in the labor market (if employees have allegiances to groups beyond their own individual self-interests, the efficiencies of a market mechanism supposedly begin to break down).

Although Japanese are more collective than Americans, they do not abandon their human identity and submerge it in the group, as *nihonjinron* theorists would have us believe. In fact, they can be quite individualistic. Soichiro Honda was a maverick, but he expressed a sentiment real to lots of Japanese when he said, "The most important thing for me, is me." According to Mr. Honda, "People will not sacrifice themselves for the company. They come to work to enjoy themselves. That feeling leads to innovation."[23] Japanese group identity is based on shared behaviors and tasks, not on shared values or allegiances. When a Japanese employee is not in sight of his group, his allegiance to the group diminishes, as does that of the group to him. This is why Japanese managers do not like being assigned to joint ventures or ad hoc intra-company projects. It is not that they feel anxiety over being loyal to two different groups. Rather they worry that they will not be welcome back to their old group if they are away for a long time. Since a group-less manager in a Japanese company lacks protection, chances for career advancement are dimmed.

Management philosophies in Japan are wonderfully elegant, but they are not quite what Americans have read about. Nor are they quite what Japanese companies say they are in their training manuals for American employees or their pronouncements for the press. Often these are riddled with fashionable *nihonjinron* writings about how unique Japanese culture is and how this uniqueness carries over into managing. In addition, pet theories of American academics have been put forward as if they were already operational in Japan. There is no attempt at deception going on here. It is all sincerity and *tatemae*, a desire to make nice, unthreatening statements which rock no one's boat and which have enough truth and genuine idealism in them to make them defensible. American executives and politicians make these kinds of statements all the time and nobody takes them too seriously. The same is true of American advertisers, who constantly trumpet mere changes as new, improved breakthroughs. Why should anyone expect the Japanese in America to be any different? After all, they cannot go around saying things like, "Work is an end in itself" or "Just do what you're told and your manager will take good care of you." So they say what is expected of them and go about their business.

NINE

What Is Profit?

Naoki Kameda is chairman of Tamon International, a small Tokyo firm manufacturing audio speakers. He and I have been friends for years and both of us have an interest in language issues. Several years ago, in discussing the concept of profit in American and Japanese business life, we were surprised to realize that the word meant something different to each of us. To find out if these differences actually reflected national thinking in both countries, we surveyed American and Japanese business students.[1] Sure enough, the differences were there. It seemed a minor issue at the time, but since the surge of Japanese investment in the United States it has become noteworthy. We will see that Americans have several definitions of profit and really can't make up their mind about it. Japanese know exactly what profit is and what to do with it.

THE BUSINESS STUDENTS

In our study of business students, Mr. Kameda and I first set out to collect every definition of profit we could find in the economics literature. Here they are.

An everyday conventional use of the term for noneconomists is called *businessmen's profits*, the difference between revenues and expenses (including taxes) of a business at the end of each year. An expanded version of this, which includes capital gains as well as gains from operations, is *owner's surplus*. Many people tend to see profit in a more limited sense, as *retained earnings*, the money left over at the end of each year which the company uses to invest in new equipment, new products, or new markets. A more sophisticated concept is *economic profit*, the money the entrepreneur gets as compensation from society for taking the financial risks which are needed to produce society's goods and services. Three other definitions are less common. Peter Drucker sees profit as *future investment*, the money society uses to foster progress.[2] Joel Dean calls profits *rewards for innovation*, gains generated by creative entrepreneurial innovation.[3] Essentially, these profits are society's compensation for developing new and improved products. A final definition is *oligopolistic profits*, which companies receive when they are able to influence prices and the supply of goods in markets. As we saw earlier, Japan is riddled with companies enjoying these kinds of gains.

We showed these definitions to several hundred business students in Tokyo and Seattle and asked them to identify those with which they agreed. We reasoned that business students would be more likely to reflect national thinking about profit in a less biased manner than managers, who might report ideas prevalent in their firm or industry rather than the country. Our results showed that businessmen's profit was the favored definition for the Americans, while the Japanese chose both future investment and rewards for innovation.

If we generalize from this small sample, which I believe we can, then Japanese have a model of profit as rewards to entrepreneurs for taking risks to produce innovations which society needs to develop the future. Americans have an impoverished sense of profit as simply what is left over after paying expenses. Why it exists and what is to be done with it are not part of the definition. Consider for a moment the problems Americans face in developing a definition. They are bombarded with portrayals of companies in movies and television which suggest, to use Jimmy Carter's term, that "obscene profits" are being generated from polluting the environment, cheating widows and orphans, and corrupting politicians. Their own experience, however, is of companies that perform routine, usually harmless, sometimes beneficial tasks and receive only small returns for their trouble. Bewildered, they turn to the schools for help—and do not get it. Americans learn almost nothing about risk, value, allocation of scarce resources, or profit in secondary or high school. Even in college most students are not required to learn any economics. The concept is something of a mystery for Americans, and they opt for a trivial idea of what profits are.

The well-educated Japanese have a concrete, functional, sophisticated idea of profit which is widespread in society. The presence of oligopolistic profits in many industries is not of any consequence, even though they come from companies charging artificially high prices and conspiring to control supplies. What Japanese focus on instead is a prosperous future and the role of profit in ensuring that it will occur. The corporation in its role as the primary social agent of orderly change enjoys wide latitude in Japanese society regarding how it generates profits and what it does with them, as long as material well being improves. Alexander Pope argued for an economic model in his poetry in which "social and self-interest are the same." The Japanese change this somewhat: "Social and corporate interests are the same."

LOW PROFITS IN JAPAN

Japanese companies invariably report low profits, although they shy away from stating losses. In the fiscal year ending in March 1990, C. Itoh, one of Japan's biggest companies, had 0.9 percent return on sales after taxes. Another giant, the Sumitomo Corporation, reported 0.2 percent. The picture looks even worse if we use an economic rent calculation in which profitability is annual profit minus what could have been gained by investing in risk-free government bonds divided by input costs for the year. A positive value means the firm is gaining rewards for the risks it takes in its line of business. A negative value suggests that the company should cease business operations and begin investing its funds in bonds. C. Itoh's profitability is −1.6 percent. The Bank of Tokyo's is −2.8 percent. Toray Industries' is −2.0 percent. Daiwa Securities' is −14 percent. These firms, chosen virtually at random from published sources, are typical. It is the kind of business environment ripe for a Carl Icahn or a T. Boone Pickens. *In theory* they could acquire these poor performers cheaply and make them profitable through ruthless cost cutting and employee layoffs. Then they could watch their stock values soar and sell them. Nothing like this currently is allowed to happen in Japan, although the 1990s could be a decade of big changes in the market for companies.

All of this is only *in theory*, because Japanese companies are not as ripe for plucking as they look, even if they could be plucked by Carl and T. Boone. For several reasons, bottom line reported net income figures are not taken very seriously in Japan, and "real" profits are likely to be much larger—"real" meaning those on which American public accountants would sign off.

One reason why Japanese do not take net income numbers seriously is that, aside from the English and Americans who developed the accounting valuation measures used to calculate net income, few people in the world take these figures seriously, and with good reason. Net income purports to be a reliable and valid estimate of the annual wealth acquisition or loss of a firm. The accounting process followed to develop an estimate requires the identification of financial concepts like depreciation, ways of measuring the variables representing the concepts, and sets of rules to guide measurement. But there are at least three different ways to define depreciation, two ways to define money (nominal or inflation-adjusted), and numberless rules. If we defined different measurement rules for depreciating assets, stating cash flows at a present value, or valuing inventory, we would get different measures of net income. We could not say which measure exactly corresponds to the real wealth acquisition that occurred because we could not determine which combination of measuring procedures and rules would be required to derive the correct measure. The best course would be to report a series of net income figures with each value accompanied by a description of how it was calculated. Each value could be assigned a probability as to its accuracy. The weighted average, called the expected value, would then be the best estimate of profit. This is not what is done, however, since accountants report a single-value estimate, net income, which is simple and easy to comprehend.

Americans tend to see the net income figure as much more accurate than it in fact is. Japanese, who love to collect numbers but are not in thrall to them, do not make this mistake. Accounting, while recognized as useful, does not have the legitimacy in Japan it enjoys in America. The head of accounting in a Japanese corporation may be a general manager on a routine assignment rather than a person with a professional commitment. By the same token, public accountants are rather casual about their audits. One Big Six American accounting firm in Tokyo tries to hire Japanese auditors right out of school, because it has found that hirees from Japanese audit firms have developed slovenly habits and require substantial retraining. As I noted in an earlier chapter, Japanese management experts think of accounting as "window dressing."

As long as it is positive, then, the value of the Japanese company's net income is not too important. But why is it usually low? Here we need to go back to the Japanese definition of profit as rewards to innovative entrepreneurs who will use the money to develop still more innovation. But there are no entrepreneurs! The risks and innovations occur in a managerial system within large corporations. No Japanese versions of Bill Gates or Steve Jobs are tucked away in corners of Tokyo tinkering in their basements. They do not even have basements to tinker in. All development is done by managers and technicians, and they capture their rewards *before* the bottom line in the form of expenses for new facilities, improved machinery, and research. The owners of corporations, mostly other corporations, are doing the same thing and so understand and tolerate what is going on. The banks which hold the company's debt want to see increased market share rather than profits, because market power lowers the risk that the company will be unable to generate enough cash to pay off its loans. Profit has to exist, but it need not be large.

Profits must be stated as positive, if possible, because negative numbers obviously suggest a drain on capital. But statements of profit or loss are more resonant than that. According to the Matsushita philosophy, "The mission of an enterprise is to contribute to society." Putting a Japanese spin on this, former president Yamashita says, "An unprofitable firm must not be doing work useful to society. Perhaps its products are lousy or maybe it is badly run. In any case, the balance sheet is both a managerial and moral scorecard."[4] At ASICS chairman Onitsuka sees profit as a sign that the company is meeting society's needs and is functioning appropriately in what he calls "adjusted capitalism" or "new socialism."[5] It is immoral not to make a profit, since morality consists of being socially useful, and losses are evidence of not being useful.

In sum, profit is a sign that the company is fulfilling its moral and material role, but the amount of profit need not be large since no one expects it to be and no one has much faith in the numbers anyway. What happens, then, when a company invests in America, where people believe in bottom lines and wonder what is going on at a firm which can't seem to make much money?

ARE U.S. PROFITS REALLY LOW?

Are Japanese profits in America really as low as reported? Or do they simply reflect casual Japanese-style reporting? More ominously, are the Japanese trying to escape U.S. income taxes by cooking their books to show weak income performance? We cannot answer these questions with certainty, but in general Japanese firms do not appear to be cheating, nor are they employing careless Japanese accounting. They really aren't making money.

If we use return on investment (R.O.I.) for foreign investors as a benchmark, only a few Japanese investors did well in 1989.[6] Foreigners' R.O.I. in banking was 3.7 percent, but Japanese banks did very well at 16.7 percent. The only substantial repatriations of profits back to Japan came from the $741 million income of the banks. Financial services companies earned 3.7 percent, about the same as other investors, and real estate did better, at 1.9 percent, than the −2.7 percent of the foreigners' total. Except for banking, however, none of these industries could be considered highly profitable. All other Japanese industries did worse than their foreign peers. The worst were retail trade, a small group of investors whose R.O.I. at −8.5 percent was substantially lower than the overall 4.9 percent figure for foreign retail investors, and what the Commerce Department calls "Other Manufacturing," which among other things covers the auto transplants. While foreigners here enjoyed 3.3 percent R.O.I., the Japanese were unprofitable at −6.4 percent. We will look at autos in detail below.

Data for 1990 show an interesting shift. Profitability at U.S. firms acquired by Japanese companies continued to be lower than other foreign investors'. But at Japanese-owned *start ups* profitability for the first time was better than that of other foreign start ups. If Japanese owners can start from scratch, then, it appears that they can do quite well. Most of Japan's direct investing in the United States, however, is now and will continue to be poor-performing acquisitions.

Japanese machinery manufacturers, including high tech and consumer electronics industries, were losers at -0.9 percent R.O.I in 1989, as were all foreigners at -1.2 percent. All other Japanese investors, in food, chemicals, metals, and wholesale trade, enjoyed profitability in the 1–4 percent range, substantially lower than the foreign totals in the 3–6 percent R.O.I. range. Some will see this data as evidence that the Japanese are foregoing profits as they buy market share in the United States. This is probably true here and there, but other data indicate a general trend of hanging on rather than triumphing. For example, most 1989 investment in machinery manufacturing was in the form of debt rather than equity. This suggests that Japanese investors are not primarily using their capital to buy American firms and their market shares. Instead, the Japanese are somewhat more focused on loaning funds to their hard-pressed American subsidiaries to develop production capabilities. Over the long term this may pay off, but it has not yet.

In the high tech electronics business, consisting of computer and communications equipment, not one Japanese-owned firm appears on the 1989 list of the fifty most profitable companies.[7] Amdahl, owned by Fuji Electric, was number fifty-two with a 7.3 percent return on sales. Cipher Data Products, a computer peripherals maker owned by Japan's Alps Electric Company, was ranked seventy-nine with 5.6 percent returns. Data on the success of Japanese investment in consumer electronics are not available, but aggregate totals for all foreigners in the electrical equipment industries tell a startling story. In the five-year period of 1985–1989, foreign investors in electrical equipment, including Japanese consumer electronics, increased their capital by $11 billion. During that period they did not have one profitable year and lost a total of $3.5 billion, an R.O.I. of -32 percent! Matsushita, Sharp, Toshiba, and Hitachi have very deep pockets, but one has to wonder, first, how deep is deep and, second, how long is long term.

The Commerce Department does not break down transportation equipment manufacturing investment figures by country, but the aggregates are revealing. Over the 1985–1989 period, over $2.7 billion was invested, almost all of it Japanese. Only in 1987 was a profit reported. Overall, net losses were $559 million, an R.O.I. of -21 percent for the period. Ordinarily such losses could not be sustained for very long, but the success of Japanese imports in the United States has provided cash which undoubtedly has been used to carry the transplants. Aggregate data for transportation equipment sales of imported cars and trucks from wholesalers and distributors to dealers show five-year profits of $5.3 billion. Since the Japanese drove many European imports out of the U.S. market during the 1980s, it is safe to assume that they captured most of these gains. While the successes of Japanese imports have been used to keep the transplants going, this is unlikely to continue. Over 60 percent of the 1985–1989 profits from selling imports occurred in 1985–1986, and profits are steadily declining. The R.O.I. for transportation equipment selling declined from 18.7 percent in 1985 to 1.3 percent in 1989. Sales of Japanese imports have remained high in the United States, but fierce competition is eroding profit margins. Soon, the Japanese auto manufacturing plants will have to show profits on their own.

Are the Japanese cheating? Are all these losses part of some kind of massive fraud designed to escape U.S. income taxes? The U.S. Internal Revenue Service has its suspicions and has targeted the use of transfer prices for investigation.

Changes in the Japanese consumer electronics industry give us a hint as to why the IRS is suspicious. By 1989 there were eighty-five Japanese consumer electronics manufacturing facilities in North America. They were served by sixty-eight Japanese component supplier plants. All of the producers and suppliers employed about 76,000 people, managed by 1,100 Japanese. One could conclude that with all those suppliers in the United States, the producers would not need to purchase components from Japan. Yet Japanese exports to the United States of electronics component devices, such as integrated circuits, went up 19 percent in 1988 and 28.5 percent in 1989. The IRS suspects that Japanese firms in the United States which do heavy importing from their Japanese parent companies are being charged much higher prices than those prevailing in America. These artificially set transfer prices are a ploy by the parents to increase the U.S. subsidiaries' costs and to lower their profits. With low profits the subsidiaries pay low taxes.

In the early 1980s the IRS concluded that both Honda and Nissho Iwai, a large trading company, were using higher than market transfer prices to reduce their American income and U.S. taxes. It ordered the firms to pay additional taxes. The companies appealed, and after almost nine years of wrangling the courts threw out the cases, supporting the Japanese claims that transactions with their parents were "arm's length." Arm's-length transactions are those in which the subsidiary pays the local U.S. market price to the parent. By 1990, the IRS was ready to try it again. A friendly congressional subcommittee studied twenty-five foreign multinational investors, mostly Japanese, and found that more than half of them had paid little or no federal income tax over the last decade. Several researchers attached to the committee attributed the low profits to exorbitant fees charged by parent companies for insurance, interest, and freight. Others raised the high transfer price issue.

Given the lax accounting practices which many Japanese firms undoubtedly have brought with them to the United States, the IRS may have trouble uncovering the paper trails it needs to support its investigation. But logic and empirical research both suggest that Japanese parents charge *low* rather than high prices to their American subsidiaries. The logic is based on the claim by the *keidanren*, the Japanese manufacturers' association, that effective corporate tax rates are lower in the United States than Japan.[8] If that is true, then Japanese parents would want to shift profits to the United States by charging low prices for exports to subsidiaries. Their domestic costs would go up and profits down, while the U.S. affiliates' profits would rise. The losses from increased payments of U.S. taxes would be more than offset by the savings from taxes which did not have to be paid in Japan. Data collected by Professor Takino Takanaga of Kibi International University support the low transfer price scenario, but for another reason.[9] His study of forty-eight Japanese multinationals revealed that one-half of them always maintained an arm's-length relationship with subsidiaries when setting transfer prices. Among those that did not use market rates as a basis for prices, the setting of high prices to escape host country income taxes was considered a trivial issue. The most important use of transfer prices for the firms that calculated a price, however, was to stabilize the competitive position of a subsidiary. In other words, about 50 percent of Japanese multinationals do not follow arm's-length transfer pricing but charge artificially low prices for supplies. With low-cost supplies, the subsidiaries can charge lower prices for their finished goods and can compete better with local firms.

If we now go back to the consumer electronics firms, which import components from Japan even though many suppliers are available in the United States, we can see what probably is occurring. The Japanese television, VCR, and other manufacturers are locked in fierce competition with each other, with other foreign investors, and with American firms. Some of them try to compete on price in the absence of an established brand name. To do this they need to reduce costs, and their parents help them with low transfer prices for imports.

Many Japanese firms having trouble generating profits in the United States turn to a less than arm's-length relationship with their parents, but it has nothing to do with avoiding taxes. They seek subsidies in the form of prices for imports of supplies from the parent lower than they would have to pay to American vendors. On a cost plus basis, their products then can be priced lower. While a very few Japanese multinationals whose subsidiaries are making large profits do try to avoid host country taxes, close to half of them try to prop up their affiliates with transfer pricing subsidization. The other, more competitive half simply charges market rates. If these worldwide figures apply to the United States, then about one-half of Japanese U.S. subsidiaries are uncompetitive and cannot generate profit successfully on their own. Professor Takanaga's survey results dovetail nicely with Commerce Department data discussed above, which show widespread weak performance of Japan's U.S. investments. The irony is that the IRS wants to label as villains a group of Japanese managers in the United States who are merely incompetent.

Profit is the reward Japanese society gives for innovation to spur further innovation. It goes to managers who take the money in the form of expenses before it appears on the bottom line. Accountants are accommodating, and no one worries much about low reported numbers. Statements of losses, however, are avoided if possible, since they suggest a socially dysfunctional institution. In America the story is different. The low profits of many Japanese-owned firms indicate a lack of competitiveness rather than lax accounting or the managerial capture of gains before they reach the bottom line. Struggling firms have depended on low-priced imports of components from their parents to lower costs and position themselves as low-price competitors. These are probably reluctant follower firms that moved rapidly to the United States and have not been able to establish brand names for their products which would enable them to compete on something more than price. They also are borrowing heavily from their parents to improve their production and perhaps marketing capabilities. With the cost of capital rising in Japan, this source of help cannot be counted on in the future.

Even worse, the Japanese public is starting to wonder where all the money went. In a late 1989 study conducted by the Dentsu Institute for Human Studies in Tokyo, researchers found that Japanese sense a growing gap between personal and national affluence. They are bewildered and angered by the fact that Japan is first in the world in per capita gross national product but is seventh in terms of per capita purchasing power. What this means is that the public has been getting only a small share of the profits from economic activity. The rest has been retained by the corporations, which have used much of it recently to invest in the United States. So far there is little to show for that investment. At 1.8 percent for 1989, overall Japanese R.O.I. in the United States is positive, but it is only half of the 3.5 percent return for all U.S. foreign investment. Some of the gap is due to the latecoming Japanese still recording large, profit-reducing depreciation expenses for buildings and equipment. Most of it is due to a lack of competitive success.

This may change, but if it does not, the people of Japan will begin to question the good sense of Japanese corporations. What is more, if losses in the United States begin to mount, the public may start to debate the legitimacy of the corporation as the prime agent of social improvement and exemplar of moral worth among Japanese institutions. Japanese managers may talk for hours about their long-term orientation in the United States, but this does not mean that the Japanese public will tolerate a lack of profits forever.

TEN

Lifetime Employment and Managerial Power

The lifetime employment system practiced at large Japanese firms, the same oligopolized giants that have come to the United States, has made American workers envious. They too are willing to give their Japanese employers loyal, motivated service in return for guarantees of job security. If the Japanese employees have it, they say, why can't we? The problem is that the Americans want something that has only existed in the imaginations of management gurus and Chrysanthemum club members. Lifetime employment was developed during and immediately following World War II as a scheme to enhance managerial power and control in the face of growing union threats to that power. In return for job security until age fifty-five, employees gave up what little autonomy they had. The trade off did not include increased loyalty or motivation, and so these things are not associated with lifetime employment. Tenured Japanese workers perform well, and that performance is indirectly associated with job security, but it is directly due to the increased control Japanese managers gain from the practice, not to loyalty or motivation. This system cannot be transferred to America in its Japanese form, but as we will see, an Americanized version of lifetime employment is developing at American- and Japanese-owned firms.[1]

RECENT EMERGENCE OF THE SYSTEM

The lifetime employment system is practiced by the bigger Japanese companies and only applies to about 20 percent of the workforce. Smaller firms, however, try to emulate the large ones, although their ability to do so is weak. The practice involves the hiring of employees directly from high school or, for managers, from college and offering them an implicit guarantee after six months or so that they will never be laid off or fired, except in the most dire circumstances, until the normal retirement age between fifty-five and sixty. The cadre of lifetime employees is limited to males; women, employees hired from other firms, and those retained after retirement are rarely given such assurances. Japanese lifetime employees are very much like tenured American college professors. They get job security, but if they decide to quit and go elsewhere, they find that few other organizations will give them the same security guarantee without a long probationary period. Since that is not a good deal, they tend to stay where they are. In effect, there is no labor market for lifetime employees, and as one might expect, their pay tends to be less than it would be in a functioning marketplace. Notice that the system of lifetime hiring only at entry levels requires all the relevant firms in the industry to practice it. If that were not so, changing jobs would occur. Disgruntled employees at lifetime employment firms would be lured away by other firms with promises of higher pay and job tenure. Soon there would be no value to companies in offering the lifetime employment guarantee, since firms could not expect increased control over employees in return. Large Japanese firms tacitly agree among themselves to offer lifetime employment to entry level people only. The benefits of doing this are a permanent work force that has little opportunity to go elsewhere and is thus more easily subject to managerial power.

The system is breaking down in Japan, and we will see why later. For now, we will examine its roots. For years an argument has raged over whether lifetime employment is a cultural artifact peculiar to Japan or a phenomenon governed by economic forces which will change when those forces change. The culturalists note that one of the essential elements of pre-Meiji (before 1868) Japan was the requirement of subordination to patriarchal authority among peasant family groups. This lifetime arrangement of submission from below and benevolence from above carried over into the Tokugawa Period (1615–1868) and the rise of the great Mitsui and Sumitomo merchant families. In the "house traditions" of these firms, young apprentices were taken in and trained. Later they would be sent out as loyal employees to manage branch houses. The company leaders could be certain that the employee was trustworthy and would act in the family's best interests. Supported by Confucian values centered on the necessity for order and authority in society, peasant and merchant practices supposedly have become embedded in Japanese cultural life so that modern corporations see it as their duty to carry on the tradition in the form of the lifetime employment system.

The story can be read this way, and there undoubtedly is some truth to it. The cultural explanation, however, looks suspiciously like a rhetorical gloss to simplify a more complex reality. This is the position of economists, who see the system emerging during and after the war in response to supply and demand conditions in the labor markets and to other factors. Even though these conditions have changed over time, a set of unexpected benefits of lifetime employment is believed to have kept the system intact.

According to this argument, Japan went into World War II with high rates of turnover in critical industries. Job hopping was common, as were firings and lay offs.[2] To better control the labor force, authorities issued a series of laws prohibiting unauthorized changes in place of employment. The Industrial Patriotic Association (I.P.A.), a national labor organization, was formed to issue *nihonjinron* statements about corporations as families with employees as loyal, submissive members. When the war ended, so did the I.P.A. and the laws restricting labor mobility, but the rhetoric about corporate families has been used frequently since then to legitimize attempts to hinder workers from exercising labor power. After December 1945, Japanese workers could legally organize trade unions. Some of the unions were quite radical, their resolve stiffened by the ideological fervor of returning prisoners of the Soviets who had learned communist ideology during captivity. American occupation authorities tried to put a damper on the left wing elements in the labor movement, but as with so much that happened during the occupation, it was the Japanese themselves who really solved the problem. In a series of labor negotiations during the late 1940s, corporations created a lifetime employment system in which employees would receive job tenure but would surrender control over job assignments, the location of jobs, and retirement age to managers. Company unions were formed whose major task was to ensure that the companies kept their part of the bargain.

During this period and the 1950s, the big companies gradually recognized that if they all hung together in offering lifetime employment only to entry-level employees, they would break the back of any incipient labor market. Workers who could not get tenure at another firm were unlikely to put themselves on the market. They had to stay where they were. Turnover fell to near zero in the large companies, and the Japanese manager's belief that turnover *should be* zero emerged. American employees have noted this fear of turnover among Japanese managers in the United States. Low turnover is a key sign in Japan that the manager is adequately controlling the workforce, while a high rate suggests a loss of power—the ultimate sin among Japanese managers. The lifetime employment system also reduced unions to one-task operations, and their interest in wages and working conditions faded until recently. Without worrisome unions and a functioning labor market, employees in the corporations came under the sway of enterprise leaders to an extent rare in the modern industrial world. In most cases Japanese managers used their power with good sense, and various other benefits of the system—or at least ideas about benefits—emerged.

ALLEGED BENEFITS

The positive dimensions of lifetime employment are more argued than proven, and they have served as the basis for American workers' hopes that the system can be transferred to Japanese-owned firms in the United States.

The first benefit is supposedly loyalty. Lifetime employment is said to increase employee commitment to the organization's goals because the employee's long-term career with the company will ensure that its interests and the worker's interests will eventually coalesce. This mutuality of outlook will inspire a communal environment filled with harmony, sincerity, and trust. A second benefit is high quality economic performance. Firms with employees who are not expected to quit can invest heavily in their training with a resulting improvement in productivity and output. Also, the absence of an external labor market gives firms a chance to develop highly efficient internal markets in which, through transfers or employee requests, workers and jobs are well matched. A third benefit is motivation. Employees with expectations of security and regular pay increases are thought to become highly motivated to work hard in a creative, innovative manner. They are aided by the constant performance feedback they receive from supervisors with whom they have a long, friendly association and by the job design skills which the organization has had an opportunity to test and implement.

The final benefit, which is the one argued for here as the only one that really counts, is control. Managers have almost unlimited power over job assignments, overtime, training, and geographical location of employees. Employees who are not satisfied will not quit because they cannot get tenure elsewhere. Appeals to the union, concerned only with protecting job security, will fall on deaf ears. One might expect employee sabotage in conditions where there are no outlets for frustration, but this is unheard of in Japan. Japanese managers involve themselves deeply in the lives of their employees, and when they see trouble coming they take steps to head it off. An unsatisfied worker will be reassigned or offered more training. Nevertheless, Japanese employees invariably score lowest in job satisfaction in cross-national studies. Apparently their dissatisfaction is not low enough, however, to menace performance. Indeed, the exceptionally high performance of Japanese workers is well known.

In a test of these various benefits at eighty-four firms in Japan conducted by the author and his colleagues, the value of lifetime employment became crystal clear.[3] The prevalence of the practice in organizations in Japan was not associated with loyalty or motivation. Instead, the greater the number of employees enjoying tenure in a firm, the greater the control over workers enjoyed by Japanese managers and the better the performance of the firm. Simply put, the system enhances managerial power, which is then used to good effect. Whatever motivation, creativity, and loyalty employees have is rooted in other things, not lifetime employment.

THE SYSTEM BEGINS TO FAIL

The people who run large Japanese organizations fear the decline in their power posed by trade unionism. To maintain power over labor they offer lifetime employment in return for increased managerial control over employee behavior. The bargain is struck within the context of culturalist rhetoric about the corporation as a family and the obligations of family members to each other. Possible union problems are dampened by this rhetoric and by creating company unions, whose main task is to monitor the bargain and do little else. Japanese workers and their unions have been well aware of the costs and benefits of the system and have accepted it for many years. When asked in a 1978 survey if they would change jobs for more pay and better conditions elsewhere, only 15 percent of Kikkomen employees in Japan said yes. In contrast to Sony president Morita's claims (noted earlier) about his American employees' loyalty, 50 percent of Americans surveyed at Sony's California facility said they would leave.[4]

The lifetime employment system now is beginning to break down. "Young people are entering our bank in Japan," said a Fuji Bank official, "and after only one year they leave. In the old days this never happened." These young people do not see any benefits in the system, and some corporate leaders are starting to agree. When Japanese economic growth levels off in the 1990s, the large number of older lifetime employees will become a burden. Remember, they are not particularly loyal or motivated, they are just easily controlled. But control is not enough in the new era, when a rapidly changing global environment demands fast, innovative responses from managers and employees working together to come up with new and improved products. In an era of modest growth and fierce competition—both new developments for Japanese managers—the availability of a vast, compliant industrial army is not enough. Moreover, the salaries of those workers constitute a fixed cost which reduces the cost-cutting options of managers. Ironically, the increased control over labor enjoyed by Japanese managers comes at the expense of reduced control over cost-based pricing strategies. On the employee side, mid-career managers and workers now find themselves waiting in long lines for promotion. The temptation is strong to abandon security for the chance to obtain better positions in other firms. This is now starting to happen. In the author's study, roughly 50 percent of the employees in the eighty-four firms surveyed had been hired after working at other firms. The young workers have joined the tightest labor market since World War II, and opportunities are limitless. Although a decline in economic growth will reduce demand somewhat, the low Japanese birth rate ensures a sellers market for labor for a long time to come. When jobs are so plentiful, the offer of job security has a hollow ring to it, and young people are becoming disinterested.

A few firms have abandoned lifetime employment, according to the flood of articles on the topic in the Japanese press. Most, however, are taking steps to retain the practice, perhaps for economic or cultural reasons. The system does seem to be associated with improved performance, and traditional assembly oriented manufacturing probably will continue to benefit from it. Also, many Japanese like the rhetoric about corporations as families and see the system as a key element in the maintenance of a communal spirit. One suspects, nevertheless, that the reduced power of supervisors in a functioning labor market is an unpleasant prospect which Japanese managers would like to avoid.

To save lifetime employment, companies are encouraging early retirement. If the overhang of older employees can be reduced, promotion opportunities will open up for younger people. Presumably they will be less likely to abandon the increased worker security-increased managerial control bargain if greater pay and enhanced status are available. Of course, the problem of heavy fixed labor costs will soon reappear, and there is nothing which can be done about the tight labor market which is now beginning to impact all levels of Japanese business. Large corporations are becoming less reluctant to hire people who have worked for competitors, and Japanese unions are focusing more on pay rather than security. The system will drag on, but the managerial power it once produced will be reduced.

JOB SECURITY IN AMERICA

In the United Auto Workers negotiations with General Motors (GM) in 1990, job security was a major issue. The resulting agreement, while enhancing managerial power, was something which no self-respecting Japanese manager would have touched with a ten foot pole. GM wanted flexibility to close plants when economic conditions warranted, and the union wanted to save jobs. After several weeks of discussions, both sides agreed on a unique solution to the problem. When GM closes a plant, it will lay off workers. They will receive unemployment benefits for whatever time period is allowed. After that, GM simply will continue to pay them close to their straight-time salary. It is unclear how long this will go on, but essentially GM will pay employees not to work as long as they do not hinder the company's ability to close plants. For GM the cost of idle workers is apparently less than that of labor strife over factory shut downs. Japanese would rather die than pay a worker to do nothing, but the Japanese auto transplants that are unionized, Mazda especially, may soon be faced with this issue.

No Japanese-owned U.S. firm offers lifetime employment. The usual reason given why they do not is that the practice is rooted in Japanese culture and is not transferable. More thoughtful Japanese, however, note that without the tacit agreement of firms in an industry to offer tenure only to entry-level people, the system does not produce the managerial control over older employees which leads to improved performance. If skilled Americans can quit and get job security at a competitor, they are not likely to be as submissive as Japanese managers would like.

Close approximates to lifetime employment have been offered by some firms for a variety of reasons. At Nissan the no-layoff-if-possible policy undoubtedly saved the company from a unionization effort in 1989 at its Tennessee plant. Why pay union dues, the company implied in its messages to employees, when you already enjoy the job security that is your major concern. This approach worked well in a high unemployment environment like central Tennessee, but how will Nissan carry it off when a really big recession hits? Sales from the plant were sluggish in the booming 1980s and declined in the 1991 economic downturn. Nissan's parent in Japan is an oligopolized giant with vast financial resources, and it could carry the Tennessee operation if it wanted to. If Nissan in America avoids layoffs, even when thousands of employees are clearly redundant, that will be a sign that the lifetime employment system has come to America.

Matsushita has no plans to offer lifetime employment in the United States, but it tries to reduce layoffs by diversifying and shifting lines in a plant when downturns occur (Nissan has done this too). When its Franklin Park plant began to feel pressure from Taiwanese and Korean producers in the 1970s and 1980s, Matsushita at first shifted manufacturing offshore. Employment fell to 750 from a high of 1300. Then the company changed its strategy. "Using what we've got" became a driving force, but so was the idea of showing commitment to employees. Soon the Franklin Park workforce was back to 1300. Throughout the United States, Matsushita's brand names of Quasar, Panasonic, and Technics are constantly developed to maintain an image of high quality and reliability. Branding of this kind keeps sales and production going, even in the face of low-priced offshore competition. It keeps employees working and offers a measure of job security. It is not the more formal system practiced in Japan, but it pays off. Moreover, as in Japan, there is a clear connection between employment security practices at Matsushita, Nissan, and other firms and performance.[5]

The link between job security and performance in Japan is enhanced managerial power, but in America the link is increased motivation. Many visitors to the NUMMI plant in Fremont, California, have noted this. In this Toyota-GM joint venture, the union contract requires the company to keep workers on the payroll unless the company's ability to survive is severely at risk. Contracts at Mazda's Flat Rock plant and at the Chrysler-Mitsubishi joint venture have similar provisions. Although managerial blunders at NUMMI and Mazda have threatened employee morale, motivation always seems to bounce back, and both plants are high performers. The Japanese managers in these firms must have been quite surprised by all this. In their experience, tenured workers are manipulable workers. Americans are less easily pushed around, but a whiff of job security made them eager to work hard and creatively. The concept of motivation is not discussed much in Japan—the system is set up for benevolent control, not inspiration or incentives—but Japan's managers in the United States will have to start paying more attention to the job security-motivation-performance process. Units of Toshiba, Sanyo, and Nomura Securities are known to have laid off American employees while shifting Japanese staff to other jobs. At Nomura the subsequent well-publicized loss of employee morale was catastrophic, since Wall Streeters were hoping Nomura would be a Japanese haven of job security in a troubled financial industry. The new Nomura of the 1990s will have to be more careful about these things.

Besides the problems of power and motivation, the head of Asahi Chemical, Kagayaki Miyazaki, has pointed out another difference. "Lifetime employment may be more characteristic of American companies than their Japanese counterparts," he says. "This is because Japanese firms get rid of older workers in early retirement while U.S. firms retain them."[6] Japanese employees are retired between fifty-five and sixty, while Americans can stay on until sixty-five. Actually the Japanese retirement age is rising while the American is declining, and both will stabilize eventually at around sixty. But for now Mr. Miyazaki's point is well taken. The overhang of older employees in Japan threatens the lifetime employment system, and Japanese firms sometimes are ruthless in letting these people go and then rehiring them as lower-paid, non-tenured workers. Giant American corporations have engaged in a similar practice, but overall, American managers do not have the stomach for this kind of cavalier treatment of employees. While few Americans are guaranteed employment, most do not have to worry about being kicked out on the street at fifty-five years of age.

Delta, IBM, and Digital Equipment are among the few American companies that have tried implicit no-layoff policies. Firms which have abandoned such policies are the Bank of America, R. J. Reynolds Tobacco, and Hewlett-Packard.[7] Those American executives who would like to institute a "Japanese" lifetime employment system see job security as stimulating motivated employees who are candidates for high level, long-term training which will benefit their companies rather than competitors. They are probably right, but there is not much Japanese about their thinking. As we have seen, the Japanese lifetime employment system does not function in a manner transferable to America. This has little to do with cultural differences and much more to do with the greater focus in Japanese managing on power. The system was originally set up to deflate the growing power of unions. It did this, and the increase in managerial control of workers was used to foster increased output. Japanese workers were well aware of the tradeoffs they were making when they acquiesced in the system, and until recently they have been content with it.

Both American executives and workers and Japanese managers in America have been thoroughly confused by the lifetime employment issue. The few American corporate leaders who have toyed with the idea have developed a vision rooted in the motivational rather than the control value of tenure and have believed they were imitating Japanese approaches. The American workers who seek Japanese-style lifetime employment do not realize that they would be giving up much more autonomy than Americans are comfortable with. And the Japanese managers who have used no-layoff tactics in the United States to break union power and to increase control over their employees have found that Americans became more motivated than manipulable. No one seems to know what he is doing, yet all have the potential to benefit greatly. In situations like these authors are wise to shake their heads, smile, and move on to the next chapter.

ELEVEN

Japanese and Americans Don't Trust Each Other

"There's a lot of language in our contract about flexibility and cooperation, but I don't trust it anymore," said Phillip Keeling, U.A.W. local president at Mazda's Flat Rock, Michigan, plant.[1] In a 1988 poll Americans were asked about their perceptions of Japanese, British, and West German business behavior. The Japanese were believed to be the most effective in business, make the best products, and even to treat their workers the best. Yet the British and West Germans were deemed to be more trustworthy.[2] For Japanese, the feeling is mutual. "It's going to take some time before we can develop confidence and rely on Americans," said Yasuhiko Sasai, a trade organization official.[3] "Trust is earned, and it takes time to earn it," said a Matsushita plant manager in the Pacific Northwest.

In a recent study, University of Michigan researchers found that cultural diversity between Japanese managers and their American employees was not strongly related to firm performance.[4] What this means is that a growing sense of cultural difference between the two groups does not necessarily lead to conflict, miscommunication, missed opportunities, or declining profits. If being different is not a problem, however, lack of mutual trust is. The Americans in the study tended not to trust their Japanese bosses, and the greater the distrust, the lower the firm's profits. Trust building is a major issue in Japan, but as one American noted, "In reality, the Japanese only trust another Japanese."[5] A senior bond trader at a Japanese firm on Wall Street also felt that Japanese managers do not trust Americans. "I feel it here sometimes," he said. "It has something to do with our individualism. They see us as pushy. We see them as stubborn." A Japanese manager of a small trading company agreed. "Americans tend to be more aggressive and very quick to make decisions. And also very quick to change their policies. That seems not good, not profitable." So, for Americans a lack of trust leads to poor profits. For Japanese, American untrustworthiness is the cause of weak performance. Are the Japanese unable to trust non-Japanese? Or are Americans unworthy of trust?

Here is a test based on a real incident. Kurt Krause was a human resources manager for a Japanese-owned company from 1976 to 1988 in California and Oregon. In an interview he recalled a meeting with a Japanese manager. "He called me into his office and flatly told me, 'The Americans don't care about this company.' "

Krause was bewildered. "What do you mean," he asked.

"There's an empty coke can sitting out near the front door. It's been sitting there for several days, and nobody has picked it up."[6]

Does this story:

a. reveal untrustworthiness in Americans

b. show a Japanese manager looking for an excuse not to trust Americans

c. both of the above

d. none of the above

The reader's success in this quiz does not depend on getting the right answer, but rather on picking the same answer as his or her counterpart in Japan, or at least understanding why the Japanese person chose a different answer. Japanese managers and their American employees do not trust each other, and we need to understand why before we can do something about improving the situation.

WHAT IS TRUST?

The shock of common humanity hits a scholar when he finds that trust among people in work groups is defined in the same way across cultures and national boundaries.[7] Both Japanese and American managers define it similarly, although Japanese clearly are more focused on developing trust than Americans. The concept has a number of elements to it, all of them focused on the way employees behave towards each other in interpersonal relations. People who trust each other are open and honest in their communications rather than feigned or insinuating. They recognize shared interests and are willing to be mutually obligated, but not in the tit-for-tat manner of economic exchange. For example, when the author does a favor for a trusted Japanese friend, he does not expect a favor in return. But he knows that if a time should come when he must call on his friend, help will be forthcoming, no matter what. Although trust and liking usually go together, it is not required. Most of us can recall a boss whom we trusted to do the right thing but did not really like. Anyone who has spent time in the U.S. military undoubtedly can come up with an example.

Everyone who has studied Japanese managerial practices has observed how important trust is. The usual explanation for this focus is that deeply rooted cultural beliefs about the need for harmony and coherence in society stimulate trust building. This is true as far as it goes, but more pragmatic interpretations exist. Japanese people are homogeneous in that they share values to a greater extent than Americans do. Trust is easy to develop in an atmosphere of shared values, but it does not matter much what those values are. Harmony and coherence are important in Japan, but so are crude racial beliefs and xenophobia. Americans share what almost everyone else in the world considers to be extreme views on individual freedom, but they do not share much else. Consequently, it is not easy to develop trust among organizational members. There just are not enough shared beliefs to serve as a base for trust building. American management gurus talk endlessly about the need to establish corporate culture—any corporate culture will do—because common values provide the opportunity to build trust, and the payoff from trust is great. The Japanese work on building corporate culture, too, but the ready at hand inventory of common beliefs makes it a rather easy task.

The benefits from a climate of trust are many. Although business books with lists often are boring , the payoffs need to be enumerated:

Trust increases the superior's ability to identify a subordinate's needs. When a subordinate is not afraid to tell the boss his or her needs, information useful in developing appropriate incentives flows freely. In a climate of mistrust, for example, Japanese managers often have not learned just how important autonomy is to their college-educated American employees.

Trust creates efficiency. Things get done faster when managers trust their employees' opinions, conclusions, recommendations, and proposals. Trust validates information in place of more information, so that units of work output per unit of information input increase. Fewer accounting checks and monitors are needed. This is a major benefit of trust in Japan, and it could be a competitive advantage in the United States.

Trust stimulates feedback. Japanese managers are not seeking or getting enough feedback from their American employees, even though feedback is a key element of managing in Japan. An increase in trust makes employees unafraid to offer information on what works and what doesn't. At the NUMMI plant in Fremont, California, for example, some workers have complained that their feedback is used to speed up the assembly line. They do not trust their Japanese managers to act in a benevolent manner to them. Overall, Japanese auto industry employees in Japan contribute 60 suggestions to every one from an American employee of the Japanese.[8]

Trust reduces personality conflicts and cross-national clashes. Employees argue with their bosses all the time, even in Japan. As long as the conflict is oriented to ideas or problems, it is a sign of health in the workplace. But conflict can easily degenerate from a "your idea is wrong" level to a "you are an ignorant S.O.B. level" unless participants trust each other to play fair and remain polite. If an American argues with her Japanese boss whom she trusts, she can speak her mind without fear of strong disagreement leading to anti-American remarks or personal attacks. The trust and lack of fear foster valuable openness and honesty.

Trust reduces stress. Two things that cause severe stress, fear of punishment for error and information overload, are dampened when employees know that the trusted boss will be fair and will give them useful, targeted information for their jobs. The effect of stress, a sense that one is unable to cope, is much less in a trust environment.

Japanese managers depend on trust, because it stimulates the flow of high quality information without increasing harmful conflict or stress. Without a climate of trust in their American operations, they must find other ways to reduce uncertainty, and they have had to move more towards formal procedures, monitoring, and evaluation systems. If a manager does not trust an American, he reduces his anxieties by making a rule, demanding adherence to the rule, and checking up on the person to see if he has adhered. Sure enough, Japanese managers report more reliance on rules and formalization in their American organizations than in Japan.[9] A frequent explanation by Japanese for this is the need to follow American custom and accounting practice, but equally important is the climate of mistrust which prevails in many firms.

THE ROOTS OF DISTRUST

In 1986 John Kageyama established a television and VCR assembly plant in Vancouver, Washington. "When we celebrated our first anniversary," he said, "I asked our American employees how they enjoyed working with us. For the most part they were happy, but I was surprised by some of the criticisms they made. One was, 'Japanese managers don't trust their American workers.' "[10] Mulling over this problem, Mr. Kageyama decided that the seeming lack of trust was due to the fact that the Japanese are simply poor communicators. They speak with great reserve and expect listeners to pick up on implied rather than overtly stated messages. "From a small bit of information that a speaker may convey—perhaps in a simple gesture or in his tone of voice—the Japanese listener gleans the whole meaning. The Japanese learn from an early age how to understand one another without direct verbal communication." Americans encountering this kind of behavior see it as secretive and feel that the Japanese managers distrust them. In his polite way, however, Mr. Kageyama makes it clear that although Japanese may need to be better speakers, the real problem is the Americans' unsophisticated approach to communication. If only they were more subtle, he gently implies, all would be well and trust would increase.

He has a point, and other observers have noted similar communication problems as a source of mistrust. "With Americans whatever is said and heard is what is real," said a Japanese securities firm manager in New York. "Trust is formed on that basis." With Japanese, many more things are taken for granted, and the unstated often is "real" and the basis for trust. Japanese managers find it hard to explain to Americans how mutual trust is formed by what is not said rather than what is. All they are asking, however, is that Americans get used to reading between the lines more. In addition, Japanese would like their American subordinates to practice *sunao*, the quality of being nonresistant or nonsuspicious. The employee who never asks why he or she is being told to do something displays *sunao*. He trusts the boss to exercise his power wisely. To ask why is to imply distrust. Unfortunately (or fortunately, if one is wary of the Japanese power focus), Americans are the greatest why-askers in the history of humankind. It is not that they distrust others. Americans just believe that knowledge should be open to everyone and information should flow freely. Actually, Japanese have similar beliefs, but not when it comes to a boss's directives. Americans who keep their queries to themselves and do their assigned jobs will exhibit trust and be trusted in return, according to Japanese commentators.

Besides reading between the lines and not questioning the boss, Americans ironically can earn Japanese trust by not feeling threatened by the barrage of questions Japanese managers throw at their subordinates. In the United States an American supervisor is concerned with end results. He or she will carefully outline a task for a subordinate and then leave that person alone to do it. The subordinate can take pride in getting a job done with minimal supervision. Japanese managers follow a different procedure. Often they will indicate a general direction rather than a specific set of goals and tasks. This leaves American subordinates unsure of what is expected of them. Why this practice? Many times Japanese bosses do not know much about the units they manage. As generalists being constantly rotated through assignments, they do not get a chance to develop expertise. Consequently, they may communicate a sense of something needing to be done without quite knowing what. The "what" is up to the more knowledgeable subordinate. Japanese managers tend to seek almost daily updates on progress, however. An American who finds her boss constantly standing over her shoulder soon will form the opinion that she is not trusted. This is not necessarily true, since the manager may be trying to learn from the subordinate or simply trying to carry on a dialogue about the project. Nevertheless, it is an annoying habit which for Americans takes getting used to, yet tolerance of vigorous questioning by Japanese bosses can foster trust.

While easy-to-solve communication problems are a source of mistrust, other problems are less easily handled. A trading company manager in Seattle noted how much American ignorance of Japan is resented. "In the past people on the West Coast where I worked did not know much about Japan. For example, when I was in Portland there was something that occurred in Japan that was of major importance, but it only got a little tiny space in the Portland newspaper. I think we Japanese have done our part in trying to make the American people understand more about Japan. Americans now have to spend about ten years learning about the Japanese for trust to be improved." If West Coast Americans bother this man, how will he react to the abysmal ignorance of Japan on the East Coast? It is true that some Japanese do not like prying eyes and would rather Americans did not learn Japanese and did not peer into some of the dark corners of Japanese society. But this manager is certainly on track in voicing the average Japanese manager's desire to be better understood. One of the difficulties that arise from ignorance is that Americans expect things from Japanese that they cannot deliver. The communal environment of Theory Z, for example, is an American invention purporting to describe a Japan which, in fact, does not exist. When American employees find that Japanese are polite but very much control-oriented, they may feel somewhat betrayed and distrustful. This need not be if Americans spend some time learning about Japanese business and managerial practices.

The ignorance is not all on the American side, however. Many Japanese believe that Americans are an untrustworthy people. This is not so. Rather Americans are less interested in developing relationships based on trust. Mostly they form business liaisons on the basis of mutual advantage. They reserve trust bonds for their personal lives. This compartmentalization of life into business and social segments is somewhat odd to Japanese managers, who see their life and work in more unified terms. They are not unfeeling workaholics who totally ignore their families (although many difficulties with home life exist). Far from it. They see themselves as fulfilling obligations sanctioned by society and by their families. It is their duty to be work-oriented. Americans have more role ambiguity and role conflict. They must be both work-oriented and nonwork-oriented. Sometimes the role requirements clash, leading to pressure, tension, and stress. For Japanese the stress of conflicting roles is not nearly as burdensome as the anxiety born of uncertainty over what the all-encompassing work role requires of them.

Japanese managers in America suffer from even greater anxieties, especially when they are deciding whether or not to develop trust with an American. What would such trust involve, they wonder? Will the American reciprocate? Not only does the Japanese not know how far to go along the road to trust, he also does not know if or when the American will get off. He sees that Americans have a duty to themselves, first, and also nonwork roles to play out. How can such duties and roles foster trust? They can't.

Japanese Manufacturer: Can I count on you to get my components to me on Saturday afternoon? We finish our run then and I don't want to have to shut down the line until Monday.

American Supplier: Ordinarily I'd have no problem with that. We want to help you in every way we can. But Saturday my kids expect me to go camping with them. I'm sure you realize I can't let them down.

Japanese: Well yes, but I hoped that we could work with each other smoothly.

American: That's right. You give a little on this issue and I'll see to it that you get a discount on the next order.

Japanese: That's kind of you, but I need to feel I can count on you, no matter what.

American: You can count on me. I will respond to every reasonable need of yours if I'm able.

Japanese: Then you'll deliver on Saturday.

American: Sorry, other commitments have to come first. But you can count on that discount. You have my word on it.

For Japanese, trust is an obligation to another willingly entered into out of mutual respect or admiration. It is not an economic exchange relationship, nor is it something to be turned on or off depending on the role one is playing. Trust endures across situations, roles, and time. This is difficult for an American to accept, and Japanese know it. Thus they don't expect Americans to be oriented to trust. Put unkindly, they do not trust Americans. While Americans are usually unwilling to make the kind of commitment to trust which Japanese make, however, this is not to say that Americans are not trustworthy. As long as a Japanese manager recognizes the limits, he will find that Americans are honest, credible, and resourceful in helping colleagues and clients. Indeed, Americans are noted for the joy they take in being generous. It is a joy born of the belief that people should do good if they are able. Being helpful is not something Americans do out of a sense of duty to another associated with a trust bond. They help because they believe in principled behavior—behavior guided by abstract ideals rooted in religious faith and republican tenets of citizenship and neighborliness. In the dialogue above the Japanese manager should not expect an American to be a Japanese. Moreover, he ought to be willing to look on the bright side. The American has his role obligations and must adhere to them. Yet he is eager to use the exchange process to ease the burden others bear because he must carry out certain role expectations. He is taking something from the Japanese, but he will compensate gladly. This behavior may not smack of allegiance and deep commitment, but it is civil and sensible. It shows a balance which Americans identify with maturity.

Americans' refusal to broaden their assigned work roles also leads to Japanese mistrust. "I was often frustrated," said a Mitsui manager, "because American employees only do a job according to its most narrow definition and nothing more." He formed the belief that he could not trust workers because of an ingrained selfishness in Americans. Only a rude shock changed his opinion. "I was in a car accident and Americans readily helped me. American people are very kind and polite." The Mitsui man received aid without any implicit demand from the Americans that he become obligated to them. In Japan this fear of unwanted obligations often keeps people from seeking or giving help to each other. The author once rescued a Japanese man in Tokyo who had fallen into the space between a subway car and the station platform. The poor man's gratitude was mixed with a look of sheer terror at the thought of the obligations which might be demanded of him. When no name and address was requested, his joy was almost as great as that from being still alive. When the Mitsui manager learned that Americans are really an unselfish people, he developed a better trust relationship with his staff, recognizing that role rigidity was a custom of the country and not rooted in selfishness.

One issue which bothers American managers and causes Japanese mistrust is the constantly shifting attitude of Japanese to the status of local employees. Invariably the Japanese see themselves as "core" staff employed by the parent firm and part of its global operations. Americans are viewed as subsidiary staff not subject to the values, rewards, or pressures of membership in the parent's organizational life. They are not allowed to attend core staff meetings focused on parent issues, are not candidates for top jobs in the subsidiary, will never be asked to serve in another country or even in another unit in the United States, are not given informal guarantees of permanent employment, and are not asked to go out drinking to build long-term bonds with core employees. Although in a few cases Americans have fought against the core-subsidiary categorization and in many cases morale may not be very high, most subsidiary employees accept the system as a given condition of working for a Japanese firm. So far, so good, but at this point a Japanese manager will say something like, "Why can't the Americans be more loyal? I want to trust them, but there's always the risk of them leaving to go with a competitor. Why can't they learn Japanese? Why do they always run off to their families at 5:00 P.M.?" The Japanese is essentially saying: Why can't they be the very thing we don't want them to be: core employees? Granted, Japanese personnel officers do not make these statements, but operations managers who do not think much about the niceties of labels often do. A bit of training in the old country is in order to sensitize Japanese to the issue. Even better, Japanese parents should offer the opportunity to some Americans to cross over from subsidiary to core employee and for Japanese to go in the opposite direction. A growing number of Japanese managers, after all, would like to get their hands on the much higher salaries paid to some Americans.

American managers sometimes protest when a subsidiary is told to work with a vendor or customer affiliated with the parent firm. Even though it makes no economic sense to do so in America, the subsidiary is assigned to help foster good relationships in Japan through its actions in the United States.[11] These practices may look at first like a global strategy working itself out, but they are really a sign of how inexperienced many Japanese corporations are in the international arena. They hire Americans for their local expertise, but then they want them to help carry out a strictly intra-Japan strategy. When the Americans protest, they are labelled as disloyal and untrustworthy. What is needed is a chance for Americans to learn what is going on in Japan so they can adapt themselves or work quietly to persuade the firm to be more rational in its decisions. Top executives from Japan need to come to America frequently to explain headquarters commitments, and Americans should be sent to Japan regularly to learn corporate culture and to give them a chance to build up their image of loyalty to the firm. Without these approaches, conflict and mistrust are inevitable. At first, Americans will object to a decision with great force, employing all the rhetoric at their command. Quite soon they will learn how distasteful open argument is to Japanese. They then will adopt a Japanese-style way of passive protest. "What I don't like I ignore and wait to see what will happen," said one American manager in Vladimar Pucik's study of Japanese-owned firms. Said another, "Maybe headquarters tells me they want to eliminate thirty-five suppliers. I'll get rid of a couple and wait and see how that works out." Passive resistance can only work for so long, however, and even if it does work, it eventually will leave a residue of mistrust.

BUILDING TRUST IN AMERICA

In 1980 Japanese managers at the Washington Courthouse, Ohio, Yusa Corporation plant were horrified to discover that their American workers were chewing gum on the job. To them, gum chewing was a sign of laziness which would not be tolerated in Japan. A gum chewer is *fumajime* (not serious enough). In their plant, a "reluctant follower" Japanese joint venture firm supplying parts for Honda cars, Japanese managers had not really made any effort to accommodate themselves to the American workplace. They believed that Americans ought to behave like Japanese workers. So they told the American supervisors to put a stop to gum chewing. When it persisted, they complained that gum might be dropped into the auto parts. Scoffed at, they then suggested that employees would concentrate better without distracting gum chewing. Eventually the Japanese gave up, but they continued to insist on the importance of concentration, devotion, and dedication. The Americans translated these directions into improved quality control procedures to turn the whole mess into a win-win situation. There are some lessons to be learned here. First of all, in some Japanese firms in the United States, probably those referred to in this book as "reluctant followers," Japanese managers may not practice the high-quality managing seen in other types of firms. Second, Japanese, as Ko Shioya notes, often value substance over form.[12] Japanese need to be a lot less punctilious, but Americans need to be a little less pragmatic if they are to trust each other.

What Japanese (at least conservative Japanese managers) want in a trusted employee are *giri, ninjo,* and *naniwabushi.* These words refer to obligation, human warmth, and a self-sacrificing, family-like attitude. When asked what Americans should do to develop the trust of their Japanese bosses, a Tokyo management consultant said, "They must develop corporate loyalty and concentrate on helping the organization meet corporate goals." According to a Japanese employee in the United States, they also should urge their fellow workers to serve corporate objectives. "I was working hard one day," he recalled, "and some other guys were drinking coffee and smoking. I said, 'Why don't you get to work.' They said I should not be saying anything to them because I was not their boss. In Japan we control each other."

So Americans need to be obliging, sensitive to rituals, friendly, and willing to broaden their vision to include organizational needs if they want to be trusted. This is what Japanese managers say, and there is no reason to doubt their word. But more elaborate research than interviews reveals additional elements to Japanese trust-building with Americans.[13] In a series of experiments, my colleagues and I found that Japanese managers will trust Americans more:

· when they, the Japanese, have power in the relationship.
· when formal rules exist to cover odd or difficult situations.
· when the company is profitable.
· when the top American and the top Japanese in the company get along well.

The ideal Japanese-owned company, then, is a profitable one in which senior Americans eagerly help Japanese to develop strong controls over American employees. These employees do not resent the control, since they know it is all in service to corporate objectives to which they also subscribe. If some kind of novel conflict occurs, say over promotion policies, the Japanese can cite a written rule that will resolve the problem without unpleasant argument. In this environment Japanese will trust Americans. A climate of mistrust will emerge when senior Americans think only of themselves or see their duties as including representation of American employees' needs, when the firm is unprofitable, when employees have unions or other mechanisms to dispute Japanese power, when workers serve primarily their own needs, and when no one has been able to write rules to resolve every difficult problem. Needless to say, this latter depiction characterizes the real life of many Japanese companies in America, and the resulting mistrust is a severe problem.

If Japanese do not seem able yet to trust Americans, perhaps they can get Americans to trust them. In Japan, the ASICS corporation builds trust through an employee-ownership plan, profit sharing, in-house hiring and promotion by merit rather than seniority, elaborate employee training, and the selection of managers based on their strong networking skills and ability to socialize with employees. This mix of American and Japanese approaches can work in America too, although Japanese investors have not shown any interest in sophisticated management to develop trust. One of the simplest things they could do but have not done is consult their American employees more. Vladimir Pucik and his team of researchers found that Japanese do seek American advice on pricing, sales, and promotion issues, but they do not want American ideas on capital allocation topics such as investment in new factories, where to borrow funds, and the kind of R & D a firm should undertake. In this sense America is like a Third World country to the Japanese, where local expertise is only used for marketing. Japanese firms often use American managers to compile information, but not to determine what the information suggests about future directions. This failure to use American talent is rooted in mistrust, and it brings out American lack of trust in turn.

Some trust-building does occur. In 1983 Bridgestone purchased Firestone's truck tire plant in La Vergne, Tennessee, for $52 million. Equality and trust became the name of the game. Executive parking and separate cafeterias were abolished, as was the punch clock for workers (who now fill out a time sheet themselves). Japanese managers worked hard to listen to workers' ideas for improvements. Daily employee output rose from seventeen to forty tires per day. In 1988 Bridgestone bought all of Firestone for $2.6 billion and moved company headquarters back from Chicago to the firm's ancestral home in Akron. New investments of $1.5 billion were made to modernize production. None of the largesse was due to Christian charity. Bridgestone got twenty-seven Firestone facilities worldwide for what it would have cost to build a new plant in Japan with its inflated land costs. Nevertheless, Bridgestone did what it could to build employee trust. In 1990, however, sluggish auto sales caused Bridgestone/Firestone to begin a staff reduction plan. Within one month Teiji Eguchi, the chairman of the company, flew to the firm's offices in Akron for an indefinite stay.[14] Then in 1991, as the recession worsened, a Japanese manager replaced the American CEO and began laying off employees. Whatever trust the company had built with its workers in the 1980s will be severely threatened in the 1990s.

Both Japanese and Americans agree that trust is the belief that another person has willingly chosen to feel obligated to help the manager or the organization carry out tasks without any thought of immediate compensation. Because of a more extensive base of shared values in Japan, trust is easier to develop than in America. Since the payoff in terms of more motivated workers producing more efficiently at lower costs is so great, Japanese managers work hard to develop trust relationships with their employees. Indeed, the combination of benevolent power plus relentless trust building is their formula for managerial success.

When they come to America, life becomes harder for Japanese. Power is not as easily exercised, and Americans, while recognizing the value of trust, do not commit themselves to developing it as eagerly as Japanese employees do. It isn't that Americans have *different* cultural values; the big problem is a *lack* of shared values which can serve as a basis for trust. In addition, Americans have obligations outside of the workplace which hinder them from making an all out effort to build trust within the company. Japanese managers will just have to get used to the fact that most of their relations with American employees will be based on tit for tat economic exchange. They can count on Americans having good will and being helpful, however, even without the existence of deep trust bonds.

Having said this, we would expect the trust issue to have moved offstage while Japanese and Americans concentrated on working out such things as power relationships. But instead we find that a debilitating climate of mistrust has developed in many Japanese-owned firms. Many explanations exist for this. Americans and Japanese are not communicating well. Both groups are ignorant of each other's ways. The core employee-subsidiary employee problem is being handled by the Japanese in a confusing and muddled manner. The situation which exists now requires action to reduce mistrust and perhaps create a base for future trust building. Japanese managers need to become better at socializing with Americans and listening to them. Top management in Tokyo and Osaka needs to travel more to the United States to demonstrate company concerns for Americans' problems. America, after all, is not Thailand or Indonesia, a place to go for inexpensive labor. It is where large Japanese companies must be if they are to survive as global organizations, and corporate leaders need to recognize this. Extending profit sharing and stock ownership to American employees are two actions which would sop up mistrust very quickly. For their part, American employees should be tolerant of more ritualized Japanese ways and seemingly intrusive information-gathering by managers. Above all, they should try to accept direction gracefully and look for ways to show their interest in helping the company attain its goals. They should accept the more vertical and authoritarian style of Japanese managing— as long as managers are benevolent and show strong interest in employee needs. Working for the Japanese is not radically different from working for Americans, but differences do exist. People need to be accommodating if they are able. If not, they should not work for a Japanese firm. As for Japanese managers, they need to keep in mind that their employees are not Japanese. Not every managerial tool they employ in Japan will work in America. If both sides work at it, mistrust will diminish. While trust cannot become the major managerial tool it is in Japan, it still can be developed.

TWELVE

Matching the Right American with the Right Japanese

Over 45 percent of top executives of Japanese subsidiaries abroad are Japanese rather than host-country managers. About 17 percent of mid-level managers are Japanese. These are much higher numbers than for foreign subsidiaries in Japan, where only 17 percent of executives and 2 percent of managers are non-Japanese.[1] A 1982 JETRO study of 150 Japanese-owned manufacturing firms in the United States revealed that 74 percent of managerial positions were held by Japanese. All of the top executives were from Japan.[2] More recent 1990 data from the Commerce Department suggest that Japanese make up about 17 percent of total employment at Japanese-owned companies, perhaps twice the rate of other foreign investors (the largest concentrations of Japanese are in non-manufacturing firms). Clearly Japanese managers have come to the United States to manage their parents' holdings. Are they prepared for the task? What kind of training do they receive? Do they train American employees adequately to work for them and with them? In general, the answers are that they are not prepared very well for their jobs in America, and they have not yet figured out how to train Americans.

TRAINING IN JAPAN

A new white collar managerial recruit is expected to learn the company philosophy; the slogans for the year, the month, and the week; how to stand when talking to a superior; and bowing. All of this social conditioning stems from two factors not present in America. First, Japan is a highly vertical society where everyone must learn his place and every place has a set of expected behaviors attached to it. One who sees the bowing and ritual formalities in Japanese movies might tend to think that this is the way Japan really is. Not quite. Interest in bowing waxes and wanes, and young Japanese are becoming increasingly ignorant of formal speech and behavior. Many companies spend weeks training recruits just to do simple things like answering the telephone in the correct manner. Plain and polite, humble and honorific language modes are as much a trial for younger people as they are for Americans trying to learn Japanese. An American can get away with using polite, neutral language in all situations, but Japanese corporate leaders want their employees to use speech in a way which shows that corporations are attentive to societal concerns about orderliness in communication and behavior. An American company will teach "interpersonal skills" simply to get employees to stop saying "Yeah, whadda ya want?" on the phone. A similar Japanese also will answer "Yeah" when he or she actually is not supposed to answer at all (at least in conservative firms). The caller speaks first, and then the answerer responds with the Japanese equivalent of "Hello. This is the Bank of Japan." The American firm is pragmatic, believing that interpersonal training fosters good communication and good company image. This is true in Japan, too, but the training also is seen to serve society's need for coherence and civility.

A second reason for the socialization training has to do with the establishment of power. Unlike their American counterparts, Japanese college graduates are often amazingly ignorant. They spend their first eighteen years memorizing things so they can pass a college entrance examination. Once in college, they relax, enjoying a well-earned four-year rest. Like many ignorant people, they develop a streak of lazy vanity that must be ruthlessly washed out if they are to fit into and contribute to the organization. Training in part becomes the development of submissive but energetic soldiers in the corporate army. At Seibu Railways new male recruits may have their heads shaved. They are put to work cleaning up trains and toilets, suffering together and building lifelong career contacts with their fellow workers and the "big brother" managers who first harangue and then console them. Americans who watch the better run of these groups as they drink their scotch after work in the bars of Osaka and Tokyo are struck by their camaraderie and joy in each other's company. When the system is working, it develops happy people.

Typically, Japanese companies spend only 0.3 percent of total labor costs on formal training, mostly during the initial indoctrination of recruits.[3] Giants like Matsushita, Sharp, and NEC do have more elaborate training regimes, but they are the exception. Only 39 percent of large Japanese firms have career development programs. In a 1980 study, formal training for 26 percent of new employees included the use of

Zen meditation. The remainder of training involved mostly lectures and discussions. Only recently have Japanese companies moved towards the use of case studies, simulations, and role play. They also are bringing managers back from the field, especially the United States, to give first-hand reports and advice. Most training, however, is done on the job by supervisors.[4] Japanese managers take their training role seriously, and it is one of their strengths. Many low-level American employees have noted how helpful their Japanese bosses have been in patiently showing them what to do (higher-level Americans are expected to pick it up on their own). This is in contrast to American supervisors, who sometimes see a trained employee as a personal threat rather than an asset. Indeed, as soon as Japanese improve their communications with Americans and begin seeing American employees as company rather than merely subsidiary workers, their superb teaching skills will start to have a big impact. The climate of mistrust described in the last chapter will disappear fast. Unfortunately, not enough Japanese managers are getting the preparation they need for American service.

WHO GETS TO GO TO THE UNITED STATES?

The future of Honda is in the United States, and its managers probably jump at the chance for a U.S. assignment. This may not be true at Toyota, which has been a reluctant follower firm whose real interests remain in Japan. To be away from the power center and out of the physical sight of important people can be a torment for ambitious Japanese managers, and until the mid-1980s a tour of duty in America was not viewed as a good assignment. That has changed somewhat now, and managers may compete for valued American posts. International experience ensures a fast track status, and the United States is a more desirable place to work than, say, Africa, where Japanese companies have set up assembly plants to take advantage of cheap labor. The United States is also better than some industrialized nations. One Matsushita executive recalled his sad experience in Australia. "I had to fire most of the workers within six months of opening the factory," he said. Weaknesses in work ethic of the Australian variety are not found much in the United States, and Japanese managers appreciate it.

At Sharp, once a year people are selected for overseas training from a list of volunteers or on the recommendation of supervisors. If they are qualified, they receive what Sharp managers call a "passport," that entitles them to one year of on-the-job training in Japan. At the end of that time, more of a weeding out process than a training exercise, those chosen for America receive a "visa." Then two month's intensive training occurs. Courses are given in English, accounting, marketing, and global production practices. The emphasis on business skills rather than cultural awareness is common at other large firms, too. At Nissho Iwai, a trading company, those short-listed for American duty must pass tests in English, trade rules and laws, accounting, and foreign exchange management. Candidates are expected to pick up knowledge of these subjects on their own with self-study. "We need both bi-lingualists and globalists," explained a Nissho Iwai senior manager. "Younger managers often have good English, but they lack a depth of international knowledge." Without having really learned anything in college, they come to a Japanese corporation lacking business training. Most firms do not send a manager to the United States until he (women are not sent) has put in at least five years with the company. This experience seasons him, but it is no guarantee that he has accumulated knowledge. Advancement in a Japanese firm depends on hard work over long hours, and little time exists for reading and study.

Twenty-eight colleges and universities in Japan offer undergraduate and graduate degrees in business administration and management science. The largest are Waseda, Meiji, Chuo, Hosei, and Keio universities. In total about 11,000 males graduate each year.[5] Since Japanese companies recruit close to 140,000 college graduates annually, it is safe to conclude that most new managers know almost nothing about business.[6] Combine this ignorance with the lack of time to study during their first five years in the company and one can see why an assignment to a responsible position in the United States fosters a series of cram courses in accounting and marketing with only a passing nod to American customs and practices. It also becomes clear why Japanese managers are always questioning their American employees and are so concerned about maintaining power. They are terribly unsure of themselves. Some of the younger men cover up their anxiety with a kind of arrogant posturing and an occasional anti-American comment. But most buckle down and for the first time in their careers actually learn something about finance, accounting, marketing, and human resource management.

One dramatic improvement over the last decade is the high quality of English many young Japanese possess. At one time students who exhibited exceptional skill in pronouncing English would be scorned by their fellows for standing out. Social pressure would drive them to mispronounce like everyone else, with the result that Japanese use of English usually was incomprehensible. Learning English correctly was something a few women did, while *macho* Japanese males gloried in their butchering of the language. Americans who came to Japan to teach English were paid poorly, and American women occasionally were mistreated. All of this is now changed, and learning English is very popular, since the biggest hurdle a manager faces in seeking an American post is his language ability.

Matsushita gives an English test to anyone who wants to take it, but passing only guarantees a closer look by managers who conduct interviews and examine comments in the candidates' files. Even when an employee is selected for formal training, he still is at risk. Two or three classes for mid-level people going overseas are held each year, with about sixty managers in attendance. About fifteen of these are dropped from the program, probably for poor English. At Matsushita's training center near Osaka, one of the key classrooms is the lounge. Here drinks are served at a bar where English is often required. Since the ability to speak a second language may deteriorate under the influence of alcohol, the lounge test is one of the most severe a manager faces. If he can still speak English with five or six whiskies in him, his instructors can be certain that he can handle an American assignment. Not all Japanese managers in America can speak English, however. Technical people often do not know the language and communicate with Americans through general management personnel. Also, many firms simply follow the sink or swim approach; a manager perfects his English on the job or else is sent back to Japan. Since it takes about two years of total immersion to develop adequate skills in a language, some Japanese are virtually useless for a substantial part of their first U.S. assignment. They do filing and are occasionally turned into chauffeurs for senior level people.

THE TRAINING REGIME

Only a few large firms do formal preparation, and even these are not sure what to do beyond putting the final touches on English skills and offering crash courses in business subjects. One approach is to send managers off to America for a visit so they can learn on their own. Several American colleges have home stay programs. In Americus, Georgia, for example, the local community college offers a six months' visit with local families to soak up culture. Japanese sometimes make useful connections on these visits. An auto parts company manager might link up with a visiting Toyota man on a Georgetown, Kentucky, home stay and develop a fruitful business relationship while getting acclimated to the United States. Matsushita occasionally sends managers for three-month visits to get their feet wet. They then go back and share what they have learned with others posted for America. One of the things Japanese want to understand is the complex regulatory environment in which American business is done. The regulation in Japan is even more excessive but is rather simple. One negotiates with the bureaucracy in charge of one's industry and that's that. American business is governed by multiple bureaucracies, and they tend to write all their laws and rules down, making negotiation less of an option. The businessman must comply, and this rigidity bothers Japanese managers who are unsure of what they are supposed to do. When they do find out what to do, they do not like it. Polls of Japanese reveal their belief that Americans are overly concerned with such things as minority hiring.[7]

Formal courses are held at a few corporations to augment home stays and visits. Canon offers a basic seven-day program on going overseas once a year. Specialized training occurs in month-long courses held twice a year. Matsushita's Overseas Training Center, the biggest and the best of the corporate training facilities in Japan, runs courses for Japanese personnel who do international work in Japan and for personnel assigned overseas. International division employees take courses in business and technical writing in English, while domestic employees can break into the international field by taking courses in any of six languages. The emphasis is on English, and proficiency exams are given twice each year. Personnel about to go to America may take an intensive three-week dormitory-lodging program in English. Management courses for these people focus on developing a global focus in strategy, marketing, laws and regulations, and personnel practices. A wives' course offers five days on living and cooking in America and five days on using English. Notice what is not offered. There is nothing on "how to motivate employees" or "how to manage your time effectively." These staples of American management training are of no interest to the Japanese, who like to hire people already motivated and who simply work longer when time pressure builds up.

DEALING WITH AMERICANS

Matsushita tries to do it right. Overseas personnel, including about fifty to sixty Americans (four to six at a time) a year, get a one-week course at the Training Center on understanding Japan and Matsushita's philosophy. Then they usually move on to a two-week course tailored to their rank. At other times Americans may return for two-week functional courses in marketing, parts control, purchasing, quality control, and so forth.[8] More technical training is given for engineering personnel and lasts a lot longer, from three weeks to two years. The Training Center also supplies course material to American subsidiaries for local in-house training in personnel management, sales, production, market research, and quality control.

Americans who come to the Overseas Training Center for the one-week introductory course see a video on what Matsushita calls "human electronics" and then visit the company's Museum of Technology. Lectures are given on Japanese history and the history of the founder, Mr. Matsushita, as well as the basic principles which constitute the corporation's philosophy. Three hours in the midst of all these value-creating activities are devoted to studying the company's business environment. Then the Americans get a tour of Kyoto. Managers who stay on for the two-week course will take either the middle or advanced management programs. In the mid-manager course two full days are spent once more on the core values of the company before getting down to case studies, lectures from top executives, an in-plant study tour, and a three-day management simulation. The Americans work as a team on the simulation exercise in competition with teams made up of other nationalities, but no one gets too up tight about it. The Center is a rather easy going place with lots of athletic facilities and a lounge.

Center director Junichi Ukita has tried to respond to American requests for more interactive training. "The Japanese way of teaching is lecturing," he says, "but our American employees like more two-way traffic." Lectures are given in English by staff people, general managers from the field, and professors from nearby universities. One of the big problems facing Matsushita, however, is how to train Americans selected to be plant managers. A few weeks' lecturing will not be enough. Mr. Ukita says, "They will probably have to come to Japan for one or two years with their families. They must develop 'bigger eyes,' as we say, and gain a wide knowledge of the company." A handful of Americans have done programs similar to this already, and more will come. A big issue is finding high quality people who also are willing to learn Japanese. "Language problems are the destiny of Japan," sighs Mr. Ukita. One half-way measure was described by Dick Kraft, the American CEO of Matsushita's American operations. "Today we're doing what we call a 'people exchange program,' " he said. "We send people from both sides to work in the environment of the other." The idea is to get managers who communicate by fax or telephone every day to meet and work with each other. Their goals are to teach and learn over a one- to three-month period. Mr. Kraft notes, "We want our American managers to understand that some things which may seem unusual by American standards are normal for Japan."

ENDURING THE UNENDURABLE

Japanese executives like Junichi Ukita think it will take years before Americans become acclimated to the Japanese way of managing. Here is an example illustrating why they are so gloomy.[9]

A recently-hired young American manager attends his first meeting of the senior staff at Nikongo, Inc., the Japanese-owned firm that hired him. He asks for time to make a statement.

"I have developed a plan to make money from our factory waste," he announces, "and I would like to share my idea with you today."

He goes on to spell out the details at great length. Finally he sits down, knowing that this great idea ought to earn him a fast track image and a quick promotion. Pleased with himself, he later approaches his boss, the Japanese general manager.

"Well, Mr. Taguchi, I hope you liked my idea. We can make a bundle from waste."

The boss stares at him for a moment. Then in a strained voice he says, "Our goal here is to eliminate waste, not profit from it. You should have proposed a plan to reduce waste."

The American's jaw drops. "But I thought . . . I mean . . . aren't we supposed to . . . . "

"You suppose too much, Mr. American. You are new here, and you should sit and listen, not bother everyone with loud speeches. It is embarrassing."

"I can't understand this," responds the American, who has regained his composure and now is getting angry. "This is a good idea."

"How can we know if it is a good idea," shoots back Mr. Taguchi. "You did not share it with us so it could be debated."

"Hey, it's my idea. I don't want anyone stealing it from me."

"Why didn't you tell me? I must know everything that will be said at a meeting."

"Wait a minute, pal. Why hold meetings if you know everything already?"

The boss sighs. "You have a lot to learn, my young friend. It is my mistake for not realizing that. Don't worry. I will teach you, and you will do very well with us." He walks off, leaving the American fuming.

The Japanese boss described here reflects both good and bad elements of the breed. He is ritualistic, preferring meetings which are puppet shows rather than substantive discourse. He is also culture-bound in having an abhorrence of waste rather than a desire to profit from it. And he is rigid in demanding adherence to a vertical system which forces silence on the lower ranks. His saving grace, however, is that he is wonderfully experienced. He knows the fires of the young. While he does not admire such ardor as much as Americans do, he tolerates it. Better than that, he is a teacher able to slowly mold the young so that passions are less likely to get out of control while their creativity serves the company and society. Indeed, his own self-discipline allows him to endure the American's abrasive tone without exploding in anger. Ritualistic, rigid, experienced, a fine teacher, self-controlled: this is what a typical Japanese manager is like, and an

American will be expected to have similar characteristics. But no one is quite sure how to develop such a person.

JAPANIZING

Some Japanese firms seek to hire people at entry level and develop them internally rather than purchasing skills as needed on the open labor market. This was Honda's strategy when it set up its first American auto plant. It looked for applicants with no prior auto industry experience. Then it formed a team of its first sixteen workers and had them build and tear down ten cars a day for two weeks. After that they spread out to show new employees how to do it. Doing things the Honda way is important to its control-oriented executives, and inexperienced hires are not burdened with ideas formed elsewhere. When companies do have to look outside for people, they follow several routes. They will look for an American with experience in Japan and language skills (very rare) or a second or third generation Japanese-American who supposedly has a "Japanese mentality" (in the author's experience, these people actually are as American as Chevrolet and apple pie).

A movement has started in the last few years to develop a different approach: hiring young American university graduates and sending them to headquarters in Japan for several years' training, socialization, and language development. According to New York University Professor Allan Bird, this strategy helps develop American managers who are loyal to the parent company.[10] They can see the whole company and its global perspective rather than focusing solely on the American subsidiary. Their headquarters knowledge and contacts serve them well when they return to work in the U.S. subsidiary, and their Japanese language skill makes them an ideal mediator between American employees and Japanese owners. They also can train newly arrived Japanese managers whose English is shaky.

Once recruited, the Americans are usually assigned to the firm's international division in Japan as contract employees for a two-year period of probation. They are paid about the same as a Japanese with similar experience and education. They may go through the same training as new Japanese recruits. At Honda, recruits spend three months on the assembly line and three months hustling cars at a dealership. One wonders whether Honda interviews at Wharton or the Harvard Business School. After training they may work in purchasing or planning. One young American spent a tour planning a major Japanese resort in the United States. He was a resource of American data for his colleagues, and they showed him the ins and outs of the corporate culture. These Americans sometimes are amazed at how weak Japanese management can be once the curtain of robotics and lifetime employment has been parted. The abacus is still used more than the calculator in many firms, and the calculator may rule in place of the spreadsheet. After several years the American returns to the United States as a permanent employee assigned to a subsidiary. He or she is now a "Japanese" manager in America, or so they are led to believe. What little anecdotal evidence there is, however, suggests that the headquarters-trained American is treated as just another local hire by Japanese executives running U.S. affiliates. This is quite demoralizing for a person who has spent two or three years becoming Japanized. The fact is that Japanese managers divide up the world ethnically: Japanese and non-Japanese. If you are white, you are non-Japanese and are treated accordingly as an outsider. You may be treated quite well, but you always will be an outsider.

Can Americans have a career with a Japanese firm after going through the Japanizing process? "Right now our headquarters is planning for more foreigners—Americans, Europeans, and Asians—as members of headquarters staff," said a securities firm manager. Other executives make similar comments, always noting that Japanese culture is "special" and "different." Clearly they are worried about *gaijin* in Japan. Young Americans worry, too, about fitting in. Craig Justice went through Mitsubishi's program and discovered the importance of finding the right sponsor. "What works well is to be trained with a sympathetic Japanese who has U.S. experience," he said. A sponsor helps the American become associated with important projects bearing on U.S. investments and identifies contacts whom the American should know. According to Justice, "You know you've arrived when people approach you with questions about business matters rather than requests for proofreading letters in English."

SENIOR-LEVEL MATCHING

The most important match-ups occur at the senior level. "When I return to America for another tour," said a sales executive in Osaka, "I will make sure I hire the best right-hand man I can find—even if I have to pay him double my own salary." The top-level American in the organization, according to the sales executive, should have extensive expertise and be able to advise on dealing with employees, customers, and lawyers and on how to negotiate with Americans. He need not speak Japanese—a criterion that calls into question all the efforts of those Japanized Americans described above.

Japanese senior managers need experts at their side because they are not experts. To become a general manager (a vice president or plant manager role) at Canon, a manager needs twenty-three years experience and must be at least thirty-eight years old.[11] No wealth of technical skill is as important as experience. "Senior Japanese executives need to have acquired a universal common sense," said a Nissho Iwai general manager. "That means the ability to give clear instructions, deal with heterogeneous people, and the ability to say yes or no—to be decisive." This executive had found these skills to be crucial in managing an important division in his firm's New York office. Few Americans realize that a well-entrenched, decisive Japanese senior manager is probably the most powerful executive they will ever encounter. In a 1987 study of eighty-eight firms, researchers looked at how Japanese companies change. They found that neither crises, attempts to restructure, nor a desire to manipulate corporate culture had as much influence on change as a turnover in top management.[12] One of the problems with senior Japanese in America, however, has been that often they are not well-entrenched and thus lack power to implement needed change. Since few other change mechanisms exist, the subsidiary tends not to adapt to the ever-shifting business environment in the United States. As we saw earlier, Japanese managers are a power-oriented group to begin with, and when their power is weak, they react in odd ways. Americans observing executives held in check by headquarters occasionally have watched them become either extremely passive or anxiety-ridden and abrasive.

A look at how these executives are evaluated gives us a sense of the pressures they face and the kind of support they need from top Americans. According to a study by Professor Takino Takanaga of Kibi International University, most Japanese overseas subsidiaries focus on long-run growth, relying on proven products rather than new technology. This makes good economic sense, since the risks of new products on top of foreign investment risks would be very high. What manufacturing subsidiary executives worry about are demand levels, actions of competitors, government decisions, and the value of the yen. They have not worried much about cost of capital, taxes, or labor costs. Revenue and profit generation are more of a burden than cost control, and performance is measured in terms of return on sales and loose adherence to constantly evolving budgets. Return on investment has not been used much, since capital costs have been so low, but this is likely to change in the 1990s. For now, top Japanese performers sell a lot of product, make at least a small profit, and keep in touch with Tokyo on budget issues. Rarely are Japanese budgets set in stone. They are constantly being discussed, and a communicative subsidiary manager is considered a good one. The American stereotype about Japanese seeking market share for its own sake is something of a myth. Growth is sought, but always with an eye to profit. As noted earlier, the profit need not be large, but sustained losses are not looked on favorably unless they have been anticipated in a plan—Japanese do not like unpleasant surprises.

The nature of the people at headquarters who evaluate subsidiary executives is nicely illustrated by the story of Toshihiko Yamashita's appointment as president of Matsushita.[13] In January 1977, he was called into the office of company founder Konosuke Matsushita.

"Board Chairman Aratoro Takahashi is resigning and my son-in-law, Masaharu, will take over his duties. I want you to become president," said the old man.

"I must respectfully decline," said Yamashita, following proper form. "I could not handle the job." Of course he obviously could handle the job. In fact he was brilliant at it when he did accept.

The ritual went on into the next day, when Yamashita turned down the job a second time. Then, according to the formula, he was deluged with calls and visits from executives urging him to accept. This all may sound like a kind of mating dance, but it is also a mechanism for building support, since not all of the top people wanted Yamashita in the job.

"Are you going to take the position?" asked Seiji Miyoshi, a former boss of Yamashita.

"It looks like I'll have to. I don't have any choice."

"If you become president, are you going to order me around?" asked Miyoshi. "If you do, I won't listen to you."

Miyoshi's commitment to seniority and rank is typical of conservative Japanese executives, who sometimes seem to value the preservation of hierarchies and control more than the effective functioning of the organization. These are the same men who make their hapless American subsidiary managers waste time in endless fax discussions with Tokyo. In any case, Yamashita went on with his dance, but he went on too long. Eventually the head of the union made an appointment to urge him to take the job. Yamashita was horrified. "I couldn't let it appear as if the union had persuaded me to accept the position." He quickly accepted.

Mr. Yamashita did a fine job in internationalizing his company, but his story gives us a hint of the tensions over status and power in the home office to which U.S. subsidiary executives must be attentive. American employees rarely are aware of these behind the scenes problems, and Japanese wonder if even Japanized Americans ever could get a grasp on them.

A 1989 JETRO survey of manufacturers revealed that 45 percent of Japanese firms would select top managers regardless of citizenship. Only 33 percent were dead set against Americans.[14] Richard Kraft is head of Matsushita's American operations, and Norman Petersen is chairman of several Fujitsu subsidiaries and a Fujitsu America board member.

Almost fifty Americans fill top spots at Fujitsu America. C. Itoh has an American executive vice president in New York who is a board member of the parent company, and Sony, Kyocera, and Toho Mutual Life all have slots for foreign directors. Normura securities put an American in charge of its American subsidiary in 1990 and gave him a seat on its board. What behavior can be expected of senior Americans which conflicts with that of Japanese executives? In a study of several hundred top managers, Jiro Nonaka of Hitotsubashi University and I found that while Japanese executives like to reach out into the whole organization for information, Americans depend on a select staff charged with feeding them data.[15] In other words, Japanese practice MWA (management by walking around); American seniors see that as an inefficient use of time. Moreover, Japanese like to talk about ideals which the firm should strive to attain, and they focus on identifying problems which must be solved. Americans talk about realistic goals involving taking advantage of opportunities.

When top-level Japanese come to America, they find it difficult to practice MWA and to talk about dreams and ideals. Language differences get in the way, as does a lack of trust that Americans will be responsive. If they expect their American executives to do the job for them, they will be disappointed. Top Americans do not get out of the office as much, and they usually do not see themselves as visionary leaders rallying the troops. These contrasts in management style and pervasive Japanese distrust have led to the "advisor" system in which most senior Americans are paired with senior Japanese. In many cases the relationship is vertical and the Americans simply take orders from the Japanese. This was the arrangement at Mazda's Flat Rock plant, and it led to the resignation or firing of most of the U.S. top management in 1989.

All too frequently, the advisor is a spy assigned to check up on the American and report to Tokyo. This demoralizing situation need not be, and several top Japanese have developed the "shadow" approach. In this the Japanese advisor gives no orders and does no spying. Instead, he acts as a protector who tells the American when headquarters is going to be troublesome and warns headquarters when to lay off. "I am in a position which assists the American president," noted a Japanese cement company shadow. "I am a window on Japan. The president doesn't know anything about headquarters, so he depends on me to inform him." The shadow runs interference so that barriers to effective action are not put up by Tokyo. Beyond being a defender and problem solver, he is a teacher who gradually socializes the American into the top ranks of the firm. Unfortunately, only a few Japanese advisors now exhibit these skills, but more will be coming along in the 1990s when many senior people with long U.S. experience retire. These executives, wise to the ways of the United States, will make excellent shadows posing as consultants to the subsidiaries. With high-value retirement yen in their pockets, they will look forward to yet another tour in the United States.

At both senior and mid-manager levels, in sum, a few firms are trying hard to match Japanese and Americans, some with formal training and selection procedures, others in an informal manner. Many Japanese companies do nothing at all and just hope for the best. Often Japanese managers sent to the United States for the first time have received little training in the business area to which they have been assigned and no training in American mores. However, their English is steadily improving. While a few Americans have sought to learn Japanese and to socialize themselves into Japanese corporate life, the lukewarm reception by subsidiary executives has been discouraging. Many Japanese do not like the idea of foreigners trying to Japanize themselves—yet another sign of how provincial and unsophisticated Japanese can be in the emerging global economy. A few big companies try to develop corporate rather than cultural values in their American managers—the object being to turn out Matsushita or Sharp managers rather than "Japanese" managers—but the status of Americans as subsidiary rather than core employees suggests that these efforts are not likely to have much impact. The biggest problem is developing senior American managers. About one-half of Japanese firms are willing to try, but many Japanese doubt that Americans can ever fill top slots in their companies. Mostly what the Japanese want from their top Americans is expertise in marketing, personnel, and regulatory issues under the careful scrutiny of advisors who pass on Tokyo's orders, many of which are designed to maintain power rather than to accomplish performance objectives. The well-developed teaching skills of experienced Japanese managers are put to good use in training Americans in a few cases, but only a few. All in all, things are not yet working out too well on the training and career development fronts.

THIRTEEN

Talking Is Not Down Time

Few things are more important in Japanese firms than communication. Where American managers see their work as actions involving thinking and doing, Japanese see it as talking. Americans often view communication as down time; Japanese view it as the essence of managing. Yet surveys reveal that communications with employees are the major problem for the Japanese in America.[1] What is going on? Who is to blame? Some sense of the difficulties involved in sorting things out can be gleaned from this mythical dialogue between a Japanese manager and a key American subordinate.

American: Sato is always engaging in endless rituals.

Japanese: Smith has such a flippant attitude. He needs to learn the proper way to do things.

American: Either Sato is droning on and on about nothing, or he clams up and I can't get anything out of him.

Japanese: I can't understand why Smith is always making such hasty judgments and wanting to act before thinking.

American: What a cold fish Sato is. He's so distant.

Japanese: Smith should realize that I'm a boss. He should respect my status. I can't be his chum.

American: He won't answer my questions.

Japanese: He pries into my private business.

American: He won't tell me what's going on.

Japanese: He is not supposed to know certain things.

American: He's covering up.

Japanese: We Japanese are a cautious, reserved people.

American: How can we work together?

Japanese: We all must develop harmony in our thoughts and actions.

American: If I'm going to contribute, I need to be able to say what I feel and let the chips fall where they may.

Is Sato cold and secretive, or is he simply formal and cautious? Is Smith flippant and rash, or is he dynamic and eager to contribute? Are communication problems the result of cultural differences which cannot be resolved? Are they due to bad managing by the Japanese or low quality American employees? We will see below that Japanese communication practices that work well in Japan do not work in the United States and that Japanese managers do not adapt to U.S. approaches, probably because of a lack of training and also their recognition that an Americanization of their managerial style would hurt them when they return to Japan. Better to blunder in America than to self-destruct at home.

THE WAY OF CERTAINTY

"The culture demands that everyone know the details," said an American executive in a Japanese firm.[2] It's true. The most remarkable characteristic of Japanese culture is a pervasive intolerance for uncertainty and ambiguity. In a society where a person is taught early on to be tentative, accommodating, and often vague in speech, everyone is driven to distraction trying to figure out what is going on.[3] The Japanese hate the unexpected and will move heaven and earth to make sure that change is planned rather than random or forced. Uncertainty is so awful that in extreme cases they will refuse to admit its existence. I once asked a group of Japanese public accountants to evaluate the financial data for a group of companies and to express their level of confidence in each rating. No matter how muddled the data, the accountants were supremely confident in their evaluations. In a corporation Japanese managers constantly "walk the halls," working all possible informal channels to pick up the detailed information which reduces their uncertainty-induced anxiety. This is necessary since the firm rarely will have extensive formal rules, policies, and procedures written down, and information systems tend to be weak. Only someone who builds horizontal relationships focused on trading information is likely to know what is happening. Americans are terrible at this, viewing managers on the same level as competitors rather than information sources. The problem for Japanese is that when they come to America, they no longer have other Japanese managers available to barter information. At one time almost all managerial slots in Japanese-owned firms were filled with Japanese. Under pressure, the firms have had to hire Americans, most of whom are not used to trading information and depend instead on elaborate computer systems.

One byproduct of walking the halls is that managers develop broad and sometimes even deep knowledge. This creates an environment in which experts are not as important as they are in America. A manager who has picked up some knowledge of contract law may be assigned to head up the legal department, while (as I have seen) one who likes to talk will be made chief of telecommunications. Naturally, specialists are always available for advice, but they are usually in a different employment category and not paid as well as general managers. The American reliance on expert managers is foreign to the Japanese. Indeed, although Japanese managers desperately seek out expert advice from Americans, the fact of expertise labels the Americans as lower ranked. One can imagine the problems which result when Americans, thinking they are raising their status by displays of arcane knowledge, actually lower it in the eyes of Japanese. Another difficulty is that when crises crop up, Japanese value fast, flexible responses (they do tend to be slow in non-crisis situations), yet experts are in the business of developing carefully considered, optimal responses. Not only will American experts be labeled as lower status, but they also will be seen as uncommunicative when needed. The Japanese in America certainly need experts, but they don't like them.

According to Makoto Kikuchi, Director of Sony's Research Center, American research experts build walls to break up the flow of information. "Let us say an American has four people on his staff—A, B, C, and D. As the group leader, he will speak one-on-one with A, B, C, and D, discussing their work and offering suggestions. But he will not explain the work A is doing to either B, C, or D. His reason is that there is no need to do so."[4] In a Japanese research group this will not do. Everyone wants to know what everyone else is doing. "In Japanese society," notes Kikuchi, "everybody feels that they share the same fate, that they and their fellows are all in the same boat, and there are times when this is extremely important to the overall working of a group." A Japan Agricultural Council official echoed Kikuchi. "When an American finds a certain thing he wants to accomplish, he tries to find the quickest, shortest, fastest way to accomplishment. After he sets out the direction, he just goes. The Japanese goes over here and discusses things with some people. Then he goes over there and talks to some other people. He never goes straight down the path to his goal. The American way is to find the most efficient way. The Japanese way is to make sure everyone understands."

The urge for certainty and understanding leads to some of the special characteristics of Japanese manufacturing management and office work. In the factory information is moved as close as possible to the people it affects. Quality charts are not kept in an executive's office on the fortieth floor. They are on the bulletin board near the production line. By the same token, *kanban* cards attached to parts carry a series of messages: where the part came from, what is to be done with it, what must happen when it is used up. Workers are never in the dark about what's happening. If they were mystified, they would demand to be enlightened. While Americans welcome this kind of information, it is not with the same fervor as Japanese. Americans tolerate uncertainty better; they can function in an environment where incomplete data exist. Japanese cannot. The Americans' strength comes out in those settings where action must occur in an uncertain environment; in an assembly factory where success requires a constant attention to minute data, Japanese do better. Indeed, in Japanese factories the rule of data is so complete that it mutes the impact of personalities, rhetoric, or plant politics. No bright young genius can come up with a great idea unless he or she has data. No supervisor can gain clout with a forceful manner without numbers. Since data collection is slow and the effect of personality can be fast, routine change in a Japanese setting can be glacial. Japanese managers recognize this problem and cope with it by planning for change ahead of time. Data are collected early in the design and engineering process on the kinds of flexibility needed in the assembly process. Then they are built into the system. What really throws the Japanese for a loop is unexpected change, the kind where no data exist. They often do not know what to do. In the more fluid economic environment of the United States, this difficulty crops up more than the Japanese are used to. If they trusted their American managers, who are comfortable with the uncertain, they would cope better.

In the typical Japanese office desks and chairs are grey, and they are usually lined up in two islands, each island consisting of two rows of desks pushed together facing each other. The boss sits at the end of the islands where he can watch his employees and share information with them. Few computers will be present, and data are collected on the telephone and in short, frequent oral communications. What is striking to an American is the absence of memos. "I like to speak directly with people," says Tetsuo Chino of Honda. "I don't believe in communicating on paper when there's an opportunity to talk in person."[5] Some observers see the tendency of Japanese managers to avoid writing as due to the difficulties of their complex writing system. A better explanation is that of a New Japan Securities manager. "I don't like to be pinned down. When something is in writing, it's hard to change later on." Face to face communicating reduces uncertainty, and it allows the manager to adapt his statements more easily to the current situation. Americans believe that what a person wrote five years ago is what he must be held to today. Japanese believe that they must adhere to the obligations of a current relationship. Words are only important to the extent that they serve the relationship. This does not mean that Japanese are casual liars—they are neither more nor less so than Americans. All it means is that what they say today is for today's conditions. They should not be held to it tomorrow. If you want to know what they believe tomorrow, you should ask then. This is exactly what Japanese do with each other, and it is another reason for the open offices and the constant chatter.

When a Matsushita personnel manager arrived in the United States in 1983, he was bewildered by the American practice of memo writing. "When we have a question or need to discuss something in Japan," he said, "we meet in someone's office. In the United States people write memos and that's it. When I first encountered memos, I couldn't handle them well. Americans want a quick response, but I couldn't do that." It is considered impolite for subordinates to fire off memos to their Japanese bosses. "The employee *must* come to the boss's office. That is required in Japanese management." This practice is completely opposite from American customs. In fact, the Matsushita manager was amazed at how useful memos could be. "They are very productive," he admitted. "They save a lot of time." This man, an experienced executive, was surprised to find out that writing is useful, and his surprise tells us just how different some Japanese practices can be from American.

So far, we have seen that the Japanese way of certainty involves an almost feverish pursuit of data and a sharing of information. Experts are shunned sometimes and memos are too slow for managers rushing about learning everything and trading what they have learned for new information. These communication practices are strange to Americans, but there are yet others which are equally bewildering.

As we saw in an earlier chapter, Americans are role-oriented in their work—if one is a machinist, that is what he does and nothing else. But when it comes to talking, an American employee is task-oriented. He wants to achieve his goal by getting to the point right away. Japanese are just the opposite. They don't worry about work roles and do whatever job is required. But their conversation may go on and on, seemingly never getting anywhere, but signaling who they are. Japanese managers will be dissatisfied with the "I only do machinist work" attitude of Americans, but Americans will criticize the apparently goalless wandering of a Japanese manager's speech as he uses words to illuminate his role as authority person, mentor, teacher, or protector.

All of these roles emerge out of the power focus that is the chief element in Japanese managerial behavior. Communicating to establish an authority role, for example, is common in older, conservative managers. "Among traditional upper echelons of Japanese management," says a Nissho Iwai executive, "bosses hand down directives and without discussion subordinates carry out the orders." That authority role is now being challenged. "Today, if a young (Japanese) staff person has the opposite opinion—believe me—there will be a discussion." With all this pressure for more consensus-style decision making, worried senior Japanese in America may be even more eager to communicate their authority role to American subordinates. On the other hand, younger Japanese bosses may be moving towards a participative approach in which their conversation invites dialogue and advice. Whatever the case, Japanese managers' role-legitimizing conversation often will seem not to be task-oriented to Americans.

Still another difference involves error. If something goes wrong, Americans believe it is only fair to find out why and to assign blame. Japanese do not do this. They seek to explain errors, but they assign blame to the entire work group (although the individual culprit will not be forgotten). Punishment may be avoided if the group leader or the erring employee writes a letter of apology to higher ups. The worst thing he can do is concoct a story excusing the error. What Japanese seek is *reconciliation* so that life can go on. They are not interested in endless "who struck John" investigations. An employee who refuses to reconcile may be transferred to a dead end job (writing the company history in a basement office is a favorite at some firms) or cut out of information flows so he does not know what is going on—the ultimate penalty for a Japanese. "American employees are very concerned about trying to protect themselves. They make lots of excuses when things go wrong," said the Nissho Iwai executive, a note of distaste in his mouth. "I try to communicate so they don't have to make excuses." What he wants is to control the future, not explain the past. In *kaizen* managing, reasons why errors occurred are crucial to improving future production, but this information is not used to punish people unless the fault is very large. Understandably, Japanese see their reconciliation approach as superior and want Americans to develop the same attitude. It is a hard sell.

We now come to the use of slogans. Although American companies are forever posting safety messages on every bulletin board, no one takes them seriously. Such is not the case among Japanese. At Matsushita each year the president creates the firm's annual slogan. In 1990 it was "Breakthrough," the first ever in English. "It was a way of saying the old Matsushita now wants to change into a global company," said Dick Kraft, head of MECA, Matsushita's American subsidiary. Every division head was asked to consult employees and to write a letter to the chairman describing the one breakthrough it would strive for in 1990. At the Overseas Training Center introductory courses include lectures on the slogans that embody the business principles of Matsushita ("service through industry," "fairness," etc.). Students listen to translations of the values-oriented speeches of the company founder, and then corporate executives show trainees how the principles embodied in the slogans are carried out day to day. "It's a program to inform people so they'll be sensitive," says Dick Kraft. "It isn't designed to convert them to anything."

Slogans bring the power of language to bear in service to performance. They have three functions. First, the slogan-creating process—Matsushita employees are asked to come up with monthly slogans for their local operations—compels everyone to step back and look at the company's purposes and processes. Highly specialized technical people, for example, must ask themselves what is going on beyond their little nuts and bolts world. Second, the slogans are rhetorical tools. They do not so much create positive attitudes as foster mental models which guide thinking. "Breakthrough" got people thinking globally, for instance. Third, slogans are a control mechanism; employees constantly exposed to them are primed to be compliant by managers imparting the slogans or requiring their repetition at morning meetings. Do American employees respond to slogans with broader thinking and improved compliance? Probably not, although certainly Matsushita has tried its best, even offering monetary rewards for the best monthly slogan in some plants. Americans distrust rhetoric and the people who use it, no matter how sensibly. The Japanese use of slogans is a good idea that does not work in the United States.

Finally, the Japanese way requires long hours of after-work communication. What do they talk about? A Fuji Bank manager, echoing many interviewees, distinguishes between older and younger managers. "When the middle-aged people go to a bar, 80 percent of the conversation is office rumors about the women or complaints about the bosses. Younger managers are different. They talk of food, clothing, and hobbies." Former Matsushita president Yamashita says, "The average Japanese corporate employee talks about his job, business conditions, and golf." If you are a Japanese manager, you may leave the office, but the office never leaves you. One reason for this is that Japanese managers do not really know enough about anything else to talk about it. They learned very little in college, having loafed after gaining admission, and what is required of them at work are long hours leaving little time for reading or recreation. "I fear many Japanese have little interest in the finer things of life," comments Mr. Yamashita sadly. A second reason is the need to reduce uncertainty. After-work drinking bouts reduce tension and loosen lips sealed during the day. The manager learns who is in, who is out, and what clique has the upper hand. Moreover, under the guise of feigned drunkenness, a subordinate can offer useful criticism to his boss and receive tough talk in return about his own performance. Americans are out of place at these sessions, because they do not have the same pressing need to reduce uncertainty and often have life interests beyond the workplace. But they ought to become more involved in them if they want to make it in a Japanese-owned firm. During social hours the Japanese way of certainty comes into its own, and the way the world really is becomes clear.

COMMUNICATION BREAKDOWN IN THE UNITED STATES?

Japanese communication practices are excellent—in Japan. Just how inappropriate they are in America has emerged in a number of research studies and interviews. Both Japanese and Americans feel that something like a communication breakdown is occurring. The research lets us know what is going wrong and what we can and cannot do about it.

The Language Curse

Americans rarely speak Japanese, but even when they do they run into problems. "My manager and I don't get along at all," noted a woman bond trader in New York. "Recently he told me, 'Don't speak to me in Japanese. It's rude.' " She found that while her direct way of speech was endurable in English, the boss could not tolerate it in Japanese. In many interviews it became clear that some Japanese managers do not want Americans to learn Japanese. The *tatemae* explanation of this, coming right out of the *nihonjinron* song-and-dance book, is that Japanese is a "language of the infinite" which cannot be used well by those not born to it. This is rubbish. Although social norms require vague, indirect speech at times, the language itself allows complete clarity if that is what one wants, and it is not hard to learn to speak it. Take the example of the sign in the shop window which says, "*Honjitsu wa yasumasite itadakimas.*" Literally, this says, "as for today resting I am humbly receiving." It is a polite way of saying, "Give me a break. I need a day off," and is not difficult for a non-Japanese to grasp. Yet this and similar phrases are often used as examples of how impossible Japanese is for outsiders. Not so. In fact, the Japanese language would make a fine world language in place of English. The grammar and syntax are easier because exceptions to rules are fewer than in English.

Japanese managers occasionally will hold meetings in English with all staff. Then the Americans are excused so the Japanese can meet by themselves to talk in Japanese. "You wonder what they're talking about," said a securities firm employee. A Japanese manager in the same firm answered, "We discuss global policy issues sent from Tokyo. Subsidiary employees are not told these." In this firm one of the subsidiary employees, however, was a Japanese national hired in New York. She was included in the meetings. Obviously, being Japanese and knowing the language was the entry ticket, not being parent company staff.

Most Japanese managers are more sensible and less ethnocentric in their attitudes to the language issue. "Our communication is done in Japanese by telex with the parent," said a trading company branch manager in Seattle. "We cannot hire an American who cannot read Japanese." Such people have been hard to find, so the company is weighing a big decision. "We may begin communicating more in English. Our textiles managers abroad are now communicating on our network about 60 percent of the time in English, but their telexes to Japan are still in Japanese." Soon everything may be in English. It would be nice, say Japanese executives, if Americans learned Japanese, but it is not going to happen, particularly when a few managers like the idea of having their own secret code which Americans cannot understand. The language curse, it seems, is going to be lifted by shifting to English. This is rather a sad development for those of us who have learned some Japanese. It is an enriching experience, and more Americans should have made the effort.

Bypassing

When Jane Brady arrived at the plant that morning, her new boss, Mr. Sato, looked worried. He had only recently arrived in the United States on his first tour of duty outside of Japan. His English was good, however, and his superiors were confident that he could handle the job.[6]

"Why so glum, Mr. Sato?" asked Jane, as she seated herself across from him in his office for their morning conference.

"Last night I received a telex from Tokyo," he replied. "Here, take a look."

She reached across the desk and took the paper. The message was short and assertive, just like all the others she had seen in her two years working for Tegami America, a firm organized to supply the Japanese parent with printing machinery for its giant publishing business in Japan.

YOU MUST NOT LET INVENTORY BUILD UP. YOU MUST MONITOR CAR-RYING COSTS AND KEEP THEM UNDER CONTROL. SHIP ANY JOB LOTS OF MORE THAN 25 UNITS TO US AT ONCE.

As she read the letter she nodded. "This is no problem, Sato-san. I can get right on it."

"How many lots do we have to ship? I want to get them out of here right away."

Jane consulted a printout in the manila file folder she had with her. "No problem. We've only got three lots. I'll start the paperwork and get everything moving today. They'll be on the ship in Portland within two weeks."

Mr. Sato smiled weakly. He liked Americans, but he had been told that they were generally not as trustworthy as Japanese. It was not that they were bad people. It was just that they saw everything as a deal or an arrangement—you do this for me and I'll do this for you. They didn't do things simply because they were sincere. Miss Brady, however, seemed different. She always did the job, and he didn't have to spell everything out for her. All he needed to do was give her a general goal and she took care of the rest. He relaxed, turning his attention to the important trip to New York he would soon undertake.

Six weeks later Jane was at the other end of the plant when the summons came. She hurried to Sato's office. He sat behind his desk, his face a mask. She knew something was wrong.

"I thought you were a good person, Miss Brady," he said sadly. "This is very bad." He handed her a telex.

WHY DIDN'T YOU DO WHAT WE TOLD YOU? YOUR QUARTERLY IN-VENTORY REPORT INDICATES YOU ARE CARRYING 40 LOTS WHICH YOU WERE SUPPOSED TO SHIP TO JAPAN. YOU MUST NOT VIOLATE OUR INSTRUCTIONS.

Jane could not believe what she was reading. "Sir, I shipped every lot more than twenty-five. Those were my orders and I carried them out."

Mr. Sato grabbed the telex out of her hand. "What about this? This doesn't lie," he shouted. "I checked this morning. We have forty lots of more than twenty-five units each."

"That's not so. We don't."

"We do!"

"No we don't!"

They stared at each other. Finally Jane said softly, "Please, let's go and look."

Sato got up silently, and Jane followed him out of the office. In the warehouse they began with the first lot. Both of them counted. There were twenty-five units in the lot.

"Miss Brady, why didn't you ship this lot as you were told to do?"

Her eyes widened. She felt herself losing control. Before answering she breathed deeply. "Tokyo's instructions referred to lots of more than twenty-five. Is that correct?"

"Yes, exactly."

"Well, this lot only has twenty-five. In fact, many of the lots are like this one. They have twenty-five units."

"But you should have shipped them," he said, his voice tightening. "You should ship anything that's twenty-five, twenty-six, twenty-seven and so forth."

"What? Since when does 'more than twenty-five' include twenty-five?"

His face became twisted in a look of withering scorn. "More than twenty-five always includes twenty-five. It's simple enough. Once again, your American education system has let you down."

"How dare you! Why don't you take the trouble to learn English if you are going to work in this country?"

They stared at each other. Sato sighed. "I think we need to have a long talk, Miss Brady." She nodded.

Mr. Sato and Miss Brady are not bad managers. They do not really have serious problems with communicating in English. And they do not have debilitating personality differences. Yet in their "long talk" that's what will be discussed. What's really gone wrong for them is that they have *bypassed* each other. Bypassing occurs when people miss each other with their meanings. They use the same words but attribute different meanings to them. When a Japanese colleague of the author was an MBA candidate at an American university, he was penalized by an American professor over the "more than 25" bypassing problem. The professor could not accept the fact that in Japan "more than X" very often includes X. He was a bit like the British philosopher in the Middle Ages who could not understand why the French persisted in saying *chien* when everyone knew the word was *dog*. Bypassing is a serious problem in managerial communications, and in the emerging era of globalism everyone must be attentive to it. When my Japanese friend was doing some business with an American firm a few years ago, he tried to head off bypassing problems by asking for their definitions of key terms which would be used in their trade correspondence. For *delivery* the American CEO replied, "I take this to mean delivery to the store. So if I promise a September delivery, it means I will deliver products to the customer's store in September." For a Japanese trader this is not what delivery means. To him it refers to the shipment of the goods on board a vessel. Several serious problems were resolved because of this clarification. When even the hint of misunderstanding exists, Japanese or Americans should define words for each other.

Argument

If as an American I say that people argue all the time, most Americans would agree. But many Japanese might find the assertion difficult to accept. The problem is that Americans assign a much wider range of behaviors to the concept of *argument* than Japanese do.

In a Japanese subsidiary where English is the language used, an American has a discussion with a Japanese colleague. Both express differing views about an issue, and they part without any resolution to the disagreement. In casual conversation later on, the American might say, "My Japanese colleague and I had an argument about inventory levels." His Japanese colleague would not use such a word and might be quite upset to hear that the American had used it.

To a Japanese, an "argument" is not simply a mutual sharing of views leading to a disagreement. It is a break in the harmonious relationships among people and a threat to the communal nature of the organization. As such, argument is intolerable and to be avoided at all costs. Indeed, it appears that many Japanese who have argued with other Japanese simply stop communicating with each other. Their harmonious relationship has been broken, and to attempt to patch it up would be to admit that a flaw has appeared in the social fabric of the community. Silence is preferable to such an admission.

Americans, on the other hand, view the concept of "argument" as encompassing everything from minor disagreements to serious conflict. But even when defining an argument as a serious conflict, Americans will not view the conflict as so intolerable as to be avoided or muted at all costs.

American-Japanese differences about what constitutes an argument reveal something about how each party copes with conflict. Americans in conflict will often work to establish mutual equality. They will try to come down (or up) to the level of the other guy. They sense that if they respond to each other as equals, conflict can be dealt with. Even if the conflict is not resolved, at least their personal relationship will be one of mutual and satisfying equality. Such a relationship is viewed as a basis for coping with future conflict.

Japanese in conflict often will work to establish mutual inequality. They will retreat into the formality of a vertical relationship, if possible.

Even if the current conflict cannot be resolved, the vertical relationship guarantees that future conflict can be muted through the exercise of decision making by the senior person and of subordination by the junior.

We can construct a scenario of an American and a Japanese working together. A dispute arises, and both parties meet to resolve it. The American cites rules and procedures as evidence for his position. The Japanese talks about the need to create a consensus. The American allows himself to become excited, but before any serious anger occurs the Japanese claims a prior commitment and excuses himself. They agree to meet for dinner to discuss the matter further.

At dinner the American is pleasantly friendly. He talks about "us all being in the same boat together" and the need to "march arm-in-arm together." He reveals personal details of his life which he would only talk about with friends. The Japanese is delighted at the opportunity to become friendly and to dampen the disagreement before it can be an argument. But he talks about how headquarters wants very much to do the right thing and how he will collect all the American's opinions and transmit them to the home office for a decision. He knows that he will be able to communicate a decision to the American which will be the proper one. He urges the American to come to him at any time when he has a problem. "We must confer with each other," he says.

They finish their dinner and leave. The American is happy that their "argument," while not yet resolved, led him to become friendly with his Japanese colleague. He sincerely feels that they can look at each other "eye to eye, man to man" in the future. The Japanese is happy that an "argument" was avoided. Their disagreement, while not resolved, led them to identify the senior (Japanese)-junior (American) relationship in which they should exist. Now that the relationship is clear, it should govern how disagreements will be resolved in the future—before arguments occur.

We can see that both the American and Japanese think they have been successful in coping with conflict. The American "let it all hang out, cleared the air," and established a working relationship based on mutual equality. At least that is what he believes. The Japanese kept the disagreement from threatening harmony and established a vertical relationship which will guarantee that harmony will be maintained in the future. At least that is what he believes.

What are we to make of all this? How long can both parties go on with different perspectives about arguments and conflict? My guess is that they can go on for a long time. The American's desire to use friendliness to resolve conflict (if citing rules and procedures does not have any effect) will be valued by the Japanese. And the Japanese person's desire to "keep a lid on" things and to proceed in a systematic fashion will be valued by the American (although he may think of the Japanese as "slow"). When really serious conflict arises, however, and the Japanese strongly invokes the vertical relationship, the American will feel that their friendly, equal relationship has been betrayed. He may become angry. The Japanese may react with total silence. Their relationship will be at an end.

COMPLIANCE-GAINING WITH KEY SUBORDINATES AND THE ROOTS OF ARROGANCE

The language problem can be solved by using English. Bypassing can be avoided by defining terms. Argument can be muted by Americans learning to be less vigorous in their disagreeing. What about the day to day communication of Japanese managers as they tell key American subordinates what they want done? This kind of talk is referred to as compliance-gaining, and it is the key to mobilizing people to accomplish goals.[7] When American managers direct key subordinates, they rarely use a "Do this, do that," order-giving approach. Instead they rely on reasoning and friendliness. This involves stating what needs to be done and then backing up the request with explanatory facts and statements about the positive benefits of the desired action. This rhetoric is delivered in a pleasant manner designed to convince the subordinate that the boss is a friend as well as a supervisor. Key subordinates are so important to the boss's success that it pays to be nice to them.

In Japan, managers, who have a good deal more power over employees, do not need to be so friendly. They usually provide some reasons (not as much as Americans) for their directions, but the friendliness is replaced by an assertive tone. They deliver orders in a forceful, demanding manner, often setting deadlines for compliance. Less frequently, they use "do it for the sake of the company" loyalty appeals. When they come to America, do they adapt a local style and replace the assertiveness with friendliness? They do not. Not only do they retain their forceful style, they also still use loyalty appeals, which must seem bizarre to American employees. Not all Japanese talk like this, but enough do to raise the issue of "arrogance." Dick Kraft of Matsushita admits that some managers carry their Japanese habits to America. "In Japan you treat your employees like children. You lecture them. You scold them. You never pat them on the back and thank them for a good job unless you are drinking heavily with them late at night," he says. NUMMI executive Mikio Kitano also sees room for improvement. "The most important thing is communication," he says.

"How to explain, how to send a message. Sometimes we are not so careful about perceptions, how it will be accepted."[8]

Does the rough tone turn friendly as Japanese spend a few years in America and learn to sound more friendly? It does not. Both the newly arrived and the old hands tend to use the same kinds of compliance-gaining tactics with key American subordinates. Little wonder the Japanese worry about turnover. One reason why they do not change their communication habits is an unwillingness to give up the language markers which signal and even legitimize their power. A related reason is the habit of using abrupt speech with subordinates with whom one has a *good* relationship. It works this way. A manager in Japan hands his new secretary something to copy. He says, "*Warui, utsusu,*" which literally means "Bad, make a copy." He means, "I feel bad about bothering you, but please copy this." This shorthand way of speaking becomes even more clipped when he develops a friendly relationship with her. Then he will simply say "Copy" and nothing else. The secretary is not offended, since his curt remark signals closeness, not distance (but closeness, of course, in a vertical, power relationship). In America, however, his abrupt tone is unacceptable, and he may be labelled as arrogant. Indeed, the closer he feels he is getting to his employees, the more shorthand will be his speech and the more arrogant he will seem to Americans. Some Japanese are truly arrogant and overly assertive as they let employees know who is in charge, but many of them are simply blundering. They talk the way a caring manager talks in Japan and end up creating bad feelings among Americans. If Japanese received better training before coming to the United States, these communication errors could be avoided or at least reduced.

DOING IT THE RIGHT WAY

The Japanese do not have far to go to get it right. They already believe that communication is not down time, which is an advance over the thinking of many American managers. A trading company manager has learned that he must treat Americans somewhat differently. "I give feedback very softly, in just a few words," he says. "In comparison with my Japanese subordinates I give more feedback to Americans." Americans are more tolerant of uncertainty than Japanese are, but even Americans are uncomfortable with the close-mouthed stonewalling they encounter with many managers. Honda America combats this by encouraging *waigaya* (chattering) meetings in which everyone gets a chance to freely express his or her ideas and to share important information with the group. At other firms frequent social events are held to build communication channels. The important thing is to get more communicating going on between Japanese and Americans. If they talk more, the problems of bypassing, arguing, and arrogance will be troubling at first. But over time they will be dealt with. A Fuji Bank official who has learned from his years in America says, "I don't think it's hard for me now to communicate with Americans. It's harder to talk with mainland Chinese and Koreans, even though we are all orientals."

Other techniques exist for increasing communication. One important tool in large Japanese companies is the house organ.[9] Typically in America these newsletters and magazines are designed to communicate the corporation's message to employees. In other words, they are propaganda machines at best. At worst they are trivial summaries of retirements and softball team scores. In Japan this is not the case. The house organ is a creature of the labor-management communication system. It tells employees about management's policies and provides information on operations and the economic climate. Since many employees are permanent, they have a deep interest in getting a picture on where the company has been and where it is going. Management wants to keep them informed, and usually assigns high quality middle managers to do the house organ. A posting of this kind is considered an important task. One of the first house organs in Japan, *Iron*, in the firm which is now Nippon Steel, began appearing in 1913. Its first issue discussed ways in which employees could use the personnel office and how the workers' cooperative was organized. The main article, however, gives us a sense today of how far Japan has come. It is entitled, "How to Prevent Cholera." Another steel firm house organ, *Friends of Steel*, was designed to reduce labor-management feuding by stressing friendliness, harmony, and unity. In the 1990s the leading topics are management policy, mutual understanding in the workplace, and quality control discussions. A survey conducted by the Japan Federation of Employers' Associations revealed that house organs are quite successful in building awareness and acceptance of company policies. As Japanese firms like Honda and Toyota develop in America, they may use house organs in a more productive manner than U.S. firms do, and this could improve communication. It is certainly worth a try.

Still another approach involves letting Americans come up with ways to foster good communication. In 1990 a group of twenty-five Americans working for Japanese-owned firms in and around Palo Alto formed the Kaisha Society of Silicon Valley (*kaisha* means corporation). Their goal is to promote learning and information exchange among Japanese and American employees. It was no accident that their first meeting focused on ways to improve communications and that the founding managers work for Mitsubishi Electric, which has been trying hard to do it right in America. The firm has begun hiring male and female Americans right out of college and assigning them to Japan for seasoning as headquarters employees. Its goal is to Americanize its U.S. subsidiaries. Once these people take up duties back in the states, they will act as a stimulus to improved communication between Japanese and Americans. Other Japanese firms have been more reluctant than Mitsubishi to admit that a problem exists, but they will have to take action eventually if they want to succeed in America.

The extensive set of communication skills of Japanese managers does not help them much in the United States, yet their communication weaknesses hurt them. Look at their skills. They are excellent at collecting information. Managers are especially good at horizontal data trading with other managers. They emphasize high-quality face to face, hands on discourse. They work hard to mute conflict and focus on reconciliation rather than blame when groups make mistakes. They like to use rhetoric to create a vision of what the organization is and does. They learn English and usually do not ask employees to learn their language. They want very much to build close communicative relationships with employees. But in America information is collected through systems and doled out by experts. Memos are crucial to managing. Conflict is often encouraged as a stimulus to creativity and progress. Rhetoric is distrusted. People who speak English in an abrupt, clipped manner are thought rude. And employees don't like work relationships to be as intimate as non-work relations. The poor Japanese simply cannot win. Better training would help, but even trained managers do not like to change their Japanese ways. After all, they must spend most of their careers in Japan.

At the least, the severe communication problem between Japanese and Americans could be softened a bit. One thing the Japanese could do is ease up on *tatemae*—the "tell them what they want to hear" approach. Workers hired at Mazda's Flat Rock and Toyota's NUMMI plants, for instance, were told they were joining some sort of warm, communal environment. The harsh reality of a highly controlled assembly operation was a shock for inexperienced young Americans. Better to tell people what to expect than to put a gloss on things. The emphasis on slogans in some subsidiaries probably should be dropped. It is a good idea, but Americans will not buy into it. Japanese also should expand their discourse, stressing explanation and payoffs more to employees. Above all, frequency of communication needs to be increased. Japanese managers do not have enough dialogue with employees, vendors, or American customers. Indeed, the lack of profitability of Japanese firms in the United States may be tied to communication problems. Success will not come until those problems are solved.

FOURTEEN

Decision Making as an End in Itself

"I find a lot of problems," said a Japanese bond trader in New York. "The people at headquarters don't understand American ways. They complain to us." In Tokyo decisions are made at large meetings where senior department heads discuss things at great length. "Here in New York, trading and operating managers at American firms make decisions on their own. But if I make an important decision by myself, Tokyo says, 'why didn't you consult us?' " This refrain is repeated endlessly by Japanese managers throughout the United States. One even hears it in Japan from people uninfluenced by American practices. Could it be that the supposedly cultural value of consensus decision making is not quite what it seems? No and yes. Getting things worked out in groups is very Japanese, but Americans define "consensus" differently from Japanese. In America it signals participation, discourse, persuasion, and the weight of argument. In Japan it means letting everyone in on what has already been decided so that they all get a chance to express obeisance to the bosses. The longer and more frequent the meetings, the greater the homage. Granted, this is not the case at every Japanese firm, but it is pervasive. Japanese corporate culture involves power maintenance and hierarchy, not equality and freedom of expression. In Japanspeak consensus is a form of control, like so many of the managerial techniques we have examined so far. Thus, consensual decision making is an end in itself. It exists to further legitimize the power of power holders. There is nothing particularly sinister in this, since a control style of managing is often workable and attractive to many employees. But lots of Japanese managers on the receiving end resent it. Americans are outraged.

JAPANESE DECIDE

Dennis Pawley resigned as Mazda's top American manager at its Flat Rock plant in 1988. His reason: he had no real authority. Decisions were made by the Japanese "advisors," and American executives were supposed to carry them out after ritual meetings to establish "consensus."[1] Pawley's replacement and many senior executives also eventually left, replaced by Japanese. Even at the worker level decision making by Americans was not allowed. American unit leaders at Mazda are salaried, nonunion people who give orders, cajole, threaten, whine and do whatever it takes to carry out Japanese directives—all under a veneer of team spirit, pushing decisions down to lower levels, and consensus. Similar practices have been reported at NUMMI.

A few years ago several top-ranked Americans resigned from NEC Electronics in California, citing "dictatorial and arrogant" interference by Tokyo headquarters.[2] The seeming arrogance may have been due to the language problems described in the last chapter, but the dictatorial approach was probably no more nor less than that experienced by mid-level managers in Japan. As the Japanese have blundered in America, however, they are learning what works and what does not. Two solutions to their problem have been undertaken. The first is to hire more submissive Americans. Firms that employ batteries of tests and extensive interviews with potential employees often are looking for compliant personalities rather than specific skills. The second is simply to establish a genuine consensus approach. "When I first went to our Memphis plant in 1985," said a Sharp staff manager in 1990, "I was in charge of the monthly managers' meeting. At that time we did not show Americans profit and loss statements. But that is changed now, and this information is shared. So now Americans take part in big decisions." This was not such a big step for Sharp, since it is a well-run firm and prudent managing would require consensus. But the fact that in 1985 the Japanese managers never thought to do it suggests just how foreign the idea of participative decision making was to them.

GETTING ON BOARD

The vision of Japanese management prevalent in the popular press is that of a group of orientals sitting around a table, each exquisitely sensitive to the others' ideas and opinions and all energetic in their efforts to reach a communal decision. While Japanese are group-oriented and do try to share information, theirs is still a highly vertical society in which the boss is very much the boss. "I don't know where this writing on group decision making comes from," said a Japanese manager turned teacher. "My boss simply told us what to do and we

obeyed." Americans have noted that vertical authority is more powerful than horizontal groupism. "There is less consensus here than in a
typical American firm," said one U.S. employee. Another noted, "The
Japanese CEO . . . is not a good listener, nor does he want an open
and free discussion."[3]

If the Japanese manager does not know what to do, the decision
process may look like the participation model described in textbooks.
But when he has already decided, the group meetings will look rather
strange to American eyes. The textbook approach requires a rational,
integrated discussion of problems, solution options, data bearing on
each option, and possible costs and benefits. The decision emerges as
the result of the method, not the will of any one person. This is not
what the Japanese manager wants, since he has already chosen the
path to take. Often he will simply inform the group, ask for advice,
and implicitly demand acceptance. But sometimes he will sit silently,
encouraging discussion. Of course, the subordinates already know from
"no surprises" informal discussions what has been decided, but they
will go through the ritual of discourse to create the appearance of debate leading to the same decision. The process makes the will of the
boss look like a rational, calculated act. Most of the time it *is* rational
and calculated, but the group meeting validates everything in a way
which maintains his power to carry out his will. This process can work
well when the boss is intelligent and experienced and when subordinates do not mind ritual meetings to give everyone a chance to get on
board.

Now assign the boss to the American subsidiary. He knows virtually
nothing about the environment, and his American managers are unfamiliar with Japanese decision processes. He can institute the textbook
model, which he knows and which Americans like. This happens frequently. But at times Japanese managers resort to the unilateral deci-
sion-ritual meeting approach. Americans hate this and resist.

In the parent firm in Tokyo a new boss is not usually an expert, and
all employees quietly help him to avoid poor decisions so that choices
he seemingly makes alone are not really unilateral. The Japanese practice of training generalists requires this subtlety. Managers in America,
however, are supposed to possess expertise, and employees are much
less active in offering gentle, informal guidance. The new Japanese
manager in the United States is left on his own, dumped into a job
about which he knows nothing with an American staff awaiting his
expert ideas so they can debate them in meetings. Some Japanese react
by asking for help and getting it—Americans, after all, are the world
champions at responding to pleas for aid. Others simply make unilateral decisions and adopt a veneer of arrogance to cover up their anxiety. When Americans do not adopt a submissive pose at the ritual

meeting, they are told in so many words that this is a Japanese company and don't you forget it.

Americans can become quite arrogant when they think they know it all, while Japanese strike the same pose when they fear they do not. Since American employees are hired for their knowledge and Japanese are often assigned to America without having a clue, two sets of very arrogant people can collide. What is needed is a wise senior executive, American or Japanese, who has seen it all before. He can take the parties aside, tell them how they appear to each other, and ask them to cool it. Better decision making, then, is the result of a senior executive who can turn the newly arrived Japanese into learners and the Americans into group-oriented helpers. Unfortunately, Japanese parents currently do not have on hand a large inventory of executives experienced in managing American operations. Japan is just too new in America. Time will solve the problem, but some very bad decisions are likely to occur in the subsidiaries in the meantime as Japanese flounder and Americans complain.

What is crucial to Japanese managers is that the decision process not threaten their power. Keisuke Nishimura was formerly an assistant personnel director at a Japanese brewery. At one point in his tenure he developed proposals to amend the plant's administrative rules. "It was very useful to know the overall impact of our proposals in advance," he said. "So I held informal meetings with sections before holding a formal meeting." American management consultants call this "feedforwarding." What is different about feedforwarding in Japan is that the informal meetings go on until everyone has given his general agreement. Only then is a formal meeting held. The obvious value of this process is that it reduces conflict later on and speeds up implementation. But another major reason, typically Japanese, is to reduce the chance of threats to the power of the senior person who will lead the formal meeting and supervise the implementation. Americans would do well to remember that what looks like consensus building is also a carefully crafted way of avoiding challenges to the boss's power. In the example of Mr. Nishimura, he played the role of *shunin*, the person in charge of getting things done and getting everyone mobilized. The boss's job is to give the stamp of approval to what he probably wanted done in the first place. It is the *shunin's* task to see to it that nothing occurs which threatens the carrying out of the boss's needs.

For Japanese, then, decision making is the exercise of power. What happens when this is not possible and genuine consensus is required? When Japanese and American companies are fifty-fifty partners in a U.S. joint venture, decisions can be difficult. "We have three Japanese and three Americans who meet to decide major issues," said a Japanese cement company executive. "That makes it hard to come to an agreement sometimes. But this is an American company operated in the United States. Japanese have to respect American ways of doing things." This man's "when in Rome" approach soon revealed itself as a mask covering terrible frustration. "If I say that I think this way is better, they can say they disagree because of their experience here in the States. They imply that because of their knowledge of the laws or customs here, my comment cannot be acceptable. So they are very powerful. This fifty-fifty ownership is not good. It just doesn't work well." It does not work well for him because either decisions are consensual or the result of American claims of expert power. Only if he were in control would he feel comfortable with the process.[4]

RIGIDITY

According to investment banker Roy Smith, once a Japanese company has made up its mind to do something after an interminable decision-making process, nothing, not even price, is allowed to stand in its way.[5] Knowing this, crafty Americans increase the price of the assets the Japanese want to buy. When the dollar is low, it doesn't matter much, but if a low-yen period develops, the Japanese can be victimized by their decision making. A boss decides to do something and then sets in motion a lengthy process of feedforwarding and getting everyone on board. Eventually the decision is legitimized in a ritual meeting. It is now set in stone and must be carried out. Regardless of whether or not the environment has changed, the executive's power would crumble if he did not forge ahead. In the mid-1980s Japanese insurance companies decided to purchase billions of dollars worth of U.S. bonds. They went ahead even when it became obvious that the dollar was about to fall. The decision had been made, and nothing was going to change it. After a 50 percent dollar decline, the insurance companies' portfolios soon fell by the equivalent of $13 billion. Executive power, however, was secure. This rigidity in service to power often looks like a commitment to the long term in contrast to Americans' short-term focus. In reality it is simply intransigence.

Roy Smith in *The Global Bankers* notes that Goldman, Sachs has had a service-oriented relationship with Sumitomo Bank for many years. In 1985 Sumitomo realized that it had weak capability to help its clients as they sought to enter international capital markets. In addition, as Japanese manufacturing firms moved to the United States, they would need help for such things as financing their dealers' inventories. The bank decided to form an overseas finance company which could issue securities to raise capital as a base for loans to manufacturers and for investing in merger and acquisition activity. It also wanted to invest in an international investment bank with which it would set up joint ventures in London and Tokyo. The president approached Goldman, Sachs, which, he knew, needed a capital infusion. The Goldman, Sachs partners analyzed the Japanese bank's goals and realized that profitability was not one of them. Sumitomo wanted to position itself so that when Japanese laws changed and the barriers between investment banking and commercial banking were lifted, it would be ready. It would have a structure in place and it would have learned how to do the business. The Goldman, Sachs team concluded that Sumitomo would pay a premium for the chance to learn and for the glory and prestige of being associated with Goldman, Sachs. The deal was made, although the Federal Reserve squelched the joint venture opportunity. Moreover, Sumitomo only was able to loan funds to Goldman, Sachs and was not able to send trainees to the firm. Sumitomo got very little for its trouble, but it went ahead anyway, driven by its strategy even though the environment had changed. One could see this as (1) an admirable long haul approach or (2) as a less than admirable rigidity. The reader can pick either—or both.

THE SLOW FACTOR

"The number one problem for our American employees is Japanese decision making," said a personnel manager in a consumer electronics firm. "The slow speed bothers them. A Japanese manager gives a problem to his people for them to generate ideas. But an American tells subordinates the target and a rough outline of the solution. In the Japanese case when the employees present ideas, a solution is determined. Only then is the target identified and action undertaken. The American manager's staff, however, take action right away."

An example of the lengthy and slow decision process followed by conservative Japanese firms follows.[6] A trading company realized in 1970 that a certain product in short supply was enjoying 2 percent annual growth in demand outside of Japan. It decided that increased access to this product would lead to increased profits on the Japanese market and elsewhere. A study team was formed that eventually issued three reports. Attention became focused on one natural resources firm, and a joint venture proposal was invited from this company. At this point the wheels began to turn very slowly. The Investment Administration Office had to decide whom to send to study the proposal. Two teams were selected, one technical and one financial/legal. Eight people studied the proposal. Their job was to bring back information to be further studied. Note that the teams were simply information collectors rather than advisors or negotiators. No negotiations could take place until all of the general managers had had a chance to study the data. Each of them appointed a specialist to a new "core" team, which had to be approved by the personnel department. As if this team were not enough, the lead department appointed a team to monitor and coordinate with the study team. When all of these people finally agreed on how to respond to the joint venture proposal, the division head went before the Project Comprehensive Policy Committee. Naturally it requested further study, so the core team went back to work. Finally, a letter was drafted setting out the Japanese firm's response to the proposal. Negotiations ensued, and a contract was signed in December 1980, ten years after the initial idea arose.

In America what legitimizes decisions is success. In poorly run Japanese firms it is often study. As long as an interminable process of analysis has occurred, the decision makers are protected. Researchers call this the "risky shift," which refers to the use of groups to relieve persons from making risky decisions. An organization might never undertake high risk-high reward endeavors without using groups in this way, so the Japanese approach has an element of good sense to it. But the overanalysis, as noted above, suggests ritual rather than rational behavior. Luckily, most Japanese firms use groups in a more productive manner.

Another reason for slow decisions cropped up in the observations of a Japanese bond trader. "Japanese take more time than Americans on Wall Street to make a decision because we require more information," he said. "We think about lots of things, especially what the other Japanese firms are doing." A follower firm focuses on trying never to be first, but always imitating requires lots of knowledge on what the other companies are up to. This is not competitive strategy as Americans know it. Rather it is a way of life based on a theory of the marketplace as ordered and static. One works to hold on to one's place by adjusting to and accommodating other placeholders. Not all Japanese firms are like this, but it is important to realize that the relentless pursuit of expanding market share is not universal.

Some firms, the more competitive kind, have learned to adopt in America. "We are moving away from a traditional bottom up decision making strategy towards a top down strategy, mainly because this approach allows the company to act quickly," said a commodities trader. "If we want to see what everyone thinks, which is what happens in a bottom up process, we may miss valuable opportunities. This company used to take a long, long time before it was certain about which direction to move." Note the former need for certainty he mentions: the boss's certainty that everyone is on board and the firm's certainty that its actions are the right ones. This typical Japanese intolerance of uncertainty has had to be muted in an American business environment where uncertainty cannot be regulated and managed away. The slow, steady march towards the right path is giving way to an American-style scramble full of uncertainty and risk.

DECIDING ON AMERICA

When a large trading company wanted to explore opportunities for a resort investment in the Pacific Northwest, it sent a senior vice president to wander around the countryside talking to developers and ordinary citizens. An American firm (if it even bothers to collect data) would have assigned an MBA to do a study with a budget and staff. A 200-page memo would have resulted. When Matsushita wanted to build a television plant on the West Coast, it reassigned an experienced general manager from Mexico to find a site and install the machinery. He did it in nine months. No complex accountability systems had to be implemented to monitor spending. Some intelligent, trusted person simply goes out when a Japanese firm wants something looked into. He collects every scrap of information he can on markets, customers, technology, labor issues, and so on. All of the data go back to Japan, where they are poured over by everyone with an interest in the project. Every so often these people will collect in a conference room and go over the idea from every conceivable angle. After a number of these marathon go rounds, a course of action will emerge. Senior executives will provide direction and vision in some firms, while in others they will see to it that their will is done.

Once a plan emerges, the process becomes more like an American operation.[7] Objectives and time line charts are drawn up and monthly reports issued. Outcome to plan meetings are held and variances are dealt with. Individuals are held very much accountable for the achievement of assigned tasks, although bonuses usually go to the group. Within this general framework Japanese researchers have described different types of firms. Some firms are very much influenced by government regulation and fiat. Examples of these "old wave" firms are NKK and Kawasaki Heavy Industries. "New wave" firms such as Sony, Honda, and Matsushita are more market oriented.[8] Another distinction is whether or not a firm comes from the Tokyo area. Tokyo companies are said to be driven by market share considerations, perhaps because the government smiles more favorably on firms with clout, while non-Tokyo firms are bottom line profit makers. An American working for an old wave, Tokyo-type firm might find its strategy-setting process regarding American investments to be market share-driven and super sensitive to political issues. An American working for a new wave, Osaka firm like Matsushita would find the decision process quite familiar.

JAPANESE PROBLEMS AND AMERICAN OPPORTUNITIES

Japanese executives tend to see themselves as beset by problems, whereas American senior managers see the world as full of opportunities.[9] The Japanese focus probably is rooted in the need to gain and hold on to power. Labeling an economic condition as a problem is a way of saying, "We are not in control and we must do something about it." Americans worry less about these things and tend to be more confident. Seeing the world as full of opportunities, they say, "We have ability and we are on the lookout for ways to apply it."

Kaoru: Well, Tom, just as we suspected, our sales of Osaka Brand are down this quarter. That's a loss for three quarters in a row.

Tom: Clearly we will have to take some action.

Kaoru: How can we get those sales back? When our other customers and competitors see our sales down, they will not respect us. Also, headquarters will never leave us alone after this. We will be powerless.

Tom: Don't worry about that. We'll be okay. Look at it this way. We can adjust to lowered sales by cutting our marketing expenses. This will widen our net margin and give us the same amount of profit we had before. No one will bother us if we still generate the same profits.

Kaoru: No, absolutely not. We have a *problem* and we must solve it. We can't pretend it isn't there and look the other way.

Tom: Let's not look backward. We have an *opportunity* to reduce managerial effort and still reap the same profits. What a chance! Let's not blow this one.

"In Japan," says social critic Michihiro Matsumoto, "patience is the name of the game and one must learn the art of reacting."[10] Japanese managers create information systems which identify problems or barriers to a goal. Then they react to them. Americans often act as a first step, and as a disturbed environment sends out information, they look for opportunities. Let us return to Kaoru and Tom again.

Kaoru: Tom, our *kaizen* program is starting to pay off. The information we're collecting will tell us what our defect rate is in a more reliable manner than before. We can be more confident in our corrective actions.

Tom: Oh, it's fine, and we will be able to make lots of little changes, but real cost cutting will take forever with *kaizen*. Why don't we just shake things up and see what happens? How about shifting the workers in our Des Moines plant to a basic hourly rate with a bonus based on a low defects rate? We'll see what happens. Who knows, perhaps we will see dramatic cost improvements.

Kaoru: Let's not create more problems, Tom. All we want to do is get a handle on the problems we have now.

Tom: Sometimes managers have to be agents of change, Kaoru.

Kaoru: Perhaps, but change must always be orderly. That is the Japanese way.

It is not that Tom and Kaoru do not understand each other. They do, and both have taken defensible positions. Their conflict is really about how to make a decision. Kaoru is empirical and inferential. His is a scientist's approach. Data are gathered that identify problems. Then explanations for the problems are sought, and action is based on the explanations. It is no accident that Japanese revere Darwin, the great empiricist. Tom is more of a tinkerer like Edison or Henry Ford. He probes and pokes and sees what wiggles—just as he probably did with his car when he was a teenager. Based on his intrusion into a system and its reaction to him, he decides what to do next.

Kaoru and Tom are stereotypes used to reveal general tendencies rather than predict the behavior of specific managers. But both characters tell us something real. Kaoru scans the environment in search of threats to his managerial control. His scanning often is unsystematic—mostly a go-look-report operation—but he is very systematic in then developing explanation tools (e.g., the *kaizen* procedures) in reaction to problems. Tom identifies opportunities, often without any data collection. He acts immediately to try out his bright ideas to see what happens. If good things result, he pours it on. If bad things occur, he tries something else. Whatever power Tom has as a manager comes from his successes, not his ability to maintain control, which is the case with Kaoru. Kaoru's approach to things is not necessarily cultural. It is simply the current style of Japanese managers that emerged during the post war years of labor strife, when all parties were grasping for power. In the United States, the Kaorus can adapt to American ways rather easily if they want to. This would involve either systematic data collection and quantitative analyses, as is common in a few large firms, or the seat of the pants opportunity grabbing which most American managers admire. Whatever the case, Japanese managers will have to change their ways in the rough and tumble American economic environment. So far they have not done so.

Japanese consensus, to sum up, is information sharing in informal meetings so that everyone knows and accepts what has been decided. Ideas are welcome, but obedience is crucial and is expressed in ritual meetings. Decisions are driven by the subtle exercise of power, not collective discourse. In Japanese-owned American firms often a veneer of team spirit aided by a cadre of "advisors" covers up what is really decision making by fiat. Some firms look for American hires who are comfortable in a controlled environment. Others adopt American-style discourse in the decision process. Americans, however, may expect expert pronouncements from the Japanese boss during deliberations. When they do not get them, they lose confidence in him instead of providing gentle guidance. Experienced senior executives are needed to train American employees to be helpful and Japanese managers to ask for help. The better firms carry their fast, flexible decision making to America, but in most Japanese companies actions are taken very slowly and are implemented regardless of environmental changes. This is okay in the managed economy of Japan. It is not so okay in the more turbulent American economy.

FIFTEEN

The Rule of Personnel

Nothing in Japan is horizontal. Indeed, "no Japanese feels at ease in an organization that is not vertical," says Hideo Inohara in his excellent *Human Resource Development in Japanese Companies.*[1] Personnel departments are not really staff activities existing side by side with operations. Rather they control operational employees in terms of hiring, evaluation, training, promotion, and transfer. This increased power of personnel is new to Americans in Japanese subsidiaries.

To get some idea of personnel department power, consider the case of Fuji Bank, with branches in New York, Atlanta, Houston, Chicago, Los Angeles, San Francisco, and Seattle. Japanese managers assigned to branches may return to Japan after three years or they may be transferred to another branch. "Only the personnel division in Tokyo knows these things," says one manager. "Out-out" transfers were increasing in the early 1990s. These refer to moves from one location outside of Japan to another post outside Japan. "Out-in" transfers back to Japan were less prevalent. Fuji managers usually bring their families to a U.S. post if the children are of elementary school age or below. When they are older and ready to enlist in what some Japanese call "education war," the wife and kids stay home, and the manager becomes a "temporary bachelor." If personnel decrees an out-out transfer for him, he may not see his family, except for brief vacations, for years.

Throughout the post-war period Japanese personnel departments have ruled the roost, often with great success. While Japanese workers have not been highly productive, they have been easily controlled and quality focused. Turnover was low and acceptance of training was high. Most training, however, was not the kind one usually sees in American firms. According to a 1990 Economic Planning Agency study, Japanese personnel departments use training mainly to improve morale, build loyalty, create team spirit, and to provide a break from routine.[2] Skill building has not been their primary preoccupation—perhaps one reason why labor productivity still is only two-thirds that of American workers. But loyalty is not high either. A 1990 Ministry of Labor survey found that only 26 percent of young workers wanted to stay with the company that first hired them. Among all workers, 44 percent were dissatisfied with their life, mainly because of low wages and long hours.[3] Personnel departments are beginning to falter in their mission in Japan, and personnel managers are looking to America for ideas. This is ironic, since Americans spent the 1980s looking to Japan for direction. As Japanese companies move to the United States, their personnel practices are in a time of transition. This is a polite way of saying they don't know what to do.

GLOBAL, LOCAL, OR JAPANESE?

Should Japanese personnel and personnel practices dominate American subsidiaries? Or should American approaches be used? Is there a global model which can be applied worldwide, so that French, American, and Japanese employees all come under the same rules for hiring, compensation, promotion, and so forth? Matsushita plans to have standardized personnel evaluation policies in place in each of its three regions (North America, Europe and Africa, Asia and the Middle East) by 1993. Promotion, for example, will be based on adherence to Matsushita's management principles, leadership ability, crisis management skills, and other criteria. While these are similar to practices in Japan, it appears that one set of rules will prevail there and another set in foreign investments.

American subsidiary employees often are in the same position as female workers in Japan. Two kinds of job categories exist at large companies, *ippan-shoku*, which refers to jobs which may or may not be managerial and which do not involve the possibility of relocation, and *sogo-shoku*, which are managerial positions subject to relocation. Virtually all women employees hold *ippan-shoku* jobs, and no possibility exists for shifting categories.[4] Some firms may have applied these categorizations to their worldwide employee cadres. One could look on this practice as a protection for workers who want to stay where they are *or* as a way of institutionalizing second-class citizenship in corporations. Put another way, if Japanese multinationals want to develop global personnel practices, they will have to treat all employees alike. All employees, by the same token, will have to understand that they are subject to transfer at the personnel department's pleasure.

Americans ought to be given a choice as to whether they want to be *ippan-shoku* or *sogo-shoku*. This is not what is happening, however. Under pressure from the U.S. government, Japanese firms are Americanizing their operations. While this localization of personnel practices is generally good, it probably signals a move towards *ippan-shoku* for Americans.

"When we build new factories in America," said a Sharp personnel manager, "the plant manager, administrative staff, and the marketing staff will be American. Engineering and accounting staff will be Japanese. That is a good way for us now, but only as a start. We eventually will transfer all authority to Americans." In 1985, thirty of 750 of Sharp's Memphis plant's employees were Japanese. By 1990 only twenty-one Japanese were on hand, filling slots for the president, accountants, quality control people, and engineers. Essentially, their job was to report back to headquarters. Hitachi America had Americans in three of its 14 general manager positions in 1989 and had plans to reduce Japanese participation in the workforce from 17 to 10 percent. Mitsubishi International had announced similar plans. "Our personnel systems should be Americanized," said a Bank of Tokyo manager. "Since we are in the United States, we should follow the American way. I know some American firms in Tokyo, and they are trying to change because they are hiring Japanese staff into top management." All of these companies are developing local rather than global or Japanese approaches.

The transition to localization of personnel management has been described by a number of researchers. One group visited the Fort Custer Industrial Park in Battle Creek, Michigan, where they found twelve Japanese firms. Interviews with managers revealed Japanese-style use of quality circles, information sharing, and job sharing. But American personnel practices also were in use. Decisions were not tied as much to groups, women were being treated as equals, and ability rather than simply effort and docility was valued. Other studies come up with similar results. Promotion by seniority is not practiced as much in America, and frequent performance appraisals, rare in Japan, occur now in many Japanese-owned firms.[5] All in all, localization is well under way. But personnel departments will not give up their Japanese model so easily, and the hand of Tokyo lies heavily on managers as they try to Americanize. Global personnel models are out and local models are in, but the Japanese model will not get off stage without a fuss. Things really are quite muddled.

RECRUITING AMERICANS

The Japanese approach is reflected in the comments of a personnel manager at a consumer electronics firm. "When I recruited Americans," he said, "my number one criterion for hiring was patience. Number two was the ability to be team-oriented. Number three was being bright. But being bright is not very important. Bright but impatient individuals would soon leave the company in frustration." When this manager hired patient, cooperative mediocrities, he knew that they would be unlikely to job hop. With an employee committed to the long term, he then felt comfortable spending time and money on training. The idea here apparently is that training can overcome ability problems. Japanese personnel managers look for people who are flexible and accommodating. While they often say they want innovative employees, the ideal person is someone who is not a boat rocker. This employee is self-effacing and sensitive to the unspoken needs of superiors. He or she accepts the control environment of Japanese management, even though control often is expressed in an unstructured and implicit manner.

When it comes to experience versus knowledge, most Japanese opt for the former. "Our management style is experience-oriented," said the consumer electronics personnel manager. "If we hired MBAs, we would not fully utilize their knowledge. They would get frustrated and leave." A staff manager at another firm had a similar viewpoint. "We do hire some MBAs," he said, "but it isn't a regular recruiting practice." The American CEO of a Japanese subsidiary was blunt about it. "I'm not a great admirer of MBAs," he noted. "They're financial instrument-oriented and not thinking in terms of making a product." Most of this firm's staff accountants and analysts are promoted from within and trained by the company. Few MBAs are recruited.

Since Japanese firms cannot always find patient, experienced people, they pursue other recruiting options. Nissho Iwai Corporation seeks U.S. college graduates, as does Matsushita. Nomura, unafraid of American business education, sends thirty or more Japanese for MBAs at U.S. business schools. Part of their task is to make connections leading to the identification of possible American hires. Both NEC and Toshiba send thousands of managers abroad each year on "fact-finding" missions. Their job is to get data on competitors and to look for high quality Americans interested in working for them. Some companies look for bilingual Americans graduating from Japanese universities. Since there were only thirty-eight of these in 1989, this approach will not solve many problems.[6] A few firms have recruited Japanese citizens graduating from U.S. universities. These Americanized Japanese are a worry. "Perhaps they will lack patience," said one executive. "Will they be willing to start at the bottom like graduates of Japanese universities?"

Once potential employees have been identified, an elaborate screening process may occur at some firms (although small companies simply hire through headhunters and hope for the best). At Honda, interviewers of job candidates want to know about the person's flexibility, likelihood of good attendance and long-term tenure, and willingness to work lots of overtime. Since skills can be taught, these are secondary. The candidate will be asked, "How do you and your family feel about working fifty hours a week?" and "If you were working on the assembly line and couldn't keep up with it, what would you do?"[7] Careful screening of this kind leads to a very low 2 percent turnover rate.

When Mazda started its Flat Rock, Michigan, plant, it received 96,500 applications for 3,100 jobs. This enormous labor supply allowed the company to pick and choose its employees with great care. The hiring process consisted of five evaluations. First came a two-hour test covering comprehension and numerical skills. Next was an interview to determine whether the candidate would fit into the Mazda environment. Third was a social assessment testing the candidate's interpersonal skills. Then came a medical examination screening for drug and alcohol abuse. Finally a physical test simulated the actual job tasks the person would perform. A complex set of hurdles like these not only will identify workers who can do the job. It also will uncover people who are likely to be submissive and to respond to any demands made of them. Competent workers who do what they are told without complaint are the *sine qua non* of Japanese managerial approaches.

One major problem with all of this is that Japanese managers go into the testing process with some strong biases. I once endured a war movie in Tokyo which recounted the sufferings of Japanese soldiers during the Pacific War. At one point in the film the hero is accused by the Americans of being a war criminal. He is thrown into a filthy jail cell, where he is beaten, tortured, and generally mistreated. Some of his American guards, however, secretly give him food and try to comfort him. In fact, the film was designed to show one-half of the Americans as bestial and the other half as saintly. Guess what the skin color of the bestial soldiers was. This film never would be shown outside of Japan, so the producers did not worry too much about letting their prejudices show. Anti-black beliefs are common in Japan. In 1988 Michio Watanabe, a leading politician, told a political rally that American blacks were more likely than whites to declare bankruptcy. These remarks echoed the 1986 statements of the prime minister, Yasuhiro Nakasone, that blacks were pulling down educational levels in the United States. Japanese companies feel no qualms about doing business with South Africa, and a few Japanese auto firms have systematically located plants to avoid urban black populations as sources of workers. In 1988 Honda agreed to a $6 million settlement for 377 blacks and women who were denied jobs because of race and sex. Similar cases occurred at Toyota and Nissan.[8]

Hiring practices, then, are often as much a screening out as well as a selecting in, characterized by a preference for compliant white people. A black MBA would be hard to find at Japanese-owned firms. This is all changing, however, as American personnel practices are adopted both in the United States and Japan, but the influence of headquarters personnel departments is still strong.

Why do Americans accept offers from Japanese firms? In a 1989 study those surveyed indicated the growth opportunities in these firms.[9] Getting in on the ground floor is a terrific advantage if the firm has a parent which can fund growth with immense capital resources. A second reason is the employment security Japanese offer. In an era when large American firms are downsizing—perhaps 500,000 managers were let go or retired in the 1980s at the Fortune 500—many Americans find it attractive to encounter firms which believe in the value of a stable work force. Note that these security-oriented people—looking for low-risk jobs at growth-oriented companies—seem to be just what the Japanese corporations want. As we will see below, nevertheless, personnel problems are occurring, especially in non-manufacturing firms.

LOCATION IS EVERYTHING

Japanese manufacturers have been extremely cautious in choosing locations for their plants. They often deliberately seek out rural settings where workers are poorly educated, have few opportunities, and are in need of work. Conditions like these are ideal for the application of Japanese personnel methods, which operate best with careful selection of highly compliant workers who are unlikely to be resistant to training or job assignment. In these manufacturing settings team approaches to complex set up and assembly tasks work well. Contrast these conditions with those facing service firms, which must locate in large cities where potential American employees are usually better educated, less desperate for a job, and less compliant. Careful selection procedures do not work well when the choices are limited, and hired Americans in cities are more likely to want to "discuss" directives and task assignments. Japanese human resource management is likely to be just as flawed in urban service firms in America as it is in Japan, and these difficulties may explain why the ratio of Japanese staff to total employees in banks and trading firms occasionally is as high as 45 percent, while in manufacturing firms it is usually under 10 percent. The service firms cannot handle Americans very well and depend on Japanese as much as possible.

A 1990 study of 107 Japanese-owned goods producers and service firms in the United States found that manufacturers tended to have selective hiring procedures, an emphasis on work teams and small groups, a formal information sharing system, and a mechanism for re-solving employee complaints.[10] Service firms tended not to have these. What service firms did emphasize, in contrast to manufacturers, were performance-based wages and annual bonus incentive plans. Turnover rates were much higher in service firms, and service firm personnel reported tight control by the Japanese parent and little American participation in major decisions. Not surprisingly, compared to manufacturing firm managers, American service firm managerial employees were less happy with their jobs, their pay, and their chances for promotion. The better educated they were, the unhappier they were. It may be that if Japanese service firms want to improve their management of Americans, they need to be more careful in hiring—as noted above this is difficult—more forthcoming with information, more participative, more attentive to complaints, and more generous in pay and promotion. As the rule of personnel from Tokyo diminishes, these things will happen. But since Japanese firms will never Americanize completely, the employee problems of banks, trading companies, and financial services firms in the big cities are likely to remain. Rural American workers will continue to be more accepting of Japanese firms than urban employees.

MOTIVATING

Inbreeding is a way of life in a large Japanese company, and most managers will have joined right after graduation from college. These are called "true-born" (*kogai*) employees. Over 78 percent of directors of major firms are true-borns.[11] No long-term employment contracts exist in Japanese firms—they are not allowed under the Labor Standards Law—but unwritten agreements are common. The greatest sin a Japanese manager can commit is to allow his turnover rate to rise, since it could be a sign that true-borns are rejecting the company because of managerial incompetence or poor treatment of people. While conditions in U.S. subsidiaries are different, the same fear of turnover exists. Managers will do almost anything to keep turnover rates low lest Tokyo become alarmed. At manufacturing firms, especially in rural and small town localities, companies have told workers that they would try to keep them on even in downturns. The effect of these promises at places like Nissan's Tennessee plant or Honda's Marysville facilities has been a dramatic increase in motivational levels. This must have come as quite a shock to Japanese executives, who use permanent employment as a control technique in Japan rather than a motivating tool. What they are getting now in rural plants are both easily controlled *and* motivated employees. Some days it pays to get out of bed.

Another motivational activity is promotion and the use of career development paths. The experiences of Japanese along these lines in Japan are rather bizarre, and they will not have much success applying their home-country ideas in the United States. George Graen of the University of Cincinnati and Mitsuru Wakabayashi have been studying this issue for almost twenty years. What they have found is that long-term career promotion prospects for a Japanese manager are determined in his first three years with the firm and are based on his relationship with his first supervisor.[12] These early interpersonal and communication skills are a major influence on speed of promotion, salary, and bonus levels for many years afterwards. Another big influence is the prestige of the university attended by the employee.[13] Startling findings such as these, if applied in the United States, suggest that Japanese firms will promote pleasant, communicative graduates of well-known universities who have had the good fortune to start off their jobs under Japanese managers who speak English well and like to talk. Ten years later these people will be highly placed. Since this is no way to run a business, observers have noted that upper mid-level managers in Japanese-owned firms, American and Japanese alike, are likely to be somewhat ineffective.[14]

Motivating senior Americans has been a problem, although Matsushita seems to have hit on a successful technique. At its Panasonic subsidiary, started in 1959, there are ten vice presidents. Eight of them are Americans, averaging eighteen years of service. "We always try to keep Americans for a long time," said a personnel officer at Matsushita's headquarters near Osaka. "We have done it by creating a family environment." In the 1960s this was done by keeping the staff small and depending on outside contractors and sales reps. As Panasonic grew in the 1970s, most of the Americans had the chance to advance. Then in the 1980s the divisional system was instituted. Americans with seniority were asked to submit business plans and to take over a number of units. They became eligible for cash bonuses of up to 40 percent of annual income based on performance and the attainment of their plans. Seniority rather than youthful friendliness or alma mater was the criterion used to identify these fast trackers. While this is certainly a better approach, it still reflects home-country personnel tactics. The idea of motivating Americans through performance-based rewards, however, was a good one. Japanese managers of business units do not get such compensation. Instead, they receive four- to five-months salary as a bonus if the whole company has done well.

The most interesting attempt to build motivation is at Honda in Ohio. New employees and their families are given orientation training to develop a family as well as an employee commitment to the company.[15] The idea apparently is to build family member support for the tough demands Honda makes of its associates. Families then serve as part of Honda's motivational process. If the employee is asked to work overtime for long periods, the company hopes that the spouse will convince the worker to keep at it. In a company that offers job security and that does not want to hire employees except for long-term growth, temporaries and overtime are used to cope with spot demand pressures. This is why it becomes crucial to motivate employees to accept overtime. Fostering spousal pressure, it is hoped, will work in the United States because it works so well in Japan. "Why are you home so early?" the Japanese wife will ask. "It's still daylight."

CUSTOMARY COMPENSATION AND SLOW RESPONSES

American compensation systems are built around job content, supply and demand for labor, and the level of performance. A person doing a demanding job well in a tight labor market should receive high wages with regular raises. In fact, the system rarely works this way for two reasons. First, complexity creeps in. A person doing a hard job well in a weak labor market may or may not receive high compensation. It all depends on how the company weights the different elements of the system. American organizations are notorious for their flightiness along these lines. One year performance is weighted highly, but the next, after yet another change in management, the market drives things. No one knows what the right system should be, so many combinations of weighting are tried randomly. Second, and to some extent because of complexity and randomness, compensation is often based on custom rather than on job content, market, or performance. In many American industries wages hardly change, regardless of labor demand and supply or industry productivity. Only in extreme situations of oversupply of workers or exceedingly strong demand for skilled people does the compensation system respond. Neither managers nor employees like to admit the reality of customary compensation. The managers do not like to give up power, and the employees do not cherish a process in which ability and effort count only a little. If custom dictates pay, managerial motivation activities will be generally ineffective, and "merit" will have but a small impact.

Japanese managers in the 1990s are torn between trying to prop up their own failing compensation system, rooted in modest seniority-based pay and job security promises, and moving towards an American system which, beyond its simple manifestations, they know is riddled with hypocrisy and self-deception. In an increasingly competitive world with its dramatic swings in demand, permanent employment is not viable. Moreover, the great need for highly skilled engineers and technical people is forcing Japanese firms out of a seniority system towards a content-market-performance system. In a Japanese firm the star middle manager might receive only 20 percent more than his weakest colleague, whereas the difference in America could be 100 percent. Eventually, American differentials will prevail in Japanese firms, especially those located in the United States. In one securities firm in New York the American chief bond trader makes well over $500,000, while a Japanese trader working alongside may get $40,000 plus bonuses and overseas allowances. It is a safe bet that the American's pay will not come down much. It is also a sure thing that the Japanese manager over time will begin to want what is "customary." When he is told that his performance is not worth that much and that there are lots of traders on the street, he will point to the American and say, "So why does he get so much? He isn't much different than I am in performance." When he is then warned that the permanent employment system cannot sustain such compensation, he will say, "The system cannot endure much longer anyway. Let's drop it now."

Gradually, Japanese firms will lower the maximum age at which seniority-based raises occur. The American system will take its place, as will the complexity, randomness, and fallback on custom. In Japan the company will control "custom" through early retirements. As employees leave, new customs can be institutionalized. In its American subsidiaries laws hinder the firm from compelling early retirement, and so customary wages will become as entrenched as they are in other American organizations.

In the meantime, current compensation practices exhibit the typical slow pace of the Japanese personnel department. "One of the first things that happened to me when I took over my section in America," recalled a consumer electronics firm manager, "was that an American manager came to me and said, 'I am thinking of quitting the company.' This was a shocking and embarrassing experience for me." The American pointed out that Nabisco had offered him $5,000 more. Before the Japanese boss could match the Nabisco offer, he had to have personnel evaluate the man's salary in accord with a point system grading performed by the compensation manager. The outcome was slow in coming, so the man left. This minor incident illustrates major flaws in Japanese human resources management in America. It is slow and focused too much on cost control. These problems are trivial in Japan, where turnover is low. They are not so trivial in job-hopping America.

PERFORMANCE APPRAISAL

With the growing emergence of custom as the basis for wages, performance appraisal will become less important. It still counts, however, and Japanese firms are trying to come up with workable systems.

An evaluation system that has promise is that practiced by some trading companies.[16] A manager is evaluated in two ways: performance evaluation and evaluation of potential. The performance evaluation is an assessment of the manager's short-term achievements, expressed as a deviation above or below a mandated company average. Outstanding performers receive somewhat more bonus that year or half-year than poor performers. The difference is not large and is only a one-time award, but the singling out of a person in a small way is very important to Japanese. If Americans are properly socialized in the firm, it will become important to them too. A second evaluation, less frequently undertaken, assesses a manager's potential in the organization. It has a major impact on future job assignment and promotion. The record of performance evaluations are taken into account, but they may not carry much weight if the employee has been assigned to very easy tasks which he did well or to hard tasks with which he had trouble. Neither case is a fair test of potential. This system ensures that managers will be willing to accept assignment to difficult tasks, since their career advancement will not be hurt by a few years of less than average performance.

The content of Japanese performance appraisals is different. "What did you do this year?" is not as important as "What are you doing to improve yourself in the long run?" Also important is "What have you done to help others in your work team improve?" Effort and team spirit are more significant than ability or task accomplishment, at least in the short term. Not much feedback is given to avoid embarrassing or antagonizing anyone, and final decisions on pay and promotion are made by personnel, which tends to raise up the low and lower the high so that the range of evaluation narrows. Hot shots and flashes in the pans do not fare well at Japanese companies. Genuine achievement by an individual working alone is often downplayed, however, and high performers are bound to feel resentment when they do not receive feedback or reward for their work. They may get token recognition in the form of having their name mentioned in some kind of public announcement. While this is valued by Japanese employees, high-performing Americans usually want more.

RATIONAL GROUP LIFE

No one would dare write a paper about Japanese management and not discuss Japanese groupism. The usual practice of writers is to illuminate Japanese group life as if it were unique, something of which Martians might be capable. Japanese find this odd, since they consider their approach to collective action as often flawed but generally sensible. Indeed, if we look at American group behavior, it is the Americans who begin to look rather odd.

According to economic theory, "the existence of a common interest

need not provide any incentive for individual action in the group interest."[17] If a group is large enough so that a person's failure to contribute
makes no real difference in outcomes and if that person can benefit
whether or not he contributes, it would be irrational for him to engage
in collective action in the interest of the group.

What is to be done, then, to get groups in organizations to function?
One idea is to make them small enough so that "free riders" can be
singled out and penalized. Risk-averse managers will join in their group's
work if they fear penalties for avoiding work. A more positive approach is to reward individuals specifically for engaging in collective
action. Thus, group bonuses must be augmented by the possibility of
individual bonuses. But all recipients in the group must receive the
same bonus. Otherwise the exploitation of the great by the small will
occur. What this means is that a person with a big bonus expected has
a greater incentive to see to it that the group's work gets done than
someone expecting a small bonus. The little guy is very likely to sit
back and simply watch the big guy produce the group's output. Groups
are likely to function, then, only if they are small and if a group bonus
is complemented by a set amount being available to each group member for contributing. Additionally, the people in the group must be
smart enough to recognize how the system works and to maintain it,
and they must have good communications with each other.

In Japanese companies groups are managed in accord with economic
theory developed by Americans. They are small enough so that communication flows easily. Careful hiring provides bright group members
who understand the connection between behavior and reward. Bonuses (in addition to the twice a year company bonus) are often given
to groups, and an individual can get a little more if he or she has demonstrated a cooperative spirit. Usually this involves things like regular
attendance (no sick days, little vacation), a willingness to work on holidays, and acceptance of overtime without complaint. These individual
bonuses are small and do not vary much from person to person. While
some of this groupism is cultural, it is better to see it as rational. That
way, we can point out some of the irrationalities of American attempts
to manage groups. Reward for collective action rarely occurs. Bonuses
are awarded for individual more than group merit. Training on the
benefits of a cooperative spirit occurs, but infrequently. All of this brings
out the free riders, those who do not share information or tasks but
who eagerly seek any rewards given for collective performance. Clearly
the best way to think about Japanese group management practices is
that they are sensible and ought to work well in America.

Will they? Perhaps not. In the first place, American managers and
employees sometimes do see groups as useful in improving performance but more importantly as a way to share risks during tasks where

failure is a real possibility. Japanese managers in well-run, progressive companies often focus on groups as performance enhancers. This difference in perceptions about the function of groups is not too big a problem, but differences in the range of individual bonuses are. Research conducted by my Japanese colleagues and myself suggests that American managers award much higher bonuses to individuals than Japanese do, and exhibit greater variation in their awards.[18] Collective action will not flourish in such an environment, and Japanese approaches to group management will flounder. Since Japanese groupism is rational, however, it ought not to be abandoned. New American employees can be trained better to understand collective behavior, and rewards and recognition can be expanded somewhat to accommodate American individualism. The worst thing for Japanese to do is to tell Americans, "Our way is best and you must follow it." Actually, it is best (at least as far as groups are concerned), but that kind of posturing is unhelpful.

Personnel department power, then, is waning somewhat, but it still prevails. Confusion and muddle, however, reign. Japanese firms would like to develop global personnel systems but will not give up Japanese home country practices. They are being forced to localize human resource management in America, but that will ensure second class status for American employees.

The rule of personnel shows up in U.S. recruiting for submissive and cooperative rather than able employees. MBAs are not wanted in many firms. Mediocre people are easy to control and do not leave, keeping turnover low. In spite of themselves, however, Japanese-owned firms employ lots of able Americans, who join up because they see strong growth possibilities. Many of these hard chargers work for non-manufacturing firms in the big cities. They are a dissatisfied group of people and are putting pressure on their employers to improve pay, promotion, and decision participation practices. American employees in rural manufacturing plants, in contrast, are quite satisfied with their Japanese employers.

Although compensation based on custom rather than market conditions or performance is prevalent in the United States, and Japanese firms are moving towards a U.S. approach, they still use more traditional techniques, some good, some bad. It is bad to develop compensation systems which respond too slowly, focus mainly on cost control, and do not give enough reward to individual merit. It is good to do two performance evaluations, one for short-term performance and one for long-term potential. It is also good to foster collective action using group bonuses with small individual increments for cooperative behavior. The problem is to figure out how to take American individualism into account without losing the excellent Japanese collective action emphasis. Japanese corporations in the United States have not solved this problem yet, nor have they solved most other personnel problems. They have failed to develop global approaches, blundered somewhat in applying techniques used in Japan, and have set up local, American HRM (human resource management) which Americans eventually will recognize as demeaning. Their only successes have come in rural settings with Americans who need jobs and are willing to give strong allegiance to companies which offer secure employment.

SIXTEEN

Manufacturing Management

Manufacturers in Japan in the 1970s were overcapitalized in many industries. They had benefitted from a modest export-driven strategy, but little was coming of it except complacency. At Matsushita a huge American-style bureaucracy had emerged, with endless "get on board" meetings between countless layers of managers and slower and slower reaction times. Out of forty-eight operating units in the company, only two were profitable. One of these, the electric iron division, became a model for the company's subsequent turnaround in the 1980s and an exemplar of "Japanese management." In an era of declining market it had somehow reduced costs and developed new products. How did they do it?

The electric iron division has 400 employees, one-half in production. The production employees are organized into twelve teams, one for each stage in the production process.[1] Each team is an independent accounting unit treated as a kind of profit and loss (P & L) center. Monthly team P & L reports show the added value created by the team before passing the product on to the next stage. These "sales" are matched against costs, which the team leader is responsible for reducing to produce "profit." All team members are kept aware of costs and the consumer demand that drives their "sales." At the end of the production process and in close touch with it is marketing, which identifies new product needs. The sales staff takes the new irons developed and conducts seminars for retailers, showing clerks how to iron clothing properly. The clerks in turn show customers.

One of Matsushita's problems is its practice of offering permanent employment to many employees. This produces easily controlled workers and reduced union problems, but it also creates complacency. The company has attacked the issue in many ways. One approach favored by Toshihiko Yamashita when he was president in the 1980s was to create a sense of crisis. "If your division is closed," he would tell workers, "you will face transfers and separation from friends you have worked with for years." That worked well, as did the claim that successful products earned society's respect, whereas unsuccessful products showed that Matsushita employees were not esteemed by the community. This rhetorical gambit is not likely to work in America, and Matsushita Electric Company of America does not use it. It does not offer permanent employment either, however.

How good is Japanese manufacturing management in the United States? It may be too soon to tell. Only 29 percent of the Japanese electronics industry's foreign plants are in the United States and Canada (most are in East and Southeast Asia), and most of them were established after 1985. Although fully integrated manufacturing operations have appeared in auto, television, steel, and tire operations, many plants still are only assembly oriented. While Japanese manufacturers vary widely in terms of labor productivity, most seem to follow a "Japanese" approach focused on process control, quality, flexibility, and careful relations with vendors. Most of these techniques, however, are simply sensible practices rather than cultural artifacts, and well-run American firms use them too.

"HOKA NO HI, HOKA NO DORU"

The Japanese above means "another day, another dollar." It is not a Japanese proverb, but it should be. The major focus of process manufacturing in Japanese-owned companies is a slow, steady, incremental drive towards quality, efficiency, and flexibility. Sometimes tradeoffs have to be made—quality and flexibility often dominate efficiency—but the *kaizen* process never stops.

Professor Hideo Inohara sums up the typical Japanese firm's approach. "What matters to the company is not so much the individual employee's efficiency and productivity, but the crucial factors are quality of the final product and total corporate productivity."[2] In other words, let machines enhance productivity. The job of people is to concentrate on quality, which means serving customer needs and reducing defects.

Quality in a Japanese manufacturer becomes a company-wide program.[3] Where Western executives may make ritual noises about quality and then go back to decisions based on price-cost-quality calculations, the Japanese go all out. Top management appoints one of its own as the quality control manager and establishes a high-level committee to oversee the development of a program and its implementation. In one firm managers were told to identify 200 problems each involving quality and to prepare detailed plans for solving them. Workers were ordered to find 100 problems each. Through the joint union-management committee, the union is brought on board to give its advice on how to improve quality. Everyone is trained on how to develop Pareto diagrams, control charts, and checksheets. When employees are comfortable with those, they learn to develop affinity diagrams and process decision program charts. These tools, developed by W. Edwards Deming, J. C. Juran, and Kaoru Ishikawa, are ways of storing and analyzing accumulating knowledge of processes and outcomes. Such knowledge is usable because almost everyone can understand it in its visual format, everyone had a hand in collecting the information, and it is immediately available on a desk or bulletin board near the shop floor.

Quality management does not depend on quality circles (QC). While those QCs which collect data and do Pareto diagrams are immensely valuable, most do not undertake such projects. Japanese researchers have found that most QC activity focuses on improving human relations, building team spirit, and whipping up enthusiasm for management's improvement efforts.[4] Since formal training by personnel departments also concentrates on these issues, the quality improvement skills of employees in Japanese-owned firms depend on the education they bring into the plant (good in Japan, poor in the United States) and on-the-job training by managers.

Quality also depends on restructuring the organization so that it becomes the number one priority. The cross-functional committee is a mainstay at Toyota and other large manufacturers. The members are top managers from each department involved in a particular cross-function. The committee's pronouncements are second in importance only to those of the board of directors, and it has the power to order cross-functional audits to see that its goals and procedures are being attended to. Each step in the manufacturing process, from product planning and design to sales and service, is given a set of activities it must undertake. Product planners at Toyota, for example, might be told to establish and allocate optimum quality and cost targets for a new product. Once announced, these cannot be altered, and it is up to designers, production engineers, purchasing agents, operations people, and marketing managers to make sure that targets are met. At Komatsu, control points are set up to monitor quality assurance at major steps in production. Each month in a plant all managers meet in a lengthy session to review the data. The quality assurance manager, possessing much more clout than in an American firm, represents the cross-functional committee's wishes at these meetings and has the power to make change occur.

The *kaizen*, or continuous improvement, approach to manufacturing quality is either simple or very simple. In its very simple form an employee suggests that a ramp be built from floor to work station so she can dolly heavy parts herself from their pallet without help from her neighbor. The ramp is built and her expected work output is increased to account for the time saved. In case she has thoughts about not making further suggestions, her work team, whose bonus partially depends on her output, puts pressure on her to keep contributing. In *kaizen's* simple form the work team meets to identify research questions which need answering if improvements are to occur. One question might be, "Are production errors related to the day of the week?" To answer it, each worker keeps a tally sheet of defects recorded by day. The tally sheets are combined and analyzed both statistically and graphically. The team meets to examine the analysis and finds that Mondays and errors are related. New research questions are generated: "Is it because of hungover workers?" and "Is it due to poor setups on Monday morning?" The team figures out how to collect data to answer these questions, perhaps through surveys or direct observation. Once the answers have been found, ways of reducing errors can be devised. Then the team moves on to the next issue.

The process is neverending, and as Peter Drucker notes, *kaizen* works because of the structural and social changes it brings about in factory work.[5] Workers are no longer viewed as either operators or nonoperators (such as inspectors). Both roles are combined and workers become producers and monitors of production at the same time. They are doers, information collectors, analyzers, and change agents all rolled into one. American workers in Japanese-owned plants are both ready and not ready to assume this new role. Their American culture makes them ready in the sense that it gives them values emphasizing progress through change instituted by individuals. They are not ready, however, because of our miserable education system's failure to teach them the necessary skills: how to collect information, how to analyze using statistics and graphs, how to communicate in groups, how to write a brief analytical report. Managers of these workers must become trainers to bring out skills and leaders to inspire values. The problem is that Japanese managers are good at the first but poor at the second, while American managers are just the reverse. The solution is simple: Japanese should set up training environments, both formal and informal, while first-line American supervisors keep their groups motivated.

It appears that Japanese managers in America are not particularly effective in hands-on-managing. Their real strengths lie elsewhere. One of these is their focus on price-driven rather than cost-driven manufacturing. The marketing people tell the plant what price maximizes revenues. It is then up to manufacturing to figure out how to develop a cost structure which maximizes profitability. The same process applies to quality, delivery, and service. Whatever levels maximize are the levels required of production. Another strength is the emphasis on time as the best measure of production. The Japanese manager's goal is to reduce production times per unit as much as possible given quality constraints and also to cut downtime for changeovers. A third strength is a faith in unending incrementalism, the belief that improvement goes on as a matter of course in small continuous steps. A price orientation which drives production costs, accounting based more on time than costs, and the veneration of small, continuous changes: these are the major skills of Japanese manufacturing managers in America.

SPC, BENCHMARKING, AND CORE COMPETENCIES

Japanese are a people peculiarly intolerant of uncertainty. Often a Japanese will break out into a sweat when he encounters some kind of unexpected event which requires a spontaneous response on his part. This cultural tendency helps explain the intense commitment to the manufacturing management methods of W. Edwards Deming, which focus on variability and its management.[6] Uncertainty and variability go hand in hand, and control of one leads to control of the other. The idea is not so much to reduce defects or flaws in production to zero. Rather it is to develop an understanding of the productive capability of a system. Such things as average output per employee per day and the variability of output around the average are determined, and these yield information which provides starting point data for learning how to reduce variability, which is the key to increasing quality and, through fewer defects, quantity. Variability reduction must occur in the system, not outside of it. Thus quality inspectors do not solve problems; they simply add costs. They should be replaced by a better system in which production workers work, collect statistical data, analyze the data to discover the underlying system, and then alter the system, if necessary, or more likely figure out ways to reduce variability.

To get workers to commit to this form of workplace organization, Japanese managers follow Deming in reducing employee fears that changes may lead to redundancy. Job security promises, either overt or more usually implied, take care of this problem. The Deming method of statistical process control (SPC) is static, however, in that it is built on the assumption which underlies all statistical theories: The world tomorrow will look pretty much like the world today. Therefore, statistics about the past can tell us how the future will look. If we do not like the look, we can act now to change it. In a world, say, of Matsushita of 1979, with standardized products being cranked out for a mass market in predictable numbers, SPC and job security work well. They are not so fine in the world of the 1990s, in which markets are fragmenting and changing rapidly, new producers with low costs are entering the scene, and governments take an active hand in managing economies and international flows of goods and capital.

The late 1990s are not going to look like the early 1990s, so current statistics are not very useful as predictors. Also, job security cannot be offered in an environment of such uncertainty. The pillars of the Deming method are crumbling, but Japanese managers have nothing else to turn to. When sales declined, Toyota's NUMMI workers in California were warned that their jobs depended on improving productivity. When costs rose in Matsushita's VCR plant in Washington State, supervisors told employees that production could be shifted elsewhere. When fear creeps in, workers lose interest in collecting data to reduce variability. They worry instead about holding on to their jobs. Sure enough, quality problems arose at NUMMI, but management was unable to turn to SPC to identify variability and ways to reduce it. The information collectors and analyzers were not interested (when sales picked up, so did quality).

The total commitment to quality, which is a hallmark of Japanese management, does not work in the United States, where markets are freer than in Japan. Under rapidly shifting sales conditions, high quality cannot be attained through statistics which often are irrelevant and job security promises which cannot be made. Moreover, a focus on quality alone may work in Japan where consumers worry that their grocery bag seams may be a bit ragged (yes, they actually do have such worries). But American consumers are more conscious of price-quality tradeoffs. This does not mean that Toyota should start building rattletraps à la GM of the 1960s, but it does mean that quality issues will have to become part of marketing strategy and manufacturing cost issues. Unlike Japan, where firms like Toyota can obtain highest quality components from captive vendors who will humbly absorb the added costs, Japanese-owned U.S. manufacturers often have to pay a market price to U.S. suppliers which in part reflects their costs. The widespread practice of importing high-quality, low-cost components from Japan is unlikely to continue much longer, as public pressure is building to force Japanese firms to focus on U.S. sourcing. When quality cannot be obtained through compliant vendors, motivated workers, or a reliance on statistics, how will it be obtained? If American consumers are not the quality fanatics Japanese are, need it be obtained?

One practice which both Japanese and American firms have turned to, not in place of SPC but certainly complementary to it, is competitive benchmarking. The idea is to obtain models from one's competitors and then set production targets based on the features, options, and price of the competition. Xerox bought ten Canon Personal Copiers when they first came out and determined that the photoreceptor was strong enough to give about five years' service before breaking down.[7] In another case engineers tore down Kodak's Ektaprint 250 when it appeared and concluded that they need have no fear of it from a technical standpoint. Each office is issued a benchmarking book telling what to benchmark, how to benchmark, and how to use the information to improve Xerox products and manufacturing. Xerox learned the technique from its independent affiliate, Fuji Xerox, in 1980. As a result of its Japanese investigation, the company set as its goals: .6 overhead workers to every direct labor hourly worker, instead of the then current level of 1.3; 99.5 percent on parts quality (SPC probably helped here); and 1.0 months of inventory instead of the 3.2 current level. In a benchmark study of Japanese processes, Xerox found that production lead times were kept low by using a selected supplier base, paying attention to their design suggestions, and eliminating time-consuming price quotes. Quality was kept high by getting vendors to commit to excellence and then training them as needed. Tooling costs were controlled by avoiding expensive redesigns and hand tooling.

Japanese prototyping practices tend to differ from American. An American firm often does not make a prototype until all the problems its engineers can think of have been discussed and resolved. This takes a long time. Japanese slap together a prototype as soon as possible and then use its failures as a learning tool. Abstract reasoning is replaced by trial and error learning. With this approach the Japanese engineers need not be as specialized as Americans, since all they have to do is watch what happens and then tinker. The American engineer operating in a prototypeless world must rely on expert knowledge developed from theory and experience.

When Japanese managers in America use benchmarking, then, they may have troubles. Their American engineers may be more theoreticians than tinkerers who can play with a prototype as information comes in from the benchmarking survey. Moreover, establishing the kind of vendor relations which competitors have may not be as easy as it is in Japan. That is why Japanese firms import so much and then compel or persuade their vendors to locate in the United States. As noted above, these moves seem to be only a short-term solution to the problem. Eventually, Japanese will have to work on building long-term relationships with American suppliers. Benchmarking also has the same inherent problem as SPC. It provides a picture of what was and what is, not what will be. In an era of short product life-cycles these typical Japanese manufacturing management strategies are not enough. Flexible, rapid response to markets becomes critical. While many Japanese firms are good at this, many are not. Kao wants to break into the personal care products market in the United States and purchased Jergens, the hand-cream manufacturer, in 1988. It spends 4.5 percent of sales on

R & D, while rivals Procter and Gamble and Unilever spend about 2.5 percent. This spending supposedly will foster new products, lower cost manufacturing, and higher quality. But in the fickle world of women's products, giving the customer what she wants right now is more important than telling her what great things you have developed. Kao may have fallen in love with its factory instead of its customer and may be slow to respond. At other firms Japanese scorn the use of marketing techniques such as focus groups and elaborate surveys to spot changing trends. They rely instead on gut feelings developed by actually sending managers and engineers out into the community. The most famous case was the Japanese engineer who rented a room from a family in California so he could spy on their car use habits. While this subjective, unstructured approach may work, by itself it is not enough to identify subtle developments in tastes and desires.

A third manufacturing approach for which some Japanese companies are famous is the reliance on core competencies.[8] NEC bases its manufacturing and marketing success on core competencies rather than specific processes or products. The company decided early on the range of industries in which it would compete. Then it determined the set of competencies it would need. Core competencies support core products, which in turn foster business units selling end products. Manufacturing in this view is not primarily successful because it gets low-cost, high-quality products out the door fast. Competitors are doing the same thing. Instead, or in addition, the best manufacturing management works with R & D to rapidly build up and utilize core competencies that can spawn new and even unanticipated products. Managers do not focus mainly on the production line, as they do in SPC, nor do they keep their eye on competitors, as benchmarking requires. Their main interests turn to the work of the scientists and designers. It is their job to bring together the streams of technology being developed. Honda managers did this with small motors. Sony does it with miniaturization. Kao is trying to do it with cosmetics. At NEC digital technology is crucial. For these firms the amount of funds allocated to R & D is not as important as the organization's ability to harmonize its R & D efforts, and manufacturing managers are at the center of this effort. Will this approach work in Japanese-owned U.S. firms? Yes, and probably much better than in Japan. American engineers who go into manufacturing management are trained at places like MIT in basic theories and models. Then they develop highly focused expertise in an area and apply it on the job. Unlike many Japanese engineers, who try to get into non-manufacturing management after a few years, Americans tend to stay with technical work. They are ideally prepared, then, for the core competencies approach. The breadth of their training allows them to understand the technology streams and how they can be combined, and then long experience with every nook and cranny of a specific manufacturing process readies them to get the core competencies (CC) into action. Firms built around CC like Honda and Sony have been very successful in America because they have linked Japanese managerial theories to American engineering talent.

If core competencies is the key to successful Japanese manufacturing in America, should firms stop emphasizing SPC and benchmarking? Of course not. The employees should still keep track of output and defects and hold meetings to pore over graphs and statistics. And they should be sent out to examine competitors' products, bring them back, and figure out how to do it better. But all of this should go on within a CC context. If miniaturization is what drives the organization, then statistics should tell stories about how to get even smaller. So should benchmarking reports. Everything should be directed at ways to make core competencies pay off.

ENGINEERS AND WORKERS

After World War II engineering education in the United States began to emphasize the role of engineers as innovators and theorists. Not so in Japan. "Even the top engineer goes to the production line to learn from the manufacturing process," says Masaaki Morita, head of Sony of America.[9] He notes that American engineers rarely leave their desks, with the result that bold, creative ideas are developed that are hard to put into practice.

The differences between American and Japanese engineers at first seem striking.[10] Americans seek out the jobs they end up doing, while Japanese tend to be assigned to them as part of company job rotation plans. Americans thus occupy their positions longer and develop specialty skills. Japanese are sent to research, design, development, production, and marketing more frequently than Americans and develop breadth. The Americans, however, make up for their narrowness by developing strong intra-firm networks and exchanging lots of information. The Japanese make up for their shallow knowledge by sending people to conferences. On their return, these engineers share what they have learned with their group members.

Differences, then, are not quite as great as they appear at first glance. The only important distinguishing feature between American and Japanese engineers is the Americans' greater theoretical grounding. Mr. Morita undoubtedly is correct in saying that his American engineers are desk-bound, but that is probably because their jobs require it. Japanese engineers usually are assigned to production line operations in the United States, so they get their hands dirtier. Since English skills of engineers are often poor, however, office work for them is out of the question. The only place left to go is operations. All in all, Japanese-owned manufacturing will benefit from their American engineers, especially when they broaden themselves a bit through job rotation. As noted in the last chapter, American professional and managerial employees sometimes are very dissatisfied with their lot. They are not consulted on decisions, and career development paths are unclear. This will have to change.

American plant workers usually like working for Japanese firms, but all is not always rosy. Consider the interesting problem of Mr. K., the good Japanese plant manager described in Chapter 1. He instituted a suggestion system in his plant in which workers wrote out their ideas and passed them on to team leaders, who forwarded them to Mr. K. He was surprised to see that the team leaders invariably recommended against implementing even good ideas. Unsure of their positions, they worried that they might be replaced by hard chargers working for them. "But that cannot happen," said Mr. K. to a visitor. In Japan a manager or team leader's position is inviolable. He cannot be replaced simply because a superior wants to give a worker a shot at it in the hope that slightly better supervision will result. That is the way Mr. K. looks at the world, so he did not expect team leaders to be so threatened by good worker suggestions. American managers, however, rarely feel secure in their jobs and constantly worry about being pushed out. The suggestion system should have either bypassed team leaders or, better yet, used team leaders as the source of suggestions from the team rather than from individuals. Rewards could have been given to the team leader to dole out to individuals or to the group. This approach would have been less threatening to them and more likely to gain their participation.

"But I can't do it," said Mr. K. "I have my instructions." Once again, the heavy hand of a headquarters personnel department has reac'ied out to touch a Japanese manager and hinder him in his duties.

If Japanese manufacturing management prospers in rural areas where workers are uneducated and low labor demand makes workers submissive, what happens when conditions change? In the mid-1980s Vancouver, Washington, on the Columbia River across from Portland, Oregon, was languishing.[11] People in the small community needed jobs, and Japanese manufacturers like Kyocera and Matsushita provided them. While Matsushita's 200 employees did not have to do morning exercises or sing the company song, they were expected to contribute slogans and to submit to a strict discipline. Absenteeism was discouraged, pay was low, and no long-term employment guarantees were given. Nonetheless, a job was a job, and the plant was clean and warm in the winter. The highly competent manager spoke excellent English and took pains to create a pleasant environment. Monthly parties were held to celebrate employee birthdays, and the event gave the employees a chance to give informal advice and criticism to the boss. He often joined them for lunch. The nine other Japanese engineers, however, spoke little English and had few contacts with American employees. Plans were underway to institute training for Japanese engineers assigned to America and also for American managers to familiarize the Americans with Matsushita ways. Little was being done, however, because of the almost pathological Japanese anxiety of Americans quitting and giving trade secrets to competitors.

At this point another thing Japanese manufacturers fear occurred: labor demand grew. Starting pay of $4.80 an hour, which had looked good to workers a few years earlier, now could be earned in McDonalds after a few months. Worker turnover began rising a bit in 1990, and complaints about pay and working conditions rose. Rhetoric about participation and quality gave way to occasional threats of automation and some harassment of those who took sick leave. A worker who was criticized for only 85 percent attendance argued that if 15 percent absenteeism was accepted in the local school system, it ought to be accepted at Matsushita. "I told him school children aren't paid," said the frazzled manager, who would never have heard such things from Japanese employees. Pressure to improve productivity grew. Workers were allowed to go to the bathroom only on breaks, and the firm began paying $50 for the best monthly slogan. American managers began to take part in higher level decision making, and plans were speeded up to begin sending them to Japan for training. Although the plant could become more automated than it is, labor as a percent of unit costs is so low that little would be gained. By the same token, a wage raise would not be much of a burden. Yet although a small increase was authorized, substantial wage hikes to end turnover did not occur. The reasons probably had to do with the low-labor input in terms of effort and skills. Most of the employees perform low-level assembly activities, and the loss of a disgruntled worker is not a problem as long as there still are bag ladies at Safeway or pump bunnies at the Seven-Eleven looking to advance themselves. Moreover, although turnover is occurring, it really is quite low and morale is good. It only seems large to the Japanese, who are used to almost zero levels. The real problems for Matsushita at the Vancouver plant and elsewhere will occur when the shift to fully integrated manufacturing in an aging America occurs. Then young, skilled workers will be in demand and will have labor power. The whole control focus of Japanese management will be threatened, and more American-style approaches will have to be tried.

THE "MENACE" OF UNIONS

Managers who began their careers in the late 1940s and 1950s in Japan are super sensitive to union issues, and with good reason. After a particularly bitter encounter with his unions in the late 1940s the head of Japan National Railways disappeared. A few days later parts of his body were found sprinkled along the tracks near Tokyo Station. Unions were tough and very left-leaning then, and rhetoric about "capitalist bosses" was common. Executives would emerge from residences in the morning to find anti-management handbills stuck on the walls of their homes. One way unions were tamed was the institution of lifetime employment. Workers became company men rather than union men, and company unions were turned into job security watchdogs rather than advocates for improved pay and working conditions. In a nation-wide study conducted in 1987, employees expressed strong dissatisfaction with their unions, although they clearly were happy with union efforts to maintain job security. Generally, workers felt that unions were not putting a check on the companies' drive for growth at the expense of employee well-being.[12]

One bright side to the study was a relationship between worker beliefs that their union was effective and a willingness to accept changes initiated by management. Effective unions foster rather than retard organizational change in Japan, as elsewhere.

Mazda's experience in Flat Rock, Michigan, is an example of how not to deal with unions.[13] Because of its relationship with unionized Ford, to which it sells most of its Flat Rock output, Mazda's plant became a union shop. But when Mazda began negotiating with the U.A.W. in 1984, it got off to the wrong start by insisting that the term "bargaining committee" not be used. "Study teams" were formed instead. This small but significant action revealed Mazda's strategy, the same approach Japanese companies use in Japan. The union would be co-opted, changed from an economic agent negotiating at arm's length into an organizational team player helping the company achieve its goals. As in Japan, the emphasis on cooperation and trust to achieve plant success in return for promises of job security opened the gates to allow management control of wages, benefits, compensation, attendance, job assignment, and so forth. While many of these were covered by the contract, the union, which shared offices with the company's labor relations staff, was helpless to protest violations. In 1989, dissidents took over the union leadership. They found that the discretionary power of Japanese managers had replaced mandated powers based on negotiation. Without functioning policies and procedures and in an environment where worker complaints were seen as a form of disrespect, a cronyism had emerged in which team leaders could favor sycophants and the compliant over other employees who had no way to protest unfair treatment.

One way to mute union influence is through the quality circle. Ostensibly set up to share ideas about quality, the group can be a vehicle for developing a pro-company attitude. "The creation of sound labor-management relations in Japan often depends on building up a small core of workers at the shop floor level who are able to reconcile their dual roles as loyal employees and loyal union members," says productivity consultant Maasaki Imai.[14] "The loyal employee wishes to work hand-in-hand with management to create better products and bigger profits."

None of these cooptation and end-run strategies for weakening unions are necessary. All Japanese companies need to do is pay attention to their own experiences in Japan, where an active union working on behalf of its members actually is a help not a hindrance. Sharp has not had much problem with unions in America. International Brotherhood of Electrical Workers officials and workers seem to get along well with management in Sharp's Memphis plant. Why? "Well, we have family day once a year at an amusement park near our plant," explained one labor relations manager with a straight face. Japanese put great store in these once-a-year things and in events such as birthday parties. Whatever the explanation, Sharp has had little union trouble.

In one electronics firm union negotiations stalled when the company followed the advice of an American union-busting consultant. It then invited the union local head to sit down in private talks. A successful contract soon emerged.[15] In the NUMMI plant the company offered job security promises and got union agreement for team approaches, broad job classification, multi-skill development, and continuous improvement. All is not well at NUMMI, but at least the union seems to be functioning and is listened to. At a large tire company the union agreed to what the Japanese call PDCA (Plan, Do, Check, Action). This involves special attention to shop floor activities in which each production stage has "customers" and "producers," learning from errors, constant surveying of workers, and lots of training.

The success of these management-union activities depended on the Japanese giving up their fear of unions and actively dealing with them. Information was freely shared, and the focus was on tying wages and benefits to productivity increases emerging out of human resource management and technology management. Japanese managers call this "humanware" development. Basically, the employee becomes more productive through broad-based training, increased communication with other workers and supervisors, and through bonus opportunities. The goals are increased output without sacrificing quality. What the Japanese want unions to do is help them develop employees who are flexible, motivated, and communicative. As I have noted elsewhere, Japanese labor productivity is low, so the humanware idea is more of a rescue plan than an in-place, ongoing program. But those companies that implement it and deal fairly with American unions should do quite well in the United States.

WAIT IN THE STREET

In some Japanese assembly line manufacturing, parts suppliers deliver "just-in-time" components three, four, or even ten times a day. The pressure on suppliers is intense, and they often will locate their plants within a few miles of their customer to ensure delivery. The chief reason a manufacturer such as Toyota uses just-in-time is to avoid inventory carrying costs in an environment where warehousing is expensive due to high land values. But the same holds true for suppliers clustered around the Toyota plants. These firms reduce carrying costs by placing some inventory on trucks and having the trucks wait in the street until called in by Toyota. One sees the same practice in New York City's garment district in mid-town Manhattan, where small companies put their inventory on trucks and then park them on the street until needed by a purchaser. Not only does the system foster almost 100 percent availability of parts, it also shifts some of the costs onto the public. Management gurus and Chrysanthemum clubbers rarely discuss this element of just-in-time when they sing the praises of Japanese management.

Such systems cannot work unless the manufacturer has great power over vendors in its *keiretsu* group. As Japanese companies have come to the United States, they often have invited suppliers to locate near their American facilities so that just-in-time practices could continue. What with lower land values, however, the need to escape warehousing is not as great, and the system is not likely to be of much importance in the United States. Moreover, it is dying out in Japan. Taiichi Ono, the developer of *kanban* and just-in-time at Toyota, passed away in 1990, and Toyota's commitment to just-in-time has been rapidly declining since then.

The big problem with having suppliers clustered around a factory is that they compete for labor with the manufacturer. When labor demand rises and the richer manufacturer sucks up the available manpower with high wages, suppliers cannot find people to staff the labor-intensive just-in-time delivery system. This happened in Toyota City in 1990–1991, and Toyota began moving away from just-in-time. Suppliers were dispersed, and automated warehousing was developed. Vendors will deliver once a day, instead of ten times a day, to a warehouse instead of directly to an assembly line. Computer-operated forklifts driven by *kanban* information will pick parts as needed and deliver them to the line without human intervention. Manpower and delivery costs will go down, although Toyota's carrying costs will go up substantially.

During the just-in-time era, for every hour of assembly line overtime, direct suppliers to Toyota worked 1.3 hours extra. Their sub-contractors worked 1.4 hours.[16] The system trades off increased labor costs for suppliers for decreased inventory costs for producers. It will not work in America, where labor costs are high and power over vendors is weaker than in Japan. Toyota's American approach to dealing with vendors is NUMMI's "kanban plus" system, which is based on a parts distribution hub in Chicago. Orders are placed a week or two ahead instead of a few days.

Japanese vendors are often captive, with the purchaser owning stock in the vendor firm, buying most of its product, placing its own retired executives in the vendor's hierarchy, and controlling its financing through an affiliated bank. When dealing with American vendors, such control is out of the question. Nevertheless, Japanese managers try. At Honda a potential vendor fills out an extensive application form, is interviewed at the plant, and opens up its own facilities to a "Quality Assurance Visit," as Honda calls it. Honda employees look at production capacity, financial stability, quality consistency, and plant cleanliness. Only when Honda is satisfied that its standards are met will the firm be allowed to make a bid. Honda rigorously tests sample components, looking for durability, corrosion resistance, and functionality. When it eventually contracts with a vendor, it seeks a long-term relationship. In Japan large Japanese companies tend to squeeze vendors, so their profits and wages are often quite low. This does not seem to be the case in the United States, where more freely functioning markets exist. Honda does insist, however, that quotes be broken down into prices for raw materials, fabrication, packaging, and transportation. In Japan a breakdown like this gives the purchaser information to use against the vendor. Let us say costs are increasing at the assembly plant, and the manufacturer wants to reduce supply costs. A manager will visit the vendor and say, "Your transportation costs are too high. We want you to lower them. Why not take out a loan from our affiliated bank and build a plant closer to ours?" The vendor has little choice in this scenario. Undoubtedly Honda would like to use the information it collects in a similar way in the United States.

Controlling costs by controlling American vendors is a major ingredient in Japanese manufacturing management in the United States. One way to increase control is to constantly badger them about quality. Not only does this tactic lead to good products, it also keeps the vendors in a perpetual state of anxiety. They are thus primed to comply with demands for price cuts or other concessions. When this game does not work, the ultimate threat can be employed, "We will bring our *keiretsu* suppliers from Japan over and set them up in the United States." Clearly this approach is effective, but not for long. American public opinion will not put up with power plays that have worked in Thailand or Indonesia but that are not acceptable in the United States. Japanese manufacturers will have to depend less on cost control through the exercise of market channel power over vendors and more on in-plant cost management. Since they do not like to lay off people who become redundant, they are headed for trouble which only can be resolved through low wages. The 1990s may be characterized by a growing number of successful unionizations of Japanese-owned plants, as workers look for ways of increasing their incomes to match inflation. The alternative to unionization is layoffs with high wages for remaining workers. In the coming decade, then, Japanese manufacturers in the United States will begin to look very similar to American businesses, what with more arm's-length relations with vendors, increasing unionizations in some plants, and avoidance of unions through high wages in others. The Japanese really aren't very different now, and the time will come when they are indistinguishable from American firms.

RESEARCH AND DEVELOPMENT

"We are shifting from a Japanese company with operations all over the world to a global company," said Matsushita's Dick Kraft. "We want companies which are owned by Japan but managed locally. That's a shift for us." The individual divisions of Matsushita are autonomous to the point of almost being independent companies, so the process of localization and globalization will take time. Each division is centralized, with the center in Japan and a high degree of standardization throughout the world, but the divisions have little contact with each other. The small screen TV division, for example, has few links to big screen TV. What holds them together is a series of R & D labs serving the whole company. Each division competes with the others for the services of an R & D lab. If a division does not bid enough funding for a project at one lab, it may find another one to do the research. The labs are independent from each other and often work on duplicate projects, an expensive undertaking but often fruitful. "If things get tough and margins get small, we may have to forego some of the redundancy," noted Mr. Kraft. "But the system now is very effective for stimulating innovation."

Big Japanese manufacturers were on an R & D binge in the late 1980s and early 1990s. Hitachi spent 10.7 percent of sales on R & D in 1990, up from 9.1 percent in 1988.[17] Other firms have made smaller but equally dramatic increases. Matsushita will have a $2 billion center housing 2,000 information and communication researchers up and running by 1993. Hitachi's R & D staff is already at about 12,000. Basic product research will be done in Japan, with the subsidiaries doing everything else. Both Sharp and Matsushita are moving towards fully integrated manufacturing in America, leaving only knowledge creation in Japan.

The better Japanese firms do not wait for vendors to come up with an innovation. They develop it themselves and then tell vendors what to do.[18] In the new global R & D system being pioneered by Matsushita, senior management will decide on companywide projects which the R & D center in Japan will pursue. Smaller projects will be developed at the foreign subsidiaries and sent out for bid from R & D units scattered throughout the world. Or the units themselves may come up with a plan and look for a "buyer." As at Matsushita, these R & D buyers and sellers will come together perhaps once a year at a "fair" held in Japan by headquarters. Funding "prices" will be negotiated and deals made. With R & D material in hand, the subsidiaries will tell vendors what to make and how. This system institutionalizes both global innovation and local adaptation. Its drawbacks are its costs, which are much higher than is common in American firms, and the passivity required of vendors. If they stop innovating and simply wait for directions and plans from Honda or Toshiba, then those big companies will have to depend solely on themselves for new technology ideas from fixed cost R & D operations. Some corporations have reduced their risks by becoming knowledge seeker firms in America as well as competitors. They buy into technologically innovative U.S. firms to get sources of fresh ideas in case their own R & D should go dry. This is a smart move, since firms' headquarters often emasculate R & D in Japan when Japan's domestic economy has a downturn.

ACCOUNTING IS NOT STEWARDSHIP

One of the biggest stumbling blocks Japanese investors face in managing American plants is not the American worker. Rather it is the American accountant. Managerial and cost accounting in America have traditionally focused on measuring and controlling labor and material costs. Overhead costs, which in the past have been low, are arbitrarily assigned to units. But labor costs in consumer electronics and other manufacturing industries have fallen to less than 10 percent of total costs, and overhead costs of R & D, sales, and marketing have soared. Japanese manufacturers cope with this shift better than Americans, since they often create a target cost and then do what it takes to get to that cost. Measuring overhead correctly to establish the real cost of a unit is not as big a headache, since the percent changes in costs over time are what count. As long as measures are consistent over time, it doesn't matter too much whether they are fair or valid. For the Japanese, accounting is not allowed to interfere with their philosophy of constant tinkering to achieve continuous improvements. As one Japanese accounting professor put it, exaggerating somewhat, "Japanese accounting is what you Americans call 'window dressing.' " According to a Tokyo Metropolitan University study, the big cost in Japan is subcontracting, which is typically 40 percent of total manufacturing and has steadily replaced labor costs, which fell from 20 percent in 1950 to 3 percent in the 1990s.[19] Accounting for subcontractor costs is rather easy when you think about it. You get X amount of components for Y yen (or dollars in the United States), giving X/Y unit costs. One of the hidden benefits of Japanese reliance on subcontracting is the elimination of the regiments of accountants which one usually finds in large American firms. With target costing and subcontracting, only small platoons of accountants are needed.

American managers tend to use a budget as a control and monitoring tool. This is not a budget's use to Japanese. Instead, they constantly revise budgets during a fiscal year, using the process as a trigger to stimulate discussions over where the unit is and where it should be going.[20] Japanese budgets may be more detailed than is usual in America, but the numbers are not hard and fast. In fact, Japanese managers like to do long-range plans which use numbers of little reliability. But again, the process is a communication stimulus, not a control. The numbers do not drive action—people do that. Japanese firms have little interest in accounting as a stewardship on behalf of owners' interests. It is a purely managerial function, focused on future gains rather than the protection of assets. This will change as a market for ownership develops in Japanese equity markets and new owners become concerned about getting their money's worth, but for the next decade or so, Japanese accounting will be a help rather than a hindrance to American operations. American accountants will find that their watchdog role will not be valued in Japanese-owned firms. Only their contribution to managerial decision making will count.

The average Japanese manufacturer in the United States is less profitable and has lower labor productivity than the average American manufacturer. It probably has more satisfied workers but less satisfied engineers, managers, and accountants. It has better relations with vendors but poorer relations with unions. If we add up all the pluses and minuses, Japanese- and American-owned firms are not too dissimilar.

That is the broad picture. When we narrow the frame, concrete differences emerge, most of them evolving out of the Japanese firms' greater need for power and control. Employees are carefully selected, and they are controlled rather than motivated thereafter by the use of team rhetoric and a tradeoff of limited job security for unhindered managerial decisionmaking regarding tasks, roles, and so forth. The workers don't seem to mind. Unions are usually co-opted or avoided, but some Japanese firms seem to work very well with them. Vendors are put into a position where they lack bargaining power, but they often are treated fairly.

The development of benevolent but firm control is not just a characteristic of Japanese culture, although Japan is an authoritarian society. Power is needed to manage the highly coordinated production process so that the firm is instantly responsive to market demand at one end of the production chain and R & D innovations at the other. The *kaizen* process and its chief tool, statistical process control, cannot function without constant vigilance by managers to ensure that no one slacks off. For example, SPC applied to the time a worker takes to do a task requires a baseline standard. Japanese managers create elaborate descriptions of the movements a worker should perform and then demand that those movements are followed on the assembly line. Deviations from the baseline then can be observed and explained. Absolute adherence to baseline behavior is required in the Deming method, and Japanese firms seek power to require continuous adherence.

The strengths of Japanese manufacturing in quality and flexibility probably will not be as important in the United States as they are in Japan. Americans make price-quality tradeoffs more than Japanese do, and American firms soon will learn how to be more flexible. What really will count are core competencies. Honda's ability to produce remarkable engines will keep Americans buying, after all, not rapid model changes. Japanese firms sense this and are investing heavily in R & D and are working hard to harmonize R & D with manufacturing and marketing. The approach taken by many of the bigger firms is risky and expensive, depending as it does mostly on in-house efforts which often are duplicated in various labs, but risks are offset by knowledge-seeking purchases of American high tech firms. Also, American engineers are ideally trained to take part in basic research. Unlike their Japanese counterparts, who are good at trial and error tinkering on the assembly line and in the development lab, American engineers often have solid theoretical grounding and deep expertise. Japanese manufacturers need to do better, however, at keeping these engineers happy. That will be their biggest challenge of the 1990s in America.

SEVENTEEN

Autos, Where Something Has to Give

Worldwide overcapacity in automobile manufacturing will lead to a reduction in the number of firms in the 1990s. All manufacturers will try to produce for all markets. This will be a big change for the Japanese, who have focused on selling compacts and subcompacts in America. They will move more into small pickups and luxury cars and probably will seek to break into the full-sized pickup, van, and car markets now dominated by American producers.

One of the key elements in the success of Japanese auto manufacturing has been flexibility. Lead times have been continuously shortened to adjust to an ever-changing marketplace. Yet flexibility may soon become less relevant. As vehicle prices rose dramatically during the 1980s, consumers extended their loan periods. The average maturity for auto loans is about 56.2 months. As consumers keep their cars longer to avoid negative equity—owing more on their loans than the vehicles are worth—a longer, less volatile cycle for autos will emerge.[1] Quick adaptation to rapid changes will not be as important as building quality into cars so they retain value longer. This is where the bigger Japanese firms excel. As noted in the last chapter, however, Americans make price-quality tradeoffs more than Japanese do. Firms like Honda and Toyota hope that Americans will continue to pay high prices for high quality. If they do not and begin to want low price-modest quality cars, Japanese strategies will have to evolve. They produce at low cost in the United States now because of low retirement and medical costs for workers and perhaps due to low costs of components from captive Japanese suppliers, but all of that will change as employees age and suppliers break free of *keiretsu* relationships which do not benefit them. As costs rise, can they keep prices down?

A NEW, COMPETITIVE INDUSTRY

Subcompact cars made in Mexico, Brazil, Thailand, and South Korea compete in the United States with the autos of both Japanese-owned and American manufacturers. Under this kind of pressure, domestic producers are moving more towards intermediate and luxury market segments. Honda, producing in Ohio, led the way in this, but Toyota and Nissan soon followed. When the dollar falls, however, the price of Nissan's and Toyota's luxury imports will rise, while Honda's price can stay the same. It is thus ideally positioned to reap most of the benefits from the Japanese rush away from compacts. Things can change fast, however, if Toyota continues to pour capital into U.S. production. Should it choose to do so, it can become the dominant foreign auto firm in America in all markets, replacing Honda. With its near-monopoly status in Japan and $13 billion in cash available, Toyota can do just about anything it wants in the United States.

If firms are in all market niches, there will be nowhere to go if competition gets too tough. In the 1990s firms thus will eventually have to compete in their markets rather than flee to other markets, and the low-cost, high-quality producers will win big. This scenario is already being played out, as the biggest high cost producer, General Motors, announced major plant closings in 1990 and 1991. GM and other producers can no longer count on overall market growth as their salvation. Auto sales in 1988 were 10.54 million vehicles. U.S. government forecasts for 1994 are 10.45 million.[2] In the 1991–1992 recession they were under 7 million. Consumers probably will buy even fewer cars than forecast, so competition will occur in a declining market. Only a few bright spots exist. Light truck sales are expected to increase from about 4.6 million vehicles in 1990 to 4.9 million in 1994. Domestic producers took some of this market share away from imports over the latter half of the 1980s, due mostly to the high-yen, high-price environment and to trade barriers against Japanese two-door sport-utility vehicles. A low dollar and new product offerings from U.S. producers should ensure continued American success, although the Japanese will move into the market to a greater extent with new passenger vans and four-door sport-utility vehicles.

Another moderately bright spot is in the auto parts business. New equipment sales may not grow, but the large total vehicle fleet in the United States will ensure a stable market. American-owned firms have lost business for original equipment as GM sales declined in the 1980s and Japanese producers turned to their affiliated suppliers who also have located in the United States. But the Japanese eventually will go with whomever gives them the best deal, and Americans will regain some of the lost business. Exporting of auto parts, aided by a low dollar and Congressional pressure on Japan to lower barriers, will also help. Nevertheless, competition will increase from over 300 Japanese parts suppliers who have built facilities in America. As these firms see their *keiretsu* bonds weaken in the face of a new global business regime, they will seek business from American Big Three producers as well as from transplants.

LEAN, MEAN, OR BOTH?

After an extensive study of worldwide auto manufacturing practices, MIT researchers came to two conclusions.[3] First, Japanese producers varied widely in their performance; some were superb, while others were among the worst firms studied. Second, the best of the Japanese manufacturers practiced a "lean" style of management—somewhere between mass and customized production—which was the model for the future.

What is lean auto manufacturing? In the Japanese approach it is the replacement of arm's-length, horizontal economic relationships with employees, dealers, and suppliers by vertical arrangements based on benevolent treatment from the manufacturer in return for high performance responses from those beholden to it. The MIT researchers refer to this system as "rational," a sign of their obvious distaste for presumably "irrational" market mechanisms.

The lean manufacturer in Japan takes equity positions in supplier companies, loans them money, and shares executives with them. In response the suppliers open up their books and production operations, creating a transparency that fosters close coordination, especially in the product development process. A similar transparency is built with dealers. The system produces short development times, reduced engineering effort, and low-cost parts.

Another key element of the lean approach occurs internally. Job security is offered to employees, and in return they supposedly become loyal and motivated, willing to accept increased responsibility for tasks and problem solving. The workers become eager to cut waste in time, effort, and resources (hence "lean"), and they take control of their work in a productive manner.

The lean manufacturers, which operate without much of the hierarchy we find in Western companies, try to make employees understand that their capacity to solve increasingly difficult problems is the most meaningful type of advancement they can achieve, even if their titles don't change.[4]

The implication here is that Japanese car producers have figured out a way to make Charlie Chaplin feel fulfilled after being dragged around by all that machinery.

The lean work environment is supposedly peopled by employees with secure jobs who adopt company goals of high quality and flexibility as their own goals. Each worker is respected as an individual, but willingly submerges himself or herself in the work group. Fully trained, they perform multiple tasks, unconstrained by rigid job classifications and work rules. They do high-level analyses of data collected on the job, eagerly sharing the data on both intra- and inter-group levels. Unafraid of risks in their communal, supportive environment, the employees use trial and error to develop innovations which are quickly adopted by the firm's managers, whose main job is to coordinate rather than be directive.

Nevertheless, even those in favor of lean managing admit that the crucial element in the system is pressure: pressure on employees to avoid waste, maintain quality, and cut idle time; pressure on suppliers to reduce unit costs; pressure on dealers to collect market information. Pressure and stress replace economic exchange relations as the driving forces behind lean manufacturing. At the NUMMI plant in Fremont, California, which Toyota manages on behalf of a Toyota-GM joint venture, some employees have complained that work injuries are invariably blamed on them; absenteeism is a serious offense; performance is machine-driven rather than self-paced; groups exist to harangue, not support; unions are mouthpieces for management, not representatives of worker interests; speed up is the name of the game; and fear and intimidation forestall grievances.

Something is wrong here with the "lean" approach, and a closer look at NUMMI reveals what it is. According to the 1985 contract between NUMMI and the U.A.W. Local 2244, the firm offers employment security to employees and must take several steps in economic downturns before laying off workers.[5] It must reduce managers' salaries, reassign subcontract work to union employees, and seek voluntary layoffs. In return for these guarantees, employees are to focus on continuous improvements in productivity and quality. This arrangement, although more formally stated, is very similar to the kind of deal Japanese workers have struck with large companies in Japan. American workers did not know what they were getting into, however. In return for job security they traded off control over tasks, work pace, and virtually every other aspect of their jobs. Where GM workers actually work only thirty-five to forty-five minutes each hour, NUMMI workers work for fifty-six minutes. If they develop sore arms or suffer a minor injury, they may fall behind and be fired. What they owe to management is not loyalty and commitment, but rather submission. What their work groups, which depend on every member contributing if group bonuses are to be gained, do for them is exert peer pressure to perform rather than give mutual support. This is the way Toyota's production system works in Toyota City in Japan, and it is no surprise to see it transplanted.

Make no mistake about what is going on in NUMMI's lean system. Toyota is not exploiting anyone, nor is it treating Americans any differently than Japanese workers. Americans made a deal in which they gave up most of their autonomy in the workplace in return for job security. Management got what it wanted: control. We hear lots of talk about team spirit and cooperation in Japanese management, but the reality often is that managers in Japanese-owned organizations seek and get much more control over workers than is usually possible in America. Since American workers were unfamiliar with the control tradeoff for job security, they went into the NUMMI situation blind. Events of the last seven years have been eye opening. Rather than blame the Japanese, however, who are acting in good faith, American workers should either accept the reality that benefits come with costs, or they should renegotiate.

What is called "lean" manufacturing may be the model for high-performance auto production in Japan, but it works because power is concentrated in the hands of manufacturers to a much greater extent than is common in America. Unions are weak, as are suppliers and dealers. Moreover, Japanese government auto inspection procedures are so onerous that consumers find it easier to trade in cars after about four years rather than pay the exorbitant inspection fees. The four-year trade-in is so prevalent that companies can easily predict sales well in advance. Since three or four companies hold 80 percent of the market, and shares don't change, they know almost exactly what to expect. Thanks to government help, then, Toyota and Nissan know pretty much what the future holds. This knowledge is brought to bear in product development, parts production, and labor relations. Indeed, lean production cannot work without predictability. Delivery times, inventories, and staff can all be cut to the bone because wild swings in demand—common in the United States—do not and cannot occur in Japan.

"Power" manufacturing is a better description than "lean" of the Toyota-style approach. It is characterized by the following:[6]

· *Increased regimentation of the work force.* Often described as *management by stress,* the aim of this management method is to locate weak points in the system by having a worker signal a lighted *andon* board when he or she falls behind. The *andon* board shows the status of each work station on the assembly line. If the cord is not pulled again within a set period of time (e.g., a minute), the line stops and a management team focuses on solving the problem.

· *Tightened specifications and monitoring of how jobs are done.* The management team responsible for the design or, in the case of a frequently lighted *andon* board, subsequent redesign of an assembly task must break the required task down into the tiniest of separate *acts* and come up with a detailed written specification of how each worker is to do each job. This specification is posted near the line so the group leader can check to see that the worker does not vary his or her methods.

· *Minimized work force with no replacements for absentees.* Since each task is broken down into simple actions that require little special training, mastery of assembly tasks is accomplished quickly. As a result, workers can change tasks quickly, thus eliminating the need for absentee replacements, and the work force is kept to a minimum.

· *Continued and systematic speedup of the line.* This is accomplished by constantly looking for ways to either minimize the time it takes a worker to complete an assembly task or maximize the number of assembly tasks a worker can complete.

Integration and coordination can be added to power as the other important dimension of auto management by the best Japanese firms. At Honda's Ohio plant, stamping, welding, painting, plastic injection molding, assembly, and quality assurance all occur under one roof. Honda's American designers work on a model all the way from the drawing board to the production line. Perhaps most important of all, Japanese auto makers try to produce more than one model on an assembly line. This lowers investment costs, fixed costs, and thus breakeven costs. A firm with low breakeven costs can compete well in a price-cutting war or it can withstand low market share for a long time while it builds a customer base. The problem is to train workers to handle multiple (although simple) tasks in a complex assembly process, and as noted, firms like Toyota, Honda, and Nissan work hard at this.

POWER OVER SUPPLIERS

Transplants have concentrated in the Midwest and border states. Honda is in Ohio, Toyota in Kentucky, Fuji Heavy Industries and Isuzu are in Indiana, Mitsubishi/Chrysler is in Illinois, Mazda in Michigan, and Nissan in Tennessee. Only the Toyota/GM joint venture is located elsewhere, in this case California. The attraction of these states is their proximity to markets and inexpensive labor, not state subsidies or the nearness of suppliers. Indeed, Japanese auto makers have shown a preference for their own affiliated vendors, and they either import parts from Japan or buy from the suppliers' American subsidiaries. About 48 percent of transplant parts come from Japanese-owned American companies, and 40 percent are imported from Japan. Only about 12 percent are purchased from American-owned firms.[7] NUMMI buys engines and transaxles from Japan, but it has 65 percent local content for all parts. One hundred percent of steel sheet components used in Toyota's U.S. cars and 80 percent of Nissan's are procured locally. Nissan's policy has been to rely on domestic suppliers, and it did not invite Japanese parts makers to follow it to America. Many did, however, and they are utilized. Mazda has a local content ratio of 70–75 percent, as does Honda. TRW, an American-owned supplier to Honda of electronic controllers, also sells to the parent in Japan, as do three other U.S. firms which produce batteries, filters, and ignition plugs. Honda's goal is to unify parts purchasing as much as possible for its U.S. domestic production and its exports to the United States—a move which might lead to more business for U.S. suppliers.

The few American-owned firms that do business with the transplants soon find out what power manufacturing is. The Japanese producer often demands proprietary information on costs and production techniques and then works with the supplier on ways to cut costs and improve quality. The idea of gross margin as something set mostly by marketplace conditions soon disappears, replaced by an amount the Japanese firm considers reasonable.[8] Most American suppliers seem to be making good money, however, so the Japanese companies cannot be accused of cheating. Power to them is to be used wisely, not greedily.

So powerful do the Japanese manufacturers become that they feel confident in shifting much of the responsibility for engineering and producing most parts to suppliers. In Japan, Toyota adds only 27 percent of the value of a car, while GM, with less control over vendors, adds 70 percent. GM could take more power if it wished, but like most American manufacturers it prefers market-based relations with suppliers. This is clearly not what the Japanese prefer. American transplants single-source 98 percent of their parts, almost all from Japanese or Japanese-owned vendors tied to them in *keiretsu* or other relationships. Only manufacturers with great control over suppliers would do such a thing. While just-in-time is not as important as in Japan, these vendors still deliver more than twice as many parts that way than do vendors for Big Three manufacturers. Their lead time for installing new dies is about nineteen weeks, almost half the time Big Three vendors take. Die-change times average twenty-one minutes—it is 114 minutes for Big Three suppliers. These data suggest the remarkable speed, flexibility, and performance which increased control over suppliers gives the Japanese transplants.[9]

The vendors will not stay captive forever, however. Many of them are what were referred to in an earlier chapter as reluctant followers.

As they see just how good they are in comparison with some weak American-owned firms, they will become less passive and seek Big Three business. Some firms are doing this by forming joint ventures with American parts makers. Nagoya Screw Manufacturing Company, a Honda supplier, joined with Elco Industries in 1989. Elco wanted a chance to sell to Honda, and Nagoya wanted access to Elco's Big Three customers. One reason for the suppliers' need to grow has to do with the module-focused procurement practices of auto makers. Instead of making single parts of dashboards, for example, some suppliers now are required to produce a whole complex unit. High volume is needed to keep unit costs low, so the transplant vendors have to look beyond the Japanese purchasers. Honda and the others probably will not resist this movement, since lower-cost components will result.

As the Japanese parts suppliers look outward, American suppliers seek Japanese business. Transplants produced 1.1 million cars in 1990, about 11 percent of the U.S. market. Growth is predicted, mostly at the expense of GM and Chrysler. Their U.S. vendors will try to obtain business from Japanese firms, and as the Japanese vendors branch out, openings for Americans will occur. But in order to handle expanded business, American parts makers will have to become bigger. This is happening; the number of U.S. suppliers shrunk from 3,400 in 1979 to 2,200 in 1989. These larger firms are better positioned to meet exacting Japanese demands.

The perils of small size were evident in the tale of Variety Stamping, which became a Honda supplier in 1987.[10] Honda's business increased employment in the firm from 100 to 183 employees, and growth accelerated. But under pressure from Honda, Variety had to purchase parts and technology from Japanese subcontractors. Honda also forced Variety to open its books on overhead and material costs; after a time unit gross margins fell. Then Honda began to reject shipments because of poor quality. Cash flow problems occurred almost at once. Soon a twenty-person Honda team showed up and virtually took over the plant, forcing Variety to ignore other orders while it dealt with Honda's needs. Eventually everything fell apart and the company went bankrupt. Variety probably could have survived Honda's power play with adequate working capital to carry it through the initial rough spots as it learned to manage quality and cost better. Over time it would have fit itself into Honda's system and prospered. The lessons of all this are two. First, when you do business with Japanese car makers, you do not simply deal with them—you work for them. Second, you need to be big enough to finance organizational learning about efficiency and quality.

In their drive to gain power over suppliers in America, a move which has naturally led them to summon captive Japanese vendors to the

United States, the transplants may be making a fundamental error. By depending so much on compliant, single source suppliers who can only make one or two deliveries a day instead of eight, the Japanese assemblers have no backup when defective parts arrive. They must rework them on the spot. Problems with suppliers appear to be the source of rather startling findings by researchers at MIT's International Motor Vehicle Program. They found that the best American-owned company takes 18.6 hours to produce a vehicle. The best Japanese transplant takes 18.8 hours.[11] Although the Japanese gain productivity from greater automation in welding and painting, they lose it because of difficulties with supplies. If these problems continue, the transplants will move away from single-sourcing, and opportunities for American-owned firms will emerge. The assemblers will still practice power management; it will simply be a bit more awkward with the less submissive Americans.

POWER OVER EMPLOYEES

Total incomes of transplant workers in 1989, including overtime, bonuses, and profit sharing, ranged from a low of $28,038 at Mitsubishi/Chrysler to a high of $36,013 at NUMMI. At the Big Three, the range was $35,371 to $37,434. If we factor in medical and pension costs, which are large for the American assemblers and small for the Japanese, we can see why transplants can build a car for $500–$700 less. This gap cannot continue for more than a few years. As the young, healthy Americans hired at transplants age and begin to suffer from the inevitable perils of assembly manufacturing, Japanese labor costs will rise. They will also increase as workers seek parity with union wages as the price to be paid for non-unionization.

Within ten years, then, labor will cost the same at both Japanese-owned and American plants. Also, by that time the few low-productivity American plants will have caught up to the American and Japanese leaders or have gone under. This is a most probable scenario which the Japanese would like to avoid. Highly controlled but generally benevolent management of people is their declared strength, and they will compete on that basis. The wisdom of this is open to debate.

Let us begin with Mazda's Flat Rock, Michigan, plant. By 1990 the magic of Japanese people-management had worn off. Absenteeism was up to 10 percent compared with 2 percent at Honda, and output had fallen from a high of 23,000 vehicles a month in late 1988 to about 14,000.[12] About 300 temporary full-time employees had been laid off, but the "regular" employee jobs were not threatened. To keep them busy, Mazda had slowed assembly lines, increased training, and begun using blue collar workers to help plan new model startups. A positive benefit was an increase in employee loyalty, as the workers noted that

Mazda had meant what it said when it had offered some job security to them. U.A.W. officials were unhappy, however, since they recognized that job security for core employees depended on flexibility in hiring and firing temporaries who were also union members. In a sense, Mazda officials were lucky. After a year or so of poor management, they were able to pull the job security rabbit out of the hat and magically turn most of the workforce from hostile to friendly.

A similar process was played out at NUMMI. By early 1990 sales had become sluggish, morale had dipped, and quality problems had emerged. Managers referred to workers as slipping back to "the old GM ways," and workers were complaining about unkept promises and a lack of open communications.[13] Team meetings were not being held, the assembly line was stopped up to 2.5 hours a day, and managers were using threats of layoffs to get employees back on track.

Japanese assembly manufacturing management works best in orderly market conditions. When sales suddenly fall off, the pressures mount to cut costs. *Kaizen*, the continuous improvement process, becomes a race to find ways to squeeze more output out of employees. As work efforts mount, quality problems increase. Worried Japanese give up rhetoric about innovation and every-worker-challenged-by-his-job and demand strict adherence to standardized ways of performing tasks most efficiently. The no layoff policy still brings out strong employee commitment and a grudging acceptance of pressure, but managers discourage workers from pulling the cord which stops the line. A slippage in quality is inevitable. Something of this sort seems to have happened at NUMMI in late 1989–early 1990.

At both Mazda and NUMMI, then, variations in demand—rare in Japan and thus not part of Japanese managerial thinking—threaten the system. Tasks get piled on, "waste" that did not exist before suddenly is rooted out, quality falls, workers are blamed and threats are made, and only the no layoff policy saves the operation from chaos. As discussed earlier, one of the few cultural characteristics of Japanese managers is an intolerance for uncertainty and an inability to cope well with highly ambiguous and uncertain environments. The highly cyclical U.S. auto market is such an environment, and in it the usually benevolent power of Japanese managers sometimes turns nasty.

So far Honda's American operations have been less burdened by cyclical changes because of the high quality of its output. In an orderly growth period, Japanese managers are at their best. At Honda work teams range from five to twenty employees. Each team reports to a coordinator who supervises four to five teams. Team leaders can become coordinators, who in turn can move into management. The system requires everyone to know all the jobs, so a coordinator might know how to do as many as 100 tasks (most would be quite simple).

When absence occurs, a team leader or coordinator is ready to step in as backup. The same goes for an unwanted line slowdown. Each team member rotates from job to job to relieve tedium while learning multiple tasks, and people are regularly transferred to other teams in other departments to develop breadth of knowledge.

Honda goes all out to encourage employee feedback and ideas. In addition to a quick response suggestion system (quick responses to suggestions encourage more suggestions), it operates the Now, Next, New Honda Circles program, which consists of four- to five-person problem-solving teams which voluntarily form to work on specific issues of productivity, quality, or safety.[14] Management provides guidelines on how to form a team and to conduct statistical process control and other procedures. Then it lets them do their own thing. No prior approvals or proposals are required. Twice a year teams present the results of their projects in a packed auditorium to a panel of executives. Even vendor teams are encouraged to participate. The two best teams take part in a worldwide competition held annually at Honda facilities in Japan. Team activities take place after work, but employees receive overtime pay. Perhaps that's why about one-third of Honda's U.S. workforce participates. In addition, participating in NH Circles earns points which can be converted into prizes. The program costs over $1 million a year, but Honda believes that the results are worth it.

Honda's continued success in managing its employees contrasts sharply with the up-down variations at Mazda and NUMMI. In interviews, Japanese executives blame the union for problems at these plants and point to non-unionized Honda as proof. This is almost certainly incorrect. The U.A.W. locals have been compliant and helpful at both Mazda and NUMMI. The real problem is in the system. It has no slack to absorb increased demand, so workers must be pushed hard to move the product. But it also is too rigid to cope with downturns. To establish a baseline for statistical time and motion studies, employees are required to do each task in a programmed manner within a set time period. When disturbances from the marketplace force change, the baseline disappears, and with it goes any chance of incrementally fostering increased efficiency and quality. Unused to the unpredictabilities of the American market, Japanese auto managers often don't know what to do in rapid upturns and downturns. Honda so far has seen steady and predictable growth (with some downturns during the 1991 recession). If variability enters the picture, it could experience trouble on the assembly line. Wisely, however, the company has taken steps to reduce uncertainty somewhat. It has integrated its operations in America to a greater extent than the other transplants. With a strong dealer network and extensive marketing and advertising operations, it can predict sales better than its rivals and can plan gradual adjustments.

With design and engine production in the United States, moreover, it has the ability to rapidly translate market signals into design and engineering changes. This integration buffers the manufacturing process somewhat so that change can be planned for and built into the system. Power manufacturing at its best creates "no surprises" conditions which allow *kaizen* to plod on in its steady, relentless manner. One wonders, nevertheless, what will happen at Honda should a quick, sharp recession, deeper than 1991, occur in the U.S. economy.

FALLING INTO EACH OTHER'S ARMS

During the 1980s Ford improved efficiency 31 percent, Chrysler 19 percent, and GM only 5 percent. According to industry data, Ford was making about $951 per unit in 1988, Chrysler $228, and GM $47. GM clearly has not faced up to the Japanese invasion, and it may suffer as a consequence. By 1995 transplants are expected to have three million vehicle capacity, an amount equal to predicted overcapacity in the United States. Something will have to give. Both Chrysler and GM will take the brunt of the attack, but Japanese casualties will occur also. Fuji Heavy Industries and its partner, Isuzu, will have problems, but Nissan may step in to help. As for Mazda, beset by management problems and a narrow product line, it hired a former Chrysler marketing manager to work on improving its image in the United States. To broaden its line, it turned to purchasing Ford Explorers, renamed the Navajo, to sell in the United States.

Mazda also has been seeking joint ventures and equity participation with Ford to obtain capital and reduce its risks. Ford owns about 25 percent of Mazda and has developed strong ties with it. Mazda's U.S. transplant sells most of its 626 model output to Ford, which markets it as the Probe. The company also designs new small cars for Ford and builds other models in Japan. As the auto industry consolidates in the 1990s, Mazda will become more and more a Ford affiliate.

Among the transplants, only Honda has chosen to go it alone. It is unaffiliated with American or Japanese producers. For the rest, complex interrelationships are developing. Daihatsu is partially owned by Toyota, which has the NUMMI joint venture with GM. Fuji Heavy Industries, producing Subarus with Isuzu, is in the Nissan *keiretsu*. Nissan in turn supplies minivan panels to a Ford-Nissan joint venture. Chrysler owns Mitsubishi stock. The two firms jointly own Diamond Star in Normal, Illinois, and plan to set up a Canadian joint venture to produce a car to compete against Honda. A noteworthy dimension to all of this collaboration is the one-way direction of equity stakes. As of 1990, the Japanese firms had not bought into the American Big Three.

If Chrysler fades, however, only Japanese capital from Honda or Toyota may be available to save it.

Besides joining up with the Japanese, American firms also are fleeing to Europe in the hope they can benefit from EEC barriers against Japanese vehicles. Ford added to its major European presence by purchasing Jaguar PLC, and GM did the same when it bought Saab-Scania AB's auto operations. Chrysler has failed to develop the European safe haven, and so it will have to live or die in combat with the Japanese firms on American soil. With the Japan-bashing Lee Iacocca at its head or, if he steps down, hovering in the background, Chrysler will not find strong Japanese interest in risk-sharing arrangements unless it is willing to make some very sweet deals.

Honda, unlike the other transplants, has claimed that it is developing a genuinely independent auto company in the United States. By 1991 it had over $2 billion invested in its Ohio facilities, and 9,000 employees were able to produce over 500,000 vehicles. Another $2 billion was about to be committed. Design, R & D, and engine production were already in or were moving to the United States. Yet the company still had more Japanese managers on hand (4.5 percent of employees) than Nissan (1.3 percent) or Toyota in Georgetown (2.1 percent). Heads of sales, research, and development were Japanese, and the company had shown typically Japanese attitudes towards blacks and women in its hiring. Every time Honda was criticized, it reaffirmed its U.S. commitment and made some move to drive the point home. In 1990 it named an American executive vice president to Honda of America's board and developed a similar set up at Honda Motor Co., its other subsidiary. It periodically publicizes the export of a few of its American-produced cars back to Japan. More than Nissan and Toyota, which are the oligopoly leaders in Japan and have less to worry about, Honda needs America. Indeed, the company's future depends on its success in the United States. With only 9 percent of the Japanese market and a late start in Europe, Honda has decided that it has no other choice. It is one of the few Japanese firms which actually planned its American ventures for years before moving—in contrast to those firms which simply rushed into the United States when the dollar was cheap.

What is surprising is not that Honda has been successful but that it has overcome some very bad press. Its racism in hiring received wide coverage, as has its power approach to dealing with American-owned suppliers—when it even bothers to deal with them. Every time Honda blunders, its executives promise to do better next time and to learn from the experience. Strangely enough, I and probably most Americans believe them. Honda produces great cars by making step by step, incremental, trial and error advances. The same is likely to be the case for its advances in other areas. All of the transplants, in fact—those that are likely to survive, anyway—are adapting to the U.S. environment.

What the Japanese auto makers need to do is modify their power manufacturing approach. Highly coordinated and integrated operations are difficult in the cyclical American market. An expanded focus on market research and demand control through advertising, credit management, and customer deals is required. Blaming employee problems on unions is a foolish thing to do. Better to help workers understand the trade-off they make when they get job security. Also, the *kaizen* process, which in part requires workers to perform in a rigid, standardized manner so that a performance baseline can be created, cannot cope well with wild swings in sales. Better marketing will help somewhat, but Japanese managers will have to inspire incremental changes without firm baseline data. American-style improvement incentives for workers will have to be developed.

Japanese vendors are not as captive in America as in Japan, and the transplants will have to move towards multiple sourcing, using American-owned supply firms more and more. This is sensible, especially for a transplant whose U.S. production begins to be greater than its parent's exports to America. To standardize parts, parents will want to start using American-produced components in both transplant and export-oriented output. Currently, Japan's auto makers usually export more to the United States than they produce there, so they naturally standardize parts by depending on home country vendors. This will change in the 1990s. As for the Japanese suppliers, they will seek greater economies of scope and scale by seeking Big Three business and moving into the secondary parts markets. The high performance they have developed under the Japanese power manufacturing regime will ensure that they are fierce competitors.

Japanese manufacturers will become more cost conscious. They will look at several vendors before choosing one, not simply summon a home-country affiliate to America because it is easily controlled. They will be more interested in quality-cost trade-offs. So far, according to the MIT studies, improved quality has not come at the cost of reduced productivity in Japanese auto manufacturing. But one hears rumors about quiet substitutions of inferior parts in Japan when cost pressures loom. If true, are such practices also occurring in the transplants? Hopefully not, since costs can be managed by continuing to do what Japanese managers are good at: designing cost control into the development process, speeding up changeovers, and continuously searching out ways to reduce waste. Japanese-style power manufacturing cannot be transplanted whole to the United States, but its emphasis on human resource management, production process control, and careful attention to vendor relations will serve as a firm basis for success. The transplants will make it in America by adapting, just as Big Three American firms will adapt by moving away from old-fashioned mass production towards a more Japanese approach. It isn't really a "lean" style of managing, but it works nonetheless.

EIGHTEEN

Problems in the Office

In 1989 and also in 1990, over 70 percent of Japanese investment in the United States was in non-manufacturing businesses, mostly hotels, entertainment companies, real estate, financial services, and wholesale trade. This was a move away from manufacturing investment, which dominated in 1988 and earlier years. The swing contrasts with the behavior of other nations' investors in America. They have tended to put one-half of their capital in manufacturing and one-half in non-manufacturing in recent years. Also unlike the Japanese, other foreigners invest more in insurance and retail trade. Japanese life insurance companies are sitting atop a $700 billion mountain of assets, but they do relatively little direct investing in the United States, preferring 30-year government bonds instead. The insurance giants have purchased a number of office buildings, but they have not spent anything near what they are capable of.

When we talk about Japan's important non-manufacturing direct investment, we mean banks, securities firms, trading firms, real estate speculators and trusts, movie and record companies, and some hotels. Banks and securities firms will be dealt with in the next two chapters. In this chapter, I will cover white-collar management issues, especially in trading companies.

Japanese non-manufacturing did well in 1989 after routine performance in 1988. These white-collar firms generated $1.3 billion in income, about 35 percent of all foreign investors' income in the classification. Much of it probably came from interest payments and fees generated by Japanese banks involved in financing leveraged buyouts. As for the trading firms, among the longest-term Japanese investors in the United States, their earnings were about 44 percent of all foreign traders, a sign of how good they are at making money. Compare the traders' success with that of Japanese manufacturers, who reported U.S. losses in both 1988 and 1989.[1]

In sum, manufacturers in recent years are not making money, non-manufacturers have ups and downs, and traders seem to be doing well. Paradoxically, however, manufacturing management of Americans is moderately good, while it is weak or even terrible in non-manufacturing and trading. In the long run, Japanese managers had better solve their problems in the office if they expect to continue their modest gains.

THE JAPANESE OFFICE IN AMERICA

"Productivity in Japanese offices is relatively low," admits Yoshio Hatakeyama, president of the Japan Management Association.[2] Personal computers are outnumbered by abacuses in Japan, so requests from a New York office for spending on computerization and communications equipment may receive short shrift. In one office at Nomura Securities in Tokyo thirty PCs line the walls. Some do data analysis, others do charts. Employees must manually transfer data from one machine to the other to do different tasks. Spreadsheet analysis is rare, as are linked communications and networking setups. With this kind of home-country environment, cries from distant American subsidiaries are weak indeed. Even when such cries are heard, the hardware of choice may be NEC or Sony rather than a more appropriate American make with better software.

As we saw earlier, Japanese managers do not change their behavior much when they come to America. The offices they set up in New York or Los Angeles are similar to those in Tokyo or Osaka. For example, Yaohan Department Store Company operates six stores in the United States, including a large supermarket in Edgewater, New Jersey, catering to Japanese and Asian customers. High land prices made further investment in Japan unprofitable, so the company began expanding in America and the Far East. News reports suggest that it has had labor problems with its American employees due to its insistence that they follow rigid Japanese-style rules.[3] Department store workers are among the most put upon in Japan, it should be noted.

Another example of how little things change: just as in Tokyo, some trading company managers spend 50 percent of their time entertaining visitors in golf weekends, evening parties, briefing sessions, making introductions, and coordinating tours. The only difference is that the out-of-towners have jet lag. All of this is harmless enough in Japan, where markets are carved up and competition, while fierce, is nicely constrained. In the United States, where less certainty prevails and extensive planning and analysis are required, managers need more time, and employee rules have to be more flexible. The tendency to replicate the Japanese office in America is unrealistic and a mistake.

SERVICE WITHOUT A SMILE

Are Japanese managers also replicating the famed Japanese attentiveness to service? Not really, but they don't have to.

In 1990 Kyotaru, a food services company, bought Restaurant Associates, which owns 120 U.S. restaurants, including Mamma Leone's in New York. Will Japanese managers do well in these restaurants? One chef who had worked for a Japanese firm did not think so. "The Japanese don't keep their promises," she said. "They were constantly understaffing." This is only one person's opinion about managing American service employees. Perhaps the Japanese company will be better at delivering quality food speedily to customers in clean and attractive surroundings. After all, Japan is famous for what *The Economist* calls "retail bank 'greeters,' white-gloved taxi drivers, and department store gift wrappers."[4] The Japanese should easily succeed, since American service businesses supposedly are inattentive to quality, emphasize scale economies, and focus on short-term profit maximization.

But wait. If American service businesses are so bad, the Japanese firms really do not have to pull out all the stops. They simply need to be only a little bit better than the American competitors. The chef's remarks quoted above may be generalizable. Sure enough, in a study conducted at the Berkeley Business School focused on Japanese-owned banks, hotels, and auto dealers, researchers found that Japan's service emphasis has not been exported to America.[5]

Japanese-owned banks in California do not offer the same personal service as the parent firms do in Japan. Hotel staffing levels in Japan, which often are at twice the employees per room rate as in America, have not been replicated in the United States. And Japanese car dealers in California do not usually make home sales visits or offer seven-day service. The Berkeley researchers note that it is difficult for Japanese firms to turn acquired American service firms in a direction they do not want to go. Unionized workers are sometimes inflexible. Banks do not try to get close to their customers. Car dealers have not worked very hard to build customer confidence. Worker turnover is high—and perhaps even encouraged as a weeding-out device. In these conditions successful adoption of Japanese approaches is unlikely. A better explanation, however, may be the simpler one: Rather than being hindered from developing Japanese service methods, Japanese investors do not want to. The disgruntled chef saw her Japanese bosses doing—and doing it badly—just what American bosses do: cutting costs by skimping on labor in an attempt to raise margins. Even if unions were flexible and American bankers eager to cozy up to customers, it might not be in the interest of Japanese investors to do so. They can make profits simply by being only a little bit better.

Some Japanese firms run cruise ships, and eventually they will want to enter the lucrative American trade. Will they provide better service? It certainly will not be hard to do. Some years ago, I worked as a U.S. Coast Guard inspector, and it was my sad duty to do one of the last inspections on the SS *United States*, the pride of the American passenger liner fleet.

"Why is business so bad?" I asked the captain, a thoughtful man in his forties.

"Have you ever had a first-class dinner on this vessel?" he replied. I shook my head.

"Well, let me give you a contrast. On the foreign-owned ships, you come in to dinner and a waiter sits you down. While you eat, he hovers in the background, not too close to be obtrusive but close enough to serve every need."

Having dined on both British and Japanese ships, I nodded in agreement.

"If your wine glass needs refilling, he's there. If you drop a fork, no problem. That kind of service is a treat, and it tells the customer he's getting his money's worth."

"Don't they get the same kind of treatment on your ship?" I asked.

"It works this way. You come in and get seated. The waiter is nicely dressed. He's got a clean towel over his arm. He fills your glass and does everything he can for you."

"That sounds great."

"There's only one problem. Let's say you are eating. You cut your steak and eat a piece. Then you help yourself to some mashed potatoes. You take a sip of wine. Everything's fine. Then you slip some peas onto your fork. You're just about to put them in your mouth when you realize that the waiter is leaning over your shoulder, his face only ten inches from yours. 'Hey, how about dem peas,' he says. 'Got 'em in fresh this morning.' That's why my ship is going out of business."

Does anyone want to place bets on whether or not Japanese-owned firms will get into the cruise ship business in the United States?

SERVICE FIRMS

While Japanese service firms handle customers American-style with perhaps a little bit extra, they deal with American employees in a less accommodating manner and with less success. There is nothing strange about this, since studies in West Germany, Britain, and France all have concluded that Japanese service firm managers in banking, securities, and other white-collar businesses are weak in recruitment, personnel management, communication, and the delegation of responsibility.[6]

What kinds of Americans work in Japanese-owned service companies? One 1988 study of seventy-eight managers in financial services industry firms found the following:[7]

· American managers were recruited through personal contacts, employment agencies, and newspaper ads. They are selected because of their job experience, not their knowledge of Japan.

· Forty-one percent believed their compensation was not competitive with that of a similar job in an American firm.

· Sixty percent felt they did not have access to important information, 50 percent felt they had little influence in decision making, 45 percent felt that opportunities for promotion were poor, and 39 percent felt that their skills were not being adequately used.

The results suggest that serious problems exist. The problems are rooted in the weak capabilities of the Japanese managers in these firms, who often have language difficulties and lack understanding of the U.S. business environment. What can the Japanese service firms do to hold on to their American managers? Professors Tomasz Mroczkowski and Richard Linowes of American University suggest that Japanese recruiters should be more honest about the nature of the jobs they are filling and more careful in orienting new managers. Promotions should follow career paths and be based on objective measures of performance rather than seniority.

Japanese senior managers should have longer U.S. assignments and more autonomy. Powerful, experienced general managers are more likely to know how to treat Americans sensibly and to manage recruitment, promotion, and compensation policies well. One way to boost the probability of success with American hires is to make sure they learn something about the parent firm's way of doing business through rap sessions and visits to Japan. Another approach is to appoint an American, either as an advisor to the senior Japanese or as a replacement. Thus either a *hybridization* of management into an American/Japanese mode is in order or a *localization* of management into a totally American mode is required. The problem with localization, however, is that Japanese banks, securities firms, and other service organizations often have other Japanese firms as their clients which may not have localized. This suggests that hybridization is the preferred approach.

One thing Japanese managers will have to avoid is the skimpy benefits for service-firm employees common in Japan.[8] Over 17 percent of total compensation for American service industry employees takes the form of non-mandated benefits. The figure in Japan is only 4 percent. Americans typically get health care insurance, and paid vacations and holidays. Japanese health care insurance is mandated by law, and companies add a little more in supplementary coverage. While Japanese employees get about two weeks vacation and a number of paid holidays, however, they only take one-half of the time available. They are expected to do four to six hours of overtime per week in addition to their regular forty-six hours. All of these practices will be coldly received by Americans. Some Japanese customs Americans would like, however, are company contributions toward mortgage payments, increased pay for increased family size (this may be illegal in America), commuting allowances, canteen services, and allowances for living in high-cost locales. Clever managers ought to be able to combine the best of American and Japanese benefits packages to make employment in a Japanese-owned service firm an attractive proposition.

THE TRADERS

The trading companies like to be called *sogo shosha*, because the phrase implies that they do more than trade. A firm like Nissho Iwai handles more than 20,000 products and services in its metals, machinery, energy, general commodities, and construction/realty divisions. But it also does international project management, marketing and distribution, direct investment, mergers and acquisition, and technology transfer. Fully 67 percent of revenues come from domestic business in Japan and importing. Exporting accounts for only 9 percent, and 24 percent comes from trading and other activities in foreign countries. Net income in 1989 was only 0.1 percent of revenue and 0.3 percent of assets. These low profitability numbers do not bother stockholders. Over 87 percent of the stock is owned by banks and cross-shareholding institutions. Dividends are very low (4 cents per share in 1989), but the firm's stock value increased dramatically over the 1989–1990 period, even with the 1990 fall of the market.

Nissho Iwai buys low and sells high, but it also offers a range of services to Japanese businesses. Small firms wanting to market in America can use its established channels, but large firms can make use of Nissho Iwai's willingness to cover small markets which do not warrant separate sales and service branches. The company finances trade, manages currency risks, and collects information worldwide to help advise clients. It puts together complex projects and arranges financing.

As an investor the trader conducts feasibility studies and then puts capital into long-term profit-oriented ventures in the United States and elsewhere. A second type of investing is the knowledge-seeking kind in which U.S. technology is acquired for transfer back to Japanese companies. Nissho Iwai owns Helix International, which develops antibiotics for viruses and bacteria, and Southern Research Center, which develops toxicity and metabolism testing services. Third is real estate investing, such as its $150 million multi-use complex in La Jolla, California.

One can see where Nissho Iwai gets its capital for U.S. investing. Long-term debt for 1989 was 87 percent of debt plus equity. The debt is almost all long-term loans from commercial banks, trust banks, and insurance companies. A second source of capital is profit. Japanese trading companies, probably including Nissho Iwai, reported solid profits in the United States during the late 1980s. At a time when their power in distribution channels is in decline, their ability to make money in other ways seems to have improved.

Here is one way they do it.[9] Assume that a Japanese trader in Los Angeles (called *Rosu* by the Japanese) receives a fax from an American manufacturer of injection moulding machines who is looking for a certain type of component. The trader helps the manufacturer. A short time later he hears from one of his colleagues in Chicago who needs several hundred small industrial robots for a firm which is much too small to be able to use them all. Over the next few days he pulls together all the disparate information and comes to the startling conclusion that General Electric is planning to once again manufacture televisions in the United States under its own label.

After a quick trip to Tokyo and several visits to the Japanese bank which serves his firm's *keiretsu*, he develops a plan to take advantage of the information. One of the company's American subsidiaries forms a joint venture with the U.S. subsidiary of a Japanese manufacturer of picture tubes. Together, these firms know they can produce a tube which will suit GE's needs when it announces its plan. The trading company subsidiary will be a 50 percent owner of the joint venture, but when the operation is up and running in a year or so, it will sell out at a profit to its partner.

The skill with which a Japanese trader turns raw data into information and information into action and profit has two elements to it. He must know how to separate wheat from chaff, and he must have a remarkable breadth of interest in many industries. As he goes about his routine daily business of taking and filling orders for clients and advising them on the best deals, he develops a sense of what data to file away in his memory and what to forget. Moreover, he is aware of the goings on in a number of industries and is always trying to form a picture of interrelated needs. Few Japanese in the United States have the language abilities or the training to master these skills, and the decline of Japanese trading companies as traders has occurred. They have been replaced by their former clients. Honda, for example, formed its own trading company to export a few autos back to Japan. Now it plans to export to all of East and Southeast Asia. Firms like Matsushita have developed plants and sales offices all over America and no longer need the intermediary services of traders. What all of this means is that Japanese trading companies are going to have to become even better at information processing and deal making if they expect to prosper. Simply assigning someone from Tokyo will no longer work. He will more than likely sit by the fax machine every night from 7:00 P.M. to 11:00 P.M., when Tokyo sends out orders, waiting for someone to tell him what to do. Americans with expert knowledge and MBA-developed information processing skills will have to be hired and integrated into the trading company's global operations.

Since trading companies are among the most Japanese of Japanese companies, Americans will not be absorbed easily in them, although their eventual absorption is inevitable. Consider some of the obstacles. When an American trader signs a contract, he sees it as binding. To the Japanese it is more of a guideline which should not interfere with the demands of some future context. If the American employs his expertise to argue an action he believes the company should take, he may encounter scorn from his Japanese colleagues, who see themselves as "big picture" types of a higher status than mere "specialists." The American will have to learn that "what you know" is not nearly as important for getting things done as "who you know." Yet without Japanese language skills, he or she will not be able to make the needed connections. Even with language ability many managers resist speaking Japanese with *gaijin*. And even with connections, language, and Japanese who are comfortable with non-Japanese, the American will have to get used to endless trips to Tokyo for discussions of important deals. Really significant issues always must be discussed face to face by Japanese. Finally, since the trading companies are fierce competitors with one another, it is difficult for an American to jump from one to another as a career move. He would not be fully trusted at his new firm.

Japanese traders have mixed feelings about U.S. employees. "We cannot have Americans as senior managers in our company. General managers will remain Japanese because of the deep connection of our activities with Japanese economic life and culture," asserted a senior trading company executive. However, another executive in the same company strongly disagreed. "We need local general managers. Ten years ago we could use phrases such as 'we Japanese' and 'since Japan is a small island nation . . .' to defend our failure to internationalize on cultural grounds. This is no longer true. Our American subsidiary is an American company and must be run by Americans." Defenders of the Japanized firm admit that hiring first rate Americans will be necessary but difficult if it is clear that only Japanese will fill high level slots. "How can Americans develop ways of communicating in Japanese with trading company people in Japan? It would take ten to twenty years of language development and business experience," noted a young trader.

A textile trader who had managed his firm's Los Angeles office revealed just how important American expertise can be. "American manufacturers won't use us as representatives," he said. "They don't want us to know their secrets since we also represent Japanese textile manufacturers. They only will sell to us." This firm, faced with a high yen and increasing U.S. protectionism, plans on reducing its sales of Japanese textiles in the United States. Instead it will buy from American producers and sell to American customers, thus becoming an American wholesaler. One strategy the firm engaged in during the 1970s when the yen rose was to purchase U.S. textile factories and run them with Japanese managers. "We made a huge investment. Almost all failed because we could not control the unions and we experienced disastrous pollution problems." Now the firm is again considering manufacturing investments, but this time it will depend more on American expertise. In both wholesaling and investing it will not be able to survive unless it Americanizes.

Some trading companies are getting into American M & A activities.[10] In 1990 Mitsubishi participated in a $900 million leveraged buyout of Aristech Chemical Corporation, a $1 billion company selling unsaturated polyester compounds used in auto products and high-performance resins, a field in which Mitsubishi's *keiretsu* chemical manufacturers want to become involved. The buyout of a firm with $600 million in debt ordinarily would be a poor investment, but it gives group members a way to penetrate the U.S. market through deals and acquisitions rather than greenfield. Some trading firms treat their M & A efforts as a source of profit through the buying and selling of businesses. Most, however, want to hold on to their acquisitions and use them to stimulate product trading. Sumitomo Trading owns 50 percent of Fellsmere, a citrus orchard, and also has purchased Cooke Cable Vision. Toyo Menka Kaisha owns a salmon processing firm in Alaska, and Mitsui purchased the food division of Wilsey Foods, Inc. for about $60 million. All of this M & A business will require American help, and Japanese traders who think of their firms as cultural outposts will soon have to change their tune.

Japanese white-collar investments in the United States have been more profitable than those in manufacturing in recent years, mostly because of the successes of a few banks and trading firms. But people resources ensure continued success, and here these Japanese firms are in trouble.

They do not use employees productively, do not compensate adequately, and do not give enough attention to American expertise. Too often, they Japanize their U.S. offices, giving little authority to Japanese managers to adapt to American conditions. Paradoxically, they often fail to use excellent Japanese-style service approaches in dealing with customers. What is needed is a hybridization in which Japanese white-collar firms utilize the best of American and Japanese practices. Some Japanese trading companies are resistant, preferring instead to see themselves as ultra-Japanese institutions. This will have to change as they do more and more M & A in the United States and more intra-country trading.

NINETEEN

Trouble at the Bank

In the 1980s it was common to hear talk of Japanese banks as the spear-head of Japan's attack on America's economic independence. The banks came to control about 12 percent of U.S. bank assets by the end of the decade, the largest penetration by Japanese investors of any American industry.

Much of their lending served the needs of Japanese-owned firms scrambling to establish an American presence while the yen was high and dollar assets cheap. But a substantial part of their business was focused on big American-owned corporations. Benefiting from a low cost of funds, the Japanese bankers tried to buy market share with low-priced loans. As one American working for the Japanese put it, "Whatever the American banks bid, we lowered it. If they lowered, we went down further. Eventually they gave up."

This banker lived the good life in the 1980s. "American corporations loved Japanese banks. They were lined up at our door." Loans were priced to sell, regardless of margin. "The Japanese didn't care about profit. It was of no interest to them. They were operating by other rules." The Japanese were trying to build relationships with major American firms which would be the basis for more profitable deals later on—something along the lines of "Now that we are friends, you must help us to make at least some profit." This may work in Japan, but it certainly has not worked in the United States. "American corporations look for the lowest price for a loan," noted the American banker, who left the Japanese bank for greener pastures in 1990. "When the cost of funds rose for the Japanese, their ability to outbid American banks disappeared." Relationships meant nothing to the Americans.

But for a few years money was being made. In 1988 only three large banks—Sumitomo, Tokai, and the Bank of Tokyo—were earning 50 percent or more of their profits from international lending. By 1990, nine of the twelve biggest commercial banks, called city banks, were gaining most of their profits from abroad.[1]

Clearly some of these profits had come from the United States, probably from loans to Japanese companies, lucrative M & A activity, and real estate lending. The Japan bashers were gearing up for yet another attack on the Japanese threat, and even TV journalists were looking for the financial equivalent of a natural disaster story with lots of visual impact. Then everything changed. Worried about inflation, Japan's central bank made reductions in the growth of the money supply. Almost at once interest rates rose and the stock market fell. With high costs of funds and a reduced inventory of equity-backed capital, the competitive ability of Japanese banks in the United States declined. Suddenly it became obvious that the banks were not nearly as strong as they had looked. Beneath all the glitz and glitter was a hard nut-like core of weak management and poor competitive strength. The 1990s will be a troubling time for the banks.

BANK STRATEGIES IN AMERICA

As with other foreign investors, conditions in the home country drive bank investment in the United States. The chief characteristic of Japanese banking is how oligopolized it is. America has about 14,000 commercial banks. Japan has about 158. The other characteristic of the banks is how poorly managed they are. Labor productivity is low, technological developments are few and slow in coming, and returns on equity are only about two-thirds that of American and European banks.[2] Until recently, the bankers received little trouble from borrowers, depositors, and stockholders, and competition from foreign banks in Japan was miniscule—profits of foreign banks fell steadily throughout the 1980s.[3] With these domestic conditions, the risks of foreign venturing seemed bearable, and the banks began lending heavily to the Third World and to corporations building up their American presence. Some started to acquire American banks, while others expanded their U.S. subsidiaries and branches.

In 1988 Japanese branches and subsidiaries had about $132 billion in U.S. loans booked. About 46 percent was with American firms. Another 32 percent went to foreign companies, very likely Japanese or Japanese-owned, and to financing companies probably serving Japanese manufacturers and traders in the United States. Ten percent financed Japanese real estate purchases. By 1991 the banks had increased U.S. loans to $163 billion, of which about 41 percent were for real estate and leveraged buyout financing—neither of which will be big in the 1990s.

Japanese banks employ about 25,000 people in the United States. Most of their assets are associated with branches and agencies (86 percent) rather than subsidiaries. One reason is that subsidiaries offer services to individuals and are regulated by the U.S. government. Branches and agencies do not deal with individuals and are not regulated by the Federal Deposit Insurance Corporation. Until 1990, moreover, branches offered certain other advantages. Only bank subsidiaries had to seek a payment guarantee from a Japanese parent when the bank made a loan to one of its American-owned firms. Without such a guarantee, which was not always forthcoming, the bank subsidiary had to increase loan-loss reserves, an increase which comes right out of profits. Branches did not face this problem, so the banks naturally sought to book business through them. The Federal Reserve expanded the reserve requirement to cover most branches in 1990, however.[4]

Those banks which followed a strategy of establishing mostly branches thought they would escape the loan-loss reserve requirement, which they did not. And they thought that federal laws restricting foreign-owned subsidiaries' operations to only one state would hinder them. These laws are now about to fall by the wayside, and owners of subsidiaries and affiliates probably will be able to expand out of New York and California, where they have tended to concentrate. The New Yorkers have specialized in trust business, while the Californians have offered a broad range of services. The largest are the Bank of Tokyo's Union Bank and Mitsubishi's Bank of California. These are ideally positioned to take advantage of the critical success factors in the 1990s: consumer banking, commercial loans to mid-sized firms, and fee-generating services. Those firms which have concentrated only on serving large Japanese corporate clients will have to expand their focus and depend more on American technological and marketing know-how if they are to prosper. The market for high-end corporate loans is not as profitable as it was in the 1980s, and *keiretsu* allegiances are weakening as Japanese companies do what American companies do: shop around for the best deal.

The Bank of Tokyo purchased Union Bank in California for $750 million. It also owns a New York subsidiary, the Bank of Tokyo Trust Company (B of T). In Japan B of T is a highly specialized bank. It has only thirty-two offices in its domestic operations but 295 abroad.[5] Its task over the years has been to manage Japan's foreign exchange operations, but in the deregulated new era other banks also are doing this. Without a domestic retail presence to take advantage of the growing consumer credit market—consumer credit as a share of disposable income in Japan rose from 12.1 percent in 1984 to 17.7 percent in 1988—

and with competitors overtaking them on their own turf, B of T looked for salvation in America.

Ownership of Union Bank opened up Californian and eventually American consumer credit markets to B of T. Even greater opportunities existed than in Japan, since by 1988 American consumer credit had risen to 20.9 percent of disposable income from 19.3 percent in 1984.[6] Corporate lending also was available, offering high returns to low cost money made available from B of T's Japanese funds.

B of T's success depended on its government-protected market for three-year debentures. But with deregulation, commercial banks began offering similar products, driving up rates. Profits declined, as did the competitive strength of the Union Bank subsidiary. B of T is well positioned, however, for 1990s consumer lending in America, and it seems to recognize the importance of its American employees to its future. When it took over Union, employees were somewhat anxious about the new owners from Asia. To reduce fears, B of T provided funds to Union executives so they could award a totally unexpected bonus just before Christmas. Morale soared and the Japanese got off to a good start with their new employees. By the end of 1990, most of B of T's profits may have been coming from its American operation.

Mitsubishi Bank also recognizes American managers as a key strategic ingredient. In 1989 it gave its New York office control of loan screening, revenue control, personnel assessment, and strategy—things Japanese banks usually retain for the home office. At the time, thirty-six Japanese and forty-six American managers staffed New York head-quarters—a sign of the much larger presence of Japanese managers in U.S. service businesses than in manufacturing—but eventually all will be Americans. "Globalization" is the declared goal of the highly bureaucratic and conservative Mitsubishi, which hopes to set up the New York bank as a holding company so that it can do "universal banking," meaning both banking and securities-related business. In anticipation of the fall of barriers between banking and securities, other Japanese banks are buying into investment firms, hiring American talent to advise them, or forming strategic alliances. Sumitomo has a relationship with Goldman, Sachs, while the Long-Term Credit Bank purchased Greenwich Capital Markets for $144 million, apparently to get into the M & A business in the United States.

Burdened by low-margin market-capturing loans, some Japanese banks in the late 1980s wanted to break into the lucrative M & A market, where large fees and high rates with short maturities existed. They took on less profitable co-lender positions and for a time sought to become leaders in the business. About 75 percent of Sony's 1989 purchase of Columbia Pictures was financed by Mitsubishi, Mitsui, Fuji, B of T, and the Industrial Bank of Japan. KKR's purchase of RJR Nabisco for $25.1 billion was helped by $6.2 billion from Dai-Ichi Kangyo and other banks. Profits from these ventures were sizable, but they will not continue. The big deal M & A business has declined in the 1990s, and Japanese bankers are not comfortable in it anyway. They blundered badly in making loans to finance Campeau's buyout of Federated Department Stores, and then they refused to provide enough funds for the 1989 buyout of UAL Inc., causing the deal to collapse.[7] In the 1990s the banks mostly will seek to help Japanese acquirers of mid-sized American companies.

To identify those mid-sized U.S. companies, they will first make loans to them—if they can. The strategy of most big American banks also is to move down into the mid-market, firms with sales in the $25–500 million range. To succeed, a bank needs a branch network, so the Japanese are likely to begin seeking acquisitions of American regional banks in need of capital. Another route to the middle market is the acquisition of a financial services company. Fuji Bank followed this path in 1984 when it acquired Walter E. Heller & Co., a leasing and factoring firm based in Chicago which also makes working capital loans. An American CEO was hired, aided by a Japanese "advisor" to act as liaison with Fuji. By 1990 Heller Financial Inc. was booming. Its sales were double those of 1985, and a 1985 net loss of $32 million had turned into a $102 million net income. Not only is Heller finally making money, it also is able to spot American candidates for friendly Japanese takeovers. A six-year waiting period for Heller to turn profitable, however, was too long for even the long-term Japanese, and rumors circulated that the Fuji executives who had bought Heller had been cashiered.

The acquisition of retail outlets is most developed in California. Although some wits have said that the bankers originally came to the state to be near Disneyland, their original impetus was the need of Japanese traders and manufacturers who had located there. Soon they began acquiring banks or starting subsidiaries to get into consumer lending. Now four of the top ten banks in asset size are Japanese owned. B of T's Union Bank has $5.1 billion in assets, twice the size of other Japanese subsidiaries or acquired banks. However, the *branch* offices of Dai-Ichi Kangyo and Mitsubishi by themselves have $11.6 billion in assets.[8] Since a branch office can be no more than a low-rent room with desks and telephones manned by expatriates who do not have to bother much about managing Americans, one can see why most Japanese banking in the United States is still done through branches.

Nevertheless, some bankers have bought the buildings and hired the Californians. Sanwa has 105 outlets, and 99 percent of its customers are Americans. Only forty Japanese are mixed in with the 3,900 employees. By the same token, Sumitomo has forty-five outlets with 80 percent of its customers American. Bank managers there claim they have finally learned how to do sophisticated credit analysis, and they are developing the mid-sized firm market in addition to serving consumers' credit needs.

American financial services have $1.2 trillion in financing receivables, half in commercial loans and half in consumer credit.[9] Non-bank services, such as finance companies, automakers' credit firms, and insurance companies split the commercial loan market with banks, but the banks hold about 58 percent of consumer loans. Here is where the Japanese investing in U.S. banking eventually must compete. Although some are trying hard in California, they are having trouble overall. Consumer lending is undeveloped in Japanese banking, so many bankers do not know what to do. And those that do know cannot find regional American banks to acquire. B of T, Sanwa, Mitsubishi, Sumitomo, and perhaps one or two others are the only banks whose strategy has prepared them to follow up on the opportunities of the 1990s. Other banks, now lacking capital to buy their way into retail and consumer markets, will have to develop their fee-generating businesses. These could be lucrative, but the competition will be fierce—and Japanese bankers are unfamiliar with genuine competition.

BANK KEIRETSU IN AMERICA

Japanese antitrust laws are weakly enforced. This allows horizontal linkages—relationships among firms within an industry. In addition, vertical linkages, between suppliers and manufacturers and between manufacturers and downstream firms, are also quite strong. The result is a tightly woven business matrix which trades off some economic efficiency for stability.[10] These matrices take three forms: financial business affiliations, enterprise groupings, and vertical distribution groups. A U.S. subsidiary's parent may be a member of all or none of these groups, and the type and extent of membership influences the behavior of the subsidiary's managers in America.

The financial *keiretsu* members are linked together by their relationships with major banks. The largest groups are those of Mitsui (twenty-four firms), Mitsubishi (twenty-nine firms), Sumitomo (twenty firms), Fuyo (twenty-nine firms), Sanwa (forty-four firms), and Dai Ichi (forty-seven firms). The banks and insurance companies coordinating the groups specialize in allocating credit to member firms. In autos, for example, Nissan is allied with Fuji bank. Toyota and Honda are not members of financial *keiretsu*, however. Hitachi can call on Dai-Ichi Kangyo Bank, but Matsushita has no such alliance. Group members own each other's stock and rarely sell it. This practice ensures stability and mutual coordination activities. It also keeps foreign investors out. In America these *keiretsu* firms usually do their banking with their group bank's U.S. subsidiary or branch. Part of the reason Japanese investment in U.S. banking has been so strong is the *keiretsu's* needs for services from its leaders. The Japanese big banks had to follow their friends and gear up fast to offer everything they offered in Japan.

The bank *keiretsu* are not some kind of cultural practice or institutional arrangement emerging out of the mists of history. They are simply strategic activities on the part of large manufacturers and banks looking to lower business and financial risks. Like all strategies they come and go, depending on the environment. A study by the Japanese Fair Trade Commission suggests that *keiretsu* are not as menacing as some Americans claim. Almost all economic transactions are still based on price and quality rather than group membership.[11] *Keiretsu* are powerful, however, in some fields. Almost 96 percent of the purchasers of pension fund management services are group affiliated, as are 75 percent of buyers of fire and marine insurance. Neither of these groups have much of a U.S. presence, however.

One reason for the decline of financial *keiretsu* in the 1980s was the decline of manufacturers' need for banks. When virtually all capital was raised through loans, the big bank and its group would become quite cozy. However, while debt was still important in Japan, companies began generating capital through retained earnings and stock offerings during most of the 1980s.

What may have driven some Japanese banks to the United States in the 1980s was their declining business in Japan. In 1974 large corporations borrowed 47 percent of their funds from the banks. By 1988 the amount was only 11 percent.[12] Japanese banks had to look to America. Luckily, they are positioned to serve their children again during the last decade of the century—this time in the United States. To insure the rise of their *keiretsu* strength in the 1990s, most of the leading banks began sending more of their executives to work in affiliated manufacturers. During the 1980s, for example, Sanwa Bank increased its transferred executives by 50 percent. Presumably some of these men have come to the United States and know what their task is: to give more borrowing business to Sanwa. In the Sanwa group are such American investors as Hitachi Chemical, Toyo Tire and Rubber, Kobe Steel, and Kyocera. American bankers calling on these firms may have their work cut out for them when they find that they are talking to Sanwa Bank managers on loan to Sanwa's friends. On the other hand, Japanese-owned firms may seek out the best deals possible, regardless of *keiretsu* relations. The rebirth of bank *keiretsu* could be quickly aborted.

HOW RISKY IS THE BANKS' LENDING?

Moody's Investors Services began reviewing long-term lending practices of Japanese banks in 1990. Fuji Bank and Dai-Ichi Kangyo were among the first to feel the sting of slightly lower ratings, but others were soon to follow. What troubled Moody's was the banks' real estate lending. Although the government had tried to crack down on loans to speculators, the banks had kept right on lending to intermediary financial services companies which then pushed the credit on to the real estate people. American subsidiaries probably have taken part in some of this activity, financing the purchases by Japanese high fliers of U.S. office buildings.[13] But most lending has been sensible. The banks are conservative in focusing mostly on Class A, U.S. office buildings, but they often take on risk by not requiring large prepayments, a common way of protecting oneself with up front money from unforeseen events down the road.[14]

To understand how they can take on more risk than American banks, we must examine the topic of liquidity in banking. The Japanese have both problems and opportunities here, but the opportunities probably are greater.

A bank tends to hold nonliquid assets (loans) unpredictable in value, while its liabilities (deposits) are liquid and of a guaranteed value.[15] Take the case of liabilities first. Depositors' accounts are liabilities, what the bank uses to fund its loans, which are called assets. Usually depositors can remove their cash at will and receive a fixed amount plus interest due. If bankers could, they would reduce this liquidity of deposits to reduce their uncertainty over how much money will be available next week or next month to make loans. In a competitive (e.g., United States) banking system this is expensive to do. Uncertainty can be reduced by increasing rates paid to depositors above the market rate. The greater the increase, the less the likelihood of competitors matching it, and the greater the probability of depositors keeping their money in the bank.

Until recently Japanese banks enjoyed nonliquid deposits at no extra cost. Government regulations fixed deposit rates so that no bank could increase its rates to hold on to depositors' cash or to attract new deposits. With nonliquid liabilities comes the ability to increase risky long-term line of credit loans and speculative real estate lending. For example, assume similar American and Japanese banks were competing for the same customers in the United States in 1986. With liquid liabilities the American had only a rough idea of how much would be available to lend out. It had to assume a low amount and/or be very careful to make the most judicious use of those funds. The Japanese bank, backed by its nonliquid deposits in Japan, could predict a higher amount or be a bit more risk prone if it wanted to. It did both: Lending in America soared, with some loans at greater risk.

By the 1990s, however, fixed deposit rates were almost a thing of the past, and Japanese banks were about equal with American banks in their ability to predict deposits. Since they now had loan portfolios considered to be too full and with too much risk in them, Moody's and other raters got worried. While cause for alarm is real, especially with declining property values in both the United States and Japan expected in the 1990s, and while some banks may be forced to merge to save themselves, overall Japanese banks still will be able to take on more risk than American competitors. Why? Because of their skills in the management of assets.

While banks try to make deposit liabilities more predictable, they do the same thing for assets, which are the loans they make. The key issue is the value of the loan portfolio, and the most important tool for establishing its value is the estimation of quarterly and annual losses from bad loans. This amount is subtracted from the portfolio value. For American banks it is very hard to predict. Japanese, however, have a much easier time of it. This is because Japanese bankers have a much closer relationship with their customers than do bankers in America. To put it crudely, Japanese bankers are snoops. They visit their customers regularly and often place their people on the customers' boards. They know exactly what's going on and can predict loan losses in Japan quite accurately. This domestic accuracy allows them to be less accurate in overseas lending. The upshot is that they can keep on making more questionable loans than Americans can, even though deposit rate liberalization has eroded their liability management strengths. As long as their ability to predict and endure loan losses is good in Japan, it can be weaker in the United States.

COMPETING AND MANAGING

How do Japanese financial institutions compete? A good example is the credit card market. Four companies dominate the Japan market: JCB, Million Credit, Diamond Credit, and Sumitomo Credit.[16] They process operations, service merchants, and act as settlement facilities. These companies move "in convoy." What one does, the others do, with little attempt at differentiation. Nevertheless, consumers often cannot use one card at a store associated with another card. Japanese consumers have grown used to poor service from these firms and from their banks, which make little effort to segment customers in terms of their needs. And they overcharge. A transfer of funds from one bank account to another costs over $5. To send money overseas might cost $50.[17] The banks collude to decide on fees in order to reduce competition.

In America they must compete. If they thought they could simply continue to service Japanese investors with ease, they were wrong. The big Japanese corporations spent the 1980s setting up their own financial subsidiaries, and these will be running at full speed in the 1990s.[18]

Nineteen of these companies now offer such services as financing, fund management, foreign currency management, sales credit, tax strategies, M & A advice, factoring, and leasing. They buy and sell their subsidiaries' commercial paper, bonds, and stocks, leaving very little in direct business for the banks. All the banks can really count on are their *keiretsu* friends' big loan needs.

Or can they? The Industrial Bank of Japan (IBJ) is a good example of a *keiretsu* bank. When Fuji Heavy Industries found that low American sales of its Subaru and Legacy cars were causing big operating losses, it probably first counted on IBJ to come to its rescue with increased financing and restructuring plans. IBJ had done it before in shipping and steel, and it could do it again. Or could it? Fuji Heavy executives took a second look at their plight and turned instead to Nissan, one of its major stockholders and a player in America. In typical Japanese fashion, Nissan sent over a sixty-eight-year-old retired senior manager to become Fuji Heavy's president. In the future Subaru and Nissan autos in the United States will share design, production, and marketing. Eventually, Nissan simply may absorb Fuji facilities in America. This kind of cooperation was not needed in the past, when the big banks would step in to see to it that favored customers did not go under. Bank executives would come in and virtually take over the firm, instituting rigorous cost-cutting, until the company was back on its feet. All of this worked in Japan, where the government would insure soft landings, but the American connection has changed the game. Subaru could crash quickly in America, and IBJ could not do much about it. This situation is forcing Japanese banks to become more like their American cousins, with arm's-length, no equity relationships with their customers. As clients like Fuji Heavy sense that their banks are pulling back, they will look elsewhere for saviors when they get into trouble. Currently, Japanese firms in America go to their affiliated Japanese banks for big loans as a matter of course. As their presence grows in free-wheeling American markets, however, they may look to any bank offering a competitive price and good service.

If the ties binding Japanese corporations and banks are loosening a bit in America, then, the banks will have to develop relationships with American-owned firms. "There is very hard competition among Japanese banks for U.S. corporate business," said a Fuji Bank manager. "Business promotion in Japan involves a lot of drinking and going to play golf. In the United States we don't have to provide such courtesies. But negotiation of pricing is now so hard with the Americans! They are always looking for new financial products, and we are trying to produce those in competition with other Japanese banks, U.S. banks, and the U.S. Treasury." What this manager is saying is that he is unused to complex deal making involving both asset *and* liability management occurring at the same time. American corporations want banks to advise them on how they can make money on deposits, bonds, commercial paper, and M & A at the same time as they are negotiating lines of credit, working capital loans, and long-term loans. What's more, they want high-tech information exchange tie ups, with the bank supplying them with high-quality data to enhance their financial decisions. This can be overwhelming to a Japanese manager who has seen nothing like this in Japan and who thought he would be working with placid Japanese clients out of a hole in the wall branch office in the United States.

Japanese bankers are used to doing business in person, but Americans often depend on the telephone to speed things up. Doing a deal in ten to fifteen minutes on the phone requires a different mindset from one focused on weeks of elaborate dinners and negotiations lubricated by oceans of beer and sake. Although the bankers can take on risk if they have to, they sometimes become quite worried in the strange American environment. "I feel more risk in an American borrower," noted a Bank of Tokyo executive, "because I don't know how long it will be operating. In America there are too many mergers and acquisitions." In the arm's-length world of U.S. banking, his natural urge for snooping cannot be satisfied, and he feels anxiety in the face of more uncertainty than he is used to.

Some of these bankers do not know how to read balance sheets, working capital statements, sources and uses of funds schedules, and other tools of financial disclosure common in the United States and useful in assessing risks.[19] In Japan they dealt with risk by requiring collateral, developing client relationships which yield important information, and depending on the government to save them if trouble occurred. In the United States they will have to learn to deal with accounting data better if they want to take advantage of risk.

The upshot of all this uncertainty and muddle is that the Japanese banks need American help in managing, marketing, and dealing with the U.S. government's complex regulatory system.

Begin with regulation first. In Japan the bankers must please the Ministry of Finance and the Bank of Japan. The U.S. regulatory environment contains the Federal Reserve, the Federal Deposit Insurance Corporation, the Federal Home Loan Bank Board, the Federal Savings and Loan Insurance Corporation, the National Credit Union Administration, the Securities and Exchange Commission, and state regulators. Japanese regulations encourage investment and export growth. In the United States they foster consumer borrowing. American guides are needed to wade through this swamp of legality.

Locals are also necessary to market loans. At first, the Japanese thought they could buy their way into corporate business with low rates. That is not possible in an era of high rates in Japan and high-cost funds. They also moved into the letter of credit business, guaranteeing bonds for municipalities for a fee. This was a way to form relationships with high-quality American borrowers while making a low-risk profit. Since these Americans shop around, this tactic will not pan out either. The only organizations seeking "relationship banking" are the higher-risk groups, so the Japanese will have to move more into this end of the business. They will need creative, risk-savvy American managers who will know how to provide the complex swaps, securitizations, loan syndications, and merger structurings that generate profits at the lowest possible risk.

Wisely, some Japanese have kept a low profile. At B of T's Union Bank, only seven of seventeen top executives are Japanese (in 1990), and only thirty other expatriates worked in the staff of 7,300. "We're not a Japanese bank," said a Union official.[20] Some Japanese tolerate this approach, but they are not comfortable with the loss of control. "Compared with Japanese staff people, American employees think more about their private lives," complained a B of T executive (not stationed in Union Bank). "Americans don't make the same contribution to our bank." Many banks cannot bring themselves to turn to Americans for help, and Japanese nationals fill up managerial slots. Some are not allowed to return to Japan after a four to five year tour but are thrown into a second posting because of the shortage of personnel.

Some of these managers are quite good, of course, but lots of them are simply order takers used to serving *keiretsu* clients. A Los Angeles-based trading company executive noted that he did most of his borrowing from affiliated Japanese banks. Their rates were not lower. Then why did he go to them? "If I went to the Bank of America, I would have to write down many details about my business and previous loans. I don't keep such records. But if I went to Mitsui Bank and just mentioned my company name, they would give me a loan immediately." For a group firm, some Japanese bankers do not bother with a loan proposal. They simply take the order and dole out the funds. In many cases a loan proposal requirement would not work anyway. The small or mid-sized Japanese borrower would not have the accounting system in place to support a proposal process, and the banker would not have the ability to do sophisticated credit analysis based on proposal data. Japanese banks doing business like this with American-owned firms soon will be in big trouble if they forego the services of Americans and try to depend on home-country personnel who are little more than clerks.

A former loan officer for the New York branch of a major bank listed some of the problems he faced as an American outsider in a Japanese insiders' world. "My territory was New Jersey," he recalled, "but one of the Japanese guys in another group suddenly started making calls on my clients." Faced with a loss of business in an American firm, he would have immediately complained loudly to senior management. "You don't do that at a Japanese firm. Instead, you wait for the right time. Then you nuke 'em." The time came when the chairman casually asked him one day how things were going. "I must answer honestly," said the American in good Japanese fashion. "Things are not going well." He then told the Japanese exec.tive about the attempt to horn in on his clients. Within minutes, the offending Japanese manager had received a severe dressing down. "From then on this person was paranoid about me. He practically held my chair out for me when I arrived at my desk in the morning."

The moral of this story is that an American has to seek the protection of the most senior person available. He or she cannot constantly be complaining—that is bad form—but when help is needed, it is easy enough to put oneself informally in the path of an executive, who invariably will ask, "How are things?" and—unlike many American executives—will expect an honest answer. Subtlety and honesty can have big payoffs in a Japanese firm.

This same American was stunned to find out that credit analysis in a first-rank Japanese bank is quite different than in a similar American firm. "I did a routine analysis of a big loan when I first arrived," he remembered. "Like all American bankers, I calculated a number of key financial ratios which described the client's business." He then turned his report over to a young Japanese "translator" for transmission to Tokyo, where decisions were made. For some reason, Tokyo officials eventually re-translated the report into English and sent it back to New York, where by chance it came to the American's desk. He was astonished to find that the "translator" had scrapped most of his work and re-written it to accommodate Tokyo-style credit analysis. "They don't care about ratios," said the American banker. "What they do is gather receivables data for every division in the client's company—where the sales are coming from, the trends, reasons for the trend, and expectations. They go into a level of detail that Americans would never do." This banker learned two things from this experience. "First, do things their way if you want to succeed, and second, no one will tell you what their way is. You have to learn it by yourself."

WILL THE LENDING STOP?

A bank has to have capital available to cover loans that go sour if it is to maintain its image as a going concern in the financial community. Capital usually comes from selling equity and bonds and from profits, and according to international agreements coming into force in 1992, it must be a risk-adjusted 8 percent of assets. In 1989 I asked a Fuji Bank executive if the new capital adequacy requirement would be a problem for Japanese banks. In a polite Japanese way, he made it clear that mighty Japanese banks did not concern themselves with such trivia. By late 1990, Fuji's capital adequacy ratio was at 8.01 percent—the bank was just barely coping. Only by reducing assets by $16 billion in 1990–1991 did Fuji get its ratio over 8.7 percent by early 1992.

The banks considered themselves as mighty because their loan portfolios were so huge. This asset base was easily supported by raising capital from equity sales on the Tokyo Stock Exchange. A bank simply told its corporate clients to buy its stock, and they did. About $21 billion was raised in the 1988–1990 period.[21] Most of that probably went into capital. The other big capital source was the banks' latent profits in their equity portfolios, which consisted of their clients' stocks. As the stock market soared in the late 1980s, fueled by an enormous increase in Japan's money supply, stock values rose. By late 1989, about 60 percent of the value of the big banks' equity holdings was in the form of unrealized profits.[22] They were allowed to count 45 percent of these paper profits as capital in calculating their capital adequacy ratios. For the ten biggest banks that meant about $131 billion of their capital was in the form of unrealized gains from stock.[23] By the end of 1990 about $75 billion of this capital had disappeared in the market collapse, and the average capital adequacy ratio for the big banks was about 7.7 percent—lower than the 8 percent requirement.

During the 1990–1992 period the ten largest city banks needed to raise $14 billion in capital or lower assets to achieve an 8 percent ratio; they could achieve the ratio either by selling bonds to insurance companies, reducing their loan portfolios by $175 billion or a combination of both. According to various sources, they raised about $30 billion in capital by selling bonds and reduced their portfolios by $60–100 billion. This put their ratios in the 8 to 10 percent range. But weakness in the stock market suggested that these actions may not have been enough to cover a further equity capital decline.[24]

The banks will raise more capital through bonds and may get an extension on the 1992 deadline for achieving the 8 percent ratio. But they will have to pull back on lending in America. This was evident in early 1991, when even *keiretsu* members in New York were having trouble getting loans from their affiliated banks. Moreover, the loans the banks were making had to be profitable, since profits add to capital and losses reduce it. Suddenly the Japanese were looking very much like their American competitors—only the Americans were better managed and better positioned to compete.

THE QUEST FOR FEES

"Assets will decrease for some banks," said Masahiro Nagayasu, senior vice president for planning at Fuji Bank's New York branch.[25] Big-project financing plans were cancelled in 1990 at Kyowa Bank's New York office, as were plans at a leading bank to acquire an East Coast U.S. bank in 1991. Unprofitable corporate lending to U.S. firms was cut back, and real estate and leveraged buyout financing was reduced or eliminated. Japanese bankers began admitting that their U.S. operations, profitable in the late 1980s, have not been profitable lately, and their newly raised capital in Japan was supporting home-country rather than U.S. lending.

Some of these admissions, of course, were rhetorical, designed to persuade worried Americans that the Japanese banks are really paper tigers in the United States. Though they may have troubles, they most certainly are not weaklings about whom no one need be interested. Daiwa and Sumitomo banks are in adequate shape, although Bank of Tokyo, Mitsui Taiyo Kobe Bank, and Fuji Bank may have to become very conservative.[26]

To make it in the 1990s, both conservative and aggressive bankers will seek fee-generating business. Sanwa Bank handles about $100 million annually in mergers and acquisitions of American companies by Japanese firms. It has facilitated the sale of a Chicago drug company, research labs in Illinois and Michigan, and a Chicago sheet metal manufacturer. Until recently, Sanwa did not charge for its advice. Now it probably will seek about 1 percent in compensation. Other fees are being generated in the swap markets. A Japanese bank will match up an American borrower paying variable rates with a Japanese lender receiving variable rates. They will swap income flows from the respective loans, in effect refinancing so as to reduce risk. Similar swaps occur between American companies with yen loans outstanding and Japanese corporations with dollar loans. The deal enables each firm to get the currency it needs but to still enjoy the lower interest rate which attracted it to the foreign currency in the first place. Fees from currency swaps run about $200 million a year for the Japanese.

For every 1 percent increase in fees as a share of total revenues, Japanese banks can raise their return on sales by 1 percent or more. For example, B of T's fees were 4 percent of revenues in 1990, and return on sales was 3 percent. Yasuda Trust's fees were 5.3 percent, and its return was 4.6 percent. Similar relationships hold for other banks.[27] These data drive home the importance of fees as a source of profitability. "We have three types of revenue generators in the United States," said a Fuji Bank manager in 1990. "Loans, foreign exchange, and fees. The fee business is what is now increasing the share value of the bank. This is a big change. Before, fees were a very small portion of our business."

The rush into fee-generating businesses was illustrated by Dai-Ichi Kangyo's rather expensive purchase of CIT Group Holdings, Inc., as an entree into commercial insurance, leasing, and associated credit markets. The bank's American operations, however, cannot engage in the insurance business, and CIT's insurance operations were limited by the Federal Reserve to the New York area. Also apparently unrewarding was Sumitomo's investment in Goldman, Sachs, which also was constrained by the government. Other efforts make more sense. Mitsui Bank bought 5 percent of Security Pacific's consumer and commercial services groups to gain access to knowledge which Mitsui can put to good use. Yasuda Trust acquired 49 percent of a Chicago M & A firm focused on medium-sized company takeovers.[28] And Mitsubishi Bank established a brokerage subsidiary in New York to underwrite bonds issued by Japanese companies in the United States and to sell securitized assets based on bank loans. In the 1990s both American and Japanese banks will be trying to raise their capital adequacy ratio by securitizing high-risk assets (e.g., consumer loans) and using the proceeds from the sales of securities to buy low-risk assets (e.g., GNMA mortgage-backed securities) which require less capital backup.

A relatively risk-free fee generator is servicing futures markets transactions. Fuji Bank, Sanwa, Mitsubishi, the Long-Term Credit Bank, the Industrial Bank of Japan, and several others all have subsidiaries which are members of the Chicago Mercantile Exchange. In brokering futures transactions, however, they will be competing with many other firms, including Japanese securities groups. Fees are likely to be low, although the banks probably are looking to establish relationships with clients so they can offer other services. The securities firms are not very good at anything except underwriting and sales, while the banks can offer forecasting services, information based on their deep knowledge of their clients, and more extensive technology (it is not that the Japanese bank technology is that good; rather the Japanese securities firms' technology is generally weak).

A reluctant follower like Tokai Bank came to Georgetown, Kentucky, because its chief customer, Toyota, summoned it. To some extent, this "follow the fleet" approach was common among most banks which expanded their U.S. operations in the 1980s. They came over because they were told to, or else poor business in Japan drove them. Unlike Tokai, most have tried to do business with American-owned corporations, attract American deposits, and sell services to American firms. Some big one-time profits occurred in 1989, but the 1990s will be a difficult period. Their real estate lending business is declining, and Japanese financial services firms will do much of the retail business the banks had hoped to acquire from Japanese-owned manufacturing companies.

Those banks saddled with mostly branches will look for strategic alliances and acquisitions of American banks, if they can find any. Some will lie low, content to manage the dollar-based stock and bond portfolios of Japanese clients, but others will become knowledge seekers, hiring Americans who can teach Japanese expatriates the business. Weak personnel management will hinder this move, however.

The wave of bank mergers sweeping Japan will strengthen some banks. Size tends to improve productivity, leading to increased profits and a solid capital base. Add already good asset management skills, and new giants like Kyowa-Saitama could decide to move more aggressively in the United States. Unlike the 1980s, however, any Japanese moves will have to generate profits. Not only are profits needed to beef up capital, they are required to replace depleted loan loss reserves. Estimates are that about one billion dollars in profits will be needed to cover bad loans made in the 1980s. The 1990s-style Japanese banker in the United States will look a lot like his American counterparts in his pursuit of fees, consumers, and mid-sized corporate loans. He will differ in that he probably can take on a bit more risk, but only if he has been able to hire able Americans to advise him. This is a big if.

TWENTY

Weakness on Wall Street

"Wall Street over the last decade," said a senior American bond trader, "has been pure creativity, with new products and new markets. The Japanese are great at production, not creativity. They are laggards on Wall Street." How are the Big Four Japanese at Nomura, Daiwa, Yamaichi, Nikko, and at several smaller securities firms different from British, Dutch, and Canadian businesses on the street? "The Japanese are more restrictive in their markets. There is less reciprocation," noted another trader. She also saw the Japanese securities firm managers as arrogant. "They are perceived on the street as being elitist. They act as if they have a culture and we Americans don't yet. Also, they flex their muscles more based on their many export successes. These are all no-nos among Americans right now."

Uncreative? Exclusionary? Arrogant? Braggarts? Are these the Japanese known the world over for their civility and self-effacement? In fact, because of their uncreative and exclusionary behavior, the Wall Street Japanese have no reason to be arrogant. In 1989–1990 U.S. operations of the Big Four firms contributed only about half a percent of their combined profits. Compare this with their London offices, which averaged about 4 percent, mostly due to fees generated by selling Eurodollar warrant bonds on behalf of Japanese corporations raising capital to invest in the United States. Granted, American securities firms in Tokyo do not do much better. The 1990 profits of Merrill Lynch, Salomon, Morgan Stanley, and Goldman, Sachs ranged from $1.6 million to $16 million (for Salomon, which seems poised for a break-through).[1] But no one expected them to do well. The Wall Street Japanese, however, were supposed to be the new Goliaths of the age, threatening the masters of the universe in their lair (to put a Tom Wolf-ean spin on it). They were not and they did not.

The reality is that Japanese securities firms originally were set up in New York to service Japanese customers. Their offices were not profit centers. Over time, they became knowledge seekers trying to learn how to do more than flog stocks and peddle bonds. In the 1980s arrogance indeed did grip them and they sought to become competitive and prof-itable. Japanese executives talked very big in the press and in books like Daniel Burstein's *Yen!* about their coming worldwide dominance. This lasted for a few years. In the 1990s the Wall Street Japanese will go back to a learning mode, hiring streetwise Americans to show them the ropes. The arrogance is gone, replaced by a kinder, gentler pose.

THAILAND IT'S NOT

By early 1989 the Japanese firms had realized that things were not going very well for them. "The traditional ways of doing business are just not profitable," said Shoji Hattori, head of Yamaichi Securities' New York subsidiary.[2] To learn new ways they began buying Ameri-can expertise. Nomura bought an interest in a leveraged leasing com-pany, a real-estate investment banking firm, and a mergers and acqui-sitions specialist. It also hired an American in 1990 to take over its New York office. What Japanese management has lacked on Wall Street is the ability to develop corporate and institutional relationships, skill at managing risk, and an innovative bent. Tokyo has been reluctant to commit capital to its subsidiaries, demands to be consulted on even trivial decisions, and requires a market-share focus which is often ill-considered. This is the way the securities business is run in Japan, and as we have seen elsewhere in this book, Japanese managers first try it their way and adapt only under pressure. They rarely listen to their American employees. "To tell you how bad the communication can be," said one American, "we cannot even communicate to them how bad it is." Another noted, "It's crazy because they pay us much more than they get, then aren't really interested in our judgments." What-ever image benefits they had gained through their reputation as offer-ers of job security was lost in the wake of substantial layoffs after the 1987 crash.

At Nikko the equity department was cut from forty to twenty-five employees. Corporate bonds endured a similar cut. Nomura laid off 150 out of 650 employees in research, sales, and trading. Nikko also cut back in its domestic equities business, letting go 110 people. While American-owned Wall Street firms did the same thing in the 1988–1991 period, the Japanese are likely to be hurt badly. When hiring begins again, the already reduced pool of available Americans will be a lot smaller. Who wants to work for Daiwa whose president says, "Frankly I have found Americans so hungry for money. . . . People may be excellent at what they do, but they work for themselves, not the company." This same gentleman urged Americans to learn Japanese so they could participate in important meetings. Here again is a theme I discussed earlier. Japanese managers treat an American subsidiary as if it were a Japanese firm which just happens to be located outside of Japan. They do this because of their experience in the Asian and East Asian countries where Japan has invested so much. Subsidiaries there are indeed Japanese firms with Japanese managers and an employee group made up of uneducated, often illiterate help not capable of nor expected to contribute anything but physical labor. America is not Thailand, however, and Wall Street is not some back alley in Taipei. American Wall Streeters, while a rather rough lot, have not yet reached the lascar or coolie stage of existence. They may be from Brooklyn (as I am) and have names like Vinnie, Sonny, Freddie, and Charlie, but they have much to teach the new guys on the block.

IT'S NOT TOKYO, EITHER

"The Japanese tend to get into a ghetto when they arrive on Wall Street," admitted a Japanese trader. "They don't develop the useful business contacts they need. They attend all-Japanese golfing weekends but don't get into American society." To develop American business, Japanese managers have got to avoid the Japanese pubs which now dot the New York financial district and start hitting the American watering holes. They have to become members of local social and professional groups. Above all, they have to play the game 1990s style. Wall Street isn't the bumptious boozing of *Liar's Poker* anymore, but the Japanese don't seem to know it. "Look at the hands of the Japanese guys in my office," said a chief trader. "They're bloated from heavy drinking. Those guys will party all night and die the next day. I watch them staring out the window, waiting for the next night's bash."

"They just don't have time to develop local business," noted another American. "They stay in the office until 11 o'clock communicating with Tokyo. When they're not doing that, they party with Japanese clients."

Many Japanese securities firms act as if they are still in Japan. "They don't necessarily value performance. Instead they value development of a Japanese-style relationship over five years with a broker or dealer," observed a woman who had worked for several firms as a secretary and then a bond trader (her Japanese language skills paid off for a time, but eventually she could not take the poor treatment of women and left). At times money seems to be the last thing they care about. "Being tribal seems an end in itself. I still can't understand it after all this time. What do I care if my 'friend' Masao gets my business and is happy? I care if I make a tick!" Sometimes the Japanese are bottom-line oriented and sometimes they're not. "It's very confusing if you are put in middle management between Japanese bosses and American staff. You don't know which way to go. One week everything is bottom line. The next it's 'Let's work together and be communal.' At times I'm positive the Japanese don't know what they're doing. They don't know what they want." This woman, with years of experience in both Japan and in Japanese-owned U.S. subsidiaries, still could not understand the system. But she noted the Japanese failure to grasp the American way. "Many Americans on Wall Street are very observant of the Japanese. They learn what buttons to push. This isn't true for the Japanese. They never establish that fundamental understanding of how we operate."

One problem the Wall Street Japanese face is their inability to come up with innovations, the new securities or services which can generate enormous returns. What has hampered the firms is their own conservative background, but even worse is their Japanese habit of talking everything to death. "Once something is talked about, it's on the street pretty quick," said one American, who has watched his ideas implemented by competitors while his Japanese bosses debated. There are no copyrights or patents on Wall Street, no old boy networks to guard against theft of ideas, and no leisurely pace. The Japanese are learning this the hard way. They often are able to act quickly on local issues, but for ideas with international ramifications Tokyo must be consulted, and the process is very slow. "What I do is try to link up with an American firm on a deal," said an executive. "Then I let the Americans push my Japanese bosses into quick action."

The securities business in Japan is radically different and cannot be transferred to America. The firms provide permanent employment to their new hires and start them off with focused training programs emphasizing corporate culture and groupism.[3] On the job training consists of learning how to be a "Nomura man" or a "Daiwa man." This involves developing familiarity with the structure of the firm, its resources, and roles which must be assumed in given situations—always with the understanding that if a task needs doing, everyone is available to do it regardless of role. Young employees are assigned to a *senpai*, an "older brother" who serves as a coach, mostly in after-hours drinking bouts. The *senpai* eventually introduces the employee to clients. After that the employee is given a quota and told to sell. Somewhere along the way technical knowledge of the securities business might be picked up, but no one worries much about that. The real job is constant, intense selling.

The sales function on Wall Street, however, has been a mystery to the securities firms. "They don't build sales forces here," said an American hire of his firm. "They focus on trading instead." Doing trading for the negative reason that you don't understand selling is no way to run a shop. Part of the trading emphasis is the desire to learn, but that's not a good enough reason. "They're leading with their weakest punch. In this business they won't capture market share as they did in automobiles. They have to return to sales if they want to make markets."

Differences between Tokyo and New York were illustrated when in late 1989 Tokyo Stock Exchange officials began calling the American securities firms in Japan, asking them not to do program trading. When the market started to crash in early 1990, they were quick to blame the American arbitrageurs and portfolio insurance practitioners. But as 1990 wore on, Wall Street's Japanese subsidiaries began setting up their own program trading desks and Japanese officials started to speak in accommodating terms. "The Japanese started acting in a theoretically sound manner. That surprised me," commented a Merrill Lynch trading desk manager. "Maybe something is going on behind the scenes." This could be the case in that as the Japanese securities firms in New York develop arbitrage expertise, they will transport it back to Tokyo and Osaka. If this process is well under way, we can expect the Japanese to start accepting program trading as an inevitable outcome of a well-developed market. "When we learn to do it, then it's rational" might be one way of putting words in their mouths.

Another problem in Tokyo that will hurt in America is—believe it or not—sloth. "Our Japanese managers were not close to the product. They didn't have a sense of what it takes to make money," commented an American who had logged time in her American firm's Tokyo office. "They said to themselves, 'This is why I'm here and this is what I do. We've got new products, but I don't care to understand them.' They didn't want to dig in and learn. Eventually they started to come around, but it was very slow." Other Americans report similar experiences. Even Japanese securities people admit that they often move at a glacial pace. "I need ten years to become a good bond trader in New York," said one. "If it takes more than six months," responded an American, "he'll never learn."

During an interview, another American looked out at the bond trading floor of his Japanese-owned firm. "Someone should do a time and motion study and watch the bond trading group at work. What you will see is some people hustling and some staring off into space. I work like a horse, but the Japanese are great paper pushers. They'll spend the day going over and over some form." Anyone who has visited offices in Tokyo will recognize this description immediately as an accurate characterization of white-collar work in Japan. It's now been transported to Wall Street.

Another export is imitation of one's betters. "When the firm set up this office," noted the same American, "they bought state of the art equipment—$30,000 work stations for clerks. Why? Because Nomura did it. They didn't think about using the stuff. They just imitated Nomura."

Analysis is becoming more and more important on Wall Street, but until recently it was of no consequence in Tokyo. The Big Four downplayed analysts' views, preaching sermons instead on the stock or industry of the week and then getting their customers to drive values up with their purchases. Analysts were supposed only to recommend "buy" for stocks, especially those originally underwritten by their securities firm.[4]

The companies also bought for their own accounts. "They don't sell stock much. They just put it away. The Japanese don't march to the market," said a Merrill Lynch trader. What he meant was that in a Tokyo stock market manipulated to go up, buying and holding was the only strategy. In a real market with daily fluctuations requiring buying and selling, Japanese securities firms seem bewildered. This is what happened when the bubble burst in late March, 1990 and Tokyo stocks began a long descent. For a time the Japanese did nothing, while American and other foreign firms sold quickly. "They'll buy a stock at 1800 yen," commented the trader, "and four days from now when it's 1700 yen, as far as they're concerned it's still 1800. Japanese securities firms often act like mutual funds, holding stocks for a long time."

None of this will work in New York. Stock analysis and the research to support it are crucial, as is a willingness to be in and out of markets quickly.

If New York is not Tokyo and the Japanese securities firms are only modest in their Wall Street achievements, why were so many people worried about them in the late 1980s? One reason is that they were not modest in their assertions to journalists. "We want all customers . . . all nationalities, all borrowers, all issuers, and all investors," proclaimed Yoshihisha Tabuchi, President of Nomura to an interviewer. "We wish to be like Japanese manufacturing companies which sell the same products to people in every part of the world."[5] This same interviewer then quoted another Nomura executive on Tabuchi, "If he had lived in another time period, I'm sure he would have been a shogun." With that kind of hype the Japanese could have won the Pacific War if they had been fighting American journalists instead of U.S. Marines.

THE GREEDHEADS ARE GONE

Wall Streeters of the 1990s are not the greedheads of the 1980s. "That ended when the MBAs got fired," said one old-timer. Indeed, many traders and salesmen have long-term allegiance to firms such as Merrill Lynch and Morgan Stanley. These are the men and women who survived the crash of '87. They tend to admire the Japanese spirit of loyalty, and many are willing to be loyal to Japanese employers. At one unit of an American firm that made money in 1989 while the firm lost overall, no one received a bonus in 1990, yet no one quit. Fear of not finding a job elsewhere was part of it, but loyalty counted also. "Companies were making bids for some of these guys far in excess of what they were getting, yet they didn't leave. It surprised me," said a manager in the firm.

No one sees the Japanese firms as offering lifetime employment— that illusion gave way after 1987—but their practice of trying to retain expertise for the long run is attractive. "I wouldn't mind a little less money and more security," said a young bond trader, eyeing his Japanese colleagues (most of whom would like more money without losing their job security).

Americans gradually are working their way into responsible positions at the Japanese firms. When Max Chapman took over at Nomura International in New York in 1990, the move signalled to the industry that Nomura on Wall Street wanted to become an American firm with American capital sourcing, staffing, and clients. Chapman promptly began hiring Americans for a program trading unit. His focus also will be on turning a brokerage house into an investment bank serving U.S. multinationals' needs to reduce debt loads or to restructure them with global financing. Where Nomura goes, most of the other Japanese firms are sure to follow, although they will balk at paying the $3 million or so which Chapman-like executives get.

The policy of *dochakuka*, complete localization, has only just begun to be implemented, and the Japanese have not yet figured out how to do it. "To make a go of it," noted a senior bond trader at a Japanese firm, "they have to improve their personnel practices. They don't check people out properly. They don't know how to fire people." He gave some examples."An American we hired worked his way up from runner to a good job which he couldn't possibly handle. The firm has to manage this better. We see guys lie about their former jobs. The Japanese don't check. They hire people as salesmen who can't sell." One problem is that Japanese get assigned to manage units without having a clue as to what their duties are or what kind of personnel they need. "A Japanese is pulled off the floor and told to run the back office. That's it, no training," said the bond trader.

A young Japanese manager agreed. "I did two years as a salesman in Tokyo. Then I was ordered to another job. I have to obey." He likes the Americans whom he manages, but they worry him. "They concentrate on their responsibilities but are less interested in a career than I am." What he means is that they are less interested in doing dirty work now in hopes of better things down the road. Nevertheless, he needs their expertise. "They are greatly advanced, and we have a lot to learn from them about technology and financing methods. In the securities business we are importers of American knowledge while Japanese manufacturers are exporters of products."

The American bond trader shakes his head at Japanese muddle, but he admires many of their practices. "I worked previously at a small American securities firm. I could walk into the president's office any time I wanted. Now I work for one of the largest Japanese firms and I can do the same thing." Part of the reason for this small-firm atmosphere is the corporate culture of Japanese business. The senior people are available; they do not wall themselves off. Another reason is their desperate need for American ideas. Those Japanese firms which have poor communications with Americans (news stories suggest that Daiwa and Yamaichi may have bigger problems than the other firms) will have trouble localizing—although some of them may be content to continue serving mostly Japanese clients.

Another American bond trader has watched the senior Japanese at several firms. "The Americans play poker. The Japanese play chess," he commented on differences in strategic approaches. Americans calculate probabilities and risks, but Japanese apply tried and true general rules to most situations. The Japanese executives are every bit as sharp as their American counterparts, but they resist creative leaps to new but risky ideas. Like chess masters, they have a repertoire of moves and choose from them.

Also like chess players, Japanese managers often affect an air of studied intensity. "The formality of the work day. That's the most surprising thing I noticed when I went to work for Daiwa," said a former employee. "It's not obvious until you get into a trading situation, when you have dollars flying and emotions on the line." Americans would scream and yell, while Japanese sucked wind and sat stonefaced. During lulls in the market, Americans would joke with each other. Japanese stared out the windows or read newspapers. "The Japanese are different at night. That's when they blow off steam," said the former Daiwa employee. Americans vent emotion during the day, while Japanese wait until dark to rehash the day's events with gales of laughter or tears of anguish, all lubricated by gallons of alcohol.

Besides a certain formality, the Americans are struck by the power of the Japanese bosses. "When rank speaks, that's it," observed an

American manager. "In our business that's a drawback, because they don't get legitimate input from subordinates." Employees eager to be compliant do not exhibit creativity, and they don't provide the criticism needed to develop new tactics. "Once the decision is reached on top," said the manager, commenting on "consensus" decision making, "everybody has immediate consensus." The wiser Japanese bosses keep their doors open and listen to everyone, but once a boss decides, he makes the consensus by making the decision.

The securities managers have learned by now that Wall Street is not Tokyo, and Americans are not Japanese. Clients shop around for deals rather than relationships, and employees are much less subservient. The need for analysis is much greater, and the sales function is more than just brute force (in Tokyo salesmen are told to make a hundred telephone calls; when they finish, they call the same people again). But knowing that they must be faster, broader, and more creative does not necessarily mean that the Japanese securities firms will adapt. By putting the American head of Nomura International on its forty-member board in Tokyo in 1990, Nomura initiated a process which will differentiate New York operations from Tokyo. This level of Americanization is not being tried at the other firms, however, and it may not even work at Nomura. But it is the right thing to do, given the failures of the firms to Japanize their Wall Street activities.

COMPETING

The principal competitors with Nomura and the other Japanese securities firms are the six large American wholesalers catering to institutional investors and corporate and municipal clients: Goldman, Sachs, Merrill Lynch, Salomon, Morgan Stanley, First Boston, and Shearson Lehman.[6] The Americans have been growing, both in terms of capital and services offered, in anticipation of the eventual movement of commercial banks into investment banking when the Glass-Steagall constraints are diminished. They are now well positioned to fend off both American and Japanese banks and Japanese securities firms. These U.S. firms now offer over 250 distinct financial instruments, up from sixty-two in 1982. Chief among these are bond-like products. Although competitive pressures from Europe have eroded commissions, the Japanese have not made inroads here. While the junk bond business has declined, the market for asset-backed securities has emerged. Mortgage-backed securities were invented by Salomon, but all of the larger firms now do them. One of the possibilities for the Japanese firms is to offer securities based on Japanese nonliquid assets, perhaps even the growing number of Japanese mortgages. They are certainly not going to be competitive in municipal debt offerings.

One area where the Japanese have become competitive is the U.S. government-securities market. Several firms became primary dealers, which means they were among the forty or so companies permitted to make direct bids at Treasury auctions (the rules changed in 1991). These firms serve the big Japanese insurance and trust companies which buy U.S. securities and help fund the U.S. deficit. Profits per transactions are miniscule, but the market's massive size allows money to be made. A promising future market will be underwriting of U.S. corporations' equity offerings in Asia and Japan. The Japanese are well-positioned if this form of equity financing develops.

Brokerage is what the Japanese do in Japan, and it is what they do in America for Japanese clients wanting U.S. equity. This business too will increase, since investor faith in the Tokyo Stock Exchange has been reduced after big declines in 1990. The steadier U.S. markets will attract Japanese buyers served by Japanese brokers. Currently, however, the biggest revenue producer on Wall Street is trading, and the Japanese managers, although trying hard, are weak in this field in both bond and stock trading.

Trading is essentially gambling as a way to make money rather than serving clients, and Japanese firms have not done it in the past. They now are doing it because money can be made and because many of their clients are trading and want to benefit from their securities firms' expertise. Becoming an instant expert takes a long time, as the Japanese are discovering. It may be that they will never become good traders; as we will see below, their attitudes toward risk do not foster a trading mentality. Another thing they have not been doing is research, and their clients will demand more of it. Investors want advice and traders want to calculate rough odds. Both turn to research. Goldman, Sachs, First Boston, and Merrill Lynch are research leaders, but all good investors try to maximize their incomes. Japanese, with deep pockets, clearly can become players here if they want to.

Corporate finance activities for the Japanese have focused on advising Japanese firms in America, but American banks want to get into this business. Assume you are a mid-sized Japanese firm which finds that the profitability in its overcapitalized industry in Japan is declining. You want to acquire a U.S. firm in a friendly takeover to gain entry into new and more lucrative American markets. Should you go to a Japanese bank, say Fuji Bank, or to Yamaichi Securities? Those were your choices until recently. But these firms have had trouble finding American takeover candidates. The reason is simple: they do not look hard enough and they do not have the staff. Regional American banks, especially retailers with branches all over a state or a geographic area, are ideally positioned to pull information together from their little empires and to sell it to the Japanese. That's just what some of them are doing. The American bankers can advise Japanese clients not only about takeover candidates seeking suitors but also on valuation, legal, and structuring issues. To put it politely, internal rate of return and present-value evaluation techniques are not widely practiced in Japan, where simple return on investment and growth rule the roost. Bluntly stated, the Japanese do not know the real worth of anything as well as Americans do. Our Japanese acquirer would be well-advised by an American bank rather than a Japanese securities firm.

The experience of Yamaichi in the 1960s gives a hint of the kind of trouble Japanese securities firms can get into when they focus on speculation of the kind the American firms do well. Yamaichi had underwritten equity offerings for a number of growth-oriented companies. Then it made a market for these securities, trading on its own account and reaping some capital gains. When the stock market fell, Yamaichi's holdings declined in value, but it refused to sell its clients' stocks. What was worse, it had borrowed heavily to finance its market-making and trading activities. Wall Streeters say that Japanese securities firms engage in similar practices today. The difference is that their capital base is huge, so they can afford to be Mr. Nice Guy for their clients—up to a point. Competitive strength, after all, does not come from self-immolation.

THE HORROR OF RISK

"Most of our revenues came from brokerage fees. That is changing," said a Japanese manager at a second tier firm. "We are not used to taking risks, but we must take more risk in the states than in Japan. Trading and investment banking are new areas for us." Risk management is one of the hardest things the Wall Street Japanese must learn. "There is no college training on this in Japan. I have to learn on the job," he moaned, envious of the well-trained young Americans from Wharton and Chicago still left on the street and the experienced oldtimers who know all the right moves.

"The Japanese firms have huge amounts of money, but it's often irresponsibly managed," observed an American manager of equity trading. "I see Japanese guys throwing futures around, and there's nothing strategic about it." The firms have tried to develop knowledge of risk control through joint ventures and by hiring American expertise, but more is needed. They need to develop skills in managing one risk relative to all risks, buying the whole market, focusing on indexation, developing strong research and analysis abilities, and reducing their reliance on the opinions of self-appointed gurus and "shoguns."

Risk management confusion leads to unnecessary conservatism or crazy speculation. "We don't buy any of the more speculative bond issues. Junk is totally out of the picture," a young bond trader in a Japanese firm complained. "We go for A ratings and above. We broker BAA securities, but we don't take positions in them. We just look for steady returns," he sighed. "The Japanese say, 'Hit singles, not home runs.' "

A senior bond trader saw the speculative side. "On a personal level, Japanese managers are not risk takers, but if the firm makes a decision to take risk, the amount of risk they take is often unreal. Some of the positions they will take are mind boggling." A story one hears frequently on the street concerns Daiwa's decision to develop a bond trading desk. Seven traders were hired, but no sales force was put in place to support them. Then Daiwa brought in a "hitter" from Salomon who took on huge positions. He blew himself out of the water in a year.

Securities firms, like Japanese firms in other industries, often do not develop strategy in terms of risks and rewards. Instead, they ask themselves, "What must we do to maintain our ranking relative to the other firms in our industry?" An official in a second-tier firm was quite blunt about this. "We want to compete, but we don't want to be Number 1 to do something." Doing something first is the duty of Nomura, the leader, and the follower firms will then scramble to catch up. This sounds like something emerging out of Japanese cultural values but it is not. American firms in highly oligopolized industries will do the same thing. What is peculiarly Japanese is the wild plunges a firm will take to maintain its rank. To fall a notch or two is so shameful as to be out of the question, and almost any risk is worth taking to avoid it. Couple this fear of falling with a lack of sophistication and you have at least some understanding of the Wall Street Japanese attitude to risk. When the industry is stable and the leader is quiet, everyone plays it safe and is conservative. But when 1990-style turmoil grips the markets and Nomura starts making moves, the other Japanese firms can get very nervous and primed to take some big chances.

Their success in Japan will determine how big a presence on Wall Street the Japanese securities firms will have. "If the Tokyo stock market falls, we will face hard times," noted a Japanese manager in early 1990. By the end of the year it had declined about 37 percent and was back at 1986–1987 levels. Securities firms' profits had fallen sharply, although they were still making money. By 1992, losses had started to occur, scandal had hit the industry because of its association with Japanese gangsters, and the stock market was still low.

For the 1990s the Japanese must decide what they want from Wall Street: knowledge or profits. They were barely breaking even in the 1989–1991 period, but knowledge was piling up as high-quality Americans were hired and eager young Japanese worked alongside and learned. Ordinarily one would conclude that the Wall Street Japanese eventually would carve out a small but noteworthy chunk of the marketplace for themselves. But consider their problems. Capital from Tokyo will be slow in coming in the 1990s, and the Japanese banks will not loan money as readily as they once did. Tokyo executives will be preoccupied with their domestic problems and will become annoyed with the continued lack of profitability on Wall Street. They will be in no mood to make strategic investments.

In addition, the recurring failure of Japanese financial service firms to properly manage and motivate the high quality Americans they have hired may take its toll when business picks up and more jobs become available. Without American expertise, the firms will sink back to the status of passive agents for Japanese investors and corporations rather than full-fledged competitors.

"The Japanese have had some rough years here," commented a bond trader. "As soon as they have some success, they'll improve." True enough, but can they have success? They lack customers and don't develop their sales forces. They party among themselves, foregoing the opportunity to develop American contacts. They do not take an active part in professional associations. They are slow to innovate. They are nice to their American employees but do not utilize them well. As traders they do not manage risk well. They do not use research and analytics well. It will take a long time to solve these problems.

TWENTY-ONE

Marketing and Negotiating

"In Japan perhaps I can find a firm which has in it a relative of my grandfather. I can approach them and try to sell my product, even at a high price," said a textile trader. "In America I can't use family connections, and even a stay of three or four years in the United States is not enough time to build sales relationships. We must compete on price. But when I do, my American competitors file dumping charges against us."

Competing in the United States on price is difficult in an era of high yen and low dollars—the price of Japanese exports to the United States has to go up to compensate for the rising yen value. "Many Japanese firms do 70 percent of their business in Japan and 30 percent export. They cannot survive without that 30 percent, so they give my trading firm low prices, which we pass on to American customers."

What this manager is saying is that Japanese firms (usually in oligopolized industries) often are overcapitalized and must sell abroad. In the absence of other selling points and despite the rising yen, they can only compete in the United States on price. While there are low profits in this kind of activity, it does keep the machinery and the lifetime employees busy back in Japan. It also forces companies to think about investing in America, where there is a chance to make better use of capital.

The textile trading executive's remarks probably describe the lot of many mid-sized Japanese firms in America and even some large companies. They did not come to this country with sophisticated marketing plans in place. Rather they could not go on with exporting just to cover fixed costs in Japan and saw a chance for higher returns in the United

States. How successful have they been? Not very. U.S. Department of Commerce data for 1988 show $1.8 million in sales per employee for non-Japanese foreign investors in the United States and 4.06 employees per million dollars of assets. For Japanese non-bank, majority-owned U.S. affiliates the numbers are $690,000 in sales per employee and 1.76 employees per $ million in assets.[1] Thus the Japanese are more capital intensive than other foreign investors—which should indicate high sales per employee—yet sales per employee are lower. Although revenues have been rising steadily since 1985 for Japanese-owned firms, by 1988 at least they were still not very good in comparison with those of other foreign firms.

In the 1990s Japanese firms will have to increase sales per employee by almost two and one-half times just to catch up to the other foreign firms. Using labor better in their plants won't be enough. They will have to find more customers for their products. They will have to become better at marketing in the United States.

Johny K. Johansson of Georgetown University has been watching Japanese marketing efforts in America for many years. "The successes of the Japanese almost invariably hide a number of failures. Their products do not make money," he says.[2] Shiseido has been trying for 18 years to make a dent in the U.S. cosmetics market and only recently has had some success. Although Toyota and Honda are doing well, they took a long time getting there. Who remembers the immortal Toyopet or the early Honda motorcycles that did not sell? During most of the 1980s the Bridgestone tire held only about 1 percent of the U.S. target market. For most of the time since they bought it in 1976, Matsushita's Quasar plant outside of Chicago was not profitable. The personal computers of Fujitsu and NEC are of excellent quality, but they do not always compete well against IBM. Has anyone purchased Toray's ultrasuede, Ecsaine, lately?

According to Johansson, what is common in Japanese marketing is an initial reliance on inexperienced managers from Japan who doggedly travel around to their various U.S. dealerships, talking endlessly with salesmen, retailers, and customers. Then the company invests heavily in advertising stressing a seemingly unbeatable price/quality combination. Sometimes this works, but it is quite amateurish. More sophisticated approaches usually are the result of American expertise hired when repeated failures force corrective action. Japanese executives excuse their errors by pointing out how long-term their focus is, and would not it be wonderful if American firms could be just like us.

HOW IT'S DONE IN JAPAN

In Japan roles are reversed. Japanese companies know what they are doing, and it is the Americans who sometimes need help. Take the case of Remington Japan. Today the company has a modest presence in Japan with its Lady Remington shaver, a hair remover riding a fad which began in 1989. But things were not always so smooth.

In the early 1970s Remington, then owned by Sperry-Univac, entered the Japanese market in a typical American fashion with a giant ad campaign designed to generate consumer demand which would force closed distribution channels to open. The company tried for four years and then gave up. Over half of the consumer outlets in Japan are exclusive dealers for Matsushita, Hitachi, Toshiba, and Sony, and demand for Remington shavers meant nothing to them. "If they had planned a ten-year program, maybe they could have succeeded," said Katsuhiko Saitoh, Remington Japan's current president.

After Remington had exited the market in the mid-1970s, Japanese purchasers kept on using the shavers. Inevitably, ordinary wear and tear took its toll, and people began bringing the products back to the stores for repairs. The stores could do nothing for them, but in desperation they recommended another foreign seller, Braun, which took advantage of the opening and today is Japan's leading foreign marketer of shaving equipment. After Victor Kiam bought Remington, he soon came to Japan and formed Remington Japan in 1980 with Japanese investors. Mr. Saitoh was appointed as president. His first task was to visit the retail buyers. "It's not like America, with personnel changing every two or three years," he recalled. "I wish it was, because the buyers for the stores were the same people who had dealt with Remington ten years earlier."

A typical buyer would say something like "Jesus Christ, you people again!" Then he would pull open a drawer and display the old razors returned for repairs. "I realized that we would have a hard time selling Mr. Kiam's shavers," said Mr. Saitoh. He soon found himself paying compensation to retailers instead of selling to them. "We were starting out from less than zero rather than zero." It took five years for Remington to build up its credibility again and to establish a service record. Initially advertising was used, with Victor Kiam in his bathrobe telling the audience, "I liked the shaver so much, I bought the company." This approach did not work, so the company turned to print media and advertised the shavers on the pages in newspapers and magazines listing luxury gift items.

Slowly Remington built up a brand image as a high-quality gift item. At the same time volume discount and specialty stores emerged in Japan and began to carry the product. Finally wholesalers agreed to stock it. This was crucial for Remington, which was experiencing high delivery and inventory costs dealing directly with the stores. The wholesalers offered well-established delivery systems and large warehousing facilities. Remington retained servicing activities. When the Lady Remington opened up the female users' market, the company became profitable.

Along the way, Mr. Saitoh got a chance to observe American marketing in action. One thing that surprised him was the American reliance on statistics. "Japanese market research is different. Americans collect data. But that's just what *has* happened. Japanese try to identify future trends." In Japan this is often a matter of watching trend setters in Tokyo, since Japanese consumers tend to follow the leader. Another difference concerned product attributes. "Japanese companies will sell several variations of a new product to satisfy customers. Americans are more cost conscious and stick with a uniform product." Thus Japanese marketers, lacking statistics and focus-group results that tell them what consumers want, vary product characteristics instead and learn what to drop or retain from sales. Having learned beforehand, Americans can be more targeted. Where Japanese cover business risks by expanding product variety, Americans expand market research.

Which is the better approach? In the United States the American strategy clearly is preferable. Consumers are more heterogeneous, and trial and error marketing would be too costly. Nevertheless, this is what many Japanese firms have done—and suffered for. As noted above, what looks like a long-term perspective sometimes is simply a drawn out period of incompetence as Japanese managers try to sell a product based on their own gut feelings about trends and a willingness to learn from mistakes. While learning from mistakes in manufacturing can be admirable, it can be folly in marketing if less expensive research techniques exist. What does work for the Japanese, however, is the door-opening niche approach. Remington, on the advice of its Japanese staff, repositioned itself in the small but important luxury gift market. This was a base from which it could launch assaults on bigger markets. Over and over in America, from cars to televisions, Japanese products have entered the marketplace in bottom of the line and/or small niches which were left undefended by Americans. Presumably this strategy will continue, augmented by better use of market research and more careful targeting.

GETTING INTO THE UNITED STATES

Japanese marketing strategy in the United States has been remarkably risk averse over the years. In the 1950s and 1960s American firms used Japanese as original equipment manufacturers (OEM) to supply components in a wide range of electronics, auto, and machine tool products.[3] As the Japanese learned how to make these products, they offered to produce finished goods for American companies. Eager to fill gaps in their product lines, the Americans began using the Japanese in OEM relationships, some of which are still occurring today. For copiers, IBM used Minolta, while Savin had a relationship with Ricoh. Amdahl used Fujitsu for mainframe computers (Fujitsu now controls Amdahl), and Sperry used Mitsubishi. Bendix used Murata for machine tools, while Sears used Sanyo and Toshiba for televisions. An OEM strategy gave Japanese firms a low-risk way to learn how to make products desired by Americans in high volumes at constantly reduced costs without sacrificing quality.

Once a Japanese firm had learned how to produce for America, it needed to learn how to market. Trading companies were in place and ready to help. They saw to it that new Japanese brands got into the U.S. distribution system and advised manufacturers on locating sales offices. After a time many firms went their own way, and soon most Japanese investment in America consisted of sales offices charged with building brand images. The spectacular success of firms like Sony and Matsushita (Panasonic brand) rests on a vast network of sales offices centered on marketing and advertising headquarters in the United States. This marketing infrastructure easily accommodated direct investment in production, which began to increase in the late 1970s and took off after 1985. If this all looks like an evolving process in some kind of grand Japan Inc.-type strategy, it is not. Japanese firms rarely do elaborate strategic plans, and most of their actions over the last forty years have been reactions to American moves or simply fortuitous rather than carefully worked out plans. The OEM business fell in their laps. The trading companies' main job was procuring resources for Japan, not helping Japanese exporters. Until the late 1970s a firm like Matsushita was not making much profit from American sales and only focused on America because it was doing so poorly in Japan. The shift to direct investment came about, as we saw earlier, because of American macroeconomic policies. None of this adds up to a grand marketing strategy, but in hindsight it certainly looks like one.

Today, a well-run Japanese mid-sized firm that wants to break into American markets probably would begin by exporting through a trading company which takes an equity position in the firm. The trader will find buyers, but more important, it will identify potential employees for a sales office. Eventually the sales office will be opened and staffed by Americans. Wise Japanese do not try to manage marketing outside of Japan. "American marketers should run everything," says Mr. Saitoh of Remington Japan. "The only Japanese in an American sales office should be the chairman."

The sales office would sell the same product that is marketed in Japan, with minor modifications for U.S. consumers. Different combinations of modifications would be tried to see which worked best. Armed with that information, the research findings of the American staff, and the results of the chairman's wanderings from dealer to dealer, the firm would borrow money from the trader's affiliated bank and set up a small plant, preferably in a rural area with interstate access to major West Coast urban centers (starting out in California makes for easier travel back and forth to Japan). The marketers would tell the plant what to produce, how much, and at what cost. Guidance would be provided by the equity partner, the trading firm, which would stay with the company until it started to do well and then sell out to the owners or to another friendly Japanese firm. American investors would be welcome if they had some technology or marketing to contribute.

This scenario describes a well-run Japanese firm. How many of them are there in the United States? About all we can say is a bit less than half, since the aggregate profit data shows overall poor but not catastrophically bad performance. Whether or not improvements occur depends on the ability of firms to hire sales-generating American employees, since selling is a major weakness of the Japanese in America.

SELLING

A Japanese sales executive specializing in high quality fabrics revealed just how tough it is. "I used to find U.S. customers by reading trade magazines. Then I would go to the firm and show our product. I got one sale for every twenty visits." This kind of wheel-spinning was unproductive, so he hired American salesmen to be exclusive reps. Base salary in 1990 was $2,000 per month with 3 percent of anything over $5 million in a year. In Japan such things would not be done—the boss and his office staff would be the sales force, with no thought of commissions. But he needed local expertise. "It is very difficult to find a good salesman in the United States," he observed, echoing the complaint of most other Japanese marketers.

A Fuji Bank account manager also found selling difficult. "When I telephone a Japanese client, I spend the first five or six minutes talking about weather or sports. Sometimes I only spend one or two minutes on business. The American way is very efficient. American business people don't like to share busy time talking about weather or sports— only two minutes." Japanese are often very meticulous, eager to do things right, and they want to know exactly how many minutes (four or two) they should spend on telephone small talk with a U.S. customer. Not being Americans, they often are quite ignorant of the little things.

An agricultural trader noted the speed of sales communications in the United States. "I have found business to be very quick here; in that sense it seems very easy. I like it. Back in Japan you have to follow procedures inside the company. You have to get permissions to sell an item or to spend money. My impression of business here has been good." As with other managers interviewed, however, he worried about American salesmen. "I think they tend to exaggerate the benefits of their products," he said. Other managers observed that salesmen often cut commission-generating deals with clients which do not favor their Japanese employers. Many were also disturbed by the high turnover in their sales forces.

The emphasis on selling to gain market share is common among Japanese companies. Automakers, for example, have concentrated on national television and magazine advertising, seeking volume sales, leaving local newspapers, radio, and television to dealer associations.[4] When Canon introduced a new 35mm camera in 1979, it set the retail price so low that dealers could barely keep up with demand. The company gave up profit so it could capture market share. Its plan was to keep competitors out of its market niche with a price which could not be beaten. To generate eventual profit, Canon let the price drive the cost rather than the other way around. Managers used the learning curve and economies of scale to reduce unit costs, but the presence of a clear goal helped considerably. They knew they had to get costs below the price and they did.

Selling to generate volume, then, keeps competitors at bay and fosters efficiencies in production. Also, a product's high volume supports experiments and incremental tinkering which can pay off in ideas for new applications. To a large extent, Japanese marketing is driven as much by production concerns as it is by customer desires and is both a push and pull strategy at the same time. The marketer is an intermediary brokering the manufacturer's desire to push product out the door and the customer's desire to pull it towards her. When what is pushed and what is pulled are different—often the case in a world where consumers are more unstable in their actions than producers—marketers must negotiate, coordinate, and placate rather than simply maximize quarterly or annual margins. The move towards shorter production runs and increased flexibility, which some Japanese auto companies are pioneering, resolves much of this tension, as manufacturers become more and more able to shift at the same rate consumers do.

Given these issues, we can see why selling in the United States is such a problem for Japanese marketers. As newcomers, it is hard to generate volume and market share. This failing keeps factory unit costs high and funds for product or process development low. Japanese managers are not up to selling by themselves, so they rely on Americans. But the Americans, while certainly interested in volume, will underprice to a point which cannot be supported by reductions in unit cost. They want commissions and have little interest in five-year plans to gradually lower prices as a spur to factory efficiency. Indeed, few plan on being around for five years.

What is to be done? For one thing, Americans need incentives to remain with the companies and become more attentive to sales strategy. Job security of the kind offered in Japan would accomplish this. A second tactic is to segment markets and let targeted customers' needs and interests dictate price, quality, and features rather than production managers' needs for clear cost goals and superb quality for every unit. Sometimes American customers want low-quality, very low-price products. Segmenting means that marketers abandon the high-volume/low-price approach that is designed to drive out competitors, and refocus instead on the specific customer. Who is she? What is her lifestyle? Within a market niche, say the low end, many segments can exist, and a marketer should try to serve each one's needs. Perhaps fifty segments exist in eight niches in the American car market, and Japanese automakers are now working hard to satisfy demand in many of them. This is not the case for other Japanese producers in the United States, who tend to sell standardized products with the hope that low price and high quality will see them through. It will sometimes, but not always.

THE FETISH OF COMPETITORS

Americans often express admiration for the wonderful Japanese focus on the customer, what with their quality products and exceptional service. This is true enough for some companies, but it certainly isn't a national practice in Japan, where lots of poor products exist—toasters and some room air conditioner models come to mind. Quality and service are really just occasional byproducts of the almost fanatical interest of Japanese companies in the actions of their competitors. Managerial success often is measured not by profit margin or customer satisfaction but by whether or not rankings vis-à-vis competitors have been maintained. This makes sense in a nation where everything and everyone has its place in a vertical hierarchy of existence. If a competitor improves service or quality, then a firm's managers will do the same. The customer's needs are not as important as the managers' need to maintain their organization's status.

Marketers may use gut feelings to define what customers want, but they will move heaven and earth to find out exactly what their competitors are up to. A market researcher, Bill Hall, who follows Japanese firms says that competitor analysis will uncover "how many trucks leave the warehouse per hour, how many are leased versus owned, what is the confidential floor price below the standard wholesale floor price, what percentage of sales is given as remuneration to wholesalers for the sales and inventory reports they submit, etc."[5] A firm's managers spend immense amounts of time interviewing wholesalers, retailers, trade association officials, academicians, and government researchers to learn about its competitors, and they expect their bankers to be a source of information, something with which American bankers will have trouble.

If they are doing well against the competition, Japanese marketers are happy, even though only small profits are being made. This phenomenon is the source of the oft-heard remark that the Japanese business environment is fiercely competitive. This is only partially so, as I have noted several times earlier, in the big oligopolized industries (e.g., autos and consumer electronics). Honda's executives were not bothered nearly as much by low profits as they were by their temporary fall from third to fourth place in car sales in Japan in late 1990. They probably will mount a major effort in the 1990s to hold on to third place regardless of profits, and Honda's American auto operations may find that they have to go it alone without subsidization from the parent (in 1991 production was cut due to low sales). Without help from Japan, it may have to rethink its market-capturing U.S. strategy and abandon its lead to the rapidly expanding Toyota. Risking so much just to retain rank in Japan seems bizarre, and Honda may not do it, but it is hard to envision the company's leaders passively accepting a loss of face.

MAINTAINING MARKETING CHANNELS

Early on Honda focused on developing strong channel relationships with dealers.[6] It first attracted them with excellent public relations. Whenever one of its motorcycles or cars won a race, dealers knew about it. When the *Reader's Digest* raved about the CVCC engine in 1975, Honda marketers mailed out tens of thousands of copies of the article. Once signed on, dealers are kept happy through high margins. When one has a question, he has easy access to senior Honda managers. These also make frequent visits to dealers to build personal relations and get feedforward for new ideas being considered.

Customer service is another strength of Honda. It operates "Tech Line," a cadre of skilled technicians who man a bank of telephones serving dealers. Mechanics who cannot solve a customer's problem call Tech Line for advice. The technician consults a database of problems and solutions and tells the mechanic what to do. As new difficulties arise, the database for each model grows. Not only does this system

get customers' cars fixed fast, it yields invaluable information on defects in new models. This information is quickly relayed to the plant,
where corrections are made on work in progress. Tech Line probably
is a major explanation for Honda's low-defect rate.

The care with which good Japanese firms build and maintain marketing channels is one of their strengths, but the environment is different in the United States. Retailers in Japan often will give more shelf
space to consignment goods as an incentive to producers to assume
more risk. But even non-consignment goods frequently are shipped
back with the expectation that payment need not be made. These kinds
of accommodating relationships rarely go on in America, and some
Japanese have trouble adapting. When they do adapt, however, their
communication skills become apparent. "It's nice to establish a friend-
ship with the Japanese," said an American supplier. "Once you do
that, everything falls into place. We have a relationship with Toshiba,
for example, where they order from us and don't worry about the price
until later when we give it to them. That's the kind of trust we have
developed."

Wholesaler behavior is also different in the United States. A Japanese
wholesaler usually deals exclusively with one manufacturer of a product, giving that manufacturer lots of power in the distribution channel.
This is uncommon in the United States, and Japanese producers are
caught up short when they realize that they no longer reap big margins
at the expense of other channel members. If they want more profits,
they will have to develop a larger customer base rather than attempt
to squeeze wholesalers and dealers. Honda's strategy of coddling dealers and getting them to help develop new customers is the right thing
to do, but Honda has had about 15 years to do it. Most Japanese marketers will spend the 1990s building channel relations, since only when
they are well-established will the possibility of bigger profits exist.

MAKING DEALS

Marketing, then, will be making deals for the Japanese over the next
decade. How do they react to negotiating with Americans? "They keep
their promises all right, but they are so concentrated on their targets,"
observed the branch manager of a Japanese trading company. "Americans I deal with give no concessions. They want to win on every point,
whereas Japanese want to bargain and compromise." Americans see
persuasion as a kind of conquest, whereas the Japanese look on it as a
meeting of minds. The Japanese verb "to persuade" (fukumeru) also
means "to include"—a sign of their different approach to negotiating.

The trader pointed out another difference. "Japanese negotiators want
to deal with the person who is in the highest position and really don't

respect someone in a lower position, even if that high-position individual is not knowledgeable about the deal. Americans will deal with whoever is knowledgeable." Which is more important, knowledge or status, to a Japanese manager? "In Japan, position is more important," said the trader, although he pointed out that younger Japanese expatriates are now more like their American counterparts in focusing on expertise.

A negotiation generally follows four stages: rapport building, a task-related exchanging of information, persuasive attempts on each person's part to change the other's views and requirements, and concluding concessions and agreement. When American managers sit down at the negotiating table with Japanese, is this four-stage pattern followed by both sides? Research conducted by John Graham at the University of Southern California suggests that Japanese and American managers have remarkably different approaches to face-to-face negotiating.[7]

Japanese managers put great store in establishing rapport. Americans often consider rapport building a waste of time and want to get down to business.

Japanese ask endless questions to identify the needs and preferences of both parties. The *reasons* for needs and preferences also are crucial data for Japanese, who seek to place information within an interpreted context. It is their construction of a meaningful, why-do-they-want-this context that guides their responses. The exchange of information part of negotiating is the main part of the process for them. Managers from the United States, however, use this stage simply as a brief, direct exchange. Americans say what they want and rarely offer explanations of why they want it.

For Japanese managers, persuasion as victory over another is secondary to the process of matching interests. Any persuasion necessary will be conducted behind the scenes, not during a formal negotiation meeting. Japanese intimidate, however, by asking questions that seek to expose weak positions and by resorting to uncomfortable silence. Americans view the persuasion stage as the most important; they pull out all the rhetorical stops to persuade others to modify their position.

The Japanese believe that nothing is settled until everything is settled, which is why they reveal concessions only at the end. They expect to hear second-best offers first, whereas Americans tend to make fair offers first. Americans put much more faith in an incremental build up to agreement. They use the concession stage to sum up the process that has been going on throughout negotiations.

Americans emphasize content in their negotiating. So do the Japanese, but they also look at presentation and style. They concentrate on the subtle indicators that reflect integrity, sincerity, and a cooperative attitude.

Let us look at a negotiation from the perspective of Mr. T., a securities firm manager in the United States. "We make proposals ambiguous as much as possible," he notes. His company is in a foreign country where great risks and uncertainties prevail. Committing to a rigid plan could be a disaster. During discussions, Americans like to use a "when in Rome do as the Romans do" approach to get Mr. T. to do things their way. He finds this argument quite persuasive, but when he counters, he says, "Rome was not built in a day." His main negotiating tactic, however, is questioning. "What do we need to do to be successful?" he will ask, or "What would you consider an unfair deal?" As the Americans answer, their own position may be called into doubt. In a sense he stimulates them to argue against their own points if he can.

What Mr. T. looks for are contradictions or inconsistencies in the statements of the American team members. "When I see these, I know I can get some flexibility in their offers." His team never shows anything but a unified front. Even at informal dinners, he talks about himself by saying "we Japanese" rather than "I." What worries him with Americans is silence, a tactic he likes to use. When they sit back and expect the Japanese to do the talking, he senses trouble. Then he cannot get them to talk themselves out of a position, they do not reveal more than they intended, and he can not uncover splits on the team. Another thing that worries him is the Americans' use of older, experienced negotiators. As a thirty-year old, he respects older people and feels that he must defer to them. Finally, he tries to avoid loss of control on American turf. "When a meeting is in the Americans' office, we have pressure on us. The Americans must show us where the rest room is, how we get coffee, where we eat lunch. These are small things, but they are advantages for the Americans."

A Japanese trader also mentioned the importance of silence. "Americans almost always talk initially," he said. "The Japanese don't really say anything for awhile. Then the Americans start to talk too much, saying things they shouldn't say that give away their negotiating position."

There is a story about Japanese silence told to me by a former fisheries minister of an Arab country on the Red Sea. At one time a large Japanese fishing firm approached him, seeking rights to harvest fish in the nation's coastal waters. The catch would be processed aboard ship and sold to distributors in East Africa, where food supplies are often low. It was a good idea, and the two sides met to negotiate a deal. The Japanese arrived, a hoard of them in their blue suits and white shirts, and took up positions on one side of an immense conference table. On the other side sat an equally large contingent of Arab leaders in long flowing tribal dress.

Negotiations went on for some time, with no agreement in sight on the key issue of distribution of profits in the joint venture. Finally, the Japanese leader spoke. "We Japanese are a people who ponder things long and hard," he said. "We sometimes need to sit quietly to let our thoughts develop. Would you allow us to carry out our custom of observing a period of silence in the room while we meditate on the issue? Perhaps we will be able to think of a solution." The fisheries minister bowed his head. "Of course," he said quietly. "Silence is part of Arab culture also."

With that the room fell silent. Nothing happened for a few moments, although a few Japanese lifted their eyes to see how the silent treatment was working on their hosts. What they saw were twenty Arabs as one pulling out small roots from their robes and inserting them in their mouths. They then began to slowly chew, giving every sign of being able to chew until doomsday. Japanese jaws dropped. The leader quickly ended the moment of silence so precious to "we Japanese" and got on with the negotiations. Eventually a fair deal was worked out. Later on, in an interview, the minister explained. "As soon as I heard 'we Japanese,' I knew that they had mistaken us for people like Americans, who are always willing to accept any kind of crazy behavior as long as someone says it's 'cultural.' What's more, Americans can't stand silence. As soon as those Japanese tried their silent ploy in the United States, Americans would have been climbing the walls. They would have signed any agreement. We Arabs, however, can sit and chew our roots for days if need be." The moral of this story is simple: When a Japanese negotiator tries the silent treatment, have your chewing gum ready.

While firms which have been in America for a long time are doing well, most Japanese marketing efforts are weak. It will take time and American expertise to build a customer base and strong relationships in distribution channels.

Selling solely on the basis of low price/high quality to gain market share cannot succeed by itself. Americans want products tailored to their particular needs and lifestyles, and these complex needs will require market research of a higher order than that practiced by most Japanese firms in the United States. While Japanese manufacturers love data, Japanese marketers like to rely on intuition and the often fragmented results of go-and-see field visits. They avoid elaborate statistical analyses. This must change, especially since Japanese products in American markets are more standardized than in Japan. Marketers must identify segments which want those particular products rather than trying to sell to every segment within a niche.

American expertise is needed, but incentives must be developed to get marketing and sales staffs to stick longer with Japanese companies.

Moreover, the practice of imitating competitors' moves to maintain relative status may be suitable in Japan where rank counts, but American marketers focus on maximizing unit net margins. They cannot help Japanese employers who are not willing to do things the American way.

TWENTY-TWO

Good Citizenship

"When a new Japanese manager comes to our office," said a Mitsui trader, "we used to throw a big party and spend a lot of money. Now we make a donation to the local hospital or the March of Dimes." In Tarrytown, New York, Hitachi America never joins the other major corporate resident, GM, in challenging its tax assessment. Instead it doles out scholarships, sponsors teacher exchanges with Japan, and donates to worthy causes. "We prefer the Japanese sense of community spirit to the American profit-or-perish philosophy," said Carin Rubenstein, a resident.[1]

The handwriting is on the wall and Japanese corporate leaders know it. "The most important thing we can do is have more involvement with the American business community . . . to show that we are contributing to the community," said Hisao Kondo, head of Mitsui USA.[2] This new-found community spirit has not suddenly bubbled up from the vast well spring of generosity residing in Japanese corporate hearts. No such font of niceness exists. Rather it is a calculated response by the large firms to the remarkably bad press Japanese companies have received. For every article on Japanese successes in productivity, an article or book also appears on wretched Japanese treatment of minorities and women, devious attempts to influence law making, and selfish demands for state and local subsidies as bribes for locating plants.[3]

Just as the press exaggerates Japanese productivity successes, it overstates the case against the companies as bad corporate citizens. Nevertheless, there is a case to be made. Left to themselves, Japanese managers behave exactly as they do in Japan. They see their actions as normal, we see them as unethical. Why is this?

CITIZENSHIP: WHAT IS THAT?

The concept of *polis*, belonging to a place as a citizen with allegiance to the abstract body of principles which govern the place, has been applied by Western peoples for several thousand years and by corporations for a few years. Neither application of the concept means much to a Japanese businessman.

The sense of citizenship is quite weak in Japan. Japanese have an allegiance to being Japanese and fulfill the obligations of Japaneseness. Mostly that means sticking together through thick and thin, harboring quiet and sometimes not so quiet thoughts about racial superiority, and enjoying the economic and social benefits which exclusivity may confer. They also have allegiance to their families, school chums, work groups, and employers—although loyalty to the firm is much weaker than Americans realize. They do not have much allegiance to their political structures, the towns, cities, and localities where they live and work. It is not that Japanese lack a sense of place. They do not, but place for them is concrete, observable, to be experienced and hopefully enjoyed. Place is the material reality to which a Japanese person adjusts himself. The Western idea of an *abstract* political structure embodied in buildings, processes, obligations, and values—all the paraphernalia of citizenship—is only imperfectly understood and does not energize social, legal, and business behavior.

A trip to any Japanese city will demonstrate the point rather nicely. Westerners developed the polis concept early on and take as a matter of course actions associated with the idea. They are forever ordering their cities through zoning. Like cats endlessly preening themselves, they want to present the best possible surface to the world. Westerners hold festivals associated with cities. Their athletic teams are named after cities. The political life of Western cities is raucous and seriously pursued. Little of this occurs in Japan. Tokyo is virtually zone-less. While that has its charms, it is disconcerting to find that even cab drivers lack the visceral sense of knowing and feeling for the city which any older New Yorker has. In New York the citizen spends his life learning the lore of the town and where in town the lore is attached. Almost any New Yorker, even those who have never lived there, can provide a serviceable history of the South Bronx, the "empty quarter" of New York. How many Tokyoites could speak eloquently about any place beyond their neighborhood?

In Japan two worlds exist, the inner and the outer. The inner is peopled by self, family, friends, groups, one's burden of being Japanese, perhaps one's company. The outer world is the life of the streets and the city, the life of the citizen. It must be lived in, but it is not favored. The outer world is where order is imposed rather than carefully constructed with one's fellows. It is where one is never sure of what role to play, what manners to employ, or how low to bow. While not exactly threatening, the Japanese world of the polis is troubling, and Japanese often flounder when they must act in it. In Japan, however, the problem is not very great. A well-trained army of civil servants is in place to smooth the way. If one wants to see just how good they are, go to Tokyo and watch a street repair crew. Nowhere in the world will it be done so quickly and so well, with the least disruption to Japanese people busily following out the dictates of their inner life. No neighborhood committees are needed nor screaming encounters at city hall. The system exists to make the outer world of citizenship as little a burden as possible.

When the Japanese manager comes to the United States, he is often shocked to find that citizenship is taken seriously. Corporate managers are expected to act in ways which serve the local polis as well as the company. The outer world intrudes on the inner world in a way which some find offensive. Their sense of being offended, however, may look like selfishness and greed to Americans. Moreover, when Japanese managers work to ensure that the outer world accommodates itself to the inner as it does in Japan, they come across as menacing and a potential danger to society. Selfish, greedy, a social menace? Are these the characteristics of Japanese managers and their firms in America? Of course not, but images and perceptions *are* reality in America, and Japanese firms have to recognize that the normal in Japan may be the abnormal in America because of a much stronger theory of citizenship.

When the unitary tax became an issue in the early 1980s, Japanese firms worked hard to get it repealed. They contributed to the election campaigns of state legislators and threatened to cancel plans for facilities in the affected states of California and Florida. Similar hardball lobbying also occurred over the discharges of an Alaska pulp mill owned by Japanese investors. Japanese firms often let it be known that plant openings and closings are tied to political and economic benefits mandated by government. All of this has a hollow ring to it, since numerous studies have shown that tax and subsidy issues rarely are important determinants of investment location decisions. More important are access to suppliers and markets, a well-trained labor force, and transportation systems. So when Japanese raise issues which are of only minor interest to American investors, they look greedy and selfish.

Perhaps some are, but more likely they are simply victims of two forces. First, there is the Japanese mind-set that the polis is there to be accommodative to them. Second is the "step up to the barbecue" approach of state and local development offices, which work hard to create the erroneous impression that American public bodies are as accommodative as in Japan. What the Japanese need to do is get rid of their "when in Japan" mind-set and also realize that hustlers from highly politicized state offices are not the best representatives of the American people. Americans believe that political bodies ought to represent, first, the public good and special interests only second, and then only within a system of turn-taking or *quid pro quo*. When the Japanese threaten to move their plants elsewhere, they frighten U.S. public officials, who then fall all over themselves imitating Japanese local bureaucrats back home. The American public, however, does not react like the Japanese public. It stores little pockets of resentment in its collective psyche and forms images of "pushy" Japanese.

Japanese bureaucrats want to help make the economic engine go as fast and efficiently as it can so that all of society will benefit. American officials want to create jobs to buy votes at the next election. Too often Japanese firms play into the hands of the power-seeking U.S. politicians, deluding themselves that everything will be seen as being done in the interests of the overall society. In Tennessee they get low-interest loans, job training, land improvements, tax abatements, road improvements, and grants. In Kentucky offers are made for site preparation, education for children of Japanese employees, and free land. In Michigan it is grants for sewers and rail improvements, while Ohio gives construction support and Illinois pollution control funding. Studies show that Japanese investors in manufacturing produce added-value to their products and engage in R & D at typical levels for American firms.[4] So society *is* benefitting from all those giveaways. But the American public does not pay much attention to outcomes which are hard to visualize when highly vivid inputs of special treatment are so easily observed and when Japanese firms act as if society owes them special treatment and they owe society nothing.

Part of the problem, then, is a weak idea in Japan of what corporate citizenship involves. But the situation has not been helped by the eagerness of American lobbyists and state politicians to tell Japanese executives that American public life involves the dispersal of favors rather than the fostering of the public good. All of this will change in the 1990s, however, for two reasons: the lobbyists have not delivered, and the state politicians have recognized that subsidies to Japanese firms do not create jobs fast enough.

Washington lobbyists helped Toshiba avoid millions in penalties during the late 1980s stemming from U.S. outrage at its sales of military-related hardware to the Soviets. Other benefits are described by Pat Choate in *Agents of Influence*. But while Mr. Choate and others are out to bash the Japanese (and when they say "Japanese," they mean all of them rather than just managers at big and mid-sized companies), they inadvertently make a case for Japanese ineptness. Choate, J. B. Judis, and others claim that Japanese have spent anywhere from $250 to $400 million each year since 1985 in trying to influence regulatory bodies and Congress. If that is so, then they should be earning say 15 percent each year on their total investment. That is, they should be getting benefits worth $38–$60 million each year for each year of spending. Gains in 1991 should have been around $250 million, based on five-year cumulative spending. The savings for Toshiba probably were around $100–$200 million, but that was a one-time thing. Nothing else comes close.

And if Japanese firms are not getting much of a tangible return on their investment in Washington, D.C., they are not getting much in the way of useful advice either. American public opinion usually leads Washington elite thinking rather than follows it. So when the firms listen to lobbyists, they hear what America was thinking yesterday rather than what it will think tomorrow. Moreover, lobbyists rarely give advice good for the long term. In 1990 Congress toughened reporting requirements a bit for Japanese and other foreign direct investors. It was a sign of still worse to come unless the big Japanese corporations mend their ways. How many lobbyists recommended that their clients reduce their efforts and lie low for a few years?

A better way to influence lawmaking is for the Japanese to go directly to the people. One approach is for executives to visit the congressmen in the districts where large Japanese investments reside. They are always willing to tell a constituent what is what and to help if they can. The Japanese should abandon their home-country custom of using intermediaries and deal directly themselves. Another approach is to use the media to make their case. We are seeing this already, as more and more Japanese businessmen are writing letters and op-ed pieces for *The Wall Street Journal,* appearing on television, and doing extensive interviews with local newspapers. A few years ago I advised a Japanese friend to send his ideas to *The Wall Street Journal.* He wrote an essay on his U.S. subsidiary as a Japanese company in America and the need for he and American employees to adapt to each other. His effort provoked a torrent of letters in which outraged Americans pointed out that his firm is an *American* company and that it is *his* job to adapt, not the American employees'. He learned much from this dialogue and made changes. By 1990 his subsidiary was considered one of the top performers in his company's global operations.

Moving away from the lobbyists is good, but there is no need to move away from the state politicians. They are already fleeing. The attractiveness of creating jobs by subsidizing Japanese investment had begun to wane by 1990, as Japanese companies shifted from start ups to acquisitions. In addition, those firms which did begin new companies only created jobs in one or two rural areas in a state. Few votes were being gathered, so state politicians began to focus instead on promoting exports. Every million dollars in U.S. exports creates twenty five to thirty jobs, and these jobs tend to be spread out better across a state. The glory days are over when a Japanese executive could pick and choose from a menu of state subsidies and be feted by teams of smiling men in polished wing-tip shoes and beautiful women in high fashion business suits. It really doesn't make much difference, since the subsidies probably had little impact, but at least it removes one source of irritation to the public.

A new influence strategy which is emerging—one more in line with corporate citizenship—is charity. Estimates for 1990 Japanese corporate giving in the United States were $250 million, up from $85 million in 1987.[5] To help firms decide how to do it, Keidanren, the leading Japanese employers' association, created the Council for Better Corporate Citizenship in 1989. Giving money seems to be the preferred activity, with little interest in encouraging employees' community service or participation in civic groups (individual firms, such as Mitsui USA, however, do encourage Japanese managers to get involved). Spending increased at Matsushita Electric Corporation of America (MECA), which now allocates .1 percent of U.S. sales for giving. For a company with about $4 billion in American revenues, that is still not much. But executives at MECA's 130 U.S. sales and manufacturing facilities are on the lookout for ways to expand involvement. The only other firm with a noteworthy program is Hitachi America, which funds giving through the Hitachi Foundation. With $23 million in assets, its goal is to "strengthen the infrastructure of American society" (whatever that means). Other foundations owned by Matsushita, Honda, Toyota, Sony, and Nakamichi Corporation disburse up to $1 million each annually to school learning programs, support for minorities, and the arts. Some of these activities are taken quite seriously. When the Matsushita Foundation concluded in 1990 that the Seattle School System was not using its grant in a worthwhile manner, it promptly withdrew it. There is something quite admirable in that.

Until recently, the reality has been that senior executives in Japan have had little experience in philanthropy. They see their companies as primarily dedicated to serving customers and employees. But with the failure to get much of a payoff for their Washington, D.C., lobbying and the decline in state interest in subsidizing their subsidiaries, corporate giving has by default become the major route to influence. While Japanese managers have not developed new ideas about citizenship, they are by necessity acting as if they have. Is this hypocritical? Of course, but what is new about that in corporate America? In any case, behavior drives belief rather than the other way around. As Japanese act like good citizens, they will start to develop beliefs about citizenship to justify their behavior. The workings of cognitive dissonance will foster the development of Japanese ideas about what it means to be a citizen. That will be good for the United States—and for Japan.

MOMMY AND MAIDEN TRACKS

A major citizenship issue has focused on discrimination practices of Japanese firms, especially against women. Bias against women by American firms is usually rooted in several beliefs:

- Women are not tough enough to stand the pressure of business life.
- Women and men will find it difficult to work together. Sexual tensions will lead to problems, and different ways of communicating will cause difficulties.
- Just when they become trained, women will quit to have babies.

Over the last fifteen years the first two biases have died out. The third one remains, however, because it is clear that many women do leave managerial jobs for family roles. "Mommy track" career paths have been proposed for women who want to raise children and also have a job in management. Regular career paths will remain for those women who do not plan on having children.

Japanese firms have tended to view themselves as important social institutions and upholders of societal norms and values, which is why they expect the government to be so accommodating to them. Where sex discrimination in America is rooted in the biases of individual male managers, it is part and parcel of the social mission of a typical Japanese firm. A woman's place after the age of courting (twenty-six or so) is at home with her children. Japanese society requires stability in family life, and Japanese firms are charged (so they see it) with ensuring that threats to that stability are reduced. The economic price is very high, since an immense army of bright young females is unavailable to the labor supply of managers, professionals, and technical people. The United States began accepting women into professional ranks in the early 1970s. For ten years American productivity suffered as these women learned their trades. Then, in the 1980s, productivity began to climb as the new labor supply "came on line." Economists disagree as to the extent of female contribution to this roller coaster ride in productivity, but clearly the emergence of women has counted. America in the 1990s will reap major economic benefits from a well-trained female work force.

A Japanese manager will point out that America's economic gains from females will come at the expense of social and family fragmentation and the "Californication" of society. Japanese firms will not become a party to such disintegration. They will defend social order by not accepting women in large numbers for career paths in management. In this light the actions of Sumitomo Shoji America make sense. Only males were being hired to fill executive, managerial, and sales positions in the late 1970s when thirteen female secretaries sued the firm for discrimination. The company eventually settled the case in 1987 by agreeing to end discriminatory practices, but its ten-year battle in the courts suggests the strength of feeling on both sides.

Notice that American sex discrimination is based on economic considerations. When a firm spends thousands of dollars developing a woman's skills, only to have her quit to raise a family, the economic loss is considerable. Best not hire managerial women in the first place, some firms say. Japanese discrimination is more high-minded. The family is the key unit in society, and women are the key members of the family. Take them out of the family and it falls apart, with resulting divorce, children not cared for, crime, lack of educational attainment, and so forth. Better-managed firms in Japan have dealt with the genuine conflict between their social mission to serve and protect society and the demand from some women for managerial careers by proposing a deal which goes something like this: The young woman will not initially be treated like the young Japanese men hired at the same time. She will be paid less, have less interesting work, and will not advance as fast. If, however, by her early thirties she is still without children, the company will assume that she is committed to a managerial career and will make up for its past discrimination through rapid advancement and pay increases. By her mid-thirties she will have caught up with her male peers and have been compensated for her losses. She will be treated equally from then on.

A deal of this kind, call it the Japanese "maiden track," will be made in an informal manner, which guarantees that it would be hard to sell in America. Also, it is illegal, since discrimination for several years is involved. Nevertheless, one suspects that some Japanese firms in the United States are following or would like to follow this approach. They certainly must do something, since their reputation for sex discrimination could not be any worse.

PRIDE AND PREJUDICE

Honda is noted for the pride it takes in producing excellent autos in its plants in and around Marysville, Ohio. It also is noted for prejudice. In 1988 the firm paid $6 million to settle an investigation by the U.S. Equal Employment Opportunity Commission into allegations of sexism and racism at the company. About 400 women and black workers were involved. Honda officials claim that the company has improved in its treatment of minorities since then. Mazda's Flat Rock, Michigan plant, in an area which is 29 percent black, had only 14 percent black employees in 1988. Nissan in 1989 settled an EEOC discrimination investigation in California and agreed to award management jobs to sixty-eight blacks, Hispanics, women, and older workers who were passed over for promotions between 1984 and 1987. The auto makers are not unique in their biases, however. Over the last few years claims of discrimination have surfaced at Nikko Securities, Sumitomo Corp., Recruit Co., and C. Itoh.

Japanese managers have carried their racial prejudices with them from Japan, where both political and intellectual leaders regularly make disparaging statements about U.S. minorities. Former prime minister Yasuhiro Nakasone told a group of politicians in 1986 that Japan is a more "intelligent society than the United States, where there are blacks, Mexicans, and Puerto Ricans and the level is still quite low."[6] In 1990 Justice Minister Seiroku Kajiyama compared prostitutes in Japan to black Americans who move into white neighborhoods and "ruin the atmosphere." Michio Watanabe, a leader of the Liberal Democratic Party, has expressed his belief that American blacks cannot be trusted to pay their debts. And Yuji Aida, emeritus professor at Kyoto University, one of Japan's most prestigious institutions, claimed in a 1990 article on "The Collapse of America" that the growth of the black and Hispanic population will ruin the U.S. economy because these groups lack the traits required for a modern industrial society—respect for precision, self-discipline, and self-improvement.[7]

I have heard this kind of talk in Japan on many occasions. It usually is associated with claims that America is in decline economically (it is not), and that the reasons for these things are American racial heterogeneity and Japanese homogeneity. Statements like these come and go, depending on how well the Japanese economy is doing relative to the United States. During the 1980s it was doing very well, and racial explanations were frequent. As soon as Japan cools down a bit in the 1990s, anti-black rhetoric will become muted. But it will not go away.

Only in the last few years have Japanese begun to travel to America on holiday, and so their knowledge of the country and its minorities has come from television and films. These simplistic, stereotype-laden images have fed into the Japanese propensity to categorize and arrange people in hierarchies, with the result that blacks and Hispanics now occupy the base of the human pyramid (with you know who on top). If Hollywood decides to replace these minorities as villains of the day with Italian mafia or Irish gunmen, they will push out Hispanics on the lower levels. Blacks, however, are at the bottom for the long run. So ingrained has Japanese bias against African Americans become that nothing is likely to dislodge it except the growing sophistication of Japanese as they travel more and learn about the complexity of black-white relations in the United States. That will take a long time.

Meanwhile, Japanese firms in the United States avoid black enclaves when they build or acquire a plant. There is more than beliefs about black intelligence driving this avoidance. Fear is also important. For years Japanese visitors to the United States carried large amounts of cash with them since credit cards were not used much. They were regularly mugged in the big cities, often by blacks. As a consequence, Japanese have developed a view of blacks as not just mentally lacking but also morally defective. Japanese managers tend to be afraid of African Americans, and they are unlikely to quietly accept American assignments to subsidiaries with a large number of black employees.

The corporations have got to change, and for more than reasons of good citizenship. Black people are a major source of inexpensive labor in and around big cities, and Japanese service firms interested in controlling costs (e.g., the banks) will have to make use of them. Like American-owned firms, they will have to establish basic skills training for young black workers and aggressive career development programs to help them advance. They have no choice, since the white labor pool of entry level workers is declining, as is the number of white people who will tolerate authoritarian Japanese management practices. Poor black people, like poor people anywhere, cannot afford to be picky and will eagerly accept jobs at Japanese businesses. In the rural areas, those firms which locate in poor black counties will be able to reduce overall labor costs by several percentage points. The resulting slim price differentials, which mean very little in Japan, can have a big impact on sales in a more freely competitive America. Since Japanese manufacturers appear to be focused on competing on the basis of price in the United States, they can gain an edge by moving to black areas. Will Japanese managers accept these moves? Some sensitivity training in Japan and the United States will help them, but leadership will be required. Japanese executives will have to use their extraordinary powers to see to it that biases and prejudices do not stand in the way of doing what is right from both an economic and a citizenship perspective.

GOOD AND BAD CITIZENS

American revisionists see Japan as different from the United States and unable to change its economic system. They call for America to develop a similar system, one involving a national industrial policy, managed international trade, and strong government support for business. Yet even as they speak, Japan is changing: imports are up, the bumbling management of the economy no longer looks so intimidating, and government tolerance of cartels is declining. Moreover, Japanese firms, without much of a concept of corporate citizenship, are moving to adapt themselves to modern ways of defining a corporation in terms of its obligations to society. It is all being done grudgingly, to be sure, but it is being done. The revisionist case is based on observations of Japanese *desires* not to change. They should be watching Japanese *behavior* instead, since behavior, however forced, will change attitudes eventually.

The change process can be illustrated by returning to our bad (past) and good (future) managers of Chapter 1, Mr. Moto and Mr. K., and seeing how they manage as corporate citizens.

The Bad Citizen

Mr. Moto has come to his plant early this morning to oversee the arrival of a large shipment of complex parts from his company's plant in Osaka. The parts have been purchased from the parent company by Mr. Moto's subsidiary. They are thus high value exports from Japan, and they help keep the Japanese home factory operating, even though it and similar firms are massively overproducing for the Japanese market. The Japanese government has quietly advised Mr. Moto's firm that its primary goal is to keep Japanese workers employed at high margin, added-value production and that it will develop its international policies accordingly. After the parts arrive, Mr. Moto confers with his Japanese subordinates, who fill all of the important managerial and technical jobs in the plant. They develop a work schedule requiring the adding on of several more minimum wage workers to tend to the menial chores—sweeping up, checking a few simple gauges, taking and putting—all of which the American employees perform.

The firm does have four American engineers on hand, and Mr. Moto is delighted with their work. They are really employees of a small high tech firm which his subsidiary was asked to purchase by Tokyo HQ. The firm is doing state-of-the-art software development related to the production process of the Japanese company's industry, and it was purchased to keep new developments out of the hands of American competitors. Of course the research of the engineers will be shared with the three other Japanese firms which dominate the industry in Japan. Mr. Moto's company doesn't like that, but the government people have suggested that it would be a good idea. They have promised to assign a bigger share of the American export market to his firm in return for this help.

Mr. Moto spends a productive morning sitting at the fax machine to HQ discussing his upcoming lunch with a man representing the governor of the state. The governor's man wants money for the election campaign about to get under way, and Mr. Moto is known to be influential in the American group which was formed to elect the right sort of people. In fact, Mr. Moto controls the group, or rather Tokyo does through Mr. Moto. The group operates as a series of political action committees attached to public relations and consulting firms with large Japanese clients. Mr. Moto tells the governor's man about the 10-year tax abatement his company must have if it is to continue to do business in the state. Without help, he says, his plant may have to close and move to a neighboring state where such aid is available. The governor's man is all smiles and tells him that there will be no problem. They part on the best of terms.

The afternoon is not so pleasant. He must meet with two of the American employees, both women, who are suing the firm for discriminatory practices. One of the women should have been promoted to foreman, but of course Mr. Moto could not do that. He must report all his moves to Tokyo, and they would not have been sympathetic to a woman's promotion. Mr. Moto actually would have liked to promote her, since he could have paid her several hundred dollars less than the man receives. But efficiency sometimes must give way to social considerations. Women do not belong in supervisory roles. It would encourage them to neglect their roles as wives and mothers. It is good, Mr. Moto tells himself, that my company is so socially minded.

The other woman is black, and she is being let go for slow performance. Her work really has not been all that bad, Mr. Moto knows, but Tokyo does not like to see blacks in the plant. The firm deliberately situated the subsidiary so it was in an area which is 98 percent white, and thus there should not be any blacks. This woman slipped by personnel. Mr. Moto makes a mental note to have a long talk with the young American MBA who runs personnel. The company seeks ethnic uniformity in its plants and does not make exceptions. The real reason, of course, is that Japanese people know that blacks are an inferior racial strain. Mr. Moto and his Japanese managers discuss these things among themselves at their daily meeting and their after-work social hour. Naturally Americans are not invited. After all, it isn't their company and they don't speak Japanese. Besides, Americans are not sophisticated people. They are not up to mastering the subtleties of Japanese management. However, Mr. Moto does admit the superiority of American music and dance. They have such natural rhythm, he says.

The Good Citizen

When Mr. K. arrived at the plant, his American plant manager, Miss Grace Strong, a Stanford MBA, met him in his office.

"Morning, Bob," she said. Mr. K. had adopted the name Robert at his confirmation. He is a Japanese Christian from Kyushu, where St. Francis Xavier converted his ancestors 400 years ago. He was thrilled to find that the church near his American plant is St. Francis Xavier, and he goes to mass there every Sunday. Many of the plant workers are Catholics, and he usually sits with one group or another of them. Occasionally he teaches in the Sunday School.

Mr. K.'s superiors in Tokyo are delighted to hear of his church involvement. This embarrasses him a bit, since he practices his religion the same way in Japan, where no one notices. But he is glad that HQ personnel people have assigned him to America. He knows he is the right man for the right spot. At one time the personnel department was not so sensitive about these things, and several rude shocks occurred. After these, change came rapidly, and now managers assigned to America are carefully chosen and then are given six weeks' training. Mr. K. lectures twice a year at the training center outside of Tokyo. His special topic is motivating American managers. He points out in his talks that American and Japanese managers are really quite similar, contrary to the findings of some researchers who seek to benefit by telling Japanese how good they are and Americans how much they must improve. This is mostly media hype, he says. Nevertheless, differences do exist, and he makes sure that the Japanese managers learn of them and what to do about motivation.

Actually, fewer and fewer Japanese managers are being assigned to America in supervisory positions. These are being turned over to Americans like Grace Strong, who will replace Mr. K. as general manager next year, when he moves to Tennessee to set up yet another subsidiary plant. Many young Japanese are still coming over, but they are usually assigned to American managers. The idea is for them to learn American ways under the guidance of Americans.

Many Americans are also going the other way to shadow Japanese managers. The main criterion for a Japan assignment is completion of a six-month intensive Japanese language evening course set up at the local college by Mr. K. It is an excellent screening device, he has learned, for identifying American fast trackers. Similar set ups exist in Japan. Under the firm's "localization" strategy all American operations will be run by Americans within ten years. Americans will sit on the board of the U.S. holding company which owns all American operations, they will work at Tokyo HQ, and they will sit on the executive committee.

All of these moves are simply good business, Mr. K. knows, and he bristles when he reads in the press that Japanese firms are cynically manipulating public opinion to cover up their "buying" of America. Yes, he did oversee the purchase of the small American high tech company, and those four American engineers have been a great find. He already has used some of their work to cut unit costs by 10 percent. With lower costs he can convince the marketing subsidiary to lower price and capture more market share. He secretly laughs when he hears Americans worry about all those repatriated profits leaving America and flooding into Japan. What profits? He has not seen any so far, although he is confident that they will be in the black in two years. At that point, he knows, all of the profits will be ploughed right back into R & D. With low cost Taiwanese and South Korean products scheduled to hit his American market in three years, he must position himself to fight them off. To send profits back to Japan would be unthinkable. Besides, what would HQ do with them? Mostly the firm is run to please the big banks which loan it money, and they want risk-reducing growth, not profits. If the American operations are well-entrenched and well-liked in America, the Tokyo banks will deluge Mr. K.'s firm with money.

Grace shows Mr. K. the load of components which have just arrived from the plant in Chicago. All of the company's parts are made in the United States. It is not so much a political thing as a foreign exchange thing. Tokyo got tired of trying to manage complex foreign exchange issues caused by exporting parts from Tokyo to America. Besides, American labor productivity is higher than in Japan, and the labor cost is a bit lower. Local suppliers-local production-local markets: this is the company strategy. However, Mr. K. knows that the company's overall global strategy must come first. Sometime down the road he or his successors may have to move U.S. profits not to Tokyo but to Brazil, where big development is expected in ten years or so. The overall global mission comes first. He sighs when he realizes what American politicians will say when they learn about these movements. They certainly will learn, since Mr. K. lectures about the company's global strategies once a quarter to his employees at a community center near the plant. The benefits of openness with employees, he believes, are great, but he shudders to think of the stories in the newspapers. It is so unfair, since every American multinational firm does exactly the same thing. Why is not Mr. Lee Iaccoca not criticized for moving funds about? Is not the free market system triumphant since 1989?

However, Mr. K. calms down when he reminds himself that his U.S. Congressman, Representative Bill Barrows, is on his side. He and Bill have lunched many times, and Bill has said he will run interference for Mr. K.'s firm as long as it continues to be a major economic force in his district. Mr. K. has persuaded Tokyo to commit itself to remaining in Barrows' district for at least ten more years. Although the commitment is informal, all parties agreed to leak the story to the press a few months ago. The public relations benefit was enormous. Barrows has not received any contributions from Mr. K. or from PACs controlled by Mr. K. There aren't any, but he is responsive nonetheless. Of course he is just as responsive to the other employers in his district. That's his job. Mr. K. has learned that if he wants to influence government policy, he has to do it American style. He makes speeches. He gives press interviews. He is on TV talk shows. He responds to every letter.

He argues with every critic, defending his firm as an American company with American products made by American workers. He doesn't win every fight, but he has developed a reputation as a good businessman with a good firm. Above all, he does not try to put one over on his American competitors—one of which is in the same city—by constantly seeking state subsidies of one kind or another. Every aid he has received has also been available to his competitor.

Ms. Strong and Mr. K. go over the components and decide how to fit them in to the production process. Some of the plant is a simple assembly operation manned by local people, mostly wives holding second jobs in families. Because of the successes of his R & D engineers, Mr. K. can afford to pay them more than other assembly plants. He has no trouble finding capable workers. Occasionally one of the women will come to him and tell him about her recent divorce and the economic needs she has suddenly developed. Mr. K. has heard this story before. Indeed, he has worked up a case on it for the training center. What he does is tell the woman about the training program set up by the firm at the community college. It is a one-year certificate course, four nights a week, in statistics, accounting, database management, and spreadsheet skills. If she enrolls at company expense and completes the program with a 3.0 or better grade point average, he will guarantee that she will be eligible for an office or supervisor's job either at that plant or at one of the other U.S. plants. The company will pay moving costs if she accepts a position elsewhere. Since the U.S. operations are growing, these positions are opening up all the time. When growth slows in five or six years, Mr. K. plans on offering these women positions in Brazil or Tokyo. HQ has agreed on his plan, since it thinks Japan will be a more sophisticated nation by then and ready for that most fearsome of creatures, the American Woman. He makes similar offers to the young blacks who express an interest in advancement, although he recognizes that Japan will be very slow to rid itself of racism. His company, however, is active in the Diet lobbying for less restrictive immigration laws.

The firm which employs me has changed a lot over the last ten years, he mused. The CEO gained his MBA at Harvard and has served several tours in America. He replaced a man who had formerly been a cabinet minister with extensive connections in the Liberal Democratic Party. Mr. K. often wondered just where his loyalties lay. He liked to make speeches to the executive board about Japan's rightful place in the world and the need to develop an immense trade surplus which could be used to fund takeovers in the United States. Without economic power, he said, Japan would be nothing. Mr. K. found this kind of talk repulsive. He had heard some American politicians make similar speeches, and he had read about Japanese politics prior to the Pacific

War. All of it was hogwash, in his view. An orderly global political and economic system depended on countries coordinating their fiscal, monetary, and trade policies. Japan should by no means give in to American politicians who wanted to cover up their deficit spending by having Japan accept blame for the resulting trade surpluses and Japanese investment in the United States. Instead, he wanted Japan to shift the focus away from trivial negotiations on "strategic impediments" towards discussions on joint management of the economies of both countries. As a start, he hoped Japan would open up more to U.S. imports and capital. Luckily, this was already happening. But these moves should only be a door-opener, he believed, to open a path to more important discussions. On the day when Japan and the United States formed a Joint Negotiating Committee to decide on spending, saving, and interest rates in each country, on that day he would cease playing the role of "the good Japanese manager." Instead, he could become "Bob K., that nice guy who runs the widget plant in the north end of town. I think he's Japanese."

TWENTY-THREE

Business Changes, But Do Japanese Managers?

The Japanese economic "invasion" of the United States is neither the fearful onslaught described by the Japan bashers, nor is it the trying but beneficial learning experience of the Chrysanthemum club rhetoricians, who would have us believe that Japan's approach to business and managing is something we must emulate if we are to survive. The reality is that Japanese investment in the United States is not very successful, and Japanese managers often blunder badly. The strengths they have brought from Japan do not seem to work as well in America, and their weaknesses hurt them.

Eventually Japan's investments will become more profitable as new products and production technologies emerge, customer bases are built up beyond those for autos and consumer electronics, and better use is made of American managerial and marketing skills. Japanese managers will become better at their jobs, but it will not be because they have changed much. Rather they will be helped to bring their existing strengths to bear by changes occurring in American managers. As communication, trust-building, continuous incremental improvements, and a sense of work as a meaningful human activity emerge as valued elements of American organizational life, Japanese managers will begin to look a lot better in the United States.

Moreover, they will learn to make their weaknesses work for them instead of against them. A power orientation to managing will not be harmful if Japanese managers are careful in their hiring and make sure American employees know what they are getting into. Reluctant follower firms, while remaining unprofitably tied to their *keiretsu*, still can expand into new relationships with American customers. The use of job security offers to control and manipulate workers also can be used to motivate employees to be innovative. The often debilitating distinction between subsidiary and parent company employees will be maintained, since Japanese executives seem unable to change it, but opportunities for crossover can be established. The companies will still avoid unions, but if they must work with them occasionally, they can act in good faith and make use of valuable union services. Finally, while the demands of American corporate citizenship will remain a source of bewilderment, Japanese companies at least can be compliant and use the demands to stimulate discourse among their senior leaders regarding the role of the corporation in society.

Direct investment into the United States is tied somewhat to economic conditions in Japan and the value of the dollar versus the yen. But the steady increases in capital flows since the mid-1970s regardless of the economic and financial environment suggest that the Japanese people have made a profound decision to tie themselves permanently to the American sphere of influence. The purchase of American assets can take two forms, the acquisition of highly liquid, get-in and get-out securities or the building and acquiring of U.S. companies. The latter activity is becoming more and more prominent, and it signals the development of a bond. Americans did the same thing in Europe in the 1950s, and today Americans are a more Europeanized people because of it. In 1958 I saw an American tourist in Norway bring a young waitress to tears because the girl could not answer the American's questions in English and was unable to say how much the bill was "in American money." Gauche behavior of this kind is no longer seen, as Americans have developed a broader international focus. American managers learn European languages and fit in nicely in European settings. Fears which gripped the French and others in the 1960s about "the American challenge" have faded, and managers easily travel back and forth on assignments. Japan, like America in Europe in 1955, is making its move to become part of something larger than itself, and the effort is both hard and easy. It is hard because Japanese are an island people uncomfortable outside their borders. It is easy because they are well educated (up to college anyway) and trained to be attentive to rituals and customs. Educated, well-mannered people can survive and prosper anywhere if they want to, and the Japanese seem now to want to. They are off the reservation in force, but they are not on the warpath. Indeed, as I noted at the beginning of this book, Japan's investing in America signals a general acceptance (although many Japanese managers are resisting) that it must Americanize. It will change Japan forever and for the better, just as America's "invasion" of Europe helped America to become a better country. Japanese as managers may not change much—if they are careful, they probably do not have to—but Japan will.

WE NEVER ADAPT

Japanese have been called an adaptable people, but this is not so. For 300 years, until the mid-nineteenth century, nothing changed under the shoguns. When change had to occur, the Japanese did not handle it well; the order-making political structure broke down, replaced by war lords who led the nation into an unwinnable war. After the Pacific War, a set of interlocking institutions was developed emphasizing one-party rule, an economic focus on production rather than consumption, an educational structure crafted to foster docility rather than creativity, and a legal system designed to serve the existing order rather than abstract principles of justice.[1] The managerial elites who arose in both government and business saw themselves as beholden to no one in their roles as guardians of the country. Indeed, it was society's duty to accommodate their needs and desires, which supposedly were in Japan's best interest. These elites mostly avoided scandal, led modest lives, and used their power wisely. The country prospered.

During this period Japanese businessmen adopted Western dress, eagerly sought Western technology, and borrowed Western ideas about manufacturing management. At first they were called *imitators;* then, later after they had done so well, the less-negative term *adapters* was used. Neither term is quite on the mark. It is better to think of Japanese managers as *open, rational,* and *rigid.* They are always open to new ideas and techniques. They rationally calculate the ways in which innovation will serve their goals, and they are remarkably rigid in sticking to their ordained plans. These characteristics are not rooted in cultural values. Good managers everywhere are open and rational, and Japanese rigidity comes from fear, fear of upsetting senior executives and government bureaucrats who have approved a set of goals and are not eager to have to examine another evolving set, and fear of destabilizing the carefully crafted structure of Japanese economic life.

Managers, then, enjoy an elite status, have had one success after another over the last forty years, and have learned not to do anything which challenges objectives. There is thus no pressure on them to be adaptable, and when they go overseas to manage, they do not easily adapt.

Are the behaviors of Japanese managers in the United States common only to America? Research conducted by Hideo Inohara suggests not.[2] In a 1981 four-country study of Japanese subsidiaries in Europe he found that

· Japanese service firms depend heavily on instructions from Tokyo.
· Job satisfaction is low for service firm employees but high for manufacturing employees.
· Japanese managers, unused to taking commercial laws seriously, were encountering problems in following local regulations on hiring and job assignments.
· Financial performance was modest, but managers took a long-term perspective.
· Quality was high but productivity was low. Local employees wondered if quality production was being overemphasized.
· While localization of management was a goal, it seemed unlikely to occur, since highly competent employees tended to quit.
· Where plant managers were authoritarian and rule-oriented in a traditional Japanese style, local employee complaints rose dramatically.

The Japanese behavior in Europe clearly was a virtual carbon copy of their American involvement in the 1980s and 1990s. Training was on the job rather than formal, and technical instruction manuals were few. When a problem occurred on the assembly line, European managers tended to retreat to their offices to study it. Japanese managers would descend on the shop floor in a flurry of trial and error until the line got going again. Workers who reported to a local manager felt strange, since they knew that his Japanese "advisor" was really in charge. The Japanese tended to be strict about shop floor cleanliness but slovenly in the office, with piles of boxes littering floors and desks buried under paper.

These 1981 European findings are remarkably similar to the characteristics of Japanese firms in the United States in the 1990s. What is one to conclude from all this? It seems fair to say that Japanese managers do not adapt very well to varied environments. They do what they do, and they do it in Japan, Europe, and the United States.[3] They emphasize quality production but at the expense of labor productivity and profit. They turn off locals who could help them, preferring to hire compliant employees who do not threaten their power. While they are usually liked and even admired by local employees and customers, they keep to themselves, failing to build the relationships which their own management philosophy demands.

Studies of Japanese managers in less-developed country subsidiaries show similar characteristics. Autocratic and centralized decision making is practiced. Local managers are not trusted and are promoted very slowly. Functional human resource management plans are not in place. Unions are feared and avoided. Recent 1990 research on Japanese management in Northern Mexico assembly plants showed the same kind of lack of training and blundering described in this book.[4]

In sum, Japanese managers do their thing regardless of where they are or how long they have been there. We should note, however, that while the studies tend to describe mostly vivid negative behaviors, high-quality performance also is much in evidence. Japanese foreign investment is not as successful as European or American investment abroad, but it is by no means a catastrophe. And American management approaches seem to be moving in a direction favorable to Japanese techniques.

THE "MID-PACIFIC" MANAGEMENT STYLE

One of the great success stories of the 1980s was Nordstrom, the Seattle-based retail giant famous for the great service in its stores. All of that service emerges out of an employee-management approach which is somewhat Japanese and somewhat American. It appears to be a hybrid which may signal what the mixing of Japanese and American styles of managing will lead to.

Each Nordie gets a base salary for forty hours but is expected to invest extra time and effort in stocking shelves, calling customers, writing thank-you notes, and other activities which produce sales. The employee gets a commission for his or her extra efforts if they pay off. What this arrangement adds up to is the assumption of some business risk by the employee. If the economy should turn sour, then incomes will turn sour. Employees, then, are implicit investors in the business. That is American.

What is Japanese about it is the hierarchical, even paternal nature of employee relations with management. Salespeople are encouraged to call John Nordstrom, "Mister John." Bruce Nordstrom is "Mister Bruce." On their own time the workers often attend rah-rah sessions to rev up morale and allegiance to the Nordstrom mission. Nordstrom does not yet have a company song, but that day may not be far off.

An American element of Nordstrom's employee management comes as employees deal with each other. They are fiercely individualistic and competitive, even to the point occasionally of stealing customers and manipulating information on who is to be credited with a sale. Tales of "Nervous Nordies" desperately pursuing their quotas or serving customers are legendary. My favorite is the one about the man who buys a $3,000 dress for his wife. Two days later he returns it. Even though the dress smells terrible, he gets his money back (the commission will be deducted from the luckless Nordie's pay). Curious, the company sends the dress to a chemist for analysis. He tells them the smell comes from formaldehyde—an embalming fluid. What the man had done was to lay out his dead wife in the dress. After the wake, he buried her in a slip and brought the dress back, tainted by the embalming fluid.

Like Japanese, Nordies are submissive in their vertical relations, accepting of management paternalism, and superbly service-oriented. Like Americans, they are highly competitive and individualistic in their horizontal relations. This "Mid-Pacific" style of management has been phenomenally successful, although Nordstrom has been pressured to develop more of a conventional pay-for-all-hours-worked compensation plan by state officials. Could the Nordstrom style be the wave of the future? Is it the outcome of Japanese and American blending? Perhaps, but Americans do not like Japanese-style paternalism and "loyalty," and Japanese do not accept ruthless un-grouplike competitiveness. Nevertheless, when all of those Japanese banks and securities and insurance firms eventually conclude that they cannot re-create Japan in America yet pull back from turning themselves into American firms, they may turn to the Nordstrom approach. The Mid-Pacific style may be a solution waiting for a problem to find it.

SUCCESS FACTORS IN THE 1990s

Success for Japanese direct investment in the United States means an increase in return on investment and acceptance by the American people. Concrete steps to achieve those goals are as follows:

Increase Added-Value Production in the United States

According to Japanese sources, a Japanese worker takes 133 hours to produce $1,000 of output. A U.S. worker takes only 109 hours.[5] Moreover, Japanese wage increases are starting to accelerate in the face of a severe labor shortage. In 1990 wages went up about 6 percent, the highest growth in many years.[6] With American workers producing added value at lower cost, companies ought to begin shifting more and more of this kind of work to the United States. This "hollowing out" of Japan won't last for more than a few years, until Japanese productivity improves and wage growth moderates, but it should stimulate a reduction in Japan's low margin assembly manufacturing in the United States in favor of increased higher margin added-value work.

Improve Marketing

Over the 1985–1991 period revenues of Japanese subsidiaries and affiliates rose, but profits did not. This suggests that firms have been buying customers with low prices in an attempt to build market share. While this strategy can work well if a company also has a strong brand image which will hold on to consumers, it is a mistake for most Japanese firms. More marketing research is needed on consumer needs, coupled with careful targeting to identify high profit market segments.[7]

Become American Companies

Until 1989 subsidiaries could borrow from their parents and deduct the interest payment as an expense. This is no longer allowed by U.S. tax authorities. In addition, those firms which use transfer pricing strategies to control costs will encounter a more hostile U.S. Internal Revenue Service in the 1990s. The IRS intends to require elaborate information to be provided by foreign companies so it can calculate "fair" transfer prices based on common industry profit ratios. These changes will reduce the subsidiaries' dependence on their parents and force them to become cost competitive in America. They will have to shop around for the best deals they can make for loans and supplies. A more decentralized, less Tokyo-controlled structuring will be needed. Whether Japanese executives like it or not, Americanization is in order.

The replacement of Japanese expatriates by local Americans also will have to occur and is inevitable anyway, since Japan is running out of managers. In 1990, 600,000 jobs were available to 210,000 male college graduates. The large firms filled their quotas, but the mid-sized companies poised to invest in the United States were unable to hire.[8] Even in the large firms, however, a troubling hostility to foreign assignments was starting to emerge. Strange as it may seem, some Japanese were resisting postings to places such as Kansas or South Dakota. Most companies still seem to have plenty of volunteers for work in the United States, but a turning point may have been reached in the demands companies can make on their managers. Fewer people will accept a position in a backwater without wife or family and with little or no home leave. As the lifetime employment system breaks down, they will quit and easily find a job elsewhere which does not require such "loyalty."

Demolish the Japan, Inc., Myth

Here is an example of how the Japan, Inc., myth stays alive. In 1990, Mr. Kagayaka Miyazaki, chairman of Asahi Chemicals, stated his vision of the future. "The Japanese corporate world should consist of 100 broad, relatively open groups, each supporting the lives of some one million people," he said in an interview.[9] "One hundred groups like this could effectively support one hundred million people. They could generate profits efficiently and provide commensurable tax revenues to the country. With this strength a group would also be able to consider building substantial overseas facilities." As I have noted earlier, Americans tend to treat expressions of desire like Mr. Miyazaki's as if they added up to an in-place plan being carried out. They do not.

The most interesting and terrifying Japan, Inc., legend of the 1980s concerned an alleged attempt to manipulate the bond markets.[10] The Japanese government supposedly told insurance companies in 1984 or 1985 to buy U.S. bonds to prop up the dollar and keep Japanese exports to the United States competitive. Alas, the dollar fell anyway in 1986, and the companies lost $13 billion. Then, in May 1987, a group of ruling elites is rumored to have met to hatch a plot to retaliate for U.S. tariffs imposed on Japanese products a month earlier. The idea was to boycott the May auction of U.S. Treasury bonds to teach the United States that Japan could not be pushed around. Without Japanese capital, interest rates would rise, costing the Treasury billions. No such boycott occurred, but the story fed the Japan, Inc., myth anyway.

For purely economic reasons the Japanese did flee the U.S. bond markets in 1990—and nothing happened. Indeed, interest rates soon fell, influenced more by an oncoming recession than Japanese actions. The truth is that Japanese financiers did not possess the clout they were said to have. In addition, the idea of a group of them meeting in a torment of rage to plot sweet revenge is ludicrous. Oligopolistic collusion certainly goes on in Japan, but it serves economic, not emotional, purposes. The boozy mutterings of a few insurance executives over beer and sake do not constitute a conspiracy or a world strategy.

Japanese managers and government officials must put a stop to this kind of talk by actively challenging every false rumor and allegation. Where attacks on Japan, Inc., have some substance but are overstated, as in Pat Choate's *Agents of Influence,* Japanese companies should mend their ways. When attacks are accurate, such as those centered on Toshiba's sales to the Soviets and its subsequent attempt to pressure U.S. lawmakers, the Japanese government should quietly chastise the offender the first time and go public with punishment if the offending actions persist. Complaining that Japan, Inc.-oriented attacks in the United States are based on racism will not work to stop them, nor will pious denials that Japanese elites never collude and do not occasionally entertain grandiose global visions of dominance.

Develop an Export Focus

Japanese firms in the United States will gain profits and American acceptance if they start exporting to Japan and to Europe. Their parent firms should pressure the Japanese government to lower its nontariff barriers to imports. These, which include import prohibitions, quantitative restrictions, and nonautomatic licensing, cover about 29 percent of Japanese imports from industrialized nations. Since U.S. and European barriers are about 15 percent, the Japanese wall is twice as high as it ought to be. At U.S. levels, it would import about $15 billion more a year.[11] Since about one-half of Japan's imports come from the United States, that amounts to $7.5 billion. While this increase would not end the U.S. trade deficit, it would reduce it to a politically tolerable amount.

Honda and other auto producers want to export more cars from the United States to Japan, but by 1990 little had been done. One promising area for improvement is agriculture. Japanese-owned U.S. beef producers should increase exports, although they probably will have to develop joint ventures with Japan's retail giants if they want to get into the distribution channels. Japanese demand for mandarin oranges was falling in 1989–1990, but this may have been due to high prices in a protected and subsidized domestic market. American-produced oranges and orange juice at low prices could find eager buyers. The same demand for affordable food exists in markets for apples, shrimp, lobsters, and cheese, most of which were enjoying increasing sales in 1990 in Japan even at high prices.[12] Lots of other opportunities exist for increasing U.S. exports to Japan from Japanese subsidiaries, and the companies should take advantage of them.

As for Europe, Japanese firms have every right to believe that they will be further shut out of European markets in the post-1992 era as the EEC retaliates for Japan's investment and trade barriers. The biggest European exports to Japan in 1990, after all, probably were antiques and oil paintings, and EEC direct investment in Japan was small. In response, Japanese companies have not been allowed to invest in Europe at will. Over 500 mostly small factories had been established by 1990—130 of these in Britain—but France and Italy were seeking tougher restrictions on increased investment and trade.

Less-onerous barriers are expected for U.S. companies, so Japanese-owned U.S. firms are setting up subsidiaries in Europe as bases for further investment and increased exports to the EEC. The biggest example of this strategy so far is Kubota, which purchased a large chunk of Cumins, the diesel engine maker, apparently to begin developing a gateway to European engine markets. Kubota also has bought a number of computer companies, perhaps for the same reason. Fujitsu purchased Britain's ICL in 1990. This move could lead to a link up between ICL and Fujitsu's majority-owned Amdahl Corporation, with Amdahl probably exporting computer components to ICL.

Slow Down

Americans became worried about Japanese investment in the 1980s because of its growth after 1985. While the surge really began in the mid-1970s, at a rate which did not stimulate concerns, the acceleration in direct investment in the late 1980s set off alarms. These worries will fade and Japanese companies will be more easily accepted if growth returns to its pre-1985 level. Will it? A Tokyo M & A specialist thinks so. "The government is putting pressure on the firms and the banks have reduced lending," he said. "Senior executives here are becoming very sensitive to the issue of investing in the U.S." This may be so, but the fall of the dollar in 1990 made U.S. assets very attractive. Matsushita spent over $6 billion to acquire MCA, a record amount. The 10 percent fall in the dollar just prior to the sale thus saved Matsushita about $500 million worth of yen needed to buy the dollars to complete the purchase.

If the dollar stays low in the 1990–1995 period, which is likely given the rising Japanese interest rates, the lowered cost to acquire U.S. companies may offset increased costs of capital in Japan. Will loan funds be available? Yes, because the Japanese people have continued to save. While savings levels are down from early 1980s levels, they are still substantial and probably will remain so until 2000. Savers have responded to the deregulation of deposit rates and the availability of high yield money market certificates for small-lot depositors. While the banks' cost of funds will increase, the deluge of savings will enable them to provide a ready source of capital for buying U.S. companies at bargain prices. Money will also be available to expand investments already in the United States and to build up American R & D facilities.[13]

So Japanese investment in the U.S. will continue to grow in the 1990s, probably at a rate between $10 and $30 billion per year (it was $28 billion in 1990 and about $18 billion in 1991, according to Japanese sources). A number of non-economic factors will become increasingly more important in determining whether growth is at the low or high rate. According to a 1988 poll conducted by the Japan Federation of Economic Organizations, Japanese executives have a number of worries which may hinder their move to the U.S. The questions a CEO asks himself before making a decision are (in order of importance): Will the U.S. Congress pass laws restricting further investment in the future? Will our firm be accepted in the local community? How will our managers' children be educated? What kind of environmental and affirmative action regulations will we face? Will the quality of American employees be high? Can we obtain high quality supplies? Notice that public acceptance and education for children were more important than problems in regulation, hiring, or supply.

These are not the worries of invaders come to challenge America's economic independence. Rather they are concerns of people who very much want to contribute and be liked. Paradoxically, if they feel that they are accepted, Japanese direct investment flows could increase, a move which would stimulate American worry and a corresponding Japanese pullback. What may be evolving is a kind of non-economic, self-regulating system in which Japanese companies tune their decisions to the ebb and flow of American acceptance and American concern and settle on an amount which maximizes one and minimizes the other. This system will remain in place as long as the U.S. trade deficit with Japan continues—probably until 2000 or 2005. Nothing like this system has ever happened before—U.S. investment in Europe in the 1950s and 1960s, for example, was not undertaken with much concern for European sensitivities—and it is a tribute to both the American and Japanese peoples that they are quietly developing a modus vivendi with each other. One hopes that these efforts will continue.

WHAT IF THE SYSTEM FAILS?

If the Japanese do not do what it takes to become accepted in their United States direct investments, they can expect a nasty response from the U.S. Congress.[14] Representative John Bryant of Texas has tried for several years to pass legislation establishing onerous reporting and information disclosure requirements for foreign investors. Another Texas Democrat, Representative Jack Brooks, wants to penalize Japanese auto transplants, whom he believes are engaging in unfair competition by not buying enough parts from American-owned suppliers.

Other responses involve the "national treatment" issue. Some legislators want the United States to impose the same barriers against Japanese trade and investment which Japan employs. It is difficult, for example, for American firms to purchase Japanese financial institutions or to do business in the securities industries. Japanese banks and securities firms, however, are mostly unhindered in the United States. National treatment is a principle of international business requiring each nation to treat domestic and foreign investors equally. Japan has been a flagrant violator of the principle, but clearly it is moving in the right direction now. Hopefully it will continue.

Other actions would involve increased use and broader interpretation of mechanisms to block foreign takeovers on national security grounds. The concept of national security could be extended to include just about any high tech acquisition that threatened what some legislators refer to as "essential commerce." In addition, the political lobbying of foreign investors could be curtailed by increased restrictions on their ability to fund political action committees and by public disclosure requirements of foreign agents' interactions with U.S. government officials. And Japanese-owned firms could be hit with reduced visas for Japanese managers, local content rules for their products, and barriers to their imports from parents.

All of these requirements together probably would put a stop to Japanese investment in the United States. During the 1980s it was not Japanese lobbying which kept the Japan bashers and protectionists at bay, nor was it the Reagan and Bush administrations' weak support for free trade and investment. Rather it was the energetic pleas from state and local politicians for foreign investment to come into their communities to provide jobs. In the 1990s this support will evaporate. Japanese firms are shifting to M & A rather than job-generating start-ups, and state development officials are refocusing their efforts on export promotion instead of foreign investment. No one will stand up for the Japanese, especially after the faint response of Japan to America's call for support during the Iraq crisis. Who then will argue on behalf of Japanese investment besides a few academics and writers of books? The Japanese themselves will, and they will achieve their goals if they follow the steps outlined above and fairly pursue their interests in time-honored American ways.

A FINAL WORD OF ADVICE

Americans can prosper in Japanese-owned firms as long as they are willing to make some small adjustments. Here's a list of helpful hints.

· Americans believe in reason, pluralism, progress, and the primacy of the individual. Japanese believe in only two of these, reason and progress. Pluralism and individualism are neither foreign nor abhorrent to them, but they are more used to authoritarianism and groupism. Americans thus need to be good soldiers and team players in Japanese organizations.
· Manners, social rituals, dress codes, a certain formality, and civility count. Act accordingly.
· Do not challenge an obvious lie. After all, it's supposed to be obvious. It's simply a way of avoiding unpleasant encounters. However, lying is used rarely by Japanese. Instead, they use ambiguity. Read between the lines.
· Follow up on every promise. Never let a Japanese conclude that you are untrustworthy.
· Since Japanese managers hate uncertainty, keep them posted with short, frequent bursts of communicating rather than long, infrequent bursts.
· Find a Japanese mentor to help you advance and a Japanese shadow to show you the ropes.
· The image of harmony is crucial. Work out problems behind the scenes in an incremental, step-by-step manner.

Japanese managers are used to vertically structured organizations in which the power distance between superiors and subordinates is quite large. Virtually all relationships are up-down. If a Japanese manager finds himself in a horizontal relationship, he will work hard to make it vertical with himself on top. He is not just power-driven, rather he is order-driven, and he will seek relationships which reduce uncertainty. Japanese bosses who are secure in their position are often wonderful superiors, as many Americans will testify. They can be tyrannical, however, if they sense a challenge to their power and status or if their role is unclear.

The Japanese manager is not an economic agent. He does not view work as an input to his utility-maximizing program. Work to him is simply part of life, just as leisure time is. He does not seek to trade off work for leisure or demand increased compensation to forego leisure. He works because Japanese people work. That is what they do. They also play, pray, and make love. None of these things are substitutes for the others, as they often are in America. Consequently, Japanese managers do not focus solely on economic exchange relationships within their firms and externally. They prefer to build trust relationships of mutual obligations because these make work livable and even pleasurable. Of course, they also make deals and seek bonuses and recognition. They are like Americans and all humans in having a rational calculus and a goal-oriented perspective. But unlike American economists, living for them is not solely pursuing interests. It is also just living, the day-to-day ongoingness of doing one's job in the high-quality fashion demanded by the company, one's wife, one's community, nation, and oneself.

There are rules (mostly unstated) in Japanese organizations to guide actions in service to firm goals. But they are few compared to American firms. Instead work gets done as does life, in incremental steps, with each advance based on trial and error and each cooperative effort rooted in the collaboration of trusted superiors, peers, and subordinates. Although Japanese CEOs love to articulate mission statements and vision pronouncements, these are mostly ignored by employees, who work because, as noted, work is a natural part of living. They work *well*, however, in response to an elaborate network of controls, rhetoric, and subtle coercion which I have described as the Japanese management system.

A Japanese manager who counts only on himself for success is a pariah to senior executives. Their task is to make sure that everyone fits in, everyone works on trust building, everyone seeks and shares information, and everyone learns from failure. Woe to the manager who doesn't do these things. His pay raises disappear, as does his responsibility and status. He is made to "sit by the window"—shuffled off to a dead-end, no-work job where the only thing left to do is stare out the window. What Japanese senior executives do is dole out freedom and autonomy to those who have shown they will use them wisely.

A manager always knows how much or how little control he has and how secure he should feel in his task assignment. This knowledge reduces uncertainty and thus helps to stimulate risk taking, which all good managing requires. Given the conformity required of Japanese managers, however, big risk taking is unlikely. But little risks, small rewards, and incremental progress are the order of the day. The American manager takes big risks for possible big rewards, and since every so often a risk pays off, the firm may prosper. In the eyes of a Japanese, however, the process is inefficient and destructive. Americans look at the outcomes, but Japanese look at all those managers dumped by the wayside because their risks didn't pay off. So wasteful, the Japanese thinks, and goes about his business.

Notes

CHAPTER 1: THE INVASION

1. The stories of Manjiro and the first Japanese mission to the United States are told in Marc Pachter and Frances Weid (eds.), *Abroad in America: Visitors to the New Nation 1776–1914*. (Reading, MA: 1976). More extensive treatments are in Sakamaki Shunzo, *Japan and the United States, 1790–1853*, translations of the Asiatic Society of Japan, 2d ser., vol. 18, Tokyo, 1939; Emily V. Warriner, *Voyager to Destiny* (New York: 1956); Kaneko Hisakazu, *Manjiro: The Man Who Discovered America* (Tokyo; 1956); Yukichi Fukuzawa, *The Autobiography of Yukichi Fukuzawa* (New York: 1966); Norimasa Muragaki, *Kokai Nikki: the Diary of the First Japanese Embassy to the United States of America* (Tokyo: 1958).

2. Interview with William Piez, *JEI Report*, February 2, 1990. On the friendliness of the U.S. people to Japan: favorable newspaper articles on Japan outnumber unfavorable articles, according to unpublished research at Washington State University, in all but the pre-war and war years.

3. Cited by Jim Powell, *The Gnomes of Tokyo*, (New York: 1988), p. 215. Originally published in "The Danger from Japan," *New York Times Magazine*, July 28, 1985.

4. In Douglas Frantz and Catherine Collins, *Selling Out* (Chicago: 1989), p. 125.

5. Frantz and Collins, p. 127.

6. Felix Rohatyn, "On the Brink," *New York Review of Books*, January 11, 1987, p. 3.

7. Kenneth Courtis is senior economist for the Deutsche Bank, Tokyo. He was quoted in *The Washington Post National Weekly Edition*, February 26, 1990, p. 8.

8. Daniel Burstein, *Yen!*, (New York: 1990) p. 258. In the 1990 version of the original 1988 book, Mr. Burstein, noting the inept behavior of the Japanese

on Wall Street, is honest enough to admit that things were not quite as bad as they seemed. [The full title for this book is found in the Bibliography.]

9. *JEI Report*, no. 23B, June 15, 1990.

10. Sources: Ministry of International Trade and Industry (MITI) and Bank of Japan. Cited in *Nippon 1990* (Japan External Trade Organization, 1990).

11. MITI, *1990 White Paper on International Trade*, Tokyo, June 1990.

12. The encounter with Mr. K. is real. I have made minor changes in it to protect his privacy. All quotes in this book are from real managers, not composites. In many cases they have requested anonymity, so their names are not given. Occasionally I have corrected their English syntax to smooth it out in written form.

13. My thanks to Mr. Junichi Ukita, Director of Matsushita's Overseas Training Center in Osaka, and his staff for their kind assistance. I have embellished their description of a bad manager with concrete examples taken from my interviews at other firms and from the literature.

CHAPTER 2: WHY ARE THEY HERE?

1. Michael Porter, *The Competitive Advantage of Nations* (New York: 1990).

2. Jeffrey S. Arpan and David A. Ricks, *Directory of Foreign Manufacturers in the United States* (Atlanta: 1990).

3. Data compiled from Japan Economic Institute, *Japan's Expanding U.S. Manufacturing Presence* (October 1989).

4. *The Economist*, July 7, 1990, p.30.

5. *Business Tokyo* (April 1990): p. 66.

6. The oligopolized industries we studied were (1989 data) detergents, cosmetics, beer, whiskey, color photo film, color televisions, home VCRs, camcorders, videodisc players, single-lens cameras, home telephones, passenger cars, mainframe computers, personal computers, facsimile machines, plain paper copiers, numerically controlled lathes, optical fibers, and integrated circuits. The non-oligopolized industries were tissue paper, compact discs, gasoline, ethylene, industrial robots, and crude steel. My thanks to my assistants, Patrick Lee and Gary O'Conner, who collected and analyzed these data and the data in our second study discussed below.

7. For twenty-five industries the r-squared correlation between the percent of Japanese-owned U.S. firms controlled by the top three firms and the number of employees controlled was .40.

8. "The Potential for Internationalizing the Japanese Company." *Economic Eye* (Spring 1990): p. 14.

9. The industries were paper mills, industrial inorganic chemicals, plastics materials and resins, pharmaceutical preparations, industrial organic chemicals, steel works, valves and pipe fittings, farm machinery, motors and generators, radio and TV communications equipment, electronic components, industrial control instruments, fluid meters, measurement and control instruments, general manufacturing, semiconductors, sewing machines, shipbuilding, typewriters, carbon black, organic fibers, VCRs and other audio and TV equipment, autos, trucks, motorcycles, synthetic fibers, tires, lift trucks, computers, air conditioning, cameras, construction equipment, copiers, large-scale computers,

and musical instruments. In our study we included most of the industries Michael Porter studied. See Michael Porter, "The Competitive Advantage of Nations," *Harvard Business Review* (March-April 1990): p. 82.

10. Earlier data are from the *Survey of Current Business*. Recent data are from Ministry of Finance, *Monthly Finance Review*; Bank of Tokyo, *Tokyo Financial Review*.

11. *The Japan Economic Journal*, June 30, 1990, p. 22.

12. Ministry of Construction data in *Japan 1990* Kezai Koho Center, Tokyo 1989.

13. E. M. Graham and Paul R. Krugman, *Foreign Direct Investment in the United States* (Washington, D.C.: 1989).

14. Robert N. McCauley and Steven A. Zimmer, "Explaining the International Differences in the Cost of Capital," *Federal Reserve Bank of New York Quarterly Review* (Summer 1989): pp. 7–28.

15. K. Zagor, "Alliances and Xenophobia," *Financial Times*, March 15, 1990, p. 76.

16. Japan Times, *Top 1500 Japanese Companies* (Tokyo: 1988).

17. See Keizai Koho Center, *Japan 1990*.

18. The story is told in Jeremiah J. Sullivan and Per O. Heggelund, *Foreign Investment in the U.S. Fishing Industry* (Lexington, MA: 1979).

19. Andrew Pollack, "Japan's New Farm Belt," *New York Times*, May 14, 1989, 3-1, pp.3–14.

CHAPTER 3: HOW ARE THEY DOING?

1. U.S. Department of Commerce data reported in *The Japan Economic Journal*, August 11, 1990, p. 6.

2. Bank of Japan data for 1987 in JETRO, *Nippon 1990*. (Tokyo: 1990).

3. See Keizai Koho Center, *Japan 1990*. The data are for 1985. The gap may have narrowed a bit since then but not by much.

4. See *The Japan Economic Journal*, June 23, 1990. Data based on Japan Productivity Center studies and the research of Professors Masahiro Kuroda of Keio University and Dale Jorgenson of Harvard.

5. The 1988 data are median values for five Japanese and three non-Japanese assemblers, and for three Japanese and five non-Japanese total production plants. Data provided by Electronic Industries Association, HDTV Information Center, Washington, D.C.

6.*Survey of Current Business* data for 1987 reported in JETRO, *Nippon 1990*.

7. For this section see Forbes "International 500," July 1990; JETRO, *Nippon 1990*; Keizai Koho Center, *Japan 1990*.

8. Yusaka Futatsugi, "What Cross-holdings Mean for Corporate Management," *Economic Eye* (Spring 1990): pp. 17–19.

9. These data are based on Japanese government surveys, reported in Tsutomu Nishimura, "Toward a Better Balance Between Savings and Investment," *Keidanren Review* (April 1990): pp. 3–7. A 1990 survey by the Nippon Credit Bank is not so optimistic, estimating a 1995 U.S. trade deficit with Japan of $36.7 billion. See *The Japan Times Weekly International Edition*, August 27, 1990, p. 16.

10. *The Wall Street Journal*, August 29, 1990, p. 1, and Bruce Stokes, *Japanese Investment in the U.S.: Its Causes and Consequences* (New York: 1988).

11. These are my calculations, but others have arrived at similar figures.

12. Duane Kujawa and Daniel Bob, *American Public Opinion on Japanese Foreign Direct Investment* (New York: 1988).

13. Survey results are summarized in *JEI Report*, March 2, 1990. See also *The Japan Economic Journal*, February 24, 1990, p. 3.

14. *New York Times*, July 10, 1990, p. A7.

15. *Business Week*, December 18, 1989.

16. Surveys by the Ministry of Labor in 1990 show only 56 percent of salaried workers satisfied with their life, down from 67 percent in 1985. See *JEI Report*, no. 31B, August 10, 1990.

17. This section summarizes the research of Professor D. P. Lohmann, "An Explanation of Reactions to Japanese Investment in Hawaii" (Paper presented at the Association of Japanese Business Studies Conference, Nashville, January 1990).

18. See V. Pucik, M. Hanada, and G. Fifeld, "Management Culture and Effectiveness of Local Executives in Japanese-owned U.S. Corporations," (Ann Arbor: 1989), p. 13.

CHAPTER 4: JAPAN BASHERS VERSUS THE CHRYSANTHEMUM CLUB

1. Books associated with Japan bashing are Martin and Susan Tolchin, *Buying Into America* (New York: 1989); Douglas Frantz and Catherine Collins, *Selling Out* (Chicago: 1989); Barrie G. James, *Trojan Horse* (London: 1989); Clyde Prestowitz, *Trading Places* (New York: 1988); James Fallows, *More Like Us* (a book also showing admiration for Japan) (New York: 1989); Daniel Burstein, *Yen!* (New York: 1990); Karel van Wolferen, *The Enigma of Japanese Power* (New York: 1989); and Chalmers Johnson, *MITI and the Japanese Miracle* (Stanford: 1982). Chrysanthemum club members are William Ouchi, *Theory Z* (Reading, MA: 1981); Ezra Vogel, *Japan as Number One* (New York: 1979); Robert L. Shook, *Honda, An American Success Story* (New York: 1988); and Jim Powell, *The Gnomes of Tokyo* (New York: 1988). Van Wolferen's book, although his tone is strident, is by far the best work on Japan available today.

2. Quoted in *Business Tokyo* (March 1990): p. 3.

3. Frantz and Collins, *Selling Out*, p. 20.

4. Graham and Krugman, *Foreign Direct Investment*.

5. See Graham and Krugman, who use 1983 and 1986 data from the Bureau of Economic Analysis and other Commerce Department sources.

6. 1986 data in Graham and Krugman. Most of the following data are from their work.

7. Frantz and Collins, p. 31.

8. Frantz and Collins, p. 57.

9. The story is told in Graham and Krugman.

10. Dennis J. Encarnation and Mark Mason, "Neither MITI nor America: The

Political Economy of Capital Liberalization in Japan," *International Organization* 44 (Winter 1990): pp. 25–54.

11. Chalmers Johnson, "Revisionism and Beyond," *Business Tokyo* (February 1990): p. 54.

CHAPTER 5: JAPANESE AND AMERICAN IDEOLOGIES

1. Ihab Hassan, "The Burden of Mutual Perceptions," *IHJ Bulletin* 10, 1 (1990): pp. 1–6.

2. Cited by Hassan, p. 6.

3. This passage is from "The Seventeen Article Constitution of Prince Shotoku." In R. Tsunoda et al., *Sources of Japanese Tradition* (New York: 1958), p. 50.

4. "Draft of the Basic Plan for Establishment of Greater East Asia Co-Prosperity Sphere, 1942." In Tsunoda et al., pp. 802–803.

5. Yamashita, *The Panasonic Way* (Tokyo: 1989).

6. For a summary of these comments see Edward Boyer, "Straight Talk to Japan," *Pacific Basin Quarterly* (Spring 1989): pp. 4–5.

7. Boyer, ibid.

8. JETRO, *Japanese Managers in America: A Survey Report* (June 1989).

CHAPTER 6: "THOSE WHO DEPART ARE FORGOTTEN, DAY BY DAY"

1. Japanese government surveys summarized by Yohiro Tokunaga, "An Anatomy of Japan's High Prices," *Economic Eye* (Spring 1990): pp. 20–24.

2. Management and Coordination Agency Study, reported in *JEI Report* no. 28B, July 20, 1990.

3. Yamashita, *The Panasonic Way*, p. 126.

4. See C. B. Macpherson, *The Political Theory of Possessive Individualism* (Oxford, 1962). Quotes in this section are from Macpherson.

5. The story is told in Joseph J. Fuccini and Suzy Fuccini, *Working for the Japanese* (New York: 1990).

6. Hideo Takahashi, "Japan's Price Structure," *JEI Report*, January 26, 1990. See Professor Toshimasa Tsuruta's report for the Japan Fair Trade Commission, "Reviewing Government Regulation from the Standpoint of Competition Policy," 1989 (in Japanese).

7. *The Daily Yomiuri*, June 16, 1990.

8. Kozo Yamamura, "The Significance of Japanese Investment in the U.S.: How Should We React." In Kozo Yamamura (ed.), *Japanese Investment in the United States* (Seattle: 1989).

9. In a 1989 government survey of 239 Westerners working in Japanese firms in Japan, the *gaijin* noted that employees tend to spend several hours at their desks after work and rarely take days off because they fear criticism if they leave. See *The Japan Economic Journal*. February 10, 1990, p. 10. Fear and control are often the hallmark of a Japanese office rather than loyalty and commitment.

CHAPTER 7: COMPETITORS, RELUCTANTS, AND
KNOWLEDGE SEEKERS

1. Bruce Kogut and Sea-Jin Chang, "Technological Capabilities and Japanese Direct Investment in the United States." (Paper presented at the Association of Japanese Business Studies Conference, Nashville, January 1990). In this section I am also drawing from the work of Thomas Roehl of the University of Michigan.

2. A. B. Karnani and B. Wernerfelt, "Multiple Point Competition." *Strategic Management Journal* 6, (1985): pp. 87–96.

3. See *Business Tokyo* (April 1990): p. 28.

4. See *JEI Report*, no. 24A, June 23, 1989 for a summary of Japanese R & D. See also Sheridan M. Tatsuno's *Created in Japan* (New York: 1990).

5. Toshihiro Horiuchi, "The Flexibility of Japan's Small and Medium-sized Firms and Their Foreign Investment." In Kozo Yamamura (ed.), *Japanese Investment in the United States* (Seattle: 1989).

6. T. A. Scandura and Kunal Banerji, "A Tale of Two Industries: Japanese Investment in Automobile Ancillary and Chemical Processing in the U.S." (Paper presented at the Association of Japanese Business Studies Conference, Nashville, January 1990).

7. T. Kono, *Changing Corporate Culture* (Tokyo: 1988). About one-third of the firms could not be categorized.

8. Articles that discuss the Americanization of Japanese firms are Todd Hixon and R. Kimball, "How Foreign-owned Businesses Can Contribute to U.S. Competitiveness," *Harvard Business Review* (January-February 1990): pp. 56–57; Robert B. Reich, "Who is Us?," *Harvard Business Review* (same issue): pp. 53–64; Doron P. Levin, "Motor City for Japanese in California," *New York Times*, May 7, 1990, p. C1–C2.

CHAPTER 8: JAPANESE MANAGEMENT PHILOSOPHIES: THE
BRAINLESS AND THE BRILLIANT

1. Peter Dale, *The Myth of Japanese Uniqueness* (New York: 1986). Mr. Dale's work owes much to that of my colleague, Roy A. Miller, *Origins of the Japanese Language* (Seattle: University of Washington Press, 1980).

2. Dale, pp. 193, 199.

3. Dale, p. 21.

4. Takeo Doi, *The Anatomy of Dependence* (Tokyo: 1971), T. S. Lebra, *Japanese Patterns of Behavior* (Honolulu: 1976), and Chie Nakane, *Japanese Society* (Berkeley: 1970).

5. Dale, p. 52.

6. Hiroshi Komai, *Japanese Management Overseas* (Tokyo: 1989).

7. Akio Morita and Shintaro Ishihara, *The Japan That Can Say 'No'*. I am quoting from an undated English translation in typescript which began circulating among Americans interested in Japan shortly after the Japanese publication occurred in 1990.

8. Cited in Jack Seward and Howard Van Zandt, *Japan: The Hungry Guest* (Tokyo: 1987), p. 89.

9. Seward and Van Zandt, p. 101.

10. J. R. Lincoln and A. L. Kalleberg, "Work Organization and Workforce Commitment: A Study of Plants and Employees in the U.S. and Japan." *American Sociological Review* 50 (1985): pp. 738–760.

11. These and the following quotes are from Morita and Ishihara, *The Japan That Can Say 'No'*.

12. Yotaro Kobayashi, "A Message to American Managers," *Economic Eye* 11 (Spring 1990): p. 11.

13. Hideo Inohara, *Human Resource Development in Japanese Companies* (Tokyo: 1990), Chapter 2.

14. Onitsuka's biography is by Hiroshi Tanaka, *Personality in Industry* (London: 1988).

15. Yamashita, *The Panasonic Way*, p. 88.

16. Jermiah J. Sullivan, "A Critique of Theory Z," *Academy of Management Review* 8 (1983): pp. 132–142.

17. James C. Abegglen and G. Stalk, Jr., *Kaisha: The Japanese Corporation* (New York: 1985).

18. Quoted in J. Kotkin and Y. Kishimoto, "Theory F," *INC.* (8 April 1986) 8: pp. 53–60.

19. Seward and Van Zandt, p. 195.

20. Jeremiah J. Sullivan and Coral Snodgrass, "Tolerance of Executive Failure in American and Japanese Organizations," *Asia-Pacific Journal* 8 (1991): pp. 15–31.

21. Quoted in Powell, *The Gnomes of Tokyo*, p. 32.

22. This work was done with Professors Teruhiko Suzuki and Yasumasu Kondo of Doshisha University in Kyoto. See the bibliography.

23. Quoted in Shook, *Honda, An American Success Story*, p. 13.

CHAPTER 9: WHAT IS PROFIT?

1. Jeremiah J. Sullivan and Naoki Kameda, "The Concept of Profit in Japanese-American Business Communication Problems," *The Journal of Business Communications* 19, 1 (1982): pp. 33–39.

2. Peter Drucker, "Learning from Foreign Management," *The Wall Street Journal*, June 4, 1980, editorial page.

3. Joel Dean, *Managerial Economics*, New York: Prentice Hall, 1951.

4. Yamashita, *The Panasonic Way*, p. 26.

5. See Tanaka, *Personality in Industry*.

6. The most recent years for which profit and profitability data are available are 1989 and 1990. See U.S. Commerce Department, *Survey of Current Business*, May, June, July, August, 1990 and 1991. See also *Electronic Business*, May 28, 1990.

7. Data are from Electronics Industry Association of Japan, *Newsletter*, various issues.

8. See Keizai Koho Center, *Japan 1990*.

9. Takino Takanaga, "A Comparative Analysis of Multinational Strategies in Japan." (Paper presented at the WAM International Conference, Shizuoka, June 1990).

CHAPTER 10: LIFETIME EMPLOYMENT AND MANAGERIAL POWER

1. For a review of the research on lifetime employment, see Jeremiah J. Sullivan and Richard B. Peterson, "The Japanese Lifetime Employment System: Whither It Goest?" In S. Benjamin Prasad (ed), *Advances in International Comparative Management*, vol. 5 (Greenwich, CT: 1990). For the research supporting the control use of the system, see Jeremiah J. Sullivan and Richard B. Peterson, "Theories Underlying the Japanese Lifetime Employment System," *Journal of International Business Studies* 22 (1991): pp. 79–97.

2. John W. Dower, "The Useful War," *Daedalus* 119 (Summer 1990): pp. 49–70 and A. Gordon, *The Evolution of Labor Relations in Japan* (Cambridge, MA: 1985).

3. Sullivan and Peterson, "Theories Underlying the Japanese Lifetime Employment System."

4. Survey results are in Hiroshi Komai, *Japanese Management Overseas*.

5. See the study by Pucik et al., "Management Culture and Effectiveness," 1989.

6. *Economic Eye* (Spring 1990): p. 13.

7. See *Business Week*, February 16, 1990.

CHAPTER 11: JAPANESE AND AMERICANS DON'T TRUST EACH OTHER

1. Quoted in *Business Tokyo* (March 1990): p. 26.

2. Cited in *JEI Report*, March 2, 1990.

3. Quoted in *The Washington Post National Weekly Edition*, February 26, 1990, p. 8.

4. See Pucik et al., 1989.

5. Quoted in Pucik, et al., p. 51.

6. Interview with Bill Donahue, *The Oregonian*, April 5, 1990.

7. For a review of the research and empirical data, see Jeremiah J. Sullivan and Richard B. Peterson, "Factors Associated with Trust in Japanese-American Joint Ventures," *Management International Review* 22 (1982): pp. 30-40 and Jeremiah J. Sullivan, Richard B. Peterson, and Naoki Kameda, "The Relationship between Conflict Resolution Approaches and Trust—A Cross-cultural Study," *Academy of Management Journal* 24 (1981): pp. 803–815.

8. See James P. Womak et al., *The Machine That Changed the World* (New York: 1990), p. 92 for a comparison of suggestions per employee from Japanese and American employees of Japanese firms.

9. This was a finding of the JETRO survey, *Japanese Managers in America* (1989).

10. John A. Kageyama, "Japanese Managers and American Employees," *Pacific Northwest Executive* (July 1989).

11. See Pucik et al., 1989.

12. The story of Yusa is told by Ku Shioya, "The Sticky Business of Communication." *Business Tokyo* (February 1990): p. 8.

13. See note 7.

14. R. Bruns, "Bought by the Japanese," *Business Tokyo* (March 1990): pp. 20–22.

CHAPTER 12: MATCHING THE RIGHT AMERICAN WITH THE RIGHT JAPANESE

1. MITI, *White Paper on International Trade 1987*, Tokyo, 1987.

2. Seward and Van Zandt, p. 200.

3. Inohara, *Human Resource Development in Japanese Companies.*

4. See Inohara for a thorough discussion of the data on training.

5. Business enrollment was estimated to be 20 percent of total university enrollment. Males were assumed to be 50 percent of those enrolled. I assumed that 25 percent graduated each year.

6. *Japan Labor Bulletin,* September 1, 1989, p. 3.

7. See *Business Week,* December 18, 1989.

8. My thanks to Mr. Junichi Ukita, Director, Overseas Training Center, for his assistance in obtaining this and other information on Matsushita's training.

9. My thanks to Steve Wilhelm of the *Puget Sound Business Journal* for this interesting scenario, which is based on his interviews with Japanese and American managers. I have adapted it somewhat from its original form.

10. Allan Bird, "Expatriates at Home: A New Twist in the Human Resource Management Strategies of Japanese MNCs." (Working paper, New York University, January 1990).

11. Inohara, *Human Resource Development in Japanese Companies.*

12. Kono, *Changing Corporate Culture.*

13. Yamashita, *The Panasonic Way.*

14. Tradescope (May 1990): p. 22.

15. Sullivan and Nonaka, "The Application of Organizational Learning Theory to American and Japanese Management," *Journal of International Business Studies* 17, 3 (1986): pp. 127–148.

CHAPTER 13: TALKING IS NOT DOWN TIME

1. JETRO, *Japanese Managers in America, A Survey Report.*

2. See Pucik et al.

3. G. Hofstede, *Culture's Consequences* (Beverly Hills: 1980).

4. Makoto Kikuchi, *Japanese Electronics,* (Tokyo: 1983), p. 188.

5. Quoted by Shook, *Honda, An American Success Story.*

6. This section is an excerpt from Sullivan and Kameda, "Bypassing in Managerial Communication." *Business Horizon* 34 (January 1991): pp. 71–80.

7. The research on compliance-gaining is summarized in the articles by Sullivan and Taylor listed in the Bibliography.

8. Quoted in the *San Jose Mercury News,* April 29, 1990, p. 2E.

9. My thanks to Hisanori Yokodate and the Japan Federation of Employers' Associations for this information.

CHAPTER 14: DECISION MAKING AS AN END IN ITSELF

1. The story is told in Fucini and Fucini, *Working for the Japanese.*

2. Kenneth B. Noble, "A Clash of Styles: Japanese Companies in U.S. Under Fire for Cultural Bias," *New York Times*, January 25, 1988.

3. Both quotes are from Pucik et al.

4. For an empirical study of Japanese power needs, see Sullivan, "Factors Associated with Trust in Japanese-American Joint Ventures." Japanese power is a key factor.

5. Roy C. Smith, *The Global Bankers* (New York: 1989).

6. This example is taken from Yoshino and Lifson, *The Invisible Link* (Cambridge, MA: 1986).

7. On Japanese strategic decisions see M. C. Lauenstein, "Strategic Planning in Japan," *Journal of Business Strategy*, (Fall 1985), and K. Kase, N. Campbell, and M. Goold, "The Role of the Centre in Managing Large Diversified Corporations in Japan." (Paper presented at the Association of Japanese Business Studies Conference, Nashville, January 1990.)

8. M. Tsuda, *Personal Strategy of Japanese Management.* See also D. J. Lu, *Inside Corporate Japan.*

9. Sullivan and Nonaka, "The Application of Organizational Learning Theory to Japanese and American Management." We studied several hundred Japanese and American executives in an effort to understand how they approached knowledge development.

10. Michihiro Matsumoto, *The Unspoken Way*, p. 77.

CHAPTER 15: THE RULE OF PERSONNEL

1. Inohara, p. 44.

2. See Natalie J. Ohnishi, "Japan's Corporate Culture: A Time of Transition," *Japan Economic Journal*, February 17, 1990, p. 9.

3. See *JEI Report*, no. 31B, August 10, 1990.

4. See Inohara's fine rundown on the status of women employees in Japan.

5. For the Fort Custer study, see Dicle et al., "Human Resource Management Practices in Japanese Organizations in the United States." See also James Bowman, "The Rising Sun in America—Japanese Management in the United States" and Art Gemmel, "Management in a Cross-cultural Environment: The Best of Both Worlds."

6. See *Japan Economic Journal*, February 10, 1990, p. 11.

7. Examples of questions are from Shook, *Honda*, p. 170.

8. Examples from Mazda and the data on anti-black biases are from Frantz and Collins, *Selling Out.*

9. See Pucik et al., 1989.

10. Zhuang Yang, "Internal Labor Market, Environments and Human Resource Management—A Study of HRM Policies at Japanese Companies Operating in the U.S.," San Francisco, 1990.

11. See Inohara, *Human Resource Development in Japanese Companies* for data on this issue.

12. M. Wakabayashi and G. Graen, "Human Resource Development of Japanese Managers: Leadership and Career Investment."

13. Allan Bird, "Executive Career Advancement at Japanese Banks: Who Gets to the Top?" (Nashville: 1990).

14. H. Takagi, *The Flow of Japanese Management*.

15. Shook, *Honda, An American Success Story*.

16. This section is based on the research of Yoshino and Lifson, *The Invisible Link*.

17. Mancur Olson, "Collective Action." In J. Eatwell, M. Milgate, and P. Newman (eds.), *The Invisible Hand*, New York: W. W. Norton, 1989, p. 61.

18. Sullivan, Suzuki, and Kondo, "Managerial Perceptions of Performance."

CHAPTER 16: MANUFACTURING MANAGEMENT

1. Details are from Yamashita, *The Panasonic Way*.

2. Inohara, *Human Resource Development in Japanese Companies*, p. 70.

3. Two superb studies of quality and *kaizen* are Kaoru Ishikawa, *What Is Total Quality Control?* (Englewood Cliffs, NJ: 1985) and Masaaki Imai, *Kaizen, The Key to Japan's Competitive Success* (New York: 1986).

4. See Inohara for a summary of the data.

5. Peter Drucker, "The Emerging Theory of Manufacturing," *Harvard Business Review* (May-June 1990): pp. 94–102.

6. W. Edwards Deming, *Out of the Crisis* (Cambridge, MA: MIT Center for Advanced Engineering Study, 1986). See also Mary Walton, *The Deming Management Method* (New York: Dodd, Mead, 1986).

7. Gary Jacobson and John Hillkirk, *Xerox, American Samurai* (New York: Collier Books, 1986).

8. C. K. Prahald and Gary Hamel, "The Core Competence of the Corporation," *Harvard Business Review* (May-June 1990): pp. 79–91.

9. *Business Tokyo* (December 1989): p. 2.

10. I am drawing from my own interviews and from Leonard H. Lynn and Henry R. Piehler, "Engineering Careers, Job Rotation, and Gatekeepers in Japan and the United States" (Case Western Reserve University: 1990).

11. Data was collected from author interviews and from Leslie Helm, "Japanese Way Causes Friction," *Seattle Post-Intelligencer*, May 7, 1990, p. B4.

12. Motohiro Morishima, "Japanese Employee Attitudes toward Changes in Traditional Employment Practices."

13. The story is told by Fucini and Fucini in *Working for the Japanese*.

14. Imai, *Kaizen*, p. 176.

15. Haruo Shimada, "Labor Problems of Japanese Companies Abroad," pp. 4–8.

16. *The Japan Digest*, August 28, 1990, p. 4.

17. *Japan Economic Journal*, August 11, 1990, p. 15.

18. Leonard Lynn, "Japan Adopts A New Technology: The Roles of Government, Trading Firms and Suppliers," *Columbia Journal of World Business* 19 (Winter 1984): pp. 39–45.

19. *The Economist*, March 3, 1990, p. 62.

20. Lane Daley, James Jimbalvo, Gary Sundem, and Yasumasa Kondo, "At-

titudes Towards Financial Control Systems in the United States and Japan,"
Journal of International Business Studies (Fall 1985): pp. 331–339.

CHAPTER 17: AUTOS, WHERE SOMETHING HAS TO GIVE

1. Edward B. Leviton, "Motor Vehicles and Parts," *U.S. Industrial Outlook,*
U.S. Department of Commerce, January 1990.
2. Forecasts are from Ward's Automotive Reports and the Office of Automotive Industry Affairs, U.S. Department of Commerce.
3. Womack et al., *The Machine That Changed The World.*
4. Womack et al., p. 199.
5. See Robert R. Rehder, "Japanese Transplants: In Search of a Balanced
and Broader Perspective."(Nashville: 1990).
6. My thanks to Dan Bodnar, who wrote this summary of power producing.
7. Estimates are from various sources, as reported in *New York Times,* October 11, 1990, p. C2, and *The Japan Economic Journal,* February 17, 1990, p. 1.
8. Womack, et al., p. 148.
9. Womack et al, p. 157.
10. Dana Miller, "Making Honda Parts . . . ," *The Wall Street Journal,* October 5, 1990, p. 1.
11. Womack et al., pp. 85, 87.
12. "UAW Faces Test at Mazda's U.S. Plant," *New York Times,* March 27, 1990, p. C1.
13. *San Jose Mercury News,* April 29, 1990, p. E1.
14. Shook, *Honda, An American Success Story.*

CHAPTER 18: PROBLEMS IN THE OFFICE

1. See *Survey of Current Business,* May, June, July, and August issues, 1988–1991.
2. Quoted by Jacob M. Schlesinger, "One High Tech Race Where U.S.
Leads," *The Wall Street Journal,* October 31, 1989, p. 1.
3. James Sterngold, "A Different Drummer in Japan," *New York Times,* February 19, 1990, pp. C1, C4.
4. "Japanese Management, Bigger, Not Better," *The Economist,* January 27, 1990, p. 74.
5. The work of Professor Dave Aaker and his associates is summarized in
The Economist article, above.
6. European studies are summarized in K. Shibagaki, M. Trevor, and T.
Abo, *Japanese and European Management: Their International Adaptability* (Tokyo: 1989).
7. Mroczkowski and Linowes, "American Professionals Inside Japanese Firms:
A Study of Japanese Financial Services in the U.S." (Nashville: 1990).
8. Pat Murdo, "Corporate Benefits as a Competitive Tool in Japan," *JEI
Report,* no. 40A, October 19, 1990.
9. The general outline of the example is based on Yoshino and Lifson, *The
Invisible Link.*

10. See *The Japan Economic Journal,* January 27, 1990, p. 22, and April 28, 1990, p. 13

CHAPTER 19: TROUBLE AT THE BANK

1. See *The Japan Economic Journal,* June 9, 1990, p. 30, and December 1, 1990, p. 31 for profit reports.

2. "International Banking Survey," *The Economist,* April 7, 1990. See also Terrell, Dohner, and Lowrey, "The Activities of Japanese Banks in the United Kingdom and in the United States, 1980–1988," pp. 39–50.

3. W. Hall, "Still Searching for the Right Role," *Financial Times,* March 15, 1990, p. X. Data in this and the following paragraph are from *The Economist,* June 15, 1991, p. 72 and Japanese sources.

4. *JEI Report,* no. 16B, April 20, 1990.

5. James Sterngold, "Japan's Stubborn Overseas Bank," *New York Times,* April 29, 1990, p. F5.

6. *Financial Times.* March 15, 1990, p. VIII.

7. *JEI Reports,* no. 41B, October 19, 1989.

8. *The Banker* (July 1990): p. 85.

9. The data are for 1988. See *The Economist,* April 7, 1990.

10. Douglas Ostrom, *"Keiretsu* and Other Large Corporate Groups in Japan," *JEI Report,* January 12, 1990.

11. Fair Trade Commission, "Long-term Relationships Among Japanese Companies: Report by the Study Group on Trade Frictions and Market Structure (in Japanese)," April, 1987.

12. Bank of Japan, "Financial Statements of Principal Enterprises," *Economic Statistics Monthly,* various issues. Summarized in *JEI Report,* January 12, 1990.

13. Powell, *The Gnomes of Tokyo, The Wall Street Journal,* April 26, 1990, and *New York Times,* August 14, 1990, p. C14.

14. Powell, p. 84.

15. I am drawing on James Tobin, "Financial Intermediaries." In John Eatwell, Murray Milgate, and Peter Newman (eds), *The New Palgrave,* New York: W. W. Norton, 1989, pp. 35–52.

16. Kenneth Grossberg, "Citibank Launches a Credit Card in Japan." (Paper presented at Association of Japanese Business Conference, Nashville, January 1990.)

17. *The Japan Economic Journal,* February 3, 1990, p. 32.

18. See *The Japan Economic Journal,* May 12, 1990.

19. See Suzuki, "A Comparative Study of Financial Innovation, Deregulation, and Reform in Japan and the United States."

20. R. Bruns, "Union Bank, Going for the Golden State," *Business Tokyo* (March 1990): p. 24.

21. *The Economist,* March 24, 1990, p. 81.

22. Data compiled by *The Japan Economic Journal,* April 21, 1990, p. 32, and December 1, 1990, p. 31.

23. Total unrealized gains were $290 billion. Of this $131 billion could be counted as capital.

24. According to *The Banker* (March 1990): pp. 41–42, Japanese banks had

$368 billion in loans outstanding through their U.S. offices in 1988 (agencies, branches, and subsidiaries). This amount does not include loans made by Japanese-owned U.S banks (about $100 billion). About 50 percent of these assets were held by B of T, Dai-Ichi Kangyo, Fuji, Mitsubishi, Sanwa, and Sumitomo.

25. Quoted in *The Japan Economic Journal*, October 13, 1990, p. 30.

26. See ratings on the banks and expected capital adequacy ratios in *The Japan Economic Journal*, September 8, 1990 and December 1, 1990.

27. Based on my own analysis of data for Chuo Trust, Bank of Yokohama, Dai-Ichi Kangyo, B of T, Sumitomo Trust, Tokai Bank, and Yasuda Trust.

28. *Financial Times*, March 15, 1990, p. X.

CHAPTER 20: WEAKNESS ON WALL STREET

1. *The Japan Economic Journal*, June 30, 1990, p. 40.

2. The quotes in this section are from the *New York Times*, June 11, 1989, p. F6.

3. M. Nakamoto, "Generalists, Not Specialists," *Financial Times*, March 15, 1990, p. XII.

4. See *The Japan Economic Journal*, August 25, 1990, p. 35. The number of stock analysts started to grow at an accelerated rate in 1989. By 1990 there were about 1600 people certified by the Security Analysts Association of Japan.

5. Burstein, *Yen!*, p. 180.

6. Hayes and Hubbard, *Investment Banking, A Tale of Three Cities* (Boston: 1990).

CHAPTER 21: MARKETING AND NEGOTIATING

1. Data compiled from *Survey of Current Business*, various issues.

2. Johny K. Johansson, "Japanese Marketing: Short-term Failures vs. Long-term Successes," *Pacific Northwest Executive* 2 (1986): p. 3.

3. James, *Trojan Horse*.

4. L. Meyers, "Tokyo California," *Madison Avenue* 28 (September 1986): pp. 64–66.

5. Quoted by Huddleston in *Gaijin Kaisha*, p. 71.

6. Shook, *Honda, An American Success Story*.

7. Graham and Sano, "Across the Negotiating Table From the Japanese," *International Marketing Review* (Autumn 1986): pp. 58–71.

CHAPTER 22: GOOD CITIZENSHIP

1. "The Deadbeat of America," *New York Times*, March 15, 1990.

2. *Business Tokyo* (December 1989): p. 26.

3. Attacks on Japanese corporate behavior are central themes in Pat Choate's *Agents of Influence*, the Tolchins' *Buying Into America*, Frantz and Collins' *Selling Out*, and J. B. Judis' "The Japanese Megaphone" in *The New Republic*.

4. Graham and Krugman, *Foreign Direct Investment in the United States*.

5. *JEI Reports*, no. 18A, May 4, 1990.

6. Quoted in *The Wall Street Journal*, December 1, 1987, p. 31.

7. The article was published in Japanese in *Voice* (September 1990) and summarized in *Business Tokyo* (January 1991): p. 6.

CHAPTER 23: BUSINESS CHANGES, BUT DO JAPANESE MANAGERS?

1. The best description of the modern Japanese state is van Wolferen's *The Enigma of Japanese Power*.

2. Inohara, *Human Resource Development in Japanese Companies*.

3. A review of studies from 1968 to 1984 is in Neghandi, Eshgh, and Yuen. [See Bibliography.]

4. The research was conducted by my colleague Dick Moxon and Professor Sully Taylor of Portland State University.

5. *Japan Labor Bulletin* 29 (May 1, 1990): p. 7. Calculations are based on 1987 data.

6. *The Japan Times,* June 27, 1990, p. 2.

7. Improved targeting was called for by respondents to a '90 Japan Small Business Corporation survey of small- and mid-sized Japanese investors in the U.S. *The Japan Times Weekly International Edition,* October 15–21, 1990, p. 17.

8. *The Japan Times,* June 20, 1990.

9. *Economic Eye* (Spring 1990): p. 16.

10. The story is summarized in Daniel Burstein's *Yen!*

11. Twentieth Century Fund Reports, *The Free Trade Debate* (New York: Priority Press), p. 168.

12. GATT and MITI data in *Nippon 1990* (JETRO, 1990).

13. See the results of a survey of manufacturers conducted in 1990. *The Japan Economic Journal,* June 30, 1990.

14. See *JEI Report,* no. 34A, August 31, 1990 and *Business Tokyo* (October 1990): pp. 7–8.

Bibliography

Abegglen, James C., and G. Stalk. *Kaisha: The Japanese Corporation*. New York: Basic Books, 1985.

Arpan, Jeffrey S., and David A. Ricks. *Directory of Foreign Manufacturers in the United States* (4th ed.) Atlanta: Georgia State University Press, 1990.

Bird, Allan. "Executive Career Advancement in Japanese Banks: Who Gets to the Top?" Paper presented at the Association of Japanese Business Studies Conference, Nashville, January, 1990.

Bird, Allan. "Expatriates at Home: A New Twist in the Human Resource Management Strategies of Japanese MNCs." Working paper, NYU School of Business, January 1990.

Bowman, James S. "The Rising Sun in America—Japanese Management in the United States." *Personnel Administrator* 31, (October 1986): pp. 81–91.

Boyer, Edward. "Straight Talk to Japan." *Pacific Basin Quarterly* (Spring 1989): pp. 4–5.

Burstein, Daniel. *Yen! Japan's New Financial Empire and Its Threat to America*. New York: Fawcett Columbine, 1990.

Choate, Pat. *Agents of Influence*. New York: Knopf, 1990.

Dale, Peter N. *The Myth of Japanese Uniqueness*. New York: St. Martin's Press, 1986.

Daley, Lane, James Jimbalvo, Gary Sundem, and Yasumasu Kondo. "Attitudes Toward Financial Control Systems in the United States and Japan." *Journal of International Business Studies* (Fall 1985): pp. 91–110.

Dicle, Ulku, A. I. Dicle, and Raymond E. Alie. "Human Resources Management Practices in Japanese Organizations in the United States." *Public Personnel Management* 17 (Fall 1988): pp. 331–339.

Doi, Takeo L. *The Anatomy of Dependence*. Tokyo: Kobundo, 1971.

Dower, John W. "The Useful War." *Daedalus* 119 (Summer 1990): pp. 49–70.

Encarnation, Dennis J., and Mark Mason. "Neither MITI nor America: The

Political Economy of Capital Liberalization in Japan." *International Organization* 44 (Winter 1990): pp. 25–54.

Fallows, James. *More like Us: Making America Great Again.* New York: Houghton Mifflin, 1989.

Frantz, Douglas, and Catherine Collins. *Selling Out: How We Are Letting Japan Buy Our Land, Our Industries, Our Financial Institutions, Our Future.* Chicago: Contemporary Books, 1989.

Fucini, Joseph J. and Suzy Fucini. *Working for the Japanese: Inside Mazda's American Auto Plant.* New York: The Free Press, 1990.

Futatsugi, Yusaku. "What Cross-holdings Mean for Corporate Management." *Economic Eye* (Spring 1990): pp.17–19.

Gelsanliter, David. *Jump Start: Japan Comes to the Heartland.* New York: Farrar, Straus, Giroux, 1990.

Gemmel, Art. "Management in a Cross-cultural Environment: The Best of Both Worlds." *Management Solutions* 31 (January 1986): pp. 28–33.

Gordon, A. *The Evolution of Labor Relations in Japan: Heavy Industry, 1953–1955.* Cambridge: Harvard University Press, 1985.

Graham, E. M., and Paul R. Krugman. *Foreign Direct Investment in the United States.* Washington, D.C.: Institute for International Economics, 1989.

Graham, John L., and Yoshihiro Sano. "Across the Negotiating Table from the Japanese." *International Marketing Review* (Autumn 1986): pp. 58–71.

Hassan, Ihab. "The Burden of Mutual Perceptions: Japan and the United States." *IHJ Bulletin* 10, 1 (1990): pp. 1–6.

Hayes, Samuel L., and Philip Hubbard. *Investment Banking: A Tale of Three Cities.* Boston: Harvard Business School Press, 1990.

Hexon, Todd, and R. Kimball. "How Foreign-owned Businesses Can Contribute to U.S. Competitiveness." *Harvard Business Review* 90 (January-February 1990): pp. 56–57.

Hofstede, G. *Culture's Consequences: International Differences in Work-related Values.* Beverly Hills, CA: Sage, 1980.

Huddleston, Jackson W. *Gaijin Kaisha: Running a Foreign Business in Japan.* Armonk, NY: M. E. Sharpe, 1990.

Imai, Masaaki. *Kaizen: The Key to Japan's Competitive Success.* New York: Random House, 1986.

Inohara, Hideo. *Human Resource Development in Japanese Companies.* Tokyo: Asian Productivity Organization, 1990.

Ishikawa, Kaoru. *What Is Total Quality Control?* Englewood Cliffs, NJ: Prentice Hall, 1985.

James, Barrie G. *Trojan Horse: The Ultimate Japanese Challenge to Western Industry.* London: Mercury Books, 1989.

Japan Economic Institute. *Japan's Expanding U.S. Manufacturing Presence.* Washington, D.C.: JEI, October 1989.

Japan Times. *Top 1500 Japanese Companies.* Tokyo: 1988.

JETRO. *Japanese Managers in America: A Survey Report.* Tokyo: June 1989 (in Japanese).

JETRO. *Nippon 1990.* Tokyo: 1990.

Johnson, Chalmers. *MITI and the Japanese Miracle.* Stanford: Stanford University Press, 1982.

Johnson, Chalmers. "Revisionism and Beyond." *Business Tokyo*, (February 1990): p. 54.

Judis, J. B. "The Japanese Megaphone." *The New Republic*, January 22, 1990, pp. 20–25.

Karnani, A. B. and B. Wernerfelt. "Multiple Point Competition." *Strategic Management Journal* 6 (1985): pp. 87–96.

Kase, K., N. Campbell, and M. Goold. "The Role of the Centre in Managing Large Diversified Corporations in Japan." Paper presented at the Association of Japanese Business Studies Conference, Nashville, January 1990.

Keizai Koho Center. *Japan, 1990.* Tokyo: 1989.

Kikuchi, Makoto. *Japanese Electronics.* Tokyo: Simul Press, 1983.

Kobayashi, Yotaro. "A Message to American Managers." *Economic Eye*, 11 (Spring 1990): pp. 8–12.

Kogut, Bruce, and Chang Sea-Jin. "Technological Capabilities and Japanese Direct Investment in the United States." Paper presented at the Association of Japanese Business Studies Conference, Nashville, January 1990.

Komai, Hiroshi. *Japanese Management Overseas.* Tokyo: Asian Productivity Organization, 1989.

Kono, T. *Changing Corporate Culture.* Tokyo: Kodansha, 1988 (in Japanese).

Kotkin, J., and Y. Kishimoto. "Theory F." *INC.* 8 (April 1986): pp. 53–60.

Kujawa, Duane, and Daniel Bob. *American Public Opinion on Japanese Foreign Direct Investment.* New York: Japan Society, 1988.

Lauenstein, M. C. "Strategic Planning in Japan." *The Journal of Business Strategy* (Fall 1985).

Lebra, T. S. *Japanese Patterns of Behavior.* Honolulu: University Press of Hawaii, 1976.

Levin, Doron P. "Motor City for Japanese in California." *New York Times*, May 7, 1990, pp. C1–C2.

Lincoln, J. R. and A. L. Kalleberg. "Work Organization and Workforce Commitment: A Study of Plants and Employees in the U.S. and Japan." *American Sociological Review* 50 (1985): pp. 738–760.

Lohmann, D. P. "An Explanation of Reactions to Japanese Investments in Hawaii." Paper presented at the Association of Japanese Business Studies Conference, Nashville, January 1990.

Lynn, Leonard H. "Japan Adopts a New Technology: The Roles of Government, Trading Firms and Suppliers." *The Columbia Journal of World Business* 19 Winter (1984): pp. 39–45.

Lynn, Leonard H., and Henry R. Piehler. "Engineering Careers, Job Rotation, and Gatekeepers in Japan and the United States." Working paper, Case Western Reserve University, 1990.

Lu, D. J. *Inside Corporate Japan.* Tokyo: Charles E. Tuttle, 1989.

McCauley, Robert N., and Steven A. Zimmer. "Explaining the International Differences in the Cost of Capital." *Federal Reserve Bank of New York Quarterly Review* (Summer 1989): pp. 7–28.

Macpherson, C. B. *The Political Theory of Possessive Individualism: Hobbes to Locke.* Oxford: Clarendon Press, 1962.

Matsumoto, Michihiro. *The Unspoken Way.* Tokyo: Kodansha, 1988.

Ministry of International Trade and Industry. *1990 White Paper on International Trade*. Tokyo:MITI, June 1990.

Miyazaki, Kagayaki. "The Potential for Internationalizing the Japanese Company." *Economic Eye* (Spring 1990): pp. 12–16.

Morita, Akio, and Shintaro Ishihara. *The Japan That Can Say 'No.'* Undated typescript in English, 1990.

Morishima, Motohiro. "Japanese Employees Attitudes Toward Changes in Traditional Employment Practices." Working paper, Department of Policy Management, Keio University, 1990.

Mroczkowski, Tomasz, and Richard Linowes. "American Professionals Inside Japanese Firms: A Study of Japanese Financial Services in the U.S." Paper presented at the Association of Japanese Business Studies Conference, Nashville: January 1990.

Nakane, Chie. *Japanese Society*. Berkeley and Los Angeles: University of California Press, 1970.

Neghandi, A. R., G. S. Eshgh, and E. C. Yuen. "The Management Practices of Japanese Subsidiaries Overseas." *California Management Review* 27 (Summer 1985): pp. 93–105.

Nishimura, Tsutomu. "Toward a Better Balance Between Savings and Investment." *Keidanren Review* (April 1990): pp. 3–7.

Ouchi, William. *Theory Z: How American Business Can Meet the Japanese Challenge*. Reading, MA: Addison-Wesley, 1981.

Pachter, Marc, and Frances Wein, eds. *Abroad in America: Visitors to the New Nation 1776–1914*. Reading, MA: Addison-Wesley, 1976.

Porter, Michael. *The Competitive Advantage of Nations*. New York: Free Press, 1990.

Powell, Jim. *The Gnomes of Tokyo*. New York: American Management Association, 1988.

Prestowitz, Clyde. *Trading Places: How We Allowed Japan to Take the Lead*. New York: Basic Books, 1988.

Pucik, V., M. Hanada, and G. Fifield. "Management Culture and Effectiveness of Local Executives in Japanese-owned U.S. Corporations." Working paper, University of Michigan School of Business, Ann Arbor, July 1989.

Rehder, Robert R. "Japanese Transplants: In Search of a Balanced and Broader Perspective." Paper presented at the Association of Japanese Business Conference, Nashville, January 1990.

Reich, Robert B. "Who Is Us?" *Harvard Business Review*, 90 (January-February 1990): pp. 53–64.

Scandura, T. A., and K. Banerji. "A Tale of Two Industries: Japanese Investment in Automobile Ancillary and Chemical Processing in the U.S." Paper presented at the Association of Japanese Business Studies Conference, Nashville, January 1990.

Seward, Jack, and Howard Van Zandt. *Japan: The Hungry Guest*. Tokyo: Yohan Publications, 1987.

Shibagaki, K., M. Trevor, and T. Abo. *Japanese and European Management: Their International Adaptability*. Tokyo: University of Tokyo Press, 1989.

Shimada, Haruo. "Labor Problems of Japanese Companies Abroad." *Japanese Labor Bulletin*, January 1, 1990, pp. 4–8.

Shook, Robert L. *Honda: An American Success Story*. New York: Prentice Hall Press, 1988.

Smith, Roy C. *The Global Bankers*. New York: E. P. Dutton, 1989.

Stokes, Bruce. *Japanese Investment in the U.S.: Its Causes and Consequences*. New York: Japan Society, 1988.

Sullivan, Jeremiah J., and Per O. Heggelund. *Foreign Investment in the U.S. Fishing Industry*. Lexington, MA: Lexington Books, 1979.

Sullivan, Jeremiah J., Richard Peterson, Naoki Kameda, and J. Shimada. "The Relationship between Conflict Resolution Approaches and Trust—A Cross-cultural Study." *Academy of Management Journal*, 24 (1981): pp. 803–815.

Sullivan, Jeremiah J., and Naoki Kameda. "The Concept of Profit and Managerial Communications Problems in Japanese-American Joint Ventures." *The Journal of Business Communications*, 19 (1982): pp. 33–40.

Sullivan, Jeremiah J., and Richard Peterson. "Applying Japanese Management in the U.S.A." *Journal of Contemporary Business* 11 (1982): pp. 5–16.

Sullivan, Jeremiah J. and R. Peterson. "Factors Associated with Trust in Japanese-American Joint Ventures." *Management International Review* 22 (1982): pp. 30–40.

Sullivan, Jeremiah J. "A Critique of Theory Z." *Academy of Management Review* 8 (1983):pp. 132–142

Sullivan, Jeremiah J., Teruhiko Suzuki, and Yasumasu Kondo. "The Fundamental Attribution Error in Japanese and American Performance Appraisals." *Doshisha Business Review* 35 (1983): pp. 1–34 (in Japanese).

Sullivan, Jeremiah J. "Japanese and American Business Communications: English Words with Different Meanings." *Proceedings*, Second Japan-U.S. Business Conference, Tokyo, 1984.

Sullivan, Jeremiah J., Teruhiko Suzuki and Yasumasu Kondo. "The Function of Work Groups in Japanese and American Performance Control Processes." *Proceedings*, Academy of Management, August 1985.

Sullivan, Jeremiah J., and Jiro Nonaka. "The Application of Organizational Learning Theory to Japanese and American Management." *Journal of International Business Studies* 17, 3 (1986): pp. 127–148

Sullivan, Jeremiah J., Teruhiko Suzuki and Yasumasu Kondo. "Managerial Perceptions of Performance in Japanese and American Work Groups." *Journal of Cross Cultural Psychology* 17 (1986): pp. 379–398.

Sullivan, Jeremiah J. and Jiro Nonaka. "Culture and Strategic Issue Categorization Theory." *Management International Review* 28 (1988): pp. 6–10.

Sullivan, Jeremiah J., Teruhiko Suzuki, and Yasumasu Kondo. "The Function of Work Groups in Japanese and American Control Processes." In *Applying Indigenous Research Abroad*. edited by C.A.B. Osigweh, pp. 135–151. New York: Plenum Press, 1988.

Sullivan, Jeremiah J., Teruhiko Suzuki, and Yasumasu Kondo. "Japanese and American Work Groups: Performance Enhancers or Risk Reducers?" *Doshisha Business Review* (Autumn 1988): pp. 297–315.

Sullivan, Jeremiah J., and Richard B. Peterson. "Japanese Management Theories—A Research Agenda." In *Advances in International Comparative Management*, edited by B. Prasad, Vol. 4, pp. 255–275. Greenwich, CT: JAI Press, 1990.

Sullivan, Jeremiah J. and Sully Taylor, and Terrance Albrecht. "Process, Organizational, Relational, and Personal Determinants of Managerial Compliance-gaining Strategies." *Journal of Business Communications* 27 (Fall 1990): pp. 331–357.

Sullivan, Jeremiah J., and Naoki Kameda. "Bypassing in Managerial Communications." *Business Horizons* 34 (1991): pp. 71–80.

Sullivan, Jeremiah J. and Richard B. Peterson. "The Japanese Lifetime Employment System." In *Advances in International Comparative Management,* edited by B. Prasad, Vol. 5. pp. 169–194. Greenwich, CT: JAI Press, 1991.

Sullivan, Jeremiah J., and Richard B. Peterson. "A Test of Theories Underlying the Japanese Lifetime Employment System." *Journal of International Business Studies* 22, (1991): pp. 79–97

Sullivan, Jeremiah J., and Coral Snodgrass. "Tolerance of Executive Failure in American and Japanese Organizations." *Asia Pacific Journal of Management* 8 (1991): pp. 15–34

Sullivan, Jeremiah J., and Sully Taylor. "A Cross Cultural Test of Compliance-gaining Theory in Japan." *Management Communication Quarterly* (Fall 1991): pp. 220–239.

Suzuki, Yoshio. "A Comparative Study of Financial Innovation, Deregulation, and Reform in Japan and the United States." *Bank of Japan Monetary and Economic Studies,* October 4, 1986, pp. 147–159.

Takagi, H. *The Flow of Japanese Management.* Ann Arbor: UMI Research Press, 1985.

Takahashi, Hideo. "Japan's Price Structure." *JEI Report,* January 26, 1990.

Takanaga, Takino. "A Comparative Analysis of Multinational Strategies in Japan." Paper presented at the WAM International Conference, Shizuoka, June 1990.

Tanaka, Hiroshi. *Personality in Industry.* London: Pinter Publishers, 1988.

Tatsuno, Sheridan M. *Created in Japan.* New York: Harper & Row, 1990.

Terrell, Henry S., Robert S. Dohner, and Barbara R. Lowrey. "The Activities of Japanese Banks in the United Kingdom and in the United States, 1980–1988." *Federal Reserve Bulletin,* 76 (February 1990): pp. 39–50.

Tokunaga, Yohiro. "An Anatomy of Japan's High Prices." *Economic Eye* (Spring 1990): pp. 20–24.

Tolchin, Martin and Susan Tolchin. *Buying Into America.* New York: Berkley Books, 1989.

Tsuda, M. *Personnel Strategy of Japanese Management* (in Japanese). Tokyo: Dobunkan, 1987.

Tsunoda, R., W. T. de Bary, and D. Keene, eds. *Sources of Japanese Tradition.* New York: Columbia University Press, 1958.

van Wolferen, Karel. *The Enigma of Japanese Power.* New York: Knopf, 1989.

Vogel, Ezra F. *Japan as Number One.* New York: Harper Colophon Books, 1979.

Wakabayashi, Mitsuru, and George Graen. "Human Resource Development of Japanese Managers: Leadership and Career Investment." In *International Human Resource Management,* edited by K. Rowland and G. Ferris, Greenwich, CT: JAI Press, 1988.

Womack, James P., Daniel T. Jones, and Daniel Roos. *The Machine That Changed the World.* New York: Rawson Associates, 1990.

Yamamura, Kozo, ed. *Japanese Investment in the United States: Should We Be Concerned.* Seattle: Society for Japanese Studies, 1989.

Yamashita, Toshihiko. *The Panasonic Way.* Tokyo: Kodansha International, 1989.

Yang, Zhuang. "Internal Labor Market Environments and Human Resource Management—A Study of HRM Policies at Japanese Companies Operating in the U.S." Paper presented at the Academy of Management Conference, San Francisco, 1990.

Yoshino, M.Y., and T.B. Lifson. *The Invisible Link: Japan's* Sogo Shosha *and the Organization of Trade.* Cambridge, MA: The MIT Press, 1986.

Index

About the Author

JEREMIAH J. SULLIVAN is Professor of International Business at the University of Washington Graduate School of Business. He is the author of *Pacific Basin Enterprise and the Changing Law of the Sea* and *Foreign Investment in the U.S. Fishing Industry*. His scholarly articles have appeared in the *Journal of International Business Studies, Academy of Management Journal, Journal of Management, Business Horizons, Asia Pacific Journal of Management*, and many others. Professor Sullivan is a member of the Association of Japanese Business Studies, Academy of International Business, International House of Japan, and the Academy of Management.